Determinants of FinTech Adoption and Banks' Financial Performance

Muhammad Naeem Shahid
https://orcid.org/0000-0001-7167-8386

School of Accounting and Finance, Faculty of Business and Law, Taylor's University, Malaysia

Muhammad Umar Islam
https://orcid.org/0000-0002-3328-2820

Asia Pacific University of Techology and Innovations, Malaysia

IGI Global
Scientific Publishing
Publishing Tomorrow's Research Today

Vice President of Editorial Melissa Wagner
Director of Acquisitions Mikaela Felty
Director of Book Development Jocelynn Hessler
Production Manager Mike Brehm
Cover Design Jose Rosado

Published in the United States of America by
IGI Global Scientific Publishing
701 East Chocolate Avenue
Hershey, PA, 17033, USA
Tel: 717-533-8845 | Fax: 717-533-7115
Website: https://www.igi-global.com E-mail: cust@igi-global.com

Library of Congress Cataloging-in-Publication Data

Names: Shahid, Muhammad Naeem, 1985- editor | Islam, Muhammad Umar, 1982- editor
Title: Determinants of fintech adoption and banks' financial performance / [edited by] Muhammad Naeem Shahid, Muhammad Umar Islam.
Description: Hershey, PA : IGI Global Scientific Publishing, [2027] | Includes bibliographical references and index. | Summary: "This book examines how financial technology adoption influences banks' performance, with a focus on profitability, stability, and operational efficiency. It introduces structured indices to measure FinTech adoption and applies them to assess impacts across different banking models, sizes, and ownership structures. The volume provides a rigorous framework for understanding how digital transformation shapes competitive advantage in commercial, investment, and development banking"-- Provided by publisher.
Identifiers: LCCN 2025038277 (print) | LCCN 2025038278 (ebook) | ISBN 9798337362441 hardcover | ISBN 9798337362458 paperback | ISBN 9798337362465 ebook
Subjects: LCSH: Banks and banking | Finance--Technological innovations
Classification: LCC HG1601 .D37 2026 (print) | LCC HG1601 (ebook) | DDC 332.1--dc23/eng/20260327
LC record available at https://lccn.loc.gov/2025038277
LC ebook record available at https://lccn.loc.gov/2025038278

British Cataloguing in Publication Data
A Cataloguing in Publication record for this book is available from the British Library.

Table of Contents

Detailed Table of Contents

Extraordinary growth and rapid dependence on Financial Technology (FinTech) have reshaped the entire banking system worldwide. FinTech has introduced novel business models, enhanced operational efficiency, and redefined customer preferences. FinTech, including mobile banking, digital banking, artificial intelligence-driven risk assessment, and blockchain transactions, has altered banks' exposure to stability and profitability. This chapter aims to explain how the FinTech adoption influences the financial performance of Banks. For this purpose, the chapter provides an overview of FinTech, its various dimensions and discusses the FinTech adoption in relation to different theories. The chapter offers the evolution of FinTech, the components of FinTech used in previous studies, and how such adoption enhances the financial performance of banks. Moreover, the chapter presents a Bank-Based novel comprehensive FinTech adoption Index (BBNC-FTAI) using Python software. The proposed index can best measure FinTech adoption in banks and enhance the performance of the banking industry.

The chapter explores the infiltration of FinTech into the banking sector by coming up with a multifaceted, bank-level composite index, as well as evaluating the consequences on financial performance and stability. Leaving behind uncomplicated single-proxy indicators, the paper describes FinTech adoption as a combined process that includes the uptake of digital services, data analytics, platform integration, regulatory technology, and systems of governance. The findings of the panel based empirical research indicate that the adoption of FinTech has a positive impact on the financial performance of banks, but its results on stability are inconsistent and depend on the quality of governance and sustainability oriented position. The results highlight the mediating role of the ESG performance, and support the need to have responsible and well-managed digital transformation in order to achieve sustainable and resilient banking results.

Financial technologies explosive growth has changed the global banking landscape by transforming established commercial banking models and creating new avenues for expansion, effectiveness and financial inclusion. The chapter aims at addressing the impact of fintech on the bank's financial performances and its challenges in adopting it in the system. Despite of these, there raised a challenging risk and threats in way of handling such technical aspects of bank briefing various financial technologies and its evolution over the years also it discusses about its financial inclusion and provides a way for underserved areas to explore and to incorporate the habit of saving through wide range of fintech platforms like peer-peer lending, AI integrated applications etc., along with the various available opportunities for commercial banks. Adding to this, it discusses about the crucial role of fintech in policy and regulatory compliance of commercial banks as it leads to achieve long-term financial sustainability and customer loyalty by balancing efficiency, trust and transparency.

In recent times, Fintech has been a revolutionary force that connects finance with innovative technologies. Fintech has introduced new business model innovations, innovative banking products/services, and processes, creating a landscape that has completely transformed the financial industry. FinTech-oriented banks work in a dynamic environment where FinTech firms compete with them. Moreover, the adoption of FinTech by banks is complex due to regulatory, governance, and operational environments. Therefore, it is important to understand the adoption of FinTech and its impact on banks' financial performance. The chapter examines the determinants of FinTech adoption, ranging from non-banking to bank-based components of FinTech. The chapter offers nine components that can best measure FinTech adoption in banks. The chapter also addresses the banks' FinTech adoption and financial performance from the perspectives of regulatory, governance, and stability. It has been observed that FinTech adoption enhances a bank's financial performance.

India's rapid expansion of digital finance has transformed payment systems while heightening exposure to financial cybercrime. Real-time payments, platform-based services, and fintech integration have created risk pathways that extend beyond isolated fraud incidents. This study analyses financial cybercrime in India through a systemic lens, mapping evolving fraud typologies, payment-rail vulnerabilities, organised criminal networks, and behavioural asymmetries. It also examines the capacity of regulatory, infrastructural, and enforcement mechanisms to manage these risks under real-time operational constraints. Drawing on a structured synthesis of academic and policy sources, the paper develops the Systemic Cybercrime Mitigation Framework for Digital Finance (SCMF-DF), which integrates prevention, detection, containment, recovery, and adaptive learning to address cybercrime as a financial stability concern.

The chapter explores the measurement and impact of FinTech adoption within the banking industry, presenting a structured methodology for constructing a FinTech Adoption Index (FAI) that integrates multiple dimensions such as digital presence, automation, open APIs, artificial intelligence, and FinTech partnerships. It examines how these digital innovations influence banks' profitability, operational stability, and institutional diversity across conventional, Islamic, foreign, and digital-only models. Empirical results demonstrate that higher FinTech maturity enhances efficiency and competitiveness but introduces governance and cybersecurity challenges. Through real-world cases from DBS Bank and the State Bank of India, the study validates the transformative potential of data-driven innovation in achieving sustainable financial performance and inclusive digital growth.

The emergence of Financial Technology (FinTech) as an accelerated phenomenon is reshaping the banking industry, particularly in regions such as Asia, where institutional varieties and regulatory regimes present both opportunities and challenges to digital transformation. The chapter presents a map of the FinTech Adoption Index (FAI), a comprehensive framework developed to measure the level of FinTech adoption among various banking organisations. The FAI measures various dimensions of adoption, including customer experience, regulatory compliance, technological infrastructure, and strategic alliances. The index provides banks, regulatory authorities, and policymakers with a crucial tool that helps measure progress, identify shortcomings, and inform future decision-making in digital projects. Although the adoption of FinTech has significant potential, the remnants of past systems, regulatory challenges, and concerns about consumer trust are among the graver obstacles that must be overcome.

Based on the data set collected from 2018 to 2022 from the Scopus database, this study represents a bibliometric and systematic evaluation analysis of the mobile payment system. In this study, literature classification based on theory and technology is done by extensive literature study by preparing a table in Excel. Bibliometric research is done by VOS viewer software.The findings of the study show that TAM is used by most of the researchers for theoretical framework and the "partial least square structure equation modelling" technique is the most prevalent. All the highly cited articles used the survey method in collecting the data. The text-based and keywords graphs cluster shows various keywords' relationships. The cluster analysis reveals that the primary emphasis of research is on how customers accept technology. It also highlights the need for more research into how consumers employ mobile payments and how small businesses and merchants use them. The title "Predicting the determinants of mobile payment acceptance: A hybrid SEM-neural network approach" is highly cited theme.

Financial institutions can meet client demand for better, safer, and easier money management with AI and ML.AI helps the financial sector manage risk, trade with numbers, and make investment decisions more efficiently.Thus, automated solutions

Preface

The rapid transformation of the global financial ecosystem through Financial Technology (FinTech) has ushered in a new era of banking innovation, operational efficiency, and customer-centric financial services. Across developed and emerging economies alike, banks are increasingly integrating digital technologies such as artificial intelligence, blockchain, machine learning, mobile payments, big data analytics, cloud computing, and platform-based financial systems into their strategic operations. This edited reference book, *Determinants of FinTech Adoption and Banks' Financial Performance*, emerges at a critical juncture where financial institutions, regulators, policymakers, researchers, and practitioners are collectively seeking to understand how FinTech adoption influences institutional performance, stability, sustainability, and financial inclusion.

The motivation behind this volume stems from the growing academic and practical need to explore FinTech adoption not merely as a technological shift, but as a multidimensional transformation affecting governance structures, strategic decision-making, customer behavior, risk management, cybersecurity, and long-term financial resilience. While previous studies have often focused on isolated technological variables or single-country analyses, this book brings together diverse scholarly perspectives that collectively examine the determinants, measurement frameworks, implications, and strategic consequences of FinTech integration in banking systems across multiple contexts. The chapters included in this volume contribute theoretical advancements, empirical evidence, conceptual frameworks, and methodological innovations that broaden the understanding of digital transformation within modern banking.

Another distinguishing feature of this volume is its emphasis on measurement and evaluation. Several contributors introduce innovative FinTech Adoption Indices and composite frameworks designed to quantify technological maturity and assess its relationship with profitability, institutional diversity, operational efficiency, sustainability, and financial stability. These contributions provide valuable tools for academics and practitioners seeking more rigorous approaches to evaluating digital banking transformation. Moreover, the book extends beyond traditional discussions of innovation by critically addressing contemporary concerns including cybercrime risks, behavioral nudges, governance challenges, ethical implications, and systemic vulnerabilities associated with rapid digitization.

This volume also reflects the interdisciplinary nature of FinTech research. The contributing authors represent a broad spectrum of institutions and countries, offering international and comparative insights into digital banking ecosystems. Their collective expertise spans finance, accounting, management, economics, technology, cybersecurity, and behavioral studies. Such diversity enriches the discussions presented in this book and demonstrates the increasingly interconnected relationship between technology and financial systems.

The editors sincerely appreciate the dedication and scholarly contributions of all chapter authors whose research efforts have made this volume possible. We are equally grateful to the reviewers, academic colleagues, and publishing professionals whose guidance and support contributed significantly to the development of this book. We believe this collection will serve as a valuable academic resource for researchers, postgraduate students, policymakers, banking professionals, and technology strategists interested in understanding the evolving relationship between FinTech adoption and banking performance.

CHAPTER OVERVIEW

Chapter 1: FinTech Development, Adoption, and Financial Performance of Banks; Bank-Based Novel Comprehensive FinTech Index (BBNC-FTAI)

The opening chapter introduces the evolution and conceptual foundations of FinTech adoption within the banking industry. It discusses the theoretical perspectives underpinning technological adoption and presents the Bank-Based Novel Comprehensive FinTech Adoption Index (BBNC-FTAI), developed using Python-based methodologies. The chapter establishes how FinTech dimensions such as digital banking, AI-driven services, and blockchain technologies influence profitability, operational performance, and institutional competitiveness.

Chapter 2: Measuring FinTech Adoption in Banks; Construction of a Composite Index and Its Impact on Financial Performance and Stability

This chapter develops a multidimensional composite index that captures digital service integration, governance mechanisms, analytics adoption, and regulatory technology implementation. Through panel-based empirical analysis, the authors demonstrate the positive relationship between FinTech adoption and bank performance while also highlighting governance and ESG considerations that mediate institutional stability outcomes.

Chapter 3: Balancing Efficiency and Sustainability: The Effect of FinTech on Commercial Banks' Financial Performances

Focusing on commercial banking institutions, this chapter examines how FinTech contributes to operational efficiency, customer engagement, and financial inclusion while simultaneously creating technological and regulatory challenges. The discussion emphasizes balancing innovation with trust, transparency, and sustainability to ensure long-term banking resilience.

Chapter 4: Non-Bank to Bank-Based FinTech Determinants and Banks' Financial Performance

This chapter investigates the determinants of FinTech adoption by examining both non-bank and bank-based technological factors. It proposes nine major FinTech components relevant to banking institutions and explores how regulatory environments, governance structures, and competitive market conditions influence digital transformation and financial performance.

Chapter 5: Financial Cybercrime, FinTech Adoption, and Bank Performance in an Interconnected Indian Economy: Typologies, Networks, and Systemic Implications

Addressing one of the most pressing concerns in digital finance, this chapter explores financial cybercrime within India's rapidly expanding FinTech ecosystem. The authors present the Systemic Cybercrime Mitigation Framework for Digital Finance (SCMF-DF), emphasizing prevention, adaptive learning, detection, and containment strategies necessary for maintaining financial stability in increasingly interconnected digital environments.

Chapter 6: Measuring FinTech Adoption in Banking - Constructing Indices and Assessing Impacts on Profitability, Stability, and Institutional Diversity

This chapter develops a FinTech Adoption Index integrating digital infrastructure, automation, AI implementation, and open banking capabilities. Through case studies and empirical analysis, the authors demonstrate how FinTech maturity affects profitability, competitiveness, institutional diversity, and operational stability across different banking models.

Chapter 7: Designing FinTech Adoption Index - A Strategic Framework for Measuring Digital Transformation in Asian Banks

Focusing specifically on Asian banking systems, this chapter proposes a strategic framework for evaluating FinTech adoption through dimensions such as customer experience, technological readiness, strategic partnerships, and regulatory compliance. The discussion highlights regional opportunities and challenges associated with digital transformation in diverse institutional environments.

Chapter 8: Mobile Payment Systems - Thematic Insights, Research Gaps, and Emerging Opportunities

This chapter presents a bibliometric and systematic review of mobile payment systems research using Scopus-indexed literature. By analyzing dominant theories, methodologies, and research clusters, the chapter identifies emerging opportunities and significant gaps in mobile payment adoption studies, particularly concerning consumer behavior and merchant integration.

Chapter 9: Revolutionizing Banking Operations with AI and ML Technologies

The authors examine how artificial intelligence and machine learning technologies are transforming banking operations through automation, risk assessment, fraud detection, personalized services, and data-driven decision-making. The chapter highlights both the opportunities and challenges associated with AI-enabled financial systems and their implications for future banking strategies.

CONCLUSION

The chapters presented in this volume collectively demonstrate that FinTech is no longer a peripheral innovation within banking systems; rather, it has become a foundational driver of transformation across operational, strategic, and institutional dimensions. The integration of digital technologies has fundamentally altered how banks deliver services, manage risks, interact with customers, and compete in increasingly dynamic financial environments. From artificial intelligence and mobile payments to cybersecurity frameworks and behavioral nudges, the contributions in this book reveal the breadth and complexity of modern financial transformation.

A recurring theme throughout this collection is the importance of responsible and measurable digital adoption. While FinTech adoption enhances operational efficiency, financial inclusion, customer engagement, and institutional competitiveness, it also introduces significant concerns related to cybersecurity, governance, ethical accountability, financial stability, and regulatory compliance. The frameworks and indices proposed by contributors provide valuable tools for evaluating technological maturity and understanding how digital transformation can be aligned with sustainable and resilient banking practices.

This volume further highlights the importance of interdisciplinary and international collaboration in FinTech research. The challenges and opportunities associated with digital banking transcend national boundaries and require integrated perspectives from finance, technology, economics, behavioral science, and public policy. The diverse geographical and scholarly representation within this book contributes to a more holistic understanding of how FinTech adoption evolves across different institutional and regulatory contexts.

As editors, we hope this book stimulates further academic inquiry and practical dialogue concerning the future of digital banking. We envision this volume serving not only as a scholarly reference for researchers and students, but also as a practical guide for banking professionals, regulators, policymakers, and technology innovators seeking to navigate the evolving financial landscape. The future of banking will undoubtedly continue to be shaped by technological innovation, and understanding the determinants, implications, and strategic management of FinTech adoption will remain essential for achieving sustainable financial development.

Finally, we extend our heartfelt gratitude to all contributors, reviewers, and publishing teams whose dedication and expertise made this volume possible. It is our sincere hope that this book contributes meaningfully to ongoing discussions surrounding FinTech, banking innovation, and financial performance in the digital age.

Chapter 1

FinTech Development, Adoption, and Financial Performance of Banks:
Bank-Based Novel Comprehensive FinTech Index (BBNC-FTAI)

Muhammad Naeem Shahid
http://orcid.org/0000-0001-7167-8386
School of Accounting and Finance, Faculty of Business and Law, Taylor's University, Malaysia

Mahreen Bashir
Government College University Faisalabad, Chiniot, Pakistan

Muhammad Umar Islam
http://orcid.org/0000-0002-3328-2820
Asia Pacific University of Technology & Innovation, Malaysia

Zahid Mahmood
Bahria University, Islamabad, Pakistan

ABSTRACT

Extraordinary growth and rapid dependence on Financial Technology (FinTech) have reshaped the entire banking system worldwide. FinTech has introduced novel business models, enhanced operational efficiency, and redefined customer preferences. FinTech, including mobile banking, digital banking, artificial intelligence-driven risk assessment, and blockchain transactions, has altered banks' exposure to stability and profitability. This chapter aims to explain how the FinTech adoption

DOI: 10.4018/979-8-3373-6244-1.ch001

influences the financial performance of Banks. For this purpose, the chapter provides an overview of FinTech, its various dimensions and discusses the FinTech adoption in relation to different theories. The chapter offers the evolution of FinTech, the components of FinTech used in previous studies, and how such adoption enhances the financial performance of banks. Moreover, the chapter presents a Bank-Based novel comprehensive FinTech adoption Index (BBNC-FTAI) using Python software. The proposed index can best measure FinTech adoption in banks and enhance the performance of the banking industry.

1. FINTECH AND ITS SCOPE

Financial technology refers to a set of innovative services supported by advancements in information and communication technologies and systems (Barbu et al., 2021). FinTech encompasses those revolutionary actors that provide financial services primarily through technology (Segura et al., 2020). FinTech integrates computer software and technologies to support banking services, enabling various transactions, including credit card payments, wire transfers, ATMs, e-money, and online payments (Nurlaela et al., 2020). Additionally, it signifies the use of the Internet and technological advancements in the financial sector (Zaghol et al., 2021). Therefore, FinTech is incorporating advanced technology to provide financial sector services (Gai et al., 2018). FinTech fundamentally relies on advanced technologies, including AI, blockchain, mobile wallets, IoT, and NFC (Lim et al., 2019). The know-how of such services is essential in FinTech (Suseendran et al., 2019). The availability of round-the-clock financial services, customised design, delivery, and improved consumer experience are the results of FinTech's dependence on technological innovation and the adoption of new processes, as highlighted by recent researchers (Barbu et al., 2021). FinTech represents innovation in financial business models and services (Nangin et al., 2020). Unlike traditional organisations, FinTech firms are technology-oriented and provide better, convenient, lower-priced, and faster services by incorporating digital infrastructure. Romanova and Kudinska (2016) documented that both cutting-edge IT firms and the conventional banking industry are monitoring financial technology and utilising it to enhance their offerings. Speedy and continuous growth of banks in a progressive and agile way can be expected through the use of computers and other digital technologies associated with financial services. FinTech can take several forms, such as the digitalisation of the financial services industry and the exploration of potential financial solutions through information technology (Zaghol et al., 2021). The chapter aims to: 1) provide an overview of FinTech and its various dimensions, 2) discuss the FinTech adoption in relation to different theories to explain how FinTech adoption influences the financial performance of Banks, 3) facilitate the bank's financial performance under the umbrella of FinTech adoption by offering the evolution of FinTech and the components of FinTech used in previous studies, and 4) develop and present a Bank-Based Novel Comprehensive FinTech Adoption Index (BBNC-FTAI) that can best measure FinTech adoption in banks and enhance the performance of the banking industry. The researchers can collect primary or secondary data on the components offered by BBNC-FTAI.

2. FINTECH DIMENSIONS

- Financial Inclusion

Financial inclusion is a vital aspect of FinTech because FinTech solutions (such as mobile banking, digital wallets, and peer-to-peer lending) enhance access to financial services, making them more affordable and convenient, particularly for unbanked or underserved populations. Financial inclusion refers to the process of ensuring that organisations and the general public have easy access to various financial products and services, including loan facilities, savings, funds transfers, payments, and insurance, that meet their needs at affordable prices and improve their living standards. To improve the financial well-being of the entire society, particularly the lower middle class, the primary purpose of financial inclusion is to provide businesses and individuals with easy access to financial services (Alnabulsi & Salameh, 2022). Moreover, financial inclusion enables residents to understand fundamental financial terms thoroughly and also provides security to financial consumers (Erfan et al., 2021). Alnabulsi and Salameh (2022) expanded the discussion, reporting that financial inclusion is beneficial for citizens, as it offers them numerous opportunities to make digital payments and utilise the services of SMEs. Additionally, financial inclusion enhances awareness and is beneficial in protecting the rights and interests of customers (Kartawinata et al., 2021). Finally, Financial inclusion is indispensable for the stability and development of various economic and social sectors, as well as for devising a comprehensive strategy for sustainable growth (Alnabulsi & Salameh, 2022).

- Alternative Payment Methods (APMs)

One of the significant key dimensions of FinTech is alternative payment methods (APMs), such as cryptocurrencies, contactless cards, QR code payments, and mobile wallets, which make transactions more convenient, safer, and faster compared to conventional banks and cash transactions. Such APMs support global trade, enhance e-commerce, reduce transaction costs and reshape the way money moves. In Pakistan, JazzCash and Easypaisa are the best examples of APMs. More recently, to upgrade the imbursement methods for people in different regions, situations and circumstances, the payment industry has acquired new perspectives, including improvements in cash payments, wallets and mobile wallets, direct debit, invoice and pay later solutions, online banking e-payments, cryptocurrencies, and credit and debit cards (Payment Methods Report, 2019). The APMs have further dimensions:

a) Remittances, digital wallets, and payments (categorised as Payments & Transfers).
b) Branchless banking services (categorised as Digital Banking).
c) Microfinance platforms and Peer-to-peer lending (categorised as Lending & Crowdfunding)
d) Usage-based insurance and Digital insurance platforms (categorised as InsurTech or Insurance Technology).
e) Decentralised finance (DeFi), smart contracts, Digital currencies (categorised as Blockchain & Cryptocurrencies).

- Automations

Automation can be considered a key dimension of FinTech, particularly in areas such as chatbots (utilising AI-driven customer service), fraud detection, automated trading, and robo-advisory. It offers faster and more cost-effective financial services, reduces human errors, improves efficiency, and lowers transaction costs. Thus, it makes finance more customer-friendly and scalable. Sobczak (2022) argues that organizations are quickly shifting on the IT-based solutions such as digital revolution, automatic procedures and software robots. Swan (2017) further highlighted that an automated economy centered on economic operations is relevant in contexts where robotic technology substitutes manpower. Anagnoste (2017) documented that employment structure is modified due to machine automation, demanding the reallocation of personnel for more advanced jobs for high value addition but this reallocation also requires training of some workers. Kedziora and Penttinen (2021) highlighted that robotic process automation predominantly affects banking industry. The Automation has further dimensions:

a) Asset management, Digital Trading, and Robo-advisors (categorized as Wealth Management & Investments).
b) Fraud detection, risk management and compliance (categorized as RegTech or Regulatory Technology).

3. FINTECH VS BANKING SECTOR SERVICES

Arslanian and Fischer (2019) further noted that competition between FinTech and conventional banking services negatively affects traditional banks' risk-taking, performance, and innovation. FinTech dampens the number of high interest based loan opportunities. The inclusion and development of FinTech have significant impact on the traditional banking frameworks (Petralia et al., 2019). Similarly, FinTech is expanding in various financial domains, including investments, lending, deposits, account settlements, and fund raising (Nguyen et al., 2022). The recent era is experiencing a swift global advancement in FinTech, which has entirely changed the ecosystem of the financial industry via digitalisation, i.e., cloud computing, blockchain, and AI, especially in emerging economies (Li et al., 2022). These digital developments have urged the advancement of novel financial models, meaningfully changing traditional commercial banks' operational efficiency, service quality, and profit structures (Kayed et al., 2025). Moreover, the depth of interest rate liberalisation reforms has gradually decreased the lending rate on assets, while liability has increased due to deposit costs; thus, the commercial banks are experiencing squeezed profit margins. Concurrently, the conventional business model of banks is significantly changed due to the speedy growth in FinTech. Unlike traditional systems that depend heavily on physical branches for service delivery, FinTech rely on offline branches and redefines how customers interact with financial services to fulfill the growing demand for online services (Baker et al., 2023). Furthermore, traditional commercial banks have overlooked niche targeting. Conversely, FinTech firms are competing intensely with commercial banks by focusing on micro-segmentation through flexible service models and leveraging their technological strengths.

4. NEED FOR FINTECH ADOPTION IN BANKS (TRADITIONAL AND ISLAMIC) UNDER DIFFERENT THEORIES

FinTech firms offer innovative products and services that replace traditional banking services and fulfil consumer demands (Yudaruddin, 2023). In the adoption of digital innovations, traditional and Islamic banks have faced some limitations and various benefits. The aim of maximizing gains and coping with competitors encourages conventional banks to implement FinTech tools including AI based risk models, robotic advisory services and introducing application programming interfaces at large scale. Islamic banking is based on the rules of Sharia in which profit and loss sharing, ethical and assets backed financing are prioritized. Therefore, Shariah Supervisory Boards again check and filter technology-based products before their implementation which further slowdown the innovation process (Fianto et al.,

2021). Nguyen et al. (2022) noted that FinTech allows low-cost mobile payments that decrease the long-run advantages held by commercial banks in term of payment settlements. However, Islamic banks, along with conventional banks do not have such technology (Abdul-Majid et al., 2017). Furthermore, Islamic banks have to bear high expenses tied to Sharia counsellors especially for products and auditors (Yudaruddin, 2023). Owing to the introduction of Islamic finance the intensity of innovation is stubby in Islamic banks (Panjwani & Shili, 2020). In addressing the impacts of FinTech, Islamic banks are slower as compare to conventional banks (Ali et al., 2019). However, the chapter discusses the need for FinTech adoption in banks under different theories i.e.,

- Resource-Based View (RBV)

By drawing on RBV, organizations can grab competitive edge through deploying unique, distinctive and valuable resources that are deeply rooted within the organization (Barney, 1991). The efficiency and effectiveness of banking industry can be boosted by leveraging digital competencies including open banking APIs, AI analytics and blockchain framework. As compare to traditional banks, Islamic banks face further delays in employing such resources owing to extra Shariah approval procedures that are slow but more vigilant. If all other factors remain constant, Islamic banks show relatively lower FinTech Index scores compare to traditional banks. This is due to the distinguishing operational paradigms, the built-in procedures resulting from Sharia compliance requirements and the differences in the levels of risk aversion may result in different speed of innovation adoption of both corresponding institutions. However, traditional financial institutions have less governance limitations so, they exhibit quicker growth and efficiency but Islamic institutions have to comply with sharia so they achieve similar developments in slow pace.

- Financial Stability Theory

Financial Stability Theory explains the impact of innovation on systemic resilience (Bank for International Settlements [BIS], 2021). FinTech opens new door for systematic risks in the shape of algorithmic biases and cybersecurity flaws. In accepting the same technology, Islamic banks —due to their inherent nature, asset-backed financing and risk sharing agreement—can have different stability dynamics compare to conventional banks. FinTech embracement have positive impact on stability of banks and this impact is significant and robust in Islamic banks than traditional banks. By implementing the principles of risk-sharing, asset-backed financing, and ethical banking practices, Islamic banks can better harness the potential of FinTech to increase stability. This approach may also strengthen their resilience through advanced risk management tools, all while avoiding unnecessary increases in systemic risk. Although, Stability and profitability of all banks either Islamic or conventional can be increased by adopting FinTech, Islamic banks due to their focus on asset-backed financing and risk sharing are able to achieve comparatively higher stability than profitability that is the main target of their counterparts. The relative stability gains that result from embracing FinTech may be higher for the same level of efficiency improvement because Islamic banks place a higher priority on real economic activity, ethical issues and mutual risk-sharing than traditional banks, which are primarily motivated by pure profit maximization.

- Technology spillover theory and the Disruptive theory of innovation

Technology spillover theory and disruptive innovation theory can be applied to understand the relationship between Fintech and the profitability of banks. The theoretical lens of disruptive innovation theory is widely utilized in past studies to elucidate the impact of Fintech on the profitability of banks (Siek & Sutanto, 2019; Tarawneh et al., 2024). This theory explains how new business models and technology can transform conventional industries by focusing on previously neglected market segments (Kjellman et al., 2019). These innovations typically begin with a negligible impact on the market, but over times, they grow and develop, becoming strong enough to challenge and eventually replace established players (Leo et al., 2019; Owusu & Gupta, 2024). Disruptive innovation theory is specifically suitable within the framework of Fintech and its rising impact on conventional banking (Solanki & Sujee, 2022). The innovative products and services of FinTech startups are more consumer-oriented, easily reachable, and affordable compared to the offerings of traditional banks (Nugraha et al., 2022). These products and services include blockchain-based solutions, peer-to-peer lending platforms, and mobile banking applications (Mothobi & Kebotsamang, 2024). Such innovations appeal to consumers who are dissatisfied with conventional banking products (T.-H. Chen, 2020).

Bouheni et al. (2023) found that the long-standing aggressive competition in the financial services industry is disrupted as these innovations are developed and widely accepted because they reshape customer expectations. Conventional banks lose their importance in the market, which values convenience, customer-oriented banking experiences, and speed, when they fail to adopt technological advancements. On the other hand, financial organizations that proactively incorporate FinTech solutions can significantly improve operational efficiency, customer satisfaction, and cut costs. Ibidunni et al. (2022) highlighted that banks can widen their access, particularly in less-served or far-flung geographical areas, increase their clientele, and market penetration by utilizing digital platforms and tools. The outcomes of Fintech are revolutionary in smaller and developing countries like Fiji. In such regions, banks can foster economic stability, provide inclusive financial services, and mitigate the risk of structural challenges by incorporating technology-based innovations. Avoiding innovative technologies can expose organizations to severe competition and the risk of losing market relevance. Finally, disruptive innovation theory emphasizes the importance of continuous innovation. For banks, particularly in developing economies, adopting FinTech not only gives a strategic advantage but is also necessary for sustainable growth in a quickly changing financial environment. Moreover, the performance of financial institutions can be enhanced if they invest more in FinTech. With this investment, the integration of financial services and technology will increase, which will accordingly reveal the impact of technology diffusion (Kayed et al., 2025; Von Solms, 2021). Disruptive Innovation Theory delineates that by providing relatively reachable and affordable substitutes, simpler and novel business models and technologies have ability to disrupt existing businesses. FinTech is an emerging sector and closely related to this theory as it utilizes technology to introduce innovative financial products. Solanki & Sujee (2022) argued that FinTech startups targets low access markets, offer affordable and user-friendly services that encounter conventional financial firms. Such firms address the limitations of traditional banks such as obsolete technology and high charges and accommodate larger customer groups. FinTech exemplifies disruptive models, highlighting its connection to Disruptive Innovation Theory. FinTech companies provide customized services to the unserved areas, gives innovative solutions that are accessible and cost efficient. Gradually, such technologies transfer a significant amount of risk to conventional financial institutions. The conventional banking landscape is disrupted by Fintech's technological based new financial offerings, emphasis executives to adapt it otherwise there would be risk of decreasing market share. The interaction between Fintech and Disruptive Innovation Theory is steadily displacing traditional players by exemplifying the way technology fulfills clients' needs. Ibidunni et al. (2022) highlighted that with the development of FinTech, its effect on financial institutions is extended, emphasizing the lasting importance of Disruptive Innovation Theory in current business landscape.

- Porter's Theory of Competitive Advantage

By focusing on differentiation via innovation, client-oriented financial services, following a low-cost strategy through modernized operations, FinTech startups integrate with Porter's theory of competitive advantage. Such organizations challenge conventional companies that are bound to inherited systems by emphasizing niche marketing and making new client's segments via imposing affordable prices. FinTech companies interrupt financial industry, successfully compete with and create competitive advantage by implementing strategies align with porter's ideologies. Such strategic alignment reflects porters' lasting impact, drive competition and restructure financial sector in the rapidly changing FinTech sphere (Aggarwal et al., 2023).

5. DRIVERS OF FINTECH ADOPTION IN BANKS

Drivers of adoption may range from customer demand, competition, regulatory push, to cost efficiency. FinTech adoption in banks is necessary due to increasing customer demand for digital transactions. FinTech adoption in banks can grab profits by providing digital, fast and smooth services to their clients, which not only covers customer demand but also beats competition. Banks can confront disruptive innovation by collaborating with FinTech startups to enhance clients' trust and gain added benefits (Juengerkes, 2016). Elsaid, (2023) claimed that space and time limitations in the delivery of financial services can be diminished by incorporating FinTech into traditional banking. Banks can provide instantaneous and easily available banking services by utilizing online platforms e.g., mobile payments and internet. This innovative competency of banks enables them to reach branchless channels in offering financial services and advance their operational responsiveness as well as expand target audience. Resultantly, the efficiency of banks in collecting, processing, and analyzing data is enhanced, thereby improving customer acquisition and facilitating banks' entry into the wider financial system (Gomber et al., 2018). FinTech adoption helps reduce costs in core areas. For example, Stulz (2019) noted that it minimizes channel costs by utilizing efficient and effective service delivery systems and rationalizes service locations. Likewise, C. Li et al. (2022) reported that loan decisions are improved as credit review costs diminished due to prompt and precise customer data fetching. As a result, such technological dissemination maintains operating efficiency and holds a vital position in enhancing the sustainability and profitability of Banks. Mixed findings are reported in the literature regarding the relationship between FinTech and banks' profits. For Example, Aloulou et al. (2024) and Kayed et al. (2025) reported a positive impact, whereas Lu and Kosim (2022) and Adalessossi (2023) found a negative effect. On the other hand, Bouheni et al. (2023) found no significant relationship between these two variables. FinTech and AI have reshaped international banking, restructuring the delivery of digital services, customer service, and risk management. Philippon (2016) and Arner et al. (2020) found that online platforms, blockchain-based agreements, RegTech solutions, and AI-based credit ratings are observed to boost financial inclusion and cut operating expenses. Furthermore, FinTech has intensified market competition and significantly impacted the profitability of commercial banks by reshaping their asset and liability sides, as well as their intermediary businesses (Song et al., 2023). The transformational effect of digital payments on performance of banks is supported by empirical evidence. There is positive impact of e-transaction technologies on banks' profit as it advanced financial transparency, ensures prompt services, standardized payment process (Adalessossi, 2023; Kharrat et al., 2024)

Nevertheless, the following are the main drivers of FinTech adoption in the banks that can increase bank profitability:

- Customer demand,
- Competition
- Regulatory push
- Efficiency (cost reduction, digital transactions, service delivery speed)
- Risk management (credit risk, operational risk, fraud detection)
- Customer satisfaction and retention

Conversely, these technology-based advantages pose new threats, such as algorithmic bias, complex data governance challenges, and cybersecurity risks (Bank for International Settlements [BIS], 2021; Iqbal et al., 2025). FinTech-driven finance has yielded mixed findings regarding the widening of financial access in developing countries. Although online client onboarding and mobile banking have increased financial inclusion, they have sometimes exacerbated disparities in the context of limited digital literacy and inadequate infrastructure (Demirgüç-Kunt et al., 2022). To what extent FinTech advances efficiency, depends on regulatory policies and the organization's willingness.

6. FINTECH ADOPTION AND BANKS' FINANCIAL PERFORMANCE

The banking sector is entirely reshaped due to FinTech. Therefore, the rapidly growing interest in FinTech products among clients contributed in both constructive and detrimental ways. Alliances between FinTech and banks within the financial industry have minimised transaction costs, ultimately ensuring client benefits. It appeals to new customers, upgrades approaches to clients' engagement, boosts brand loyalty, and ultimately improves performance (Obeidat & Saxena, 2015); it also bolsters the industry's competitive strength globally. Banks can enhance the availability of their products and services in the digital realm by adopting FinTech. They are offering distinct mobile banking facilities. Obeidat & Saxena (2015) found that, to offer convenient, accessible and quality services to customers in the banking sector, up-to-date channels of operations such as m-banking and e-banking are impossible without FinTech. Wonglimpiyarat (2017) highlighted the positive impact of the association between the banking industry and FinTech, which enhances efficiency and effectiveness in the financial industry. FinTech is utilising technology in the banking industry to develop products and services that meet the changing needs of consumers (Mbama, 2018). Friedline et al. (2018) documented that the progress of FinTech within a country can be attributed to its positive impact on both individuals and banking institutions, as it enables the entire population to achieve greater financial inclusion. Buchak et al. (2018) were among the first to analyse how regulatory considerations influence the impact of FinTech-provided credit services on banks' financial performance. Rita (2018) found that incorporating FinTech led to a positive change in the stock market prices for some banks.

The competition and performance of the banking industry are significantly affected by its collaboration with FinTech. Financial Technology implementation provides technology-based innovative solutions that advance service delivery, improve customers' involvement and enhance operational efficiency which ultimately challenges conventional banks customs. In banking, the nexus between competitiveness and bank performance is highly important, as competitiveness frames the way banks works, make innovations and assist their clients. Strong competition directly affects bank's performance and pushes them to struggle for efficiency and excellence. In a competitive environment, banks are encouraged to incorporate innovative and tech-based strategies for differentiation from other banks. Research shows that FinTech upgrades financial services in term of providing more secure, improved and cozier business structures, affordable transactions, and also improves the quality of these services (Nguyen et al. 2022; Yao & Song 2023). Therefore, the alliance between the banking industry and FinTech could develop an efficient financial ecosystem.

In banking industry, competition affects the combination of Fintech solutions and strategies that finally frames the way this combination influences performance of banks. Dwivedi et al. (2021) highlighted that to maintain their image in a competitive landscape, FinTech incorporation has become an essential element for banks. The highly competitive markets compel banks to maintain a competitive advantage through technologies and take more preemptive assimilation of Fintech tools. This puts significant impact on performance as these banks strive to distinguish themselves from their competitors. This motivation for innovation helps in launching novel, client-oriented products and services. Banks can enhance their performance by maintaining attractiveness and relevancy in the industry along with satisfying the changing demands and preferences of their clients. Moreover, banks are motivated for efficient management of their resources due to high competition. To cope with competition, banks should focus on operational excellence and cost management. Behl (2022) highlights that efficient management of resources and cutting costs can enhance profits, and ultimately have positive impact on financial performance. The relationship between competitiveness and banking outcomes goes beyond financial indicators, that also affects clients trust and satisfaction. In highly competitive environment, banks are more customer-oriented and improve customer services, and pay more attention to their needs.

Therefore, to improve their sustainable performance and goodwill in the market, banks should build more trust and robust brand loyalty via adoption of FinTech. However, there is a complex relationship between competitiveness and bank performance. Competition motivates banks to value customer satisfaction, make effective cost management, foster innovation, resultantly all these factors enhance their performance, where FinTech adoption may augment the competitiveness of Banks. Such links infer that competitiveness may moderate the nexus between Fintech Adoption and Bank Performance. According to Shuli et al. (2022), FinTech has a favorable effect on banks' ROE, TA, NIM, and credit risk measured through NPL. The quick evolution of FinTech has expended the strategic choices available to commercial banks regarding operational development and business management. It urged banks to embrace innovation and transformation that in turn offers new opportunities to increase profitability. It is imperative to note that, although FinTech creates new competitive pressure with in banking industry, it simultaneously provides significant platforms for growth and innovation (Tong & Yang, 2025). Along with the favorable impressions of FinTech adoption on banks' financial performance, such adoption has also many drawbacks on financial stability and performance of Banks where Nguyen (2022) reported negative impact of FinTech development on financial stability in emerging markets. As indicated by heterogeneity analysis, this negative impact of FinTech development on financial stability is greater when the extent of financial stability is low and such negative effect is smaller if foreign ownership is high. On the contrary, the influence of FinTech incorporation on banks performance may be less evident in low competitive markets. Banks working in low competitive markets might not be compelled to quickly integrate technological innovation which potentially causing a diminished influence on their performance (Chan et al., 2022). It is important to understand the moderating effect of competitiveness on the relationship between Fintech adoption and bank performance. FinTech adoption underscores the importance of evaluating the market's competitive environment, recognizing that the overall impact on performance can vary across different levels of competition.

Table 1. Non-Bank-Based measure of FinTech

S#	Authors	Measurement of FinTech
1	Li et al. (2024a)	Digital Fundraising in a country
2	Shahid et al. (2025)	Digital Capital Raising in a country
3	Li et al. (2025)	Digital Fundraising in a country
4	Li et al. (2024b)	FinTech Revenue

continued on following page

Table 1. Continued

S#	Authors	Measurement of FinTech
5	Li et al. (2024c)	FinTech Revenue
6	Ishtiaq et al. (2024)	Growth of Fintech Revenue
7	Yuan et al. (2025)	Financial Inclusion Index

7. MEASUREMENT OF FINTECH IN RECENT STUDIES AND BEST FINTECH INDEX

Presenting the components that can best measure the FinTech is one of the objectives of this chapter. Recently studies measure fintech with different indicators. Early study presents that *p2p* lending (peer-to-peer) and crowdfunding are the best measure of non-bank based FinTech (Chen et al., 2016). SMEs with low credit rating can easily get *p2p* lending services and crowdfunding. Table 1 presents the Non-Bank-based measure of FinTech used in the previous studies. Table 1 shows that mostly studies have been used Digital Find Raising, Fintech revenue growth and Financial inclusion to measure FinTech to explore the impact of FinTech on sustainability measures.

Table 2. Bank-Based Components to measure FinTech Adoption (Survey, Patents and Index-based measures of FinTech)

S#	Authors	Measurement of FinTech
Panel A (Survey Based FinTech Measures)		
1	Meero, A. (2025)	FinTech Index Score (0-7 Scale) corroborated from the study of Berg et al. (2020)
2	Alshannag et al. (2024)	Alternative payment method Automation Financial inclusion
Panel B (Patent-Based FinTech Measures)		
3	Feng et al. (2025)	The number of FinTech patents held by commercial banks
4	Liu & Hu (2025)	The number of FintTech patents held by commercial banks
5	Li et al. (2025)	The number of firm-level FinTech patents of its bank lenders
6	Pan et al., (2025)	The number of FinTech patent applications filed by banks
7	Qian et al. (2025)	The number of FinTech patent applications filed by banks
8	Wang & He (2025)	Fintech-Related Patents

continued on following page

Table 2. Continued

S#	Authors	Measurement of FinTech
9	Zhang & Li (2025)	(1) The number of patents applied for and authorized by banks (2) FinTech subsidiaries of banks can provide FinTech services or products to the parent banks.
Panel C (Index-Based FinTech Measures)		
10	Chand et al. (2025)	Mobile Banking
11	Kayed et al. (2025)	Three-dimensional FinTech Index 1) Automated teller machine services 2) Internet banking services 3) Phone banking services
12	Khanchel et al. (2025)	1) Mobile transactions 2) Internet transactions 3) ATM transactions
13	Ngo et al. (2025)	Three-dimensional FinTech Index 1) Digital platforms 2) Mobile banking 3) Customer-facing digital services
14	Duan & Liu (2025)	Six-dimensional FinTech Index 1) Artificial Intelligence 2) Blockchain 3) Cloud computing 4) Big data 5) Digitization 6) Mobilization
15	Meero (2025)	Seven-dimensional FinTech Index 1) Strategic FinTech partnerships 2) Blockchain Usage 3) Biometric e-KYC 4) AI in credit and risk 5) AI in customer service 6) Open-Banking/Public APIs 7) Digital-Only App

Similarly, Table 2 presents the survey-based and Patent-based measures of Bank-Fintech components. Panels A and B of Table 2 show that researchers have used survey-based and Patent-based components of FinTech respectively to uncover the impact of FinTech Adoption on Bank's Financial performance. It is clear from the Table that recent researchers are using different surveys (using different scales), the number of patents and filed patent applications to proxy FinTech adoption in Banks to measure the impact of FinTech adoption on Banks' Financial Performance. Mostly the researchers used single-component-based FinTech measure in their studies. Panel C of the Table 2 also presents that researchers have used different dimensions and developed FinTech Index. It is clear from the Table that Index developed by Meero (2025) is more comprehensive and versatile to measure the FinTech adoption in Banks.

Table 3 presents that the previous studies have measured the FinTech adoption in banks by blending the new and old methods, even though it is challenging to distinguish between conventional and tech-based financial services. Thus, researchers developed the bank-based FinTech adoption index using text mining (Khan et al., 2023), Keyword Frequency Analysis (Naser et al., 2024; Xu et al., 2025), Word Query Index (Drago et al., 2025) and Google Trend index (Nguyen, 2025). Khan et al. (2023) used text mining method and observe that nine different components can best measure the FinTech adoption in banks. Drago et al. (2025) used different variables and calculated the frequency of these variables mentioned in the Annual reports and non-financial statements/reports of Banks. Similarly, Table 3 shows that Naser et al. (2024) used textual analysis method which is comprised of word frequency statistics and segmentation algorithms to calculate keywords used in banks' financial statements. They used a total of 32 keywords and then divide the occurrence of each word by the total number of keywords to build Index based on the frequency of each word. Similarly, Xu et al. (2025) uses different keyword to measure FinTech adoption in Banks. Nguyen (2025) used a comparatively short index to measure FinTech adoption in Banks. The author utilized the number of fintech companies (FIN) and the search keyword "FinTech" in Google Trends to measure FinTech.

Table 3. Bank-Based Components to measure FinTech Adoption (Word Query, Keyword, and Textual analysis-based measures of FinTech)

S#	Authors	Measurement of FinTech
1	Khan et al. (2023)	Text mining 1) Focus Embracing New Technologies 2) User Experience 3) Integration Innovation Initiatives 4) Automation and Artificial Intelligence 5) Digital Payment Solutions 6) Fintech Partnerships 7) Support for Open APIs 8) Mobile Banking Capabilities 9) Digital Presence
2	Naser et al. (2024)	Keyword Frequency Analysis A. Technology input dimension 1. Artificial Intelligence technology i) Artificial Intelligence ii) Face recognition iii) Voice recognition iv) Fingerprint recognition 2. Blockchain technology i) Blockchain ii) Alliance chain iii) Distributed ledger iv) Asymmetric encryption 3. Cloud technology i) Cloud computing ii) Cloud service iii) Cloud platform iv) Cloud architecture 4. Big data technology i) Big data ii) Data flow iii) Data mining iv) Data visualization B. Innovation output dimension 1. Payment and settlement innovation i) Online payment ii) Mobile payment iii) QR code payment iv) Digital wallet 2. Resource allocation innovation i) Online payment ii) Online finance iii) Lending platform iv) Inclusive credit 3. Risk management innovation i) Customer portrait ii) predictive model iii) credit evaluation iv) Anti-fraud 4. Channel construction innovation i) Online banking ii) Mobile banking iii) Internet banking iv) Bank Ap

continued on following page

Table 3. Continued

S#	Authors	Measurement of FinTech
3	Drago et al. (2025)	Word Query Index 1) Frequency of the word "Fintech" repeated in the annual report 2) Frequency of the word "Fintech" repeated in the non-financial report 3) Disclosure of FinTech dimensions in the annual report 4) Disclosure of FinTech dimensions in the non-financial report 5) Number of financial investments in Fintech companies 6) Number of projects in regulatory sandbox; A market where the security is listed.
4	Xu et al. (2025)	Keyword Frequency Analysis 1) Bank 2) Financial performance of the bank 3) Performance of a financial institution 4) Fintech 5) Finance technology 6) Digital finance 7) Internet finance 8) Online finance 9) Mobile finance 10) Electronic finance 11) Regtech 12) Wealthtech 13) Insurtech 14) Financial inclusion 15) Cryptocurrency 16) Blockchain 17) P2P lending 18) Peer-to-peer lending 19) Shadow bank
5	Nguyen (2025)	1) The number of fintech companies (FIN) 2) The Google trend index (TRE): search of keyword "FinTech)

Figure 1. Keywords Occurrence Network

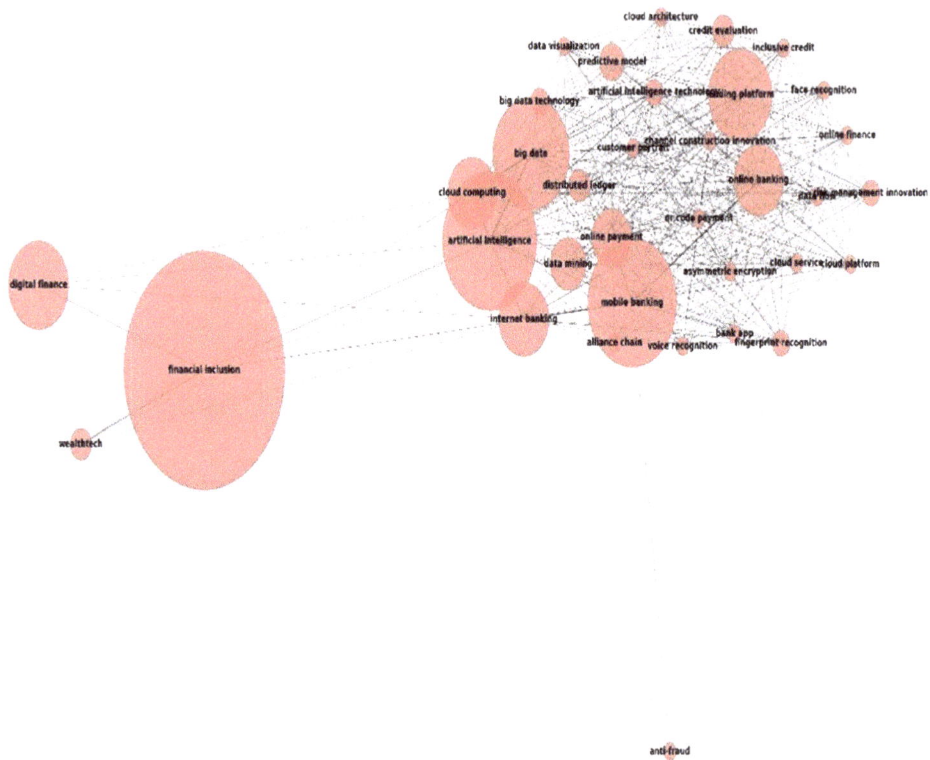

Figure 2. Keywords Communities

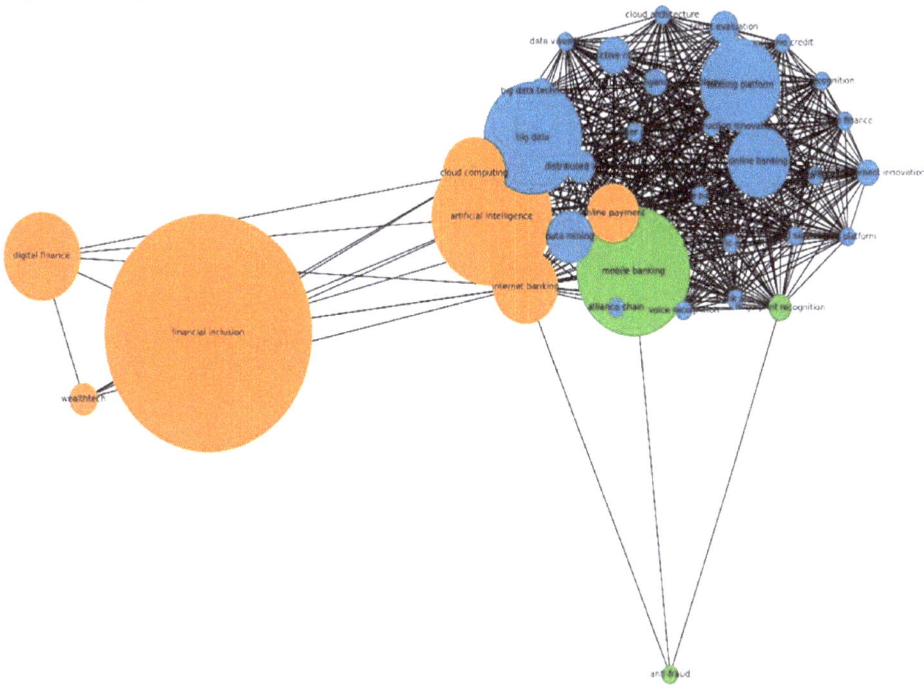

8. BANK-BASED NOVEL COMPREHENSIVE FINTECH ADOPTION INDEX (BBNC-FTAI)

After carefully analyzing the indices developed by recent researchers, the chapter creates a Bank-Based novel comprehensive FinTech adoption Index (BBNC-FTAI) that can best measure the FinTech adoption in banks and can enhance the performance of the banking industry. To construct the BBNC-FTAI, the chapter employs textual analysis using Python software. In textual analysis, the study employed word frequency via segmentation algorithms and calculated the keyword frequency using annual reports and previously published research papers from 2023 to 2025. This robust BBNC-FTAI will better measure the extent, intensity, and effectiveness of FinTech adoption in banks, evaluate banks' financial performance, make comparisons among banks and incorporate both the technological capacity and digital service utilization. The BBNC-FTAI comprises of eight domains and has the following eight dimensions, presented in Table 4.

Figure 3. FinTech Keyword Cloud.

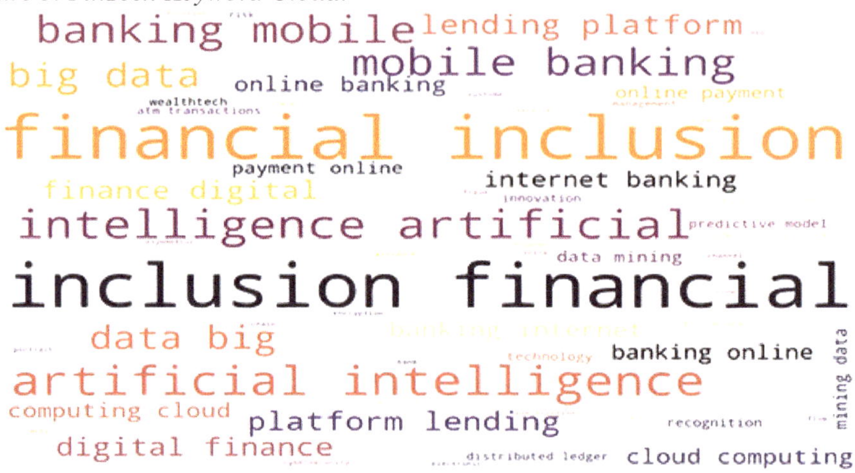

Figure 4. FinTech Keyword Cooccurrence Heatmap

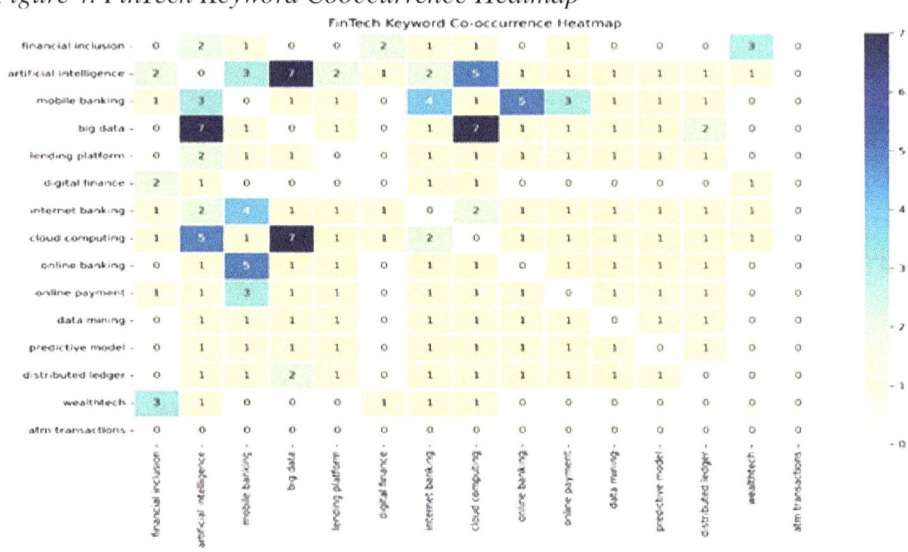

However, Figure 1 provides the FinTech keyword occurrence network, while Figure 2 displays FinTech keyword communities. Figure 1 shows how the nexus between/among keywords frequently co-occurred or co-appeared. On the other hand, Figure 2 clusters deeply connected keywords into groups of distinct themes. Figure 3 is a visual representation of keywords that occur most frequently, along with their respective sizes. The word size shows the relative frequency and importance of each word. Figure 4 represents the frequency of those keywords appearing together with the help of color intensity. The intensity of each color not only displays the depth of association but also shows the thematic linkages along with their relative importance for analysis. Similarly, to determine whether the overall tone of the text is neutral, negative, or positive, the study utilizes sentiment polarity. Figure 5 displays average sentimental polarity associated with the FinTech term, where internet banking, online banking and ATM transactions have more positive sentiments related to FinTech. In contrast, negative sentiment is reflected by the words, such as Big Data, Digital Finance and online payments.

Figure 5. FinTech Keywords by Sentiment Polarity

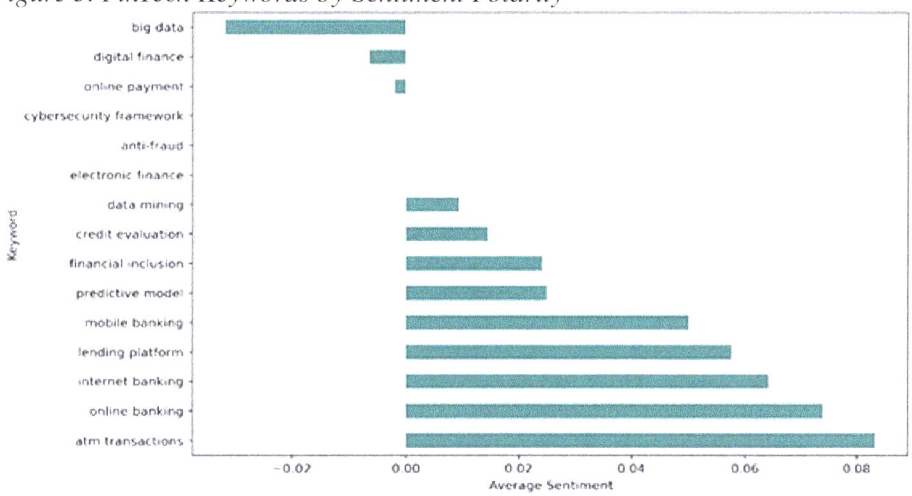

Table 4. Bank-Based Novel Comprehensive FinTech Adoption Index (BBNC-FTAI)

Domain	Sub-Domain	Dimension	Key Indicators
Measurement of how efficiently a Bank's technological backbone supports FinTech integration/adoption	Embracing New Technologies	Digital Infrastructure Readiness (DigiIR)	• Core Banking digitization level • FinTech patent applications • API banking availability • Cybersecurity framework • IT investment as % of total assets • Cloud computing use I. Cloud computing II. Cloud service III. Cloud platform IV. Cloud architecture • Artificial Intelligence technology I. Artificial Intelligence II. Face recognition III. Voice recognition IV. Fingerprint recognition • Big data technology I. Big data II. Data flow III. Data mining IV. Data visualization
Measurement of how Banks adopt digital platforms to conduct day-to-day financial transactions	Mobile Banking Capabilities/Digital Payment Solutions	Digital Payments & Transactions (DigiPT)	• Internet banking transactions (%) • Online payment • Mobile banking users (%) • QR code payment • Digital wallet integration • Real-time payment systems (RTGS/instant pay) • ATM transactions

continued on following page

Table 4. Continued

Domain	Sub-Domain	Dimension	Key Indicators
Measurement of modernization of credit and lending processes	Innovations in Digital lending	Digital Lending & Credit Scoring (DigiLCS)	• Use of AI/ML in credit scoring • Share of online loan applications (%) • Partnerships with lending platforms • Use of alternative data for risk analysis • Channel construction innovation I. Online banking II. Mobile banking III. Internet banking IV. Bank App V. Online payment VI. Online finance VII. Lending platform VIII. Inclusive credit
Measurement of digitalization of investment services	Digital Presence in investment	Digital Investment & Wealth Management (DigiIWM)	• Robo-advisory services • Online investment portals • Use of blockchain in trading/settlement • Distributed ledger • Use of Asymmetric encryption • Wealthtech
Assessment of digital transformation risk control and insurance	Risk control	Risk Management &InsurTech (RM&IT)	• Risk management innovation I. Customer portrait II. Predictive model III. Credit evaluation IV. Anti-fraud • Integration with InsurTech firms • Online insurance policy management • Automated claims and underwriting • Use of predictive analytics for risk

continued on following page

Table 4. Continued

Domain	Sub-Domain	Dimension	Key Indicators
Measurement of user interaction and satisfaction with digital services	User Experience	Customer Digital Experience & Engagement (DigiCEE)	• Customer adoption rate to I. Digital finance II. Electronic finance III. Financial inclusion • Use of AI chatbots • Mobile app usability score • Customer satisfaction with digital channels Omnichannel integration
Measurement of innovative culture and ecosystem collaboration	Integration Innovation Initiatives /Fintech Partnerships	Digital Innovation & Collaboration (DigiIC)	• Number of FinTech partnerships • Internal innovation labs • R&D expenditure on digital products • Open banking initiatives
Evaluation of compliance readiness and digital governance maturity	Regulatory Compliance and Governance	Regulatory Compliance & Digital Governance (DigiRCG)	• Adoption of digital KYC/ AML systems • Adherence to cybersecurity & data privacy laws • RegTech integration • Participation in regulatory sandboxes

In column 3 of Table 4, the study provides the abbreviations of dimensions that future researchers can use to measure the FinTech Adoption in banks and investigate the performance of banking companies. These dimensions are as follows:

1. Digital Infrastructure Readiness (DigiIR)
2. Digital Payments & Transactions (DigiPT)
3. Digital Lending & Credit Scoring (DigiLCS)
4. Digital Investment & Wealth Management (DigiIWM)
5. Risk Management &InsurTech (RM&IT)
6. Customer Digital Experience & Engagement (DigiCEE)
7. Digital Innovation & Collaboration (DigiIC)
8. Regulatory Compliance & Digital Governance (DigiRCG)

Researchers may collect data on these eight dimensions to measure FinTech adoption in banks and banks' financial performance. The researchers can collect primary data through a customer survey on digital banking usage or a survey from the bank's officials by assigning different scores/scale that may be (see Table 5):

Table 5. Score/scale for eight dimensions of Comprehensive FinTech Adoption Index (BBNC-FTAI)

Level of FinTech Adoption	Degree	Dummy
No FinTech adoption	nill	0
Initial Stage FinTech Adoption	Very Low	1
Partial FinTech Adoption	Low	2
Moderate FinTech adoption	Moderate	3
High FinTech Adoption	High	4
Full FinTech Adoption	Very High	5

The data can be collected through Text mining and word frequency analysis, where researchers can apply such techniques on published reports of banks and other sources, like:

- Central bank digital readiness report
- Interviews with digital transformation teams
- Banks' annual reports
- Financial statements and IT expenditure
- Regulatory compliance disclosures

9. CONCLUSION

FinTech firms offer novel products and services that replace services provided by the traditional banking system, therefore, encouraging conventional banks to implement FinTech tools, including AI-based risk models, robotic advisory services and introducing application programming interfaces on a large scale. The chapter provides an overview of FinTech, its various dimensions and discusses the FinTech adoption in relation to different theories to explain how FinTech adoption influences the financial performance of Banks. The chapter further facilitates the bank's financial performance under the umbrella of FinTech adoption by offering the evolution of FinTech and the components of FinTech used in previous studies. Finally, the chapter develops and presents a Bank-Based Novel Comprehensive FinTech Adoption Index (BBNC-FTAI) that can best measure FinTech adoption in banks and enhance the performance of the banking industry. The researchers can collect primary or secondary data on the components offered by BBNC-FTAI.

Future studies should incorporate the proposed FinTech adoption index into their research and investigate the relationship between FinTech adoption and the financial performance of Banks. Future studies can compare the performance of

Islamic and conventional banks using this index. Central Banks can utilize this novel index and implement it in the banking sector to ensure its adoption and enhance the performance of the banking sector. With the adoption of such a FinTech index, banks can strike a balance between rapid innovation and risk management. Future studies may investigate the adoption of this index to measure the ESG performance of banks, financial stability and sustainable performance.

REFERENCES

Abad-Segura, E., González-Zamar, M. D., López-Meneses, E., & Vázquez-Cano, E. (2020). Financial technology: Review of trends, approaches and management. *Mathematics*, *8*(6), 951. DOI: 10.3390/math8060951

Abdul-Majid, M., Falahaty, M., & Jusoh, M. (2017). Performance of Islamic and conventional banks: A meta-frontier approach. *Research in International Business and Finance*, *42*, 1327–1335. DOI: 10.1016/j.ribaf.2017.07.069

Adalessossi, K. (2023). Impact of E-Banking on the Islamic bank profitability in Sub-Saharan Africa: What are the financial determinants? *Finance Research Letters*, *57*, 104188. DOI: 10.1016/j.frl.2023.104188

Aggarwal, M., Nayak, K. M., & Bhatt, V. (2023). Examining the factors influencing fintech adoption behaviour of gen Y in India. *Cogent Economics & Finance*, *11*(1), 2197699. DOI: 10.1080/23322039.2023.2197699

Ali, H., Abdullah, R., & Zaini, M. Z. (2019). Fintech and its potential impact on Islamic banking and finance industry: A case study of Brunei Darussalam and Malaysia. [IJIEF]. *International Journal of Islamic Economics and Finance*, *2*(1), 73–108. DOI: 10.18196/ijief.2116

Alnabulsi, Z. H., & Salameh, R. S. (2022). THE IMPACT OF LAUNCHING THE FINANCIAL INCLUSION STRATEGY ON ECONOMIC DEVELOPMENT. *Journal of Management Information & Decision Sciences*, *25*(1).

Aloulou, M., Grati, R., Al-Qudah, A. A., & Al-Okaily, M. (2024). Does FinTech adoption increase the diffusion rate of digital financial inclusion? A study of the banking industry sector. *Journal of Financial Reporting and Accounting*, *22*(2), 289–307. DOI: 10.1108/JFRA-05-2023-0224

Anagnoste, S. (2017, July). Robotic Automation Process-The next major revolution in terms of back office operations improvement. In *Proceedings of the International Conference on Business Excellence* (Vol. 11, No. 1, pp. 676-686). Sciendo. DOI: 10.1515/picbe-2017-0072

Arner, D. W., Buckley, R. P., Zetzsche, D. A., & Veidt, R. (2020). Sustainability, FinTech and financial inclusion. *European Business Organization Law Review*, *21*(1), 7–35. DOI: 10.1007/s40804-020-00183-y

Arslanian, H., & Fischer, F. (2019). *The future of finance: The impact of FinTech, AI, and crypto on financial services*. Springer. DOI: 10.1007/978-3-030-14533-0

Baker, H., Kaddumi, T. A., Nassar, M. D., & Muqattash, R. S. (2023). Impact of financial technology on improvement of banks' financial performance. *Journal of Risk and Financial Management*, *16*(4), 230. DOI: 10.3390/jrfm16040230

Barbu, C. M., Florea, D. L., Dabija, D. C., & Barbu, M. C. R. (2021). Customer experience in fintech. *Journal of Theoretical and Applied Electronic Commerce Research*, *16*(5), 1415–1433. DOI: 10.3390/jtaer16050080

Behl, A. (2022). Antecedents to firm performance and competitiveness using the lens of big data analytics: A cross-cultural study. *Management Decision*, *60*(2), 368–398. DOI: 10.1108/MD-01-2020-0121

Ben Bouheni, F., Tewari, M., Sidaoui, M., & Hasnaoui, A. (2023). An econometric understanding of Fintech and operating performance. *Review of Accounting and Finance*, *22*(3), 329–352. DOI: 10.1108/RAF-10-2022-0290

Buchak, G., Matvos, G., Piskorski, T., & Seru, A. (2018). Fintech, regulatory arbitrage, and the rise of shadow banks. *Journal of Financial Economics*, *130*(3), 453–483. DOI: 10.1016/j.jfineco.2018.03.011

Chan, R., Troshani, I., Rao Hill, S., & Hoffmann, A. (2022). Towards an understanding of consumers' FinTech adoption: The case of Open Banking. *International Journal of Bank Marketing*, *40*(4), 886–917. DOI: 10.1108/IJBM-08-2021-0397

Chand, S. A., Singh, B., Narayan, K., & Chand, A. (2025). The Impact of Financial Technology (FinTech) on Bank Risk-Taking and Profitability in Small Developing Island States: A Study of Fiji. *Journal of Risk and Financial Management*, *18*(7), 366. DOI: 10.3390/jrfm18070366

Chen, L., Huang, Z., & Liu, D. (2016). Pure and hybrid crowds in crowdfunding markets. *Financial Innovation*, *2*(1), 19. DOI: 10.1186/s40854-016-0038-5

Chen, T. H. (2020). Do you know your customer? Bank risk assessment based on machine learning. *Applied Soft Computing*, *86*, 105779. DOI: 10.1016/j.asoc.2019.105779

Demirgüç-Kunt, A., Klapper, L., Singer, D., & Ansar, S. (2022). *The Global Findex Database 2021: Financial inclusion, digital payments, and resilience in the age of COVID-19*. World Bank Publications. DOI: 10.1596/978-1-4648-1897-4

Duan, D., & Liu, K. (2025). Development of Fintech, Green Credit, and Risk Taking in Commercial Banks. *Finance Research Letters*, *86*, 108687. DOI: 10.1016/j.frl.2025.108687

Dwivedi, P., Alabdooli, J. I., & Dwivedi, R. (2021). Role of FinTech adoption for competitiveness and performance of the bank: A study of banking industry in UAE. *International Journal of Global Business and Competitiveness*, *16*(2), 130–138. DOI: 10.1007/s42943-021-00033-9

Elsaid, H. M. (2023). A review of literature directions regarding the impact of fintech firms on the banking industry. *Qualitative Research in Financial Markets*, *15*(5), 693–711. DOI: 10.1108/QRFM-10-2020-0197

Erfan, N., Gangwani, S., & Belgacem, S. B. (2021). Impact of disposition effect on financial decisions among women investors. *Journal of management Information and Decision Sciences, 24*, 1-10.

Feng, J., Jiao, W., & Wang, Y. (2025). Bank fintech and lending distance: The role of information asymmetry and risk management channels. *Economic Modelling*, *151*, 107154. DOI: 10.1016/j.econmod.2025.107154

Friedline, T., Despard, M. R., & Birkenmaier, J. (2018). Policy recommendations for expanding access to banking and financial services.

Gai, K., Qiu, M., & Sun, X. (2018). A survey on FinTech. *Journal of Network and Computer Applications*, *103*, 262–273. DOI: 10.1016/j.jnca.2017.10.011

Gomber, P., Kauffman, R. J., Parker, C., & Weber, B. W. (2018). On the fintech revolution: Interpreting the forces of innovation, disruption, and transformation in financial services. *Journal of Management Information Systems*, *35*(1), 220–265. DOI: 10.1080/07421222.2018.1440766

Ibidunni, A. S., Ufua, D. E., & Opute, A. P. (2022). Linking disruptive innovation to sustainable entrepreneurship within the context of small and medium firms: A focus on Nigeria. *African Journal of Science, Technology, Innovation and Development*, *14*(6), 1591–1607. DOI: 10.1080/20421338.2021.1975355

Iqbal, M. S., Sukamto, F. A. M. S. B., Norizan, S. N. B., Mahmood, S., Fatima, A., & Hashmi, F. (2025). AI in Islamic finance: Global trends, ethical implications, and bibliometric insights. *Review of Islamic Social Finance and Entrepreneurship*, 70-85.

Ishtiaq, M., Sher, F., & Shahid, M. N. (2024). Financial Inclusion, Fintech, Green Innovation, and Social Welfare: A Perspective of Environment Quality and Economic Development in China. *Global Management Sciences Review*, *9*(4), 156–168. DOI: 10.31703/gmsr.2024(IX-IV).13

Juengerkes, B. E. (2016). FinTechs and banks–Collaboration is key. *The FinTech book: The financial technology handbook for investors, entrepreneurs and visionaries*, 179-182.

Kartawinata, B. R., Fakhri, M., Pradana, M., Hanifan, N. F., & Akbar, A. (2021). The role of financial self-efficacy: Mediating effects of financial literacy & financial inclusion of students in West Java, Indonesia. *Journal of Management Information and Decision Sciences*, *24*(7), 1–9.

Kayed, S., Alta'any, M., Meqbel, R., Khatatbeh, I. N., & Mahafzah, A. (2025). Bank FinTech and bank performance: Evidence from an emerging market. *Journal of Financial Reporting and Accounting*, *23*(2), 518–535. DOI: 10.1108/JFRA-09-2023-0526
Kayed, S., Alta'any, M., Meqbel, R., Khatatbeh, I. N., & Mahafzah, A. (2025). Bank FinTech and bank performance: Evidence from an emerging market. *Journal of Financial Reporting and Accounting*, *23*(2), 518–535. DOI: 10.1108/JFRA-09-2023-0526
Kedziora, D., & Penttinen, E. (2021). Governance models for robotic process automation: The case of Nordea Bank. *Journal of Information Technology Teaching Cases*, *11*(1), 20–29. DOI: 10.1177/2043886920937022

Khan, H. H., Khan, S., & Ghafoor, A. (2023). Fintech adoption, the regulatory environment and bank stability: An empirical investigation from GCC economies. *Borsa Istanbul Review*, *23*(6), 1263–1281. DOI: 10.1016/j.bir.2023.10.010

Khanchel, I., Lassoued, N., & Khiari, C. (2025). Untangling the skein: The impact of FinTech on social and financial performance in microfinance institutions. *Regional Science Policy & Practice*, *17*(8), 100208. DOI: 10.1016/j.rspp.2025.100208

Kharrat, H., Trichilli, Y., & Abbes, B. (2024). Relationship between FinTech index and bank's performance: A comparative study between Islamic and conventional banks in the MENA region. *Journal of Islamic Accounting and Business Research*, *15*(1), 172–195. DOI: 10.1108/JIABR-03-2022-0081

Kjellman, A., Björkroth, T., Kangas, T., Tainio, R., & Westerholm, T. (2019). Disruptive innovations and the challenges for banking. *International Journal of Financial Innovation in Banking*, *2*(3), 232–249. DOI: 10.1504/IJFIB.2019.102308

Leo, M., Sharma, S., & Maddulety, K. (2019). Machine learning in banking risk management: A literature review. *Risks*, *7*(1), 29. DOI: 10.3390/risks7010029

Li, C., He, S., Tian, Y., Sun, S., & Ning, L. (2022). Does the bank's FinTech innovation reduce its risk-taking? Evidence from China's banking industry. *Journal of Innovation & Knowledge*, *7*(3), 100219. DOI: 10.1016/j.jik.2022.100219

Li, C., He, S., Tian, Y., Sun, S., & Ning, L. (2022). Does the bank's FinTech innovation reduce its risk-taking? Evidence from China's banking industry. *Journal of Innovation & Knowledge*, *7*(3), 100219. DOI: 10.1016/j.jik.2022.100219

Li, W., Li, T., Shi, W., Long, Y., & Liu, W. (2025). A protective shield for banks: How fintech curbs earnings manipulation through information transparency and financing constraints. *International Review of Financial Analysis*, *107*, 104622. DOI: 10.1016/j.irfa.2025.104622

Li, Y., Shahid, M. N., Islam, M. U., & Deme, F. (2024a). Fintech, Financial Development, and Digitalization Derive the Sustainable Economic Recovery: COVID 19 Pandemic and Post Pandemic Perspectives. *Asian Journal Of Economics. Business And Accounting*, *24*(6), 317–327. DOI: 10.9734/ajeba/2024/v24i61364

Li, Y., Shahid, M. N., Islam, M. U., & Deme, F. (2024b). *Fintech, and Mineral Resources Deteriorate Climate Sustainability: A Significant Role of Institutional Quality and Social Capital* (No. hal-05101044).

Li, Y., Shahid, M. N., Islam, M. U., & Deme, F. (2024c). The Role of Green Technological Innovation, Fintech, and Financial Development in Environmental Sustainability: A Study on Selected Asian Countries. *Journal of Economics, Finance, and Accounting Studies*, *6*(3), 32–39. DOI: 10.32996/jefas.2024.6.3.4

Lim, S. H., Kim, D. J., Hur, Y., & Park, K. (2019). An empirical study of the impacts of perceived security and knowledge on continuous intention to use mobile fintech payment services. *International Journal of Human-Computer Interaction*, *35*(10), 886–898. DOI: 10.1080/10447318.2018.1507132

Liu, H., & Hu, J. (2025). Bank Fintech and firm leverage adjustment speed: Evidence from China. *Research in International Business and Finance*, *73*, 102613. DOI: 10.1016/j.ribaf.2024.102613

Lu, M. P., & Kosim, Z. (2022). An empirical study to explore the influence of the COVID-19 crisis on consumers' behaviour towards cashless payment in Malaysia. *Journal of Financial Services Marketing*, •••, 1.

Lv, S., Du, Y., & Liu, Y. (2022). How do fintechs impact banks' profitability?—An empirical study based on banks in China. *FinTech*, *1*(2), 155–163. DOI: 10.3390/fintech1020012

Mbama, C. I., & Ezepue, P. O. (2018). Digital banking, customer experience and bank financial performance: UK customers' perceptions. *International Journal of Bank Marketing*, *36*(2), 230–255. DOI: 10.1108/IJBM-11-2016-0181

Meero, A. (2025). Islamic vs. conventional banking in the age of FinTech and AI: Evolving business models, efficiency, and stability (2020–2024). *International Journal of Financial Studies*, *13*(3), 148. DOI: 10.3390/ijfs13030148

Meero, A. (2025). Islamic vs. conventional banking in the age of FinTech and AI: Evolving business models, efficiency, and stability (2020–2024). *International Journal of Financial Studies*, *13*(3), 148. DOI: 10.3390/ijfs13030148

Mothobi, O., & Kebotsamang, K. (2024). The impact of network coverage on adoption of Fintech and financial inclusion in sub-Saharan Africa. *Journal of Economic Structures*, *13*(1), 5. DOI: 10.1186/s40008-023-00326-7

Naser, H., Sultanova, G., & Nahar, S. (2024). The impact of Fintech innovation on bank's performance: Evidence from the Kingdom of Bahrain. *International journal of economics and financial issues, 14*(1), 136-143.

Ngo, X. T., Le, K. A., Nguyen, T. T., & Nguyen, K. D. (2025). Does FinTech curb bank risk-taking? Insights from an emerging economy. *Finance Research Letters*, *86*, 108722. DOI: 10.1016/j.frl.2025.108722

Nguyen, L., Tran, S., & Ho, T. (2022). Fintech credit, bank regulations and bank performance: A cross-country analysis. *Asia-Pacific Journal of Business Administration*, *14*(4), 445–466. DOI: 10.1108/APJBA-05-2021-0196

Nguyen, Q. K. (2022). The effect of FinTech development on financial stability in an emerging market: The role of market discipline. *Research in Globalization*, *5*, 100105. DOI: 10.1016/j.resglo.2022.100105

Nguyen, T. T. T. (2025). The Impact of Fintech on Bank Profitability and Bank Stability in Emerging Country. *Journal of Organizational Behavior Research, 10*(2-2025), 12-19.

Nugraha, D. P., Setiawan, B., Nathan, R. J., & Fekete-Farkas, M. (2022). FinTech adoption drivers for innovation for SMEs in Indonesia. *Journal of Open Innovation*, *8*(4), 208. DOI: 10.3390/joitmc8040208

Nurlaela, N., Luthfiyana, M., Sulastri, A., & Wahyunita, E. S. (2020). REVIEWING THE FATWAS RELATED TO FINTECH APPLICATIONS IN ISLAMIC FINANCIAL INSTITUTIONS IN INDONESIA. *Share: Journal of Islamic Economics & Finance/Jurnal Ekonomi dan Keuangan Islam, 9*(2).

Obeidat, M., & Saxena, J. P. (2015). Customer's acceptance of internet banking in Dubai. *IOSR Journal of Business and Management*, *17*(12), 61–80.

Owusu, A., & Gupta, A. (2024). Identifying the risk culture of banks using machine learning. *International Journal of Managerial Finance, 20*(2), 377–405. DOI: 10.1108/IJMF-09-2022-0422

Pan, X., Zhang, J., & Huang, X. (2025). How Bank Fintech Facilitates Firm-Level New Quality Productive Forces. *Available at SSRN* 5269661. DOI: 10.1016/j.frl.2025.108308

Panjwani, K., & Shili, N. (2020). The impact of fintech on development of islamic banking sector in the contemporary world. *Saudi Journal of Economics and Finance, 4*(7), 346–350. DOI: 10.36348/sjef.2020.v04i07.006

Petralia, K., Philippon, T., Rice, T. N., & Veron, N. (2019). *Banking disrupted?: Financial intermediation in an era of transformational technology*. ICMB International Center for Monetary and Banking Studies.

Philippon, T. (2016). *The fintech opportunity* (No. w22476). National Bureau of Economic Research.

Qian, S., Yang, Z., & Fang, X. (2025). Bank Fintech and Corporate Green Transformation Quality Improvement: Based on Greenwashing Governance Perspective. *Economic Analysis and Policy, 87*, 401–423. DOI: 10.1016/j.eap.2025.06.017

Rita, E. (2018). Fintech Transaction Volume Continues to Increase. Berita Satu., Retrieved October 2018, from.

Shahid, M. N., Sher, F., & Ishtiaq, M. (2025). Impact of FinTech and Control of Corruption on Environmental Sustainability. *Journal of Economic Criminology*, 100162.

Siek, M., & Sutanto, A. (2019, August). *Impact analysis of fintech on banking industry. In 2019 international conference on information management and technology (ICIMTech)* (Vol. 1). IEEE.

Solanki, R., & Sujee, L. S. (2022). Fintech: A disruptive innovation of the 21st century, or is it? *Global Business and Management Research, 14*(2s), 76–87.

Stulz, R. M. (2019). Fintech, bigtech, and the future of banks. *The Bank of America Journal of Applied Corporate Finance, 31*(4), 86–97. DOI: 10.1111/jacf.12378

Suseendran, G., Chandrasekaran, E., Akila, D., & Sasi Kumar, A. (2019). Banking and FinTech (financial technology) embraced with IoT device. In *Data Management, Analytics and Innovation* [Singapore: Springer Singapore.]. *Proceedings of ICDMAI, 1*, 197–211.

Swan, M. (2017). Is technological unemployment real? An assessment and a plea for abundance economics. In *Surviving the machine age: intelligent technology and the transformation of human work* (pp. 19–33). Springer International Publishing. DOI: 10.1007/978-3-319-51165-8_2

Tarawneh, A., Abdul-Rahman, A., Mohd Amin, S. I., & Ghazali, M. F. (2024). A systematic review of fintech and banking profitability. *International Journal of Financial Studies*, *12*(1), 3. DOI: 10.3390/ijfs12010003

Tong, X., & Yang, W. (2025). Empirical analysis of the impact of financial technology on the profitability of listed banks. *International Review of Economics & Finance*, *98*, 103788. DOI: 10.1016/j.iref.2024.103788

Von Solms, J. (2021). Integrating Regulatory Technology (RegTech) into the digital transformation of a bank Treasury. *Journal of Banking Regulation*, *22*(2), 152–168. DOI: 10.1057/s41261-020-00134-0

Wang, Q., & He, Y. (2025). Platform-Based Fintech and Bank Loan Maturity Structure: Evidence from Chinese Commercial Banks. *Finance Research Letters*, *86*, 108667. DOI: 10.1016/j.frl.2025.108667

Wonglimpiyarat, J. (2017). FinTech banking industry: a systemic approach. *foresight, 19*(6), 590-603.

Xu, F., Kasperskaya, Y., & Sagarra, M. (2025). The impact of FinTech on bank performance: A systematic literature review. *Digital Business*, 100131.

Yao, T., & Song, L. (2023). Fintech and the economic capital of Chinese commercial bank's risk: Based on theory and evidence. *International Journal of Finance & Economics*, *28*(2), 2109–2123. DOI: 10.1002/ijfe.2528

Yuan, X., Puah, C. H., & Marikan, D. A. B. A. (2025). An Empirical Study on the Impact of Financial Technology on the Profitability of China's Listed Commercial Banks. *Journal of Risk and Financial Management*, *18*(8), 440. DOI: 10.3390/jrfm18080440

Yudaruddin, R. (2023). Financial technology and performance in Islamic and conventional banks. *Journal of Islamic Accounting and Business Research*, *14*(1), 100–116. DOI: 10.1108/JIABR-03-2022-0070

Zhang, X., & Li, Z. (2025). FinTech: The disruptive force reducing bank competition pressure. *Emerging Markets Review*, *65*, 101237. DOI: 10.1016/j.ememar.2024.101237

KEY TERMS AND DEFINITIONS

Banks' Financial Performance: This refers to how banks efficiently utilize their Assets to gauge profitability, liquidity and stability.

Banks' FinTech Adoption: It refers to the degree to which Banks regularly adopt and incorporate technology into the delivery and management of financial services.

BBNC-FTAI: Refers to the Bank-Based Novel Comprehensive FinTech Adoption Index that can best measure the FinTech adoption in banks and can enhance the performance of the banking industry using eight domains and eight dimensions.

FinTech Adoption: FinTech Adoption refers to the degree to which individuals or businesses regularly adopt and incorporate technology into the delivery and management of financial services.

FinTech: FinTech refers to the use of novel technologies to provide efficient, faster and cheaper financial services as compared to services offered by traditional Financial Institutions

Chapter 2
Measuring FinTech Adoption in Banks:
Construction of a Composite Index and Its Impact on Financial Performance and Stability

KM Ashifa
http://orcid.org/0000-0003-4070-5315
Istanbul Gelisim University, Turkey

B. UmaDevi
Department of Management Studies, R.M.K. Engineering College, Chennai, India

L. Anitha
Department of MBA, Saveetha Engineering College, India

Palanivel Rathinasabapathi Velmurugan
http://orcid.org/0000-0002-0395-9060
Berlin School of Business and Innovation, Germany

R. Vettriselvan
http://orcid.org/0009-0005-1097-0806
Academy of Maritime Education and Training, Chennai, India

ABSTRACT

The chapter explores the infiltration of FinTech into the banking sector by coming up with a multifaceted, bank-level composite index, as well as evaluating the consequences on financial performance and stability. Leaving behind uncomplicated

DOI: 10.4018/979-8-3373-6244-1.ch002

single-proxy indicators, the paper describes FinTech adoption as a combined process that includes the uptake of digital services, data analytics, platform integration, regulatory technology, and systems of governance. The findings of the panel based empirical research indicate that the adoption of FinTech has a positive impact on the financial performance of banks, but its results on stability are inconsistent and depend on the quality of governance and sustainability oriented position. The results highlight the mediating role of the ESG performance, and support the need to have responsible and well-managed digital transformation in order to achieve sustainable and resilient banking results.

1. INTRODUCTION

The financial technology (FinTech) is a wave of transformation in the banking sector around the entire world, emerging due to the blistering spread of the digital payment systems, artificial intelligence-supported analytics, mobile banking solutions, big data solutions, and regulatory technologies. These technologies have not only advanced past periphery service upgrades, but now have integrated into the mainstream banking services. Consequently, the use of FinTech has essentially changed the way banks provide financial products and services, risk management, resource allocation, and retaining competitive edge in a more digitized financial ecosystem. Something that was seen as an optional or peripheral innovation, has now become a strategic requirement to banks that are eager to improve performance in a way that does not compromise financial stability. Empirical studies on the developed and developing economies show that the use of FinTech is often linked to better profitability, cost-effectiveness, and operational performance, which are often linked to a reduction in transaction expenses and improved information-processing capacity (Singh et al., 2021; Baker et al., 2023; Kaddumi et al., 2023). Yet these advantages are not unconditional or even homogenous. Previous researchers emphasize that the performance results of FinTech adoption are significantly different based on the regulatory settings, competitive factors, and the internal institutional abilities (Nguyen et al., 2022; Kayed et al., 2025). These results imply that FinTech is seen as a performance-enhancing mechanism that can only be effectively implemented in more extensive banking processes and governance structures. In addition to the performance outcomes, an emerging body of literature has discussed the consequences of FinTech on financial stability. A number of studies report that the insolvency risk mitigation and better bank resilience with the assistance of FinTech can be done through data-driven decision-making (Stankevičienė and Kabulova, 2022; Ahmad et al., 2025). Simultaneously, the issues about unintended consequences of the fast digitalization have been raised. Enhanced exposure to cyber threats, operational risks, and risk-taking through technology has been witnessed, mostly in the institutional environment with weak governance structures and and low regulation (Safiullah and Paramati, 2024; Mabe and Simo-Kengne, 2025). These opposing results indicate that the correlation between the use of FinTech and financial stability is complicated, non-linear, and extremely contextual.

These measures are a good representation of some facets of digitalization, but they do not represent the multidimensional nature of FinTech uptake by a banking institution. As a matter of fact, FinTech integration goes far beyond front-office applications to encompass back-office analytics, system integration, cybersecurity infrastructure, regulatory technologies, and governance. The recent academic works have been seeking to deal with this weakness by building FinTech-related indexes, especially within the framework of digital financial inclusion and macro-level financial development (Banik and Roy, 2023; Zheng et al., 2024). In spite of the fact that these indices are methodological improvements, they are largely country-level measures and, as such, do not take into account considerable heterogeneity in FinTech adoption among individual banks. Furthermore, most of the available indices focus on access and use aspects and pay insufficient attention to intra-operational capabilities, risk management culture, and organizational frameworks that are important determinants of both bank performance and financial stability (Kharrat et al., 2024). As such, there is still a research gap: there is no standardized, multidimensional, bank-level indicator of FinTech adoption. This is one of the gaps that should be addressed considering increasing regulatory and policy focus on sustainable and resilient banking systems. It is increasingly becoming the interest of regulators and policy-makers to know not only whether the FinTech is increasing the profitability of banks, but also the impact it now has on the risk profile of banks, on their systemic stability, and on their long-term sustainability. According to the emerging evidence, the quality of governance, environmental, social, and governance (ESG) performance, and sustainability orientations seem to have a critical impact on mediating the outcomes of the FinTech implementation (Alqudah et al., 2025; Salah Mahdi et al., 2025; Hidayat-ur-Rehman and Hossain, 2025). These understandings support the necessity to consider the concept of FinTech adoption as a component of an expanded institutional and governance system, but not as an individual technological event. In the first place, it addresses the absence of a standardized, multidimensional, and bank-level measure of FinTech adoption by creating a composition index of FinTech adoption. Second, it combines studies of financial performance and financial stability into a single and empirical study, which has been missing in previous research studies. Third, it clearly incorporates the adoption of FinTech into a wider framework of governance and sustainability, as it has a moderating effect on the outcomes. In line with this, this chapter has threefold objectives. The initial objective is to theorize the idea of FinTech uptake in banking as a multidimensional concept of digital infrastructure, analytical abilities, system integration, cybersecurity, regulatory technologies, and ethical governance. The second goal is to operationalize such dimensions with a transparent and replicable composite FinTech adoption index that can be used at the bank level. The third goal is to test empirically the twofold implications of FinTech adoption on the performance of banks and financial stability.

2. CONCEPTUAL FOUNDATIONS OF FINTECH ADOPTION IN BANKING

The move toward FinTech in the banking industry signifies a paradigm change, and not the utilization of individual digital applications. Conceptually, it is the degree to which banking institutions have integrated enhanced digital technologies in the fundamental functional, analytical and managerial processes. Contrary to traditional information technology investments, whose main goal is to promote efficiency in the back-office, FinTech implementation transforms the interaction with customers, risk management and control policies, compliance regulation frameworks, and strategic decisions. FinTech adoption must therefore be perceived as a multidimensional and an institution-wide process other than a solitary or a purely technological choice. The development of an infrastructure of digital services is one of the most apparent areas of FinTech adoption. These are online payment systems, mobile banking apps, online loan services, and online customer interfaces. The technologies enhance customer convenience and make services more accessible to the customer, as well as allow banks to expand their reach to hitherto untapped market segments. Empirical research always shows that those digital platforms drive operational effectiveness and monetary inclusion by cutting transaction prices and the extent of service provision (Aloulou et al., 2024; Zheng et al., 2023). Nevertheless, as much as customer-facing technologies represent a significant point of entry, they are not the only aspects of transforming the banking institutions into FinTech-driven entities. FinTech use may take a more substantive form in terms of adopting advanced data analytics and artificial intelligence in the main banking operations. Banks more and more rely on data-based models to enhance their credit evaluation, fraud discovery, portfolio management and managerial decisions. Such analytical functions minimize information asymmetry, improve the accuracy of risk pricing, and proactive risk management. Previous studies show that the more banks become analytically integrated, the more likely they are to convert digital innovation into the continued improvement of performance and strategic position (Yan et al., 2022; Mosayebi et al., 2024). Notably, it is a deeper dimension of FinTech adoption that is more than surface-level digitalization to embedded intelligence in organizational processes.

The other highly important conceptual element of FinTech adoption is platformization and system integration. The future of banking is becoming more of a platform-driven architecture that interoperates the internally driven systems with external service providers, such as FinTech companies and third-party technology providers. This kind of integration improves the ability to scale, to be flexible, and innovative, although it can also add complexity to the organization and technology. Empirical studies indicate that the performance advantages of FinTech adoption are the strongest when digital technologies are integrated into the main part of the banking systems, as opposed to when they are adopted as the isolated solutions (Ben Bouheni et al., 2023; Kharrat et al., 2024). Integration of platforms thus is a sign of an advanced use of FinTech, marking that a bank can organize innovation at an organizational level. With the increasing dependence of the banks on the digital infrastructures, cybersecurity and digital risk management become the inseparable conceptual dimensions of FinTech implementation. It is the amplification of the digital processes that exposes a person to cyber threats, disruptions in operations and systemic risks that might arise due to technology. Empirical evidence warns that the positive impact of FinTech on performance can be neutralized by an increase in vulnerability in a system in case of weak governance structures and risk controls (Safiullah and Paramati, 2024; Mabe and Simo-Kengne, 2025). In that regard, the use of FinTech can be viewed through the prism of not only the degree of innovation but also the efficiency of digital risk mitigation strategies. Cybersecurity preparedness and business continuity are therefore crucial elements of an all-encompassing FinTech adoption program.

Regulatory technology (RegTech) also enlarges the conceptualization of FinTech adoption to banking. RegTech is the application of digital tools to increase regulatory compliance, monitoring, and reporting. Its adoption indicates an advanced phase of the FinTech approach where technological innovation contributes to its efficiency as well as compliance with regulations. The implementation of RegTech demonstrates the interdependence of compliance requirements and digital transformation in modern banking systems, and innovation and regulation do not exclude each other and complement one another (Vettriselvan et al., 2025). In addition to the technological skills, governance, and ethical issues are the determinants of the consequences of FinTech usage. The increased application of artificial intelligence and big data analytics encourage concerns associated with the algorithmic bias, data privacy, transparency, and accountability. According to the research on AI ethics and digital governance, the responsible adoption models are essential to safeguard the stakeholder trust and guarantee the sustainability of the process over time (Fundira & Mbohwa, 2025). On performance terms, digital technologies are able to improve efficiency, cut operation costs and drive product innovation. Stability wise, better monitoring and analytics can enhance resilience, whereas greater interconnectedness of the systems can increase vulnerabilities. This duality is also present in empirical evidence, where the stabilizing and destabilizing effects are reported based on institutional context and governance quality (Stankevičienė and Kabulova, 2022; Ahmad et al., 2025). There is another level of complexity that is connected to the interrelation of FinTech adoption and sustainability orientation. According to recent researches, the efficiency of FinTech implementation depends on the condition of environmental, social, and governance (ESG) performance and sustainability strategies by determining organizational priorities, risk culture, and governance structure (Alqudah et al., 2025; Hidayat-ur-Rehman and Hossain, 2025; Salah Mahdi et al., 2025). Banks that point digital innovation at accomplishing sustainability goals are seen to be in a better position to handle digital risks and create long-term value. This interaction supports the opinion that FinTech implementation should be inbuilt into more general institutional systems and not be considered as an individual technological trend. Combining all these conceptual reflections, FinTech implementation in the banking industry is naturally multidimensional, including digital service infrastructure, analytical, system integration, cybersecurity, regulatory technology, and ethical governance. These dimensions are intimately related to each other and they collectively determine the outcomes of performance and stability related to digital transformation. This conceptualization of multidimensions is a solid theoretical basis of empirical analysis and policy assessment. Notably, it itself ensures the operationalization strategy taken in the next section, in which a composite index of FinTech adoption is built in order to reflect the degree of digital transformation and its extent at the bank level.

3. REVIEW OF LITERATURE

The existing empirical and conceptual literature on the uptake of FinTech in banking has grown faster in volume, which highlights the increasing prominence of digital technologies in the redesigning of financial intermediation, operational performance, and regulatory interactions. Although the prior literature provides useful information on the implications of FinTech to the performance and stability of banks, the literature is still rather fragmented in terms of conceptual frameworks, measurement procedures and integration of empirical studies. The systematic review of the existing studies demonstrates that there are four intimately connected strands, including FinTech adoption and bank performance; FinTech adoption and financial stability; measurement and index-based approaches to FinTech adoption; moderating roles of governance and sustainability. There exists a considerable amount of empirical evidence proving that FinTech adoption correlates with such indicators of bank performance as return on assets, return on equity, and cost efficiency. To a large extent, these gains are explained by large automation, improvement of information processing, and better service delivery (Singh et al., 2021; Baker et al., 2023). Further discussions reveal that digital technologies allow to allocate resources more efficiently and have a more competitive position by enhancing customer interaction and flexibility of operations (Ben Bouheni et al., 2023; Kaddumi et al., 2023). However, the extent and continuity of these advantages are quite different in different institutional settings. There is evidence suggesting that the quality of regulation, organisational preparations, and the presence of human-capital are very strong conditions underpinning the performance outcomes of the adoption of FinTech (Nguyen et al., 2022; Kayed et al., 2025). These results indicate that the use of FinTech alone cannot ensure the improvement of performance unless accompanied by the help of institutions. In parallel to performance-oriented investigation, there is a growing body of literature exploring the implication of FinTech adoption to financial stability. Theoretically, FinTech will facilitate greater stability by enhancing the assessment of risk, risk monitoring, and risk diversification with advanced analytics. This expectation is partially proved by empirical studies that report decreases in the insolvency risk and resurgence in the resilience in cases where the digital innovation is combined with efficient regulatory supervision (Stankevičienė and Kabulova, 2022; Ahmad et al, 2025). Other papers, though, point to the possible destabilising consequences: quick digitalization, especially in the settings of poor governance, has been linked to volatility, exposure to cyber-risks, and disruption of operations (Safiullah and Paramati, 2024; Mabe and Simo-Kengne, 2025; Yin et al., 2022). These contradictory results highlight the stabilising and destabilising nature of FinTech based on institutional quality and regulatory fit.

Conscious of the flaws of single proxy indicators, recent analyses have turned to composite measures of the FinTech adoption and digital financial development. Banik and Roy (2023) create a multidimensional digital financial inclusion index, whereas Zheng et al. (2024) build a FinTech-based financial inclusion index on the national level. These strategies show the analytical benefits of describing several aspects of digitalization simultaneously. However, current indexes are mainly macro-level indicators that hide in-homogeneity in the adoption of FinTech between individual banks. In addition, the majority of the indexes focus on the dimensions of access and use and do not represent core operational capabilities, cybersecurity preparedness, the integration of the system, and governance mechanisms (Kharrat et al., 2024).

To highlight these limitations, Table 1 synthesizes representative FinTech measurement approaches in the literature and identifies key gaps that motivate the present study.

Table 1. Comparative Summary of FinTech Adoption Measurement Approaches

Study	Level of Analysis	Key Dimensions	Main Limitations
Singh et al. (2021)	Bank-level	Digital services, IT investment	Single-proxy focus; limited multidimensionality
Banik & Roy (2023)	Country-level	Access, usage, digital inclusion	Macro-level; excludes bank heterogeneity
Zheng et al. (2024)	Country-level	FinTech-enabled inclusion	Limited governance and risk dimensions
Kharrat et al. (2024)	Sector-level	Digital intensity indicators	Underrepresents cybersecurity and internal integration
Existing ESG–FinTech studies	Mixed	Governance, sustainability	Often detached from adoption measurement

Table 1 demonstrates that no widely accepted bank-level composite index currently captures the multidimensional and institutionally embedded nature of FinTech adoption.

In the recent scholarship, the role of governance, sustainability, and ethical stewardship as determining platforms of FinTech results is paramount. Empirical studies have shown that the quality of governance has a significant influence on the nexus of the adoption of FinTechs, the performance of firms, and systemic stability, and strong ESG profiles enhance the effect of digital innovation (Alqudah et al., 2025). Corporate social responsibility analyses show even further that ethical governance structures inter-mediate the effect of uptake of FinTech on risk-taking behaviour and stakeholder trust (Salah Mahdi et al., 2025). According to sustainability-oriented inquiry, a match of FinTech efforts with the environmental and societal goals strengthens the sustainable value creation and stability (Hidayat-ur-Rehman and Hossain, 2025; Lamey et al., 2024). At the same time, the analysis of the ethics and regulatory control of AI sheds some light on the significance of ethical congruence and compliance frameworks to protect consumer protection and system stability (Fundira & Mbohwa, 2025; Vettriselvan et al., 2025). However, such insights are not integrated into FinTech adoption indices to this day. There are a number of gaps in the literature that has been preserved. To begin with, there is no bank level, standardised measure that would capture the multidimensional nature of FinTech adoption. Second, most of the empirical studies deaggregate financial performance and financial stability hence masking their dependence on each other. Third, other aspects, like governance, sustainability, cybersecurity, and regulatory technology, are often viewed as peripheral instead of being adopted as a core part of FinTech adoption. To address such shortcomings, the current chapter presents a bank level composite FinTech adoption index, combining technological, risk, governance, and sustainability facets, in a combined performance stability framework. The present methodological contribution is a direct response to the limitations of the previous study and provides a more detailed, policy-relevant evaluation of the adoption of FinTech as a banking industry.

4. THEORETICAL FRAMEWORK AND HYPOTHESIS DEVELOPMENT

To explain the consequences of the adoption of FinTech on banking performance and stability, a theory should be provided to identify both the efficiency-enhancing mechanisms and the associated risks-related trade-offs. Well beyond a technological modernization, FinTech reflects a strategic re-organisation of the banking processes, resource deployment, systems of governance and risk-management practises. To handle this complexity, this chapter combines knowledge based on innovation diffusion theory, resource-based view (RBV), financial intermediation theory and financial stability theory and establishes a single analytic framework. The innovation diffusion theory explains the reasons behind the timing, depth and scope variations in adoption of FinTech by banks. Those institutions that have increased absorptive capacity, technological preparedness, and a strong strategic thrust are the ones that are likely to adopt FinTech at an early stage where automation, better service delivery, and enhanced information processing are used to gain a competitive advantage. This position is supported by empirical evidence; digitally integrated banks oftentimes demonstrate better financial performance in the cases when their adoption is supported by strong institutional capabilities (Singh et al., 2021; Baker et al., 2023). However, the theory warns that rapid or inadequately handled diffusion may create adjustment costs, transitional inefficiencies and operational strain, particularly in cases when organisational fit is lacking. The resource-based perspective is a complement to this view because the capabilities associated with FinTechs such as advanced analytics, embedded digital platforms, and regulatory technologies are viewed as strategic assets. The competitive advantage associated with such resources is only possible when they are limited, hard to replicate, and well incorporated into the organisational practises and management skills. Those banks that effectively internalise and orchestrate these digital assets are in a better position to make the adoption of FinTechs a source of long-term performance improvements; superficial or inconsistent implementation results in only limited returns (Ben Bouheni et al., 2023; Kayed et al., 2025). In line with this, this lens highlights the criticality of conceptualising the adoption of FinTech as a multidimensional construct instead of a series of dislodged technological investments.

The financial intermediation theory can also explain how the adoption of FinTech affects the performance of banks. Digital technologies improve the principle functions of lending, payments, and credit screening and monitoring by reducing information asymmetry, minimising the cost of transactions, and enhancing credit screening and monitoring. Empirical evidence confirms that banks using FinTech are able to expand their market coverage, increase quality of their services, and increase profitability due to more efficient intermediation mechanisms (Aloulou et al., 2024; Zheng et al., 2023). These efficiency benefits provide the theoretical foundation upon which a positive association between the financial performance and FinTech adoption can be expected. Although the above viewpoints highlight the performance-enhancing effects, financial stability theory outlines the two-fold and even contradictory effects of the adoption of FinTechs on risk and resiliency. On the one hand, developed analytics, real-time control, and automated controls strengthen the ability of banks to detect, manage and diversify risks, thus lowering the chances of insolvency and increasing stability under good governance (Stankevičienė and Kabulova, 2022; Ahmad et al., 2025). On the other hand, the increased dependence on digital infrastructures may become a breeding ground of novel vulnerabilities/cyber threats, disruption of operations, and interconnectedness. Empirical studies indicate that these risks can easily overshadow efficiency improvements in the presence of weak regulatory controls and internal controls (Safiullah & Paramati, 2024; Mabe and Simo-Kengne, 2025). As a result, FinTech usage takes place on both efficiency enhancing channels and risk transmission channels, making its overall impact on stability very context-dependent. According to the recent scholarship, governance, sustainability, and ethical orientation as moderators of FinTech outcomes are also important. Banks with a strong ESG performance, sustainability strategies are more likely to responsibly implement FinTech as digital innovation becomes associated with long-term value creation and mitigating risks. It is proven that effective ESG governance increases transparency, managerial discipline, and strategic coherence thus increasing the performance returns of FinTech and mitigating the risks (Alqudah et al., 2025). The implementation of artificial intelligence and data analytics is also impacted by ethical governance frameworks, which have an effect on the trust in the stakeholders, consumer protection, and long-term resilience (Fundira and Mbohwa, 2025; Vettriselvan et al., 2025). The stabilising potential of FinTech implementation is also supported by sustainability-focused approaches, such as green finance measures that introduce the digital transformation into the overall institutional goals (Hidayat-ur-Rehman and Hossain, 2025).

Incorporating these theoretical approaches, FinTech adoption is theorised in this chapter as a multidimensional strategic construct determining banking results in interdependent performance, risk, governance, and sustainability domains. The composite FinTech adoption index is constructed based on the integrated framework directly, and the hypotheses are developed according to the results of the empirical testing. Depending on the integrated information of innovation diffusion theory, resource-based view, and financial intermediation theory, overall adoption of such FinTechs will lead to greater efficiencies, higher profits, and improved competitive standings.

> **H1:** The use of FinTech has a positive and significant effect on the financial performance of banks.
> **H2:** The use of FinTech has a great influence on the financial stability of banks.
> **H3:** ESG performance has a positive moderating effect on the association between the adoption of FinTech and financial performance of banks.
> **H4:** There is a moderating effect of ESG performance between FinTech adoption and financial stability of banks.
> **H5:** Sustainable oriented strategies enhance the positive effects of FinTech adoption on sustainable performance of banks.

These hypotheses can be combined to give a well-grounded theoretical foundation of the empirical analysis. The framework allows the direct and moderating effects to be assessed at the same time so that the composite FinTech adoption index can be measured in a context sensitive and policy-important performance stability environment.

5. CONSTRUCTION OF THE COMPOSITE FINTECH ADOPTION INDEX

The main addition made by this chapter is the creation of a multidimensional and bank-level composite index of FinTech adoption as a measure of the depth, breadth, and institutionalisation of the digital transformation in the banking industry. The available empirical data on FinTech uptake has so far been based on single proxies (e.g., the availability of digital channels, binary innovation measures, or technology expenditure ratios) that poorly capture the complexity and entrenched nature of FinTech adoption. With digital transformation surging inside the most vital banking processes, governance frameworks, and risk-control mechanisms, such limited metrics are not sufficient to the hard-core empirical analysis we hope to engage in. Based on this, the current chapter has assumed a composite-index design which summarises various indicators into a coherent, analytically sound measure of the intensity of FinTech adoption. This is where composite indices have shown specific effectiveness in the analysis of digital financial inclusion and FinTech development specifically because they can capture a multidimensional variation and should reduce measurement error when using single measures (Banik and Roy, 2023; Zheng et al., 2024). It is based on this methodological tradition and is precisely constructed at the bank level as a result of which it is possible to identify heterogeneity in digital-transformation strategies of financial institutions. With a conceptual framework, and under the influence of the existing body of empirical evidence, FinTech adoption is operationalized using six dimensions influencing each other that also sum up the technological capability and aligning governance. These dimensions do not just include conspicuous, customer-facing innovations but more subtle internal operational, analytical, and regulatory innovations which, together, define performance and stability outcomes.

Table 2 summarizes the six dimensions of the composite FinTech adoption index, their conceptual focus, and illustrative indicators used for measurement.

Table 2. Dimensions and Indicators of the Composite FinTech Adoption Index

Dimension	Conceptual Focus	Illustrative Indicators
Digital Service Infrastructure	Customer-facing digital delivery and accessibility	Share of digital transactions, mobile banking penetration, online lending services
Data Analytics and Artificial Intelligence	Advanced analytics and decision-support capabilities	AI-based credit scoring, fraud detection systems, predictive analytics adoption
Platformization and System Integration	Depth of integration into core banking and external platforms	Interoperability of systems, API usage, platform-based service integration
Cybersecurity and Digital Risk Management	Preparedness to manage technology-related risks	Cybersecurity investments, incident response systems, operational resilience tools
Regulatory Technology (RegTech)	Digital compliance and regulatory monitoring	Automated reporting systems, real-time compliance analytics
Ethical Governance and Sustainability Alignment	Governance quality and responsible digital use	ESG policies, AI ethics frameworks, data privacy and transparency mechanisms

Digital service infrastructure dimension measures the level to which the banks implement FinTech-enabled customer-facing services, including digital payments and mobile banking, which are strongly related to service efficiency and financial inclusion (Aloulou et al., 2024; Zheng et al., 2023). On this note, the spread of the digital channels is a direct conversion of the more inclusive financial system, which, in turn, increases the customer reach and throughput rates. The dimension of data analytics and artificial intelligence indicates the utilisation of sophisticated assessment instruments to assess credit, detect fraud, and make strategic choices, decreasing the informational asymmetry and raising the efficiency of operations (Yan et al., 2022; Mosayebi et al., 2024). Using data-driven intelligence, banks will be able to improve risk management procedures, and to balance resources allocation in a way that would have been impossible through traditional manual system. The dimension of platformisation and system integration is the degree to which FinTech solutions are integrated into the foundation of banking systems and interoperable platforms. It is shown that the performance benefits are the greatest in the cases when the technologies are integrated structurally, but not implemented as freestanding applications (Ben Bouheni et al., 2023; Kharrat et al., 2024). Therefore, a smooth integration becomes a precondition towards achievement of competitive advantages and operational synergies.

The dimension of cybersecurity and digital risk management deals with the abilities of banks to counter technical risks that have a growing impact on financial stability (Safiullah and Paramati, 2024; Mabe and Simo-Kengne, 2025). The ability of maintaining a high level of stakeholder trust and the integrity of the banking ecosystem in a digitally convergent environment cannot be achieved without a strong cyber-security posture. The RegTech aspect monitors the usage of electronic tools in the regulatory compliance and reporting, which is a more advanced phase of FinTech assimilation (Vettriselvan et al., 2025). The automation of compliance processes may enable banks to cut on administrative overheads, and at the same time, increase the auditability and compliance with the regulations. Lastly, the dimension of ethical governance and alignment of sustainability includes practises and ethical frameworks related to ESG that define the impact of FinTech adoption on long-term performance and resilience (Alqudah et al., 2025; Fundira and Mbohwa, 2025). By incorporating sustainability into digital transformation projects one can reduce reputational risks and overall societal goals.

Each dimension has indicators that are chosen following three criteria: relevance to core banking operations, support in the literature and availability of data. The index is a combination of quantitative indicators (e.g., ratios of digital transactions) and qualitative proxies (e.g., the use of AI-based risk management systems), which are considered best practises in measuring FinTech (Mosayebi et al., 2024). Since the indicators are heterogeneous, all the variables are normalised by means of min-max normalisation that will turn the values into a standardised range of 0 to 1. This method allows relative variation between banks but allows aggregation between dimensions. The use of the min-max normalisation is common in FinTech and digital inclusion indices because it is transparent and interpretable (Banik and Roy, 2023; Zheng et al., 2024). Following normalisation, the indicators in every dimension are summed up to acquire dimension level scores. The baseline index uses an equal-weighting programme in the event of a lack of a powerful theoretical or empirical agreement on the relative significance of individual FinTech dimensions. Equal weighting reduces subjective bias, increases transparency, and no single dimension has a disproportionate impact on the composite score, which is upheld by conventional procedures in the construction of exploratory indices (Kharrat et al., 2024). Linear aggregation then combines the dimension level scores to come up with the composite FinTech adoption index. The reason that linear aggregation is chosen is that it is simple, interpretable, and it is widely applied in the research of composite indexes. The value of the indexes is higher, which implies a more thorough and institutionally embedded adoption of Fintech.

In order to have reliability and empirical credibility, the composite index will undergo a series of validation processes. To begin with, correlation analysis will be used to determine the relationship between the proposed index and the already existing FinTech-related measures found in the literature. Second, sensitivity analysis evaluates the strength of index rankings to other weighting schemes. Third, stability tests measure the degree of the influence of extreme values on index returns. Such processes contribute to the increased level of trust in the ability of the index to be used in empirical research and policy interpretation (Kharrat et al., 2024; Zheng et al., 2024). Comprehensively, the composite FinTech adoption index that was created in this chapter offers methodologically robust, transparent, and policy-relevant bank-level digital transformation. Combining the notions of technological intensity with the aspects of governance and sustainability, the index creates a strong background to the further empirical analysis of the implications of the FinTech on the outcomes of financial performance and stability.

6. RESEARCH METHODOLOGY

This section gives the empirical strategy to be applied to test the nexus between FinTech adoption, financial performance, and financial stability in the banking institutions. The methodology combines the use of the composite FinTech adoption index created in the previous section with traditional bank-level financial and risk measures, which results in the systematic and reproducible evaluation of the outcomes of digital transformation. The study design adheres to the current quantitative traditions of research in banking and FinTech research, and it values transparency, strength and methodological soundness. The research design adopted in the study is a quantitative, explanatory research design based on the analysis of panel data that is specifically effective in the context of the study to observe cross-sectional heterogeneity among banks and temporal dynamics of FinTech adoption and banking results. The panel data methods can be used to control the institutional attributes that are unobserved and time-invariant (e.g., the managerial culture or the old systems) that can moderate the effects of digital adoption, digital performance, and digital stability at the same time. This study design increases the efficiency of the estimation, and the causal inference, which corresponds to the best practises of empirical banking studies (Nguyen et al., 2022; Ahmad et al., 2025). The sample is the empirical one, which includes commercial banks that work in the context chosen to conduct the study based on the availability and consistency of data. Banks should fulfil three strict criteria to become a part of the sample: (i) they must have full financial statements in place throughout the study period, (ii) must provide adequate disclosures to form the composite FinTech adoption index, and (iii) they must report the key performance and risk indicators. These criteria guarantee well balanced panel structure and reduce the possible estimation bias that may occur due to missing observations.

The analysis period covers several years in succession and therefore the study includes the gradual and cumulative form of digital transformation in banking. All the variables are based on the publicly available secondary sources, such as annual reports, regulatory filings, sustainability disclosures, and established financial databases. The indicators based on FinTech technology, governance, and regulatory disclosures are obtained as the result of the application of standard empirical FinTech measurement methods (Mosayebi et al., 2024; Banik and Roy, 2023).To improve clarity and replicability, Table 3 summarizes the key variables used in the empirical analysis, including their definitions and measurement approaches.

Table 3. Description of Variables Used in the Empirical Analysis

Variable Category	Variable	Description / Measurement
Dependent Variables	Financial Performance	Return on Assets (ROA), Return on Equity (ROE)
	Financial Stability	Z-score; Non-performing loan ratio (robustness)
Independent Variable	FinTech Adoption	Composite FinTech Adoption Index (Section 5)
Moderating Variables	ESG Performance	ESG scores and sustainability indicators
Control Variables	Bank Size	Natural logarithm of total assets
	Capital Adequacy	Capital-to-assets ratio
	Liquidity	Loan-to-deposit ratio
	Macroeconomic Conditions	GDP growth / inflation (where applicable)

Measures of financial performance are accounting-based measurements such as return on assets and on equity that i) summarise the profitability and managerial efficiency and have been extensively used in empirical research of the banking sector (Singh et al., 2021; Baker et al., 2023).

On the other hand, financial stability is most likely to be proxied by Z score, which is an index that attempts to measure the closeness of a bank to insolvency by combining, measures of profitability, capitalization and earnings variability. Additional indicators of risk, including non-performing loans ratio, are also included to strengthen it (Stankevičienė & Kabulova, 2022; Ahmad et al., 2025). The key explanatory variable is the composite FinTech adoption index, the operationalisation of six levels of bank-level digital transformation, including digital service infrastructure, data analytics and artificial intelligence, platform integration, cybersecurity preparedness, regulatory technology adoption, and ethical governance alignment. Higher index scores represent a more holistic and institutionalised FinTech adoption. The moderating variables put forward are ESG performance and sustainability indicators to explore whether the relationship between FinTech adoption and performance and stability is mediated by the quality of governance and long-term strategic focus. The previous study suggests that responsible governance and alignment of sustainability enhance the value-creating potential of digital innovation and, at the same time, decrease the risks associated with them (Alqudah et al., 2025; Salah Mahdi et al., 2025; Hidayat-ur-Rehman and Hossain, 2025). The common control variables commonly used in banking studies, including size, capitalization, liquidity and macroeconomic conditions, are factored in to determine the net impact of FinTech adoption (Nguyen et al., 2022).

The baseline empirical model assessing the impact of FinTech adoption on banking outcomes is specified as:

$$Y_{it} = \alpha + \beta_1 \text{FinTech}_{it} + \beta_2 \text{Controls}_{it} + \mu_i + \lambda_t + \varepsilon_{it}$$

where represents financial performance or financial stability of bank *i* in year *t*; denotes the composite FinTech adoption index; is a vector of control variables; captures unobserved bank-specific effects; denotes time effects; and is the idiosyncratic error term.

To test the moderating role of governance and sustainability, the model is extended to include interaction terms:

The given model will allow a direct evaluation of the impact of ESG performance enhancing or deterring the impact of the FinTech adoption on the banking performance. Fixed effects and random effects estimators are both used where the Hausman test is used to select the right specification. Fixed-effects estimation is desirable in cases where the unobserved heterogeneity is connected to explanatory variables otherwise random-effects estimation is used. Robust standard errors are employed to deal with the heteroskedasticity and serial correlation. To measure multicollinearity, diagnostic tests have variance inflation factors, and the standard panel tests of heteroskedasticity and serial dependence. Robustness analysis assumes reestimation of models with alternative measures of performance and stability, alternative weighting of the FinTech adoption index, and thus makes sure that the results are not caused by particular measurement choices (Kharrat et al., 2024; Mosayebi et al., 2024). The research does not engage human subjects and no confidential information is used because it uses only publicly available secondary data, which makes it in line with ethical research requirements. The possible constraints are measurement error due to the proxy indicators and lack of data. Such limitations are resolved with the help of transparent reporting and sensitivity analysis as well as with the help of voluminous robustness cheques. As a whole, the research design is based on a rigorously designed composite FinTech adoption index as well as panel econometric tools that help to form a strong empirical basis of the performance and stability impacts of digital transformation in the banking sector. It is the methodological framework that underlines the discussion and empirical results that are to be discussed in the next section.

7. EMPIRICAL RESULTS AND DISCUSSION

The data of the empirical results of the relationship between FinTech adoption, financial performance, and financial stability in banks is presented and interpreted in this section, based on the composite index of FinTech adoption, and the panel econometric model already described above. As per the aims of the study, the discussion goes beyond statistical significance to test the economic relevance, institutional implication as well as the coherence with the existing empirical data. Descriptive statistics indicate that there is a large degree of heterogeneity in FinTech adoption among banks, which proves that there is no even distribution of digital transformation in the banking sector. The composite FinTech adoption index is widely dispersed, suggesting that there is significant variance in the presence of digital tools as well as the extent of integration in regard to operational, analytical, risk-management, and governance aspects. It is this heterogeneity that confirms the index as a good bank-level indicator of the strength of FinTech and not a shallow proxy. There are also significant cross-bank changes in financial performance indicators (ROA, ROE), and financial stability measures (Z -score, non-performing loan ratio), which indicate the difference in efficiency, resilience, and exposure to risk. There is an indication that FinTech adoption and performance have a positive correlation, whereas the dependency between the FinTech adoption and stability is more complex. Notably, the correlation coefficients are not excessive and it can be concluded that multicollinearity will not pose a danger to the future regression estimates. These initial data are consistent with the previous research that has shown heterogeneous effects of FinTech in the institutional contexts (Singh et al., 2021; Ahmad et al., 2025). The answers of regression give a firm support of Hypothesis 1, which suggests that there exists a positive correlation between financial performance and the adoption of FinTechs. In the alternative model specifications, the composite FinTech adoption index shows a positive and statistically significant impact on ROA and ROE as shown in Table 4.

Table 4. Summary of Regression Results: FinTech Adoption and Bank Outcomes

Dependent Variable	Key Explanatory Variable	Direction of Effect	Significance	Interpretation
ROA	FinTech Adoption Index	Positive	Significant	Efficiency and profitability gains
ROE	FinTech Adoption Index	Positive	Significant	Enhanced shareholder returns
Z-score	FinTech Adoption Index	Positive	Significant	Increased resilience
NPL Ratio	FinTech Adoption Index	Mixed	Weak / Contextual	Heterogeneous credit risk effects
ROA / ROE	FinTech × ESG	Positive	Significant	Governance amplifies FinTech benefits
Z-score	FinTech × ESG	Positive	Significant	ESG mitigates digital risk

The sizes of the estimated coefficients indicate that FinTech adoption is not statistically significant only, but also has a substantive economic implication. The financial institutions with a higher rate of integrated FinTech use are always characterised by the increased efficiency of their operations, increased efficiency in the distribution of resources, and a greater ability to generate income. The conceptualization of FinTech adoption as a strategic organisational capability is supported by these observations, unlike a fragmented compilation of individual technological projects. Such findings support earlier empirical research that links digital innovation to improved performance of banks (Baker et al., 2023; Kaddumi et al., 2023; Kayed et al., 2025). The key feature of the current study, however, is its ability to show that the mentioned performance benefits are the result of the combined and synergistic effect of multiple FinTech dimensions, namely advanced analytics, platform integration, and regulatory technologies, but not customer-focused digitalization itself. Based on this, the paper has demonstrated the need to adopt a comprehensive approach to digital transformation that will integrate FinTech across the fundamental banking processes. Compared to the comparatively homogeneous impacts of performance, the nexus between FinTech adoption and financial stability is characterised by a more complex nature hence providing the empirical support to Hypothesis 2. Regression results indicate that the adoption of FinTech has a statistically significant impact on the stability indicators; however, the direction and the level of this impact vary depending on the risk measure utilised.

The higher the levels of FinTech adoption are, measured through the Z-score, the more robust a person is and the lower the risk of insolvency. This trend means that high analytics, automation, and real time surveillance solutions increase the risk managing skills and shock absorbing capacity in banks. These observations echo the literature available on this topic that has noted the stabilising effect of FinTech where there is strong governance and regulation of the industry (Stankevičienė et al., 2021). On the other hand, weaker or heterogenous findings are obtained with the empirical models using non-performing ratios of loans. This deviation shows that although the overall resilience may be strengthened through the use of FinTech, it may also, in parallel, lead to more aggressive lending habits or create additional operational complexity and, thus, undermine the stability benefits, at least in part. These results are in line with previous studies that recognise the dualist character of the FinTech consumption whereby efficiency gains are paralleled with increased technological and operational risks (Safiullah and Paramati, 2024; Mabe and Simo-Kengne, 2025). In turn, the information highlights the urgency of introducing multiple stability indicators in a bid to capture the multifacetedness of risks created by digital transformation. The added value of introducing ESG performance as a moderating construct to the investigation is enhanced understanding of the institutional contingencies that lead to positive results of FinTech adoption. Hypotheses 3 and 4 are strongly supported by the effect of interaction, which demonstrated that ESG performance enhances the positive effect of FinTech adoption on financial performance and financial stability. Banks that have better governance structures and a more pronounced sustainability outlook will experience more returns on digital innovation, which means that ethical governance enhances the efficiency of FinTech investments. This finding correlates with the available evidence that rigid management and strategic congruency enhance the payoffs of technology adoption (Alqudah et al., 2025).

In addition, the ESG performance will mitigate the possible destabilising effects of adopting FinTech because it will strengthen risk-management practises and improve stakeholder trust. These results align with the studies that highlight the centrality of the functions of corporate social responsibility and ethical governance in promoting banking stability (Salah Mahdi et al., 2025). In this aspect, ESG acts as a buffer system making FinTech not a possible source of vulnerability but a stabilising institutional tool. Further discussion proves that sustainability-based strategies, especially those that align with the aims of green finance and long-term value generation, enhance the long-term nature of performance effects of FinTech adoption. This fact supports the Hypothesis 5 and supports the latest results that emphasise the complementary nature of digital transformation and sustainable banking practises (Hidayat-ur-Rehman and Hossain, 2025). Collectively, the empirical data demonstrates that the use of FinTech has a consistent positive impact on the financial performance, though its impact on the financial stability depends on the quality of governance and the ability to manage risks. Using a composite FinTech adoption index provides a more finely-tuned, institutionally-based understanding of these interrelations since, at the same time, it captures both the intensity and the depth of technological integration. Compared to those studies which utilise relatively limited proxy measures, the index based methodology indicates that use of FinTech will deliver its best when it is extensive, well-managed and aligned with the sustainability goal in a strategic manner. Such revelations, therefore, support the general role of the chapter by predicting the necessity of multidimensional measurement systems in the evaluation of the true consequences of digital transformation in the banking industry.

8. MANAGERIAL, REGULATORY, AND POLICY IMPLICATIONS

Empirical results presented in this chapter have a considerable implication on the bank management, financial regulators, and officials of the state who are now working in a more digitised financial ecosystem. The findings highlight the importance of coordinated and regulated and context-specifically oriented solutions to digital transformation by showing that the adoption of FinTech can significantly improve the financial performance and have conditional and context-dependent consequences on financial stability. Managerially, these results indicate that the FinTech adoption must be viewed as an overall organisational change, and not as a messy implementation of individual digital solutions. Banks with greater composite FinTech adoption scores, on a regular basis, are associated with better performance results, which means that value creation depends on the integrated approach to the implementation of digital platforms, advanced analytics, cybersecurity services, and regulatory technologies. The top management should therefore focus on enterprise-level digital transformation plans, which would synchronise technological investments and organisational processes, strategic goals as well as human capital advancement. The evidence also warns against the adoption of FinTech solutions in a partial or ad hoc manner. Disjointed digital projects can produce little efficiency improvement and at the same time, augment operational sophistication and coordination expenses, thereby reducing long-term performance. To this end, bank executives should make sure that the investments in FinTech are integrated into more extensive organisational schemes and accompanied by change-management practises.

It is also very important to incorporate stringent risk-management models in FinTech strategies. Whereas digital innovation is able to improve monitoring and operational efficiency, it equally presents new sources of risks, especially in the areas of cybersecurity, data governance, algorithm decision-making, and interdependencies between systems. The managers ought to thus invest in risk-management structures, internal audit departments and ongoing training of staff at a pace that is appropriate with technological adoption. This congruence is particularly relevant in cases where the institutional absorptive capacity falls behind the fast-paced digital growth, thus, increasing the susceptibility to both operational and total risks. The moderating effect of ESG performance illustrates the core position of the quality of governance and ethical orientation on determining FinTech outcomes. Banks that have a strong ESG framework achieve more benefits in performance and their results become more stable after the digital transformation. It means that ESG considerations must be incorporated right into FinTech decision-making processes as opposed to being viewed as secondary compliance mandates. Making digital innovation work in alignment with the ethical principles and sustainability goals can help in building stakeholder trust, reputational capital, and help to sustain long-term value creation. Regulatory perspective the findings highlight the need to have adaptive and future oriented supervisory systems that strike a balance between promotion of innovation and maintenance of financial stability. Regulators become very central in determining the dynamics of FinTech, especially by standards of cybersecurity, data protection, algorithmic responsibility, and user rights. The heterogeneous stability impacts found during the analysis show that the regulatory oversight should change alongside technological change to avoid the concentration of systematic risks.

The increasing use of regulatory technology (RegTech) offers regulators a chance to increase the efficiency of supervising the institutions and decrease the compliance cost on the side of financial institutions. The proposed system will enhance the accuracy of reporting, facilitate the ability to monitor in real time, and enhance early warning systems by encouraging the use of the RegTech solutions. Nevertheless, regulators, together with the technological facilitation, need to come up with coherent principles under which artificial intelligence and data analytics can be used ethically. The digital practises that must be transparent, fair, and accountable will be critical in ensuring that people trust the ever-increasingly automated financial systems. The findings at the policy level emphasize the necessity of the initiatives that promote responsible, inclusive, and sustainable FinTech adoption. The policy makers ought to be concerned with the creation of digital financial ecosystems that would not only foster innovation but also enhance institutional capacity and governance standards. Cooperation between the government and commercial sectors, investment in digital infrastructure, and specific capacity-building programmes can assist banks to take advantage of the opportunities of FinTech to grow without threatening stability. The interventions are especially applicable to the context of emerging and developing banking regimes where lopsided technological preparedness and regulatory maturity may enhance the digital risks. The results also emphasize the need to incorporate sustainability goals in national and regional digital finance strategies. Green finance and responsible lending FinTech programmes that are consistent with an ESG agenda and sustainable finance strategies have a higher chance of providing sustainable performance returns and systemic stability. On balance, the implications imply that the most fruitful approach to FinTech adoption is to take it through combined managerial approaches, adaptable regulatory control, and sustainability-focused frameworks of the public policy. This alignment can help the most out of the economic and social payoff of digital transformation and limit its possible risks to financial stability.

9. CONCLUSION AND FUTURE RESEARCH DIRECTIONS

The contribution of this chapter to the existing literature on FinTech is significant because it has placed adoption as a multidimensional, institutionally-rooted and strategically-managed phenomenon, not just a set of discrete technological tools. The work fills an important measurement and analytical gap that has continued to cripple academic research by creating a bank-level composite FinTech adoption index and empirically investigating its association with financial performance and financial stability. The empirical results presented herein strongly prove that the use of FinTech has a constant positive and economically significant effect on bank performance. Banks with greater scores on integrated digital services, advanced analytics, integration of platforms, regulatory technology and ethical governance continue to record a higher score in terms of profitability and operational efficiency. These results confirm that FinTech adoption is a strategic organisational capacity, the benefits of which accrue in a cumulative manner through a process involving the orchestrated digital change, as opposed to isolated or binary markers of technological utilisation. On the other hand, the correlation between the adoption of FinTechs and financial stability is less obvious. Although increased adoption increases resilience through better monitoring, automation, and risk analytics, it also can present a number of new vulnerabilities to do with cybersecurity, operational complexity, and digital interconnectedness. The observed mixed effects in the stability metrics confirm the duality of FinTech as both stabilising and potentially destabilising influence, thus emphasising the need to have a high quality of governance and institutional capacity to influence the results. One of the core contributions of this chapter is that ESG performance and sustainability orientation are recognised as strategically important moderating mechanisms. Banks that have well-established governance structures and uncompromising sustainability policies are better equipped to turn digital innovation into a durable, stable value, which makes the ethical governance/ sustainability argument the notion that it can be viewed as the part and parcel of FinTech strategies rather than a limitation on them.

In terms of methodology, the composite FinTech adoption index is an important step in measurement practise. The index improves cross-bank comparability by incorporating technological intensity with the institutional and governance dimensions providing an empirical and scalable instrument of policy analysis. The framework proves particularly relevant to regulators and policymakers who are eager to follow digital transformation and its systemic consequences. In spite of these contributions, a number of avenues of future research come out. First, the dynamic, path-dependent nature of FinTech adoption requires longitudinal studies that can analyse the relationship between the different phases of the adoption, including initiation, consolidation, and maturity, and performance, risk-taking, and stability. There may be a need to use dynamic panel models and time-varying methods to shed light on the feedback effects between digital innovation and bank behaviour. Second, external validity would be enhanced by the comparative cross-country study that would investigate how the regulatory setting, market structure, and degrees of economic development precondition the outcomes of FinTech. Third, the measurement structure of the future might be further developed with the consideration of such measurement dimensions as open banking involvement, data-sharing structures and platform governance, possibly by using machine-learning methods without sacrificing interpretation. Ethical governance, algorithmic accountability, and data privacy should be the focus of future studies due to the increasing use of artificial intelligence effects, which increase the concerns about bias and transparency. Lastly, it would be more beneficial to focus the analysis on the traditional financial outcomes, but expand these indicators to include levels of customer trust, operational sustainability, and systemic networkedness, which would give a more detailed picture of the general implications of FinTech. Overall, this chapter proves that FinTech adoption is most effective in its complex and holistic form with sound governance and in connexion with the goals of sustainability, and thus, it provides academic and policy-relevant information to the topic of digital transformation of banking systems.

REFERENCES

Ahmad, R., Xie, C., Wang, P., Liu, B., Zainir, F., & Mohsin, M. I. A. (2025). FinTech innovation, stability and efficiency: Evidence from Malaysian bank industry. *International Journal of Finance & Economics, 30*(1), 221–241. DOI: 10.1002/ijfe.2917

Aloulou, M., Grati, R., Al-Qudah, A. A., & Al-Okaily, M. (2024). Does FinTech adoption increase the diffusion rate of digital financial inclusion? A study of the banking industry sector. *Journal of Financial Reporting and Accounting*, *22*(2), 289–307. DOI: 10.1108/JFRA-05-2023-0224

Alqudah, M. Z., Sierra-García, L., & Garcia-Benau, M. A. (2025). The moderating role of ESG scores on the relationship between FinTech adoption and financial performance: Evidence from Middle East banks. *Economic Change and Restructuring*, *58*(6), 1–50. DOI: 10.1007/s10644-025-09927-7

Baker, H., Kaddumi, T. A., Nassar, M. D., & Muqattash, R. S. (2023). Impact of financial technology on improvement of banks' financial performance. *Journal of Risk and Financial Management*, *16*(4), 230. DOI: 10.3390/jrfm16040230

Banik, B., & Roy, C. K. (2023). Measuring fintech-driven financial inclusion for developing countries: Comprehensive Digital Financial Inclusion Index (CDFII). *Economic Journal of Emerging Markets*, 143-159.

Ben Bouheni, F., Tewari, M., Sidaoui, M., & Hasnaoui, A. (2023). An econometric understanding of Fintech and operating performance. *Review of Accounting and Finance*, *22*(3), 329–352. DOI: 10.1108/RAF-10-2022-0290

Fundira, M., & Mbohwa, C. (2025). AI ethics in banking services: A systematic and bibliometric review of regulatory and consumer perspectives. *Discover Artificial Intelligence*, *5*(1), 1–25. DOI: 10.1007/s44163-025-00432-4

Hidayat-ur-Rehman, I., & Hossain, M. N. (2025). The impacts of Fintech adoption, green finance and competitiveness on banks' sustainable performance: Digital transformation as moderator. *Asia-Pacific Journal of Business Administration*, *17*(4), 987–1020. DOI: 10.1108/APJBA-10-2023-0497

Kaddumi, T. A., Baker, H., Nassar, M. D., & A-Kilani, Q. (2023). Does financial technology adoption influence bank's financial performance: The case of Jordan. *Journal of Risk and Financial Management*, *16*(9), 413. DOI: 10.3390/jrfm16090413

Kayed, S., Alta'any, M., Meqbel, R., Khatatbeh, I. N., & Mahafzah, A. (2025). Bank FinTech and bank performance: Evidence from an emerging market. *Journal of Financial Reporting and Accounting*, *23*(2), 518–535. DOI: 10.1108/JFRA-09-2023-0526

Kharrat, H., Trichilli, Y., & Abbes, B. (2024). Relationship between FinTech index and bank's performance: A comparative study between Islamic and conventional banks in the MENA region. *Journal of Islamic Accounting and Business Research*, *15*(1), 172–195. DOI: 10.1108/JIABR-03-2022-0081

Lamey, Y. M., Tawfik, O. I., Durrah, O., & Elmaasrawy, H. E. (2024). Fintech adoption and banks' Non-Financial performance: Do circular economy practices matter? *Journal of Risk and Financial Management*, *17*(8), 319. DOI: 10.3390/jrfm17080319

Mabe, Q. M., & Simo-Kengne, B. D. (2025). The impact of FinTech risk on bank performance in Africa: The PVAR approach. *Journal of Risk and Financial Management*, *18*(8), 456. DOI: 10.3390/jrfm18080456

Mosayebi, P., Nejad, S. M., Minoei, M., & Mehrani, A. (2024). Evaluation of Financial Technology (FinTech) Indicators Using a Mixed-Methods Approach in the Banking Industry. *Management Strategies and Engineering Sciences*, *6*(5), 52–58. DOI: 10.61838/msesj.6.5.7

Nguyen, L., Tran, S., & Ho, T. (2022). Fintech credit, bank regulations and bank performance: A cross-country analysis. *Asia-Pacific Journal of Business Administration*, *14*(4), 445–466. DOI: 10.1108/APJBA-05-2021-0196

Safiullah, M., & Paramati, S. R. (2024). The impact of FinTech firms on bank financial stability. *Electronic Commerce Research*, *24*(1), 453–475. DOI: 10.1007/s10660-022-09595-z

Salah Mahdi, I. B., Bouaziz, M., & Boujelbène Abbes, M. (2025). The moderating effect of fintech on the relationship between CSR and banks' financial stability: Baron and Kenny's approach analysis. *EuroMed Journal of Business*, *20*(2), 300–324. DOI: 10.1108/EMJB-03-2023-0082

Singh, R., Malik, G., & Jain, V. (2021). FinTech effect: Measuring impact of FinTech adoption on banks' profitability. *International Journal of Management Practice*, *14*(4), 411–427. DOI: 10.1504/IJMP.2021.116587

Stankevičienė, J., & Kabulova, J. (2022). Financial technology impact on stability of financial institutions. *Technological and Economic Development of Economy*, *28*(4), 1089–1114. DOI: 10.3846/tede.2022.17093

Vettriselvan, R., Velmurugan, P. R., Regins, J. C., Maheswari, S. U., & Joyce, R. (2025). Best Practices, Ethical Challenges, and Regulatory Frameworks for AI Integration in Banking: Navigating the Future. In *Artificial Intelligence for Cloud-Native Software Engineering* (pp. 377-410). IGI Global Scientific Publishing.

Yan, C., Siddik, A. B., Yong, L., Dong, Q., Zheng, G. W., & Rahman, M. N. (2022). A two-staged SEM-artificial neural network approach to analyze the impact of FinTech adoption on the sustainability performance of banking firms: The mediating effect of green finance and innovation. *Systems*, *10*(5), 148. DOI: 10.3390/systems10050148

Yin, F., Jiao, X., Zhou, J., Yin, X., Ibeke, E., Iwendi, M. G., & Biamba, C. (2022). Fintech application on banking stability using Big Data of an emerging economy. *Journal of Cloud Computing (Heidelberg, Germany)*, *11*(1), 43. DOI: 10.1186/s13677-022-00320-7 PMID: 36093281

Zheng, C., Rahman, M. A., Hossain, S., & Alam Siddik, M. N. (2024). Construction of a composite fintech index to measure financial inclusion for developing countries. *Applied Economics*, *56*(52), 6498–6515. DOI: 10.1080/00036846.2024.2313600

Zheng, C., Rahman, M. A., Hossain, S., & Moudud-Ul-Huq, S. (2023). Does Fintech-driven inclusive finance induce bank profitability? Empirical evidence from developing countries. *Journal of Risk and Financial Management*, *16*(10), 457. DOI: 10.3390/jrfm16100457

Chapter 3
Balancing Efficiency and Sustainability: The Effect of Fintech on Commercial Bank's Financial Performances

Mirudhula K.
http://orcid.org/0009-0009-1607-3160
Srinivasa Ramanujan Centre, SASTRA (Deemed to be) University, India

Karthikeyan S.
http://orcid.org/0000-0003-4276-2663
Srinivasa Ramanujan Centre, SASTRA (Deemed to be) University, India

ABSTRACT

Financial technologies explosive growth has changed the global banking landscape by transforming established commercial banking models and creating new avenues for expansion, effectiveness and financial inclusion. The chapter aims at addressing the impact of fintech on the bank's financial performances and its challenges in adopting it in the system. Despite of these, there raised a challenging risk and threats in way of handling such technical aspects of bank briefing various financial technologies and its evolution over the years also it discusses about its financial inclusion and provides a way for underserved areas to explore and to incorporate the habit of saving through wide range of fintech platforms like peer-peer lending, AI integrated applications etc., along with the various available opportunities for commercial banks. Adding to this, it discusses about the crucial role of fintech in policy and regulatory compliance of commercial banks as it leads to achieve long-term financial sustainability and customer loyalty by balancing efficiency, trust and transparency.

DOI: 10.4018/979-8-3373-6244-1.ch003

INTRODUCTION

In today's rapidly evolving financial system, technologies explosive growth has reshaped the commercial banks' way of handling their operations, customers and it is creating new avenues for expansion. Commercial banks, being a backbone of the financial system, operating in a highly competitive landscape, often require regulatory upgradation, innovation to offer more personalised financial products, thereby to keep up their market share and to build long-lasting customer relationships. In all these concepts, Fintech or Financial technology plays a predominant role – in general, it refers to the use of advanced digital solutions for boosting financial services, enhancing productivity and fostering new business models within the banking sector.

Fintech emerged as a powerful tool that is transforming traditional banking systems into a digital ecosystem, driven by customer-centric and cost-effective financial services. This redefined the operation of traditional banks, which had a lengthy operational process and limited access to financial services. With the advent of the digital banking system, commercial banks started to expand their area of operation across the rural sector to promote financial inclusion by leveraging fintech applications like peer-to-peer lending, mobile payment apps and other AI-integrated wealth management apps through an open banking initiative. In recent days, commercial banks have been attracting international business by integrating a decentralized financial (Defi) system to ease cross-border transactions, thereby generating higher revenues, paving a path for sound financial metrics. This in turn enhances the operational efficiency and helps in accelerating financial performances by way of opening new revenue strikes. On the other hand, the need for banks in this digital era goes just beyond their existence or maximizing profitability. It's an age where ESG concerns are more prevalent, and sustainability becomes a vital component in the banking industry for gaining long-term revenues.

Apart from reshaping the banking landscape, fintech as an essential role in striving for profitability, improved customer engagement, resulting in sound financial systems. It also has a significant impact on commercial banks' financial performances, depending on its size and stability. Fintech adoption has a direct and measurable impact on banks' financial performances, influencing both revenue generation and cost efficiency. Commercial banks are experiencing changes in key performance indicators like return on assets, return on equity, with rapid change in fintech. Fintech positively drives a larger value of total deposits and net profits in commercial banks(Baker et al., 2023b). An innovative tech-based commercial banks can improve operating income, CAR, and optimised profitability by reducing their risk-taking ability (Li et al., 2022). Digital risk control is a major factor in the development of fintech, as it greatly reduces the bank's credit risk. However, this effect is less significant in small and medium-sized commercial banks (Zhang et al., 2023)

However, these fintech advancements raised a challenging risk and threats to the commercial banks in way of handling large volumes of data, regulatory compliance in digital mode also changed the customer handling process. Commercial banks, focused on serving the rural population, struggled to keep up the stream of innovation and to make sound financial metrics. On the point of balancing efficiency gains with sustainable practices that guarantee resilience, inclusion and social trust, commercial banks are facing issues.

Despite all these challenges, Fintech remains a powerful catalyst that streamlines operational process, reduces costs, reinforces risk-bearing capacity and enhances commercial banks' profitability while enabling new revenue-generation models. (Y. Wang et al., 2021). However, Fintech also possess new risk to the credibility and financial soundness of financial institutions. Cyberattacks, in particular, have become a major risk factor, making both banks and fintech firms increasingly vulnerable in managing digital financial transactions. (AlBenJasim et al., 2024).

Financial system, fintech entrepreneurs and financial consumers, all be impacted by three drivers of fintech risk, i.e., the algorithms, cloud and the data (X. Chen et al., 2022). Beside the challenges faced by financial institution and fintech firms also raised a concerns about data privacy, time consumption, and network reliability hinder fintech consumers, underscoring the necessity of secure connection and efficient payment methods (Shah et al., 2024) To address all these endangers, collective engagement, ethical norms, and judicial relief mechanism are essential for regulating fintech environment to resolve moral and legal issues thereby to encourage sound and sustainable fintech growth (P. Chen, 2024). Fintech adoption in the face of pressure, commercial banks are stuck between their moral values of social expectations and the push of new technologies. Fintech's potential as an accelerator for rethinking finances as a tool for creating lasting value not only for its shareholder to keep up their legacy for retaining their loyal customers, communities and for the whole banking environment.

Fintech companies have a competitive edge in the market that boosts banks' sustainable performances by integrating such innovative technologies in their operational process to have a seamless progression of their performances in future. (Subanidja et al., 2022). In this digital age, Innovations like blockchain, 5G networks connectivity, AI and IoT-enabled services encourage and transform commercial banks by stepping ahead with transparent and sustainable banking practices, to provide more customer-centric products for retaining their trustworthy customers in the long-term (I.B & M B, 2025; Kapoor et al., 2024). As once said by Bill Gates, *"banking is necessary but bankers are not"*, fintech firms are replacing the role of bankers through Artificial Intelligence. It enables banks to create their own working platforms by collaborating with fintech startups, essential to shape digital banking in future. (Murinde et al., 2022).

OBJECTIVES

1. To explore how fintech plays a vital role in enhancing the financial performance of commercial banks
2. To discuss about fintech role in policy and regulatory compliance of commercial banks
3. To get insights about future prospects of fintech in achieving sustainable financial performance in commercial banks.

FINTECH EVOLUTION

The evolution of fintech is not just a tale of technological innovation or digital revolution; it is the timeline of peoples unrelenting drive to improve efficiency, accessibility and security of global financial dealings. This fintech tale, spanning from the ancient days of the barter system to wide interconnected, AI-powered financial landscapes of 21st century, which steadily transformed the way of handling monetary management, storage, exchange and utilization. The accelerated progress of digitizing banking industry in recent years deeply rooted in a prehistoric transformation, from barter era to coinage, then towards formal banking era to an e-banking era, which created a strong foundation for today's digital banking era. Hence, understanding this genesis is essential to get deeper insights into how fintech impacts on key financial indicators of commercial banks.

The Genesis:

Barter, coinage and the birth of value Exchange

An evolution of Fintech starts from the early days of *barter system*- a direct exchange of goods for goods or services. An effective system well-suited in tiny, local economies, but it is hindered by *"double coincidence of wants"*- refers to where both the parties want the same at the time of exchange. A standardized medium of exchange has been developed as a result of such inefficiency. Around 600 BCE *coinage era* was introduced in Turkey (later Lydia), the first significant advancement in financial environment. Coins offered a portable, strong and widely accepted form of exchange. These coins were made out of precious metals and stamped with government emblems.

By addressing the issue of double coincidence of wants, this era laid a foundation for developing first financial institution focused on implementing in temples and government treasuries that protect the wealth of a country and grant affordable credit. The value of coins was ensured only by the issuing entities rather than its intrinsic value.

Coinage era paved way for international trade, ease of taxation, and to maintain military payroll systems. Countries like Rome and Greece scaled their economies during this coinage periods. At the same time, early system banks were developed for safeguarding civilians' deposits, issue of loans and even a rigid Letter of Credit (LOC) given to specific merchants. All these positive aspects of the coinage era initiated a trust in value of exchange, which in-turn introduced the concept of monetary era. Though a historical concept when compared with today's fintech world, it created a core principle like *standardization, trust, liquidity and flexibility* being a pillar of modern finance.

The paper currency and institutionalisation of finances

This transformative phase started with the paper currency initiatives in China later adopted worldwide. This reshaped the financial landscape by solving the practical issues of storage, transportation and weight in coinage era with the innovation of paper currency. Moreover, it significantly separated money from the inherent value of coin, replaced it for the government trust and confidence backed by specific state. European banks started to issue bills of exchange and promissory notes during 17th and 18th centuries, served as a prototype of present-day cheques and bank notes. This led to the establishment of central banks that standardized the process credit generation, monetary regulation, and official lending systems, resulted in fostering formalized financial ecosystem.

This paper currency era marked a move towards simplification and mediation of financial system, more than just a convenience. Institutions evolved as a risk manager, allocation of capital advisors and a custodian of valuables. All these frameworks of financial institutions dominated the global financial landscapes until the evolution of digital banking, which addressed the issue of complex administration and physically accessible financial products.

The 1950s: Formal banking system and the rise of financial intermediation

The banking system was formalized and expanded as a result of the post-World War II period. In 1950s, banks began a small regional deposit holdings organization, which further developed into professional financial institution that provided investment services, consumer credit, business loans, mortgages. The primary innovation in this era referred as *"holding and lending"* rather than technological development.

Banks emerged as the key hubs of national economies by pooling of deposits from the people who save and transfers them to the people who need it through credit evaluation. Although this model worked well, it's highly reliant upon paperwork, limited within a specific geographical boundary. Moreover, it involved high manual work, so the transaction to be processed for longer days to get settlement. This process mandates the physical presence of a customer.

However, this transformation sowed a seed for automation. The first Automated Teller Machine (ATM) in 1950 and the launch of (MICR) Magnetic Ink Character Recognition in late 1950s marked the start of technological innovation in banking industry. Additionally, Americans were first exposed to credit cards in 1950s. Furthermore, this consumer revolution was aided by the advent of Interbank Card Association(ICA), now known as Master cards (Arner et al., 2015). It created significant growth in financial environment by reducing the need for cash and cheques, further increased access to banking products via digitizing financial transactions. These wide range of innovation, time reduction for processing a transaction and declined need of handling cash altogether paved way for the E-financial era.

The E-Financial era

The phrase E-finance is commonly referred to the early stages of fintech or digital finances, i.e., business utilizing information and communication technologies in financial industry (Gomber et al., 2017). Information Technology and finance witnessed a massive integration in the years 1980s and 1990s, hereby the initial wave of electronic banking made possible by widespread use of PCs, internet and telecommunication networks. In this transformative phase, paper relied process were gradually replaced by online banking portals, (ETFs) Electronic Fund Transfer and digital payment gateways focused not only on simplifying payment process also greatly improved financial performances of commercial banks. Improved profit margins, increased asset rotation and improved (ROE) Return on Equity were the results of early adopters across various financial institutions. It also involves declined cost of automation, low rates of error and quicker transaction processing.

E- financial era can be featured into 3 revolutionary phases;

Electronification - Physical certificates of stocks, bonds and other financial instruments were transformed into digital records. This dematerialization reduced the count of fraud, lowered the issuing and safe-keeping cost and real-time monitoring of valuable asset is made possible. Altogether strengthened the worth of commercial bank's balance sheets and boosted the distribution of funds.

Cutting out middleman's -Banks and consumers could eliminate conventional way of allowing intermediaries for some services. For example; trading stocks on online platforms like E-trade (1992) enabled investors and customers to buy and sell stocks without the need of brokers. Banks were forced to modernize and to increase cost-efficiency as a result of sector-wise reduction in fee structures. This pushed many commercial banks to scaleup their market share and to attain competitive edge in entire rapidly changing financial landscape, pivotal factor that drives revenue growth.
Expeditions - Prolonged transactions now possible to settle in fraction of seconds. Higher liquidity, reduced settlement periods and international banking system became quite fast. This acceleration made banks to more flexibly reinvest funds, forecasting higher value of cash inflow resulted in opening of new alternate revenue streams. All together witnessed a sudden rise in earnings and stakeholder value.

Adding to this, this phase of transformation is also referred for a raise of *"core banking system"*- commonly referred to the integration of software's into the baking operations for ease of managing large volume of customer data, loans and transaction history in digital format. Software's like (ERP) Enterprise Resource Planning and (CRM) Customer Relationship Management gained its value by boosting operational efficiency and to identify the prospect customer to pitch their innovative products, lifted the net interest margins and net income by cross-selling.

However, this era failed to cover unbanked or underbanked area due to complex infrastructural need, regulatory challenges and poor inter-connection. This E-finance era remains isolated. Even though it shot up sound financial statements actual expansion of the financial institution remains unattainable.

Revolution of UPI: The game changer of financial industry (2016)

In an era characterized by digital changes, few inventions had a significant impact on the global financial landscape. While nations struggled with scattered, rigid legacy mechanism, India was a surprising leader in developing a local solution that would revolutionize its own economy and serve as a model for inclusive, scalable digital finance globally. In 2016, (NPCI) National Payments Corporation of India, along with Reserve Bank of India, launched Unified Payment Interface (UPI), a turning point in history of global fintech. Using an effortless virtual payment address, UPI is known for its infrastructural innovation than just being a payment system. Through

UPI, peer-to-peer and inter-banking transactions is made possible without the need of account numbers, IFSC codes or any other banking information's.

UPIs were built using an open API, enables third party payment interface providers to get easily in-connect with the banking systems of their users and promoting strong market place. This created an impact on multiple aspects,

Financial accessibility - UPI allows millions of Indians who were uncovered in any form of financial services were made accessible to financial services including street vendors, rickshaw drivers, farmers able to make digital transaction and can view their transaction history.

Cost effective - Transaction done by UPI platforms resulted in cost reduction, even it provides cost-free services, promotes micro level transaction by encouraging the use of digital payment methods.

Expandability – 10 billion monthly transaction were processed by UPI, which crossed the big global players like Master card and visa. A demonstration for its strong and portable architecture.

Performance of commercial banks – significantly, UPI acted as a catalyst for recovering commercial banks' performances, since the rapid rise in digital transaction, banks started to experience a sharp decline reliance on branch and managing of physical cash expenses. Moreover, higher involvement of digital based transaction shot up the ratios of CASA (Current Account Savings Account), in-turn raised interest margins and declined cost of capital.

Overall, UPIs' ecosystem marked a phenomenal expansion, and the varied functionality of different banks and applications reflects the transformative power of digital financial systems (M, 2025).The growth of fintech aimed to widen the area of financial system by providing access to financial service in an underserved population. (Anne-Laure, 2019). Adding to this, fintech has potential to greatly boost financial performances of conventional banking institutions also promoting inclusivity, novelty and sustainability.

AI integration and transparent financial era

As fintech developed beyond the payment system, this is the stage were Artificial Intelligence (AI) evolved as a new horizon. AI powered tools began to integrate with financial system, aimed to transform every aspect of finance,

Credit scoring – Machine Learning algorithms evaluate additional data sources like payment apps, social media to determine the credit standing of their clients.

This improved the rates of loan approval and decreased non-performing loan ratios in commercial banks.

Fraud deduction –Real- time error deducting technologies decreased fraudulent activities in transactions by tracing out suspicious pattern at easy way than by manual deduction. This protects banks net interest margin and reduced losses due to operational inefficiency.

Robo – advisory services – By providing affordable, customized portfolios to individual investors, investment platforms based on algorithm expands the fee-based revenue and increased non- interest revenue for commercial banks, facilitating wealth management

Chatbots and VA (Virtual Assistants) – This improves 24/7 access to financial services at a lower operational cost by effective utilization of AI driven customer services. This, in turn, enhances Return on Asset (ROA) and Return on Equity (ROE).

Reg-tech – AI powered automated risk tracking, regulatory compliance reporting and AML (Anti Money Laundering) verifications reduces the count of human errors and regulatory challenges, thereby improving capital adequacy ratios and cutting down compliance costs.

The integrated use of Blockchain and AI transforms financial security and transparency, improving productivity, reduced fraud and building strong customer confidence (Rane et al., 2023). AI enormous effect on digital financial inclusion since it makes it easier for low-income individuals to engage in the financial system by enhancing fraud detection, oversight and customer service (Mhlanga, 2020)

The evolution of fintech from barter to blockchain, a multilayered series of innovations that build on one another than just being a straightforward progression. Started as a convenience-seeking initiative evolved as a cause for stability, openness and inclusivity. Fintech aims at widening the access to financial services for unserved populations, which aligns with both commercial success and social sustainability.

In case of commercial banks, sustainability and efficiency are the two crucial pillars of rather than being a negative force. When fintech used effectively, it increases revenue streams by promoting sustainable practices and ethical governance. The next phase of financial innovation will be led by banks, particularly those institutions that understand this contradiction and to see technology as a tool for sustainable growth rather than a disruptive force.

FINTECH APPLICATIONS

Commercial banks' operations now heavily include financial technologies, which have transformed traditional banking services into more customer-focused, quick and efficient services. Fintech applications are providing wide range of services with an objective of connecting customers to financial institutions at zero cost of intermediaries. Key fintech applications like digital payments, neo-banks, peer-peer lending, and AI-powered budgeting tools, which scale up the profitability, customer engagement, and long-term financial sustainability.

Digital payments- The backbone of modern banking:

One of the ways to exchange money digitally without using real cash is via digital payments. The use of digital payments has completely changed how people spend their money (Chauhan & Sharma, 2024). Particularly in commercial banks, the value transfers between banks or to their customers have been transformed by digital apps like PayPal, Google Pay, Apple Pay, Phone Pay and other regional vendors like Africa's M-Pesa and China's Alipay. These innovations reduced the settlement durations from days to seconds, eliminates the convention clearing house burden and resulted in offering smooth, safe and quick transaction processing. For example, ICICI bank reports 22% increase in volume of transaction done through its business banking platform, *"Instabiz"* during the fiscal year 2024, one of the leading private sector commercial banks offers wide range of services including retail, corporate and digital baking solutions and banks mobile application *"iMobile pay"* surpassed 30 million users during 2024, facilitating transaction around Rs. 11,000 billion.

Similarly, HDFC Bank, one of India's largest private sector bank known for its customer-centric approach, robust digital infrastructure for banking and financial services, witnessed a net revenue growth for the quarter ended December 31st,2024, grew by 6.3% to Rs 421.1 billion than Rs 396.1 billion in same quarter of previous fiscal year. This digital transition resulted in gaining retail fees income of HDFC for the 4th quarter of 2024, year is around 94% of the bank's fee income where whereas 34% of fee income from payments and card business. Highlighting the role of digital payment services in banks' revenue generation process. This is due to banks' digital applications like PayZapp and SmartHub, by offering secure and convenient choices for customers.

Figure 1. Digital payment transaction year-on-year growth

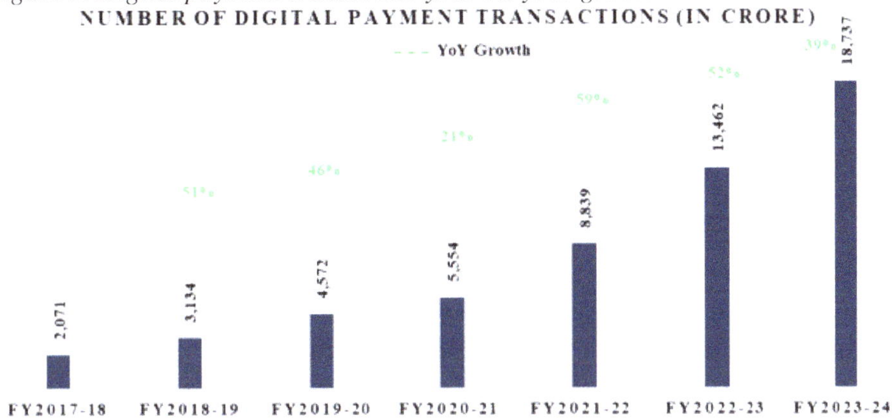

Source: Secondary data

Overall, from the above figure, the volume of all digital payment of India grew at 44% CAGR from 2,071 crore in the year 2017-18 to 18,737 crores during the fiscal year 2023-24. In recent years, the government's collaborative efforts with every participant in the banking industry led to the remarkable spike in digital payment.

Beside its ease of use to make transactions, digitization offers both opportunity and strengthens the financial performances of commercial banks and challenges in terms of adapting to dynamic environment. Similarly, for users, unmatched services push them into a financially unrecoverable situation.

Benefits to commercial banks

Operational efficiency – The use of digital payments among commercial banks has several advantages, due to lower input cost and integration into digital payment system. Commercial banks witnessed a higher-level cost efficiency, thereby enhances operational efficiency (Saroy et al., 2023). This benefits commercial banks to reduce their dependency on cash handling systems, minimized paperwork work and lower cost of maintaining ATMs and physical branches. This encouraged regional commercial banks to operate more on a customer-centric basis.

Wider customer base – The Digital payment application allows commercial banks to reach rural people, who were excluded from accessing traditional banking services. Helped in broadening their loyal customer base. Mobile payment apps played a pivotal role in gaining this benefit, promotes financial inclusion also by attracting tech-savvy younger generations.

New stream of revenue – additionally, banks can easily collaborate with fintech firms, provides predictive financial products to build customized servicing than just focusing on gaining higher revenue. By leveraging third- party payment into the intermediary business of commercial banks gets significantly impacted. It creates a new revenue structure rather than just changing the use of payment methods and customer behavior (M, 2025).

Challenges to commercial banks

High upfront cost - Adoption of digital payment apps present considerable challenges for commercial banks. The high initial investment cost of integrating digital ecosystem, a greater issue for those banks operating at lower level of profitability. This is because it requires frequent upgradation in terms like cyber security, data storage, IT infrastructure to maintain a lasting a safe digital platform.

Security threats – banks are more prone to threats like identity theft, phishing, hacking of customer accounts as the volume of digital transaction goes above. A single breach of data might result in enormous financial loss and affects banks' long-term reputation built among their customers.

Non-banking financial players – digital wallets and fintech companies frequently offer quick, easy-to-use services, which forces commercial banks to reshape their existing conventional services. Beside this, it also forces banks to allocate quite amount to invest in customer awareness programs to build trust and digital literacy among them.

Neo-banks- Redefining customer Expectations:

Neo-bank, a type of financial institution that operates entirely online without the need for a network of physical branches, whether or not it has a banking license. Innovative technology is used in this bank model to offer individualized services to specialized markets(Temelkov, 2020). Neo banks are more flexible, agile and customer-focused than traditional banks since they are not constrained by outdated systems. As a result, they frequently provide tailored financial solutions, attractive interest rates at a reduced cost (Kapliar, 2023). Neo banks are distinguished by their digital- first strategy, paperless operations, and capacity to offer easy-to access financial services at any time from any location. (S. K, 2025). By addressing underprivileged groups and providing cutting-edge tools that enables users to better manage their funds, it helps to promote financial inclusion (Voshchak, 2024). However, neo-banks being a digital only bank itself turns them to face challenges such as building trust among customers, ensuring security and overcoming regulatory barriers.

An example of this concept is the American neo-bank Chime, one of the biggest digital banks in the U.S by client base, driven by 8.6 million active members and an Average Return Per Active Member (ARPAM) of $251. Also, it reports $519 million growth in revenue for Q1 of 2025, i.e., an increase of 32% on a yearly basis. (*June 2025 Chime Investor Presentation.*) Chime achieved 67% transaction profit margin, resulted in $25 million EBITDA. As it grows into unsecured lending, insurance, and investing for households making up to $200 thousand, reaching a total addressable market of $426 billion, includes $86 billion serviceable marketing using their current products. In Europe, Revolut was established in 2015 and has since expanded to become one of the most valuable fintech firms with over 35 million customers in more than 35 countries. (*RGHL_Annual Report 31 Dec 2024-2025-04-22-17-42*). In a single app, it provides budgeting tools, stock trading, cryptocurrency and multi-currency accounts. Due to interchange fees and subscription plans, in 2023 revenue increased by60% to $ 1.3 billion. This success is derived from its unique feature of hyper-personalization, comprising saving vaults, real-time spending alerts.

According to. (Sardar & Anjaria, 2023) The global neo banking industry was estimated to be worth $47.39 billion in 2021, and it is projected to rise at an outstanding 53.4% CAGR between 2022 and 2030. The way traditional banks operate is threatened by neo-banks, commonly referred to as challenger banks.

Benefits of neo-banks

Customer-centric experience - Neo-banks prioritize the customer experience and are designed with a digital-first strategy. They provide smooth interfaces, easy navigation and user-friendly features in contrast to conventional banks with obsolete technologies. This simplified use of financial products covers younger tech-savvy customers who prefer self-service to in-person visits to branches.
24/7 accessibility – the unique feature of digital-only offerings offers flexibility to its customers to access their accounts from anywhere at any time. This benefits value to those individuals who are more time-concerned, particularly suits for urban areas where lifestyle is fast-paced. Adding to this, it also benefits global clients by using multi-currency wallets and conversion facilities.
Faster onboarding services – traditional process of account opening involves huge paper works and takes longer duration for settlement since these neo banks highly dependent on e-KYC, biometrics and providing financial service based on AI benefits their customers to open account instantly and approval within fraction of seconds. Similarly, small ticket loans and sanctioning of loan were done within seconds making financial services more accessible and faster.

Challenges of neo-banks

Regulatory hurdles – Major challenges of neo-banks is that it doesn't have full banking license. In order to offer quality services these banks have to collaborate with conventional banks, which makes obtaining regulatory permission more difficult.(S. R. K & K, 2025). Also, it operates in a quick changing landscape, subject to inspection on consumer protection, KYC norms adherence, AML regulation and data privacy issue.

Trust deficit – the lack of physical branch posts a challenging threat to lose some customer base particularly of older generation people and those who wants reassurance from a branch office. Despite of its distinguished trait i.e., offering digital only service turns into a negative force. Still there are customers hesitant to trust banks operating only on digital modes.

Raising competition from traditional banks – neo banks competitive edge being eroded as traditional banks are accelerating their process towards digitalization, resulting in making it more complex for neo-banks to hold their market position.

Peer-peer lending

Peer-to-peer online lending services provide small enterprises and individuals with alternative loan choices. These platforms have numerous competitive benefits, contributing to a significant increase in both the loan volume and value. P2P lending provides lenders a higher return rates and borrowers with restricted access to banks with cheaper credit. (A. Basha et al., 2021). When it comes to helping infra-marginal bank borrowers, peer-to-peer lending can take the place of bank lending; however, it can also be used in combination with bank lending for modest loans. These findings suggest that the expansion of credit brought about by peer-to-peer lending generally happens to borrowers who are already eligible for bank credit (Lenz, 2016). These platforms are used by small firms to obtain quick and adaptable financial solutions, but they lack knowledge of the particular financial instruments that are employed to raise loans (Anderloni et al., 2024).

To witness the crucial role of P2P lending in today's digital era, one of the first P2P lenders in the U.S, Lending Club, reported $12.5 billion in total loans originated and surpassed $ 3billion in deposits. Initially, it focused on acquiring unsecured personal loans after the acquisition of Radius Bank, and it turned into a full-fledged digital bank in the year 2020. (*Lending Club Reports Fourth Quarter and Full Year 2023 Results*). Its net revenue increased by approximately 33% in the second quarter of 2025. Overall profitability surged in the same quarter of fiscal year 2025, over

156% on a yearly basis. This resulted in its own claim credit portfolio outperforming its competitors by 40%.

According to the Federal Reserve in 2022, P2P platforms increase access to credit because 30% of Lending Club borrowers have Fair Isaac Corporation (FICO) scores below 680, a group that often banks reject. This enables to evaluation of rural borrowers and provides credit without any official credit score histories in emerging countries like China, and offers microloans based on mobile metrics.

Due to growing consumer debt and SME funding gaps, the global P2P lending market is predicted to reach $ 1.3 trillion by 2030. (*Peer-to-Peer Lending Market Size, Share & Growth | 2032*). However, risk still exists even though default rates can increase during a recession, for instance, Lending Club default rates rose over 4.1% in Q4, 2022, due to inflation. Adding to this regulatory oversight is growing in the areas of data privacy and protection of investor interest.

Benefits of the P2P platform to commercial banks

Reduced credit risk exposure – P2P platforms frequently transfer or hold the credit risk on their own, allowing conventional banks to lower their exposure to unsecured loan lending. It deals with small or retail consumer lending segments, enabling banks to focus on safer, larger ticket loans.

Additional revenue streams by partnership – Banks sometimes collaborate with P2P lending platforms by providing funds, underwriting aid, or technical integration, resulting in earning fees or interest spikes. It also generates referral fees, processing fees without the need to expand physical branches.

Simplified matching with market-driven rates - The technology automatically matches borrowers and lenders at market rates of interest that are known for each risk category, simpler for both parties to grasp (Parboteeah, 2016) Delays might occur due to imbalances, i.e., more lenders than borrowers or vice versa; however, these imbalances can be closed over time by the platform, adjusting interest rates.

Challenges of P2P platforms to commercial banks

Risk of market disruption – since a P2P lending platform is a digital financial application can rapidly innovate new credit products that easily surpass traditional banks, challenging the banks to keep up their market share. If it fails to attain, lead to depletion of the bank's market share, making it harder to regain or to maintain its growth in the retail lending market.

Pressure on interest margins – commercial banks were forced to reduce their interest rates or to enhance digital services to maintain their competitive edge with P2P platforms, contracting interest rates. More significantly, in smaller loans, this contraction of interest rates leads to a reduction in the overall profitability of the bank.

Lack of trust and knowledge – borrowers might directly contact in P2P platform rather than the bank itself, decreasing the opportunities for cross-selling products like insurance, wealth management, turn affects long-term profitability and fee income.

AI-powered wealth management Apps and budgeting tools.

AI in commercial banks can improve client focus, automate compliance tasks, enhance transaction processing and lower lending defaults (Königstorfer & Thalmann, 2020). Financial institutions that use AI-powered portfolio management techniques via Machine Learning algorithms claim a notable increase in operational efficiency, as a result of an automated system managing repetitive operations that traditionally need a high level of human engagement, like recovering tax losses and portfolio restructuring (Yaramolu, 2025). One well-known example is Robo-advisors, which employ quantitative algorithms to offer automated, tailored and inexpensive investing advice. This makes complex financial strategies more accessible to a wider customer base and allows for real-time decision-making based on data availability.

Similarly, AI-powered budgeting and forecasting enhance financial strategies by adjusting to changing market conditions, allocating resources optimally, and transforming corporate decision-making (Yaramolu, 2025). It transforms passive data into useful insights by analyzing spending trends, forecasting cash flow, and providing proactive financial solutions. Through automation and behavioral triggers, these products enable users to save, lower debt, and accumulate wealth. To illustrate, Erica, Bank of America's driven virtual assistant integrated into its mobile banking apps as it offers personalized financial insights, oversight on credit score, bill payment prediction, helps in creating budgets and sends warnings on unusual or overspending, provides foresighted suggestions using predictive analytics and Natural Language Processing (NLP).

All these benefited from the report of Q3 2023, which had over 40 million user interactions per month and served more than 20 million active users in turn contributed to a 12% increase in cross-sell rates for credit and savings products. (*Investor Relations | Bank of America Corporation (BAC)*) The automation process reduced operational costs approximately over 8 million customer service engagement per month.

One of the first international commercial bank to use AI to revolutionize wealth management and personal finance is JP Morgan Chase. The bank has intentionally integrated AI into its retail ad wealth platforms, from its self-directing investment app called "You invest" sophisticated budgeting capabilities inside its own mobile banking landscape, in light of growing need for digitalized financial services. Robo advisors are offering AI-driven portfolio recommendations based on user behavior and risk profiles. (*Investor Relations | JPMorganChase*, 2021). It created a great impact on banks financial performance by 15% year-on-year increase in retail brokerage revenue in 2021, enabled to acquire market share of fintech's like Robinhood.

The bank had led the retail banking industry in U.S profitability due to its hybrid strategy, combines AI powered advice with human assistance. This gained more profitability and sustainable.

Benefits of AI-powered applications to commercial banks

Automation of budgeting and cost tracking – AI powered apps that can automatically establish a budget and track spending include Mint, YNAB (You Need A Budget). These tools categorize expenditure patterns, analyze financial flows and provide specialized budgeting aid.

Guiding investments – by offering data-based, affordable investment methods, AI is playing a significant and essential role in Robo advisors comprising wealth maximization and improvement. (Kavitha & Krishnan, 2025) Helps in assessing investor risk tolerance, investing goals and market movements in order to make recommendation for tailored portfolios.

Personalized financial planning- an AI based application evaluates user's objective, liabilities and savings to generate personalized financial plans. (Gorai, 2025) To match the financial plan, these technologies continuously update records as their user's life being upgraded, like attaining new revenue streams.

Challenges of AI-powered applications to commercial banks

Algorithmic bias and credit risk – unfair lending practices could result from AI powered credit rating that unknowingly reinforce inequalities based on economic status, geography or gender. Such bias can lead to loss of credit, risk is misevaluated adding an extra burden to regulatory complexities.

Concerns about data security and privacy – according to 2019 Accenture poll,76% of wealth management clients expressed concerned about the use of their personal data particularly on AI-based investment platforms. In 2020, IBM released a data breach cost report that found the financial services industry had the top average cost per incident of any industry, around $5.85 million. (Tamraparani, 2022).

Overreliance on technology – overreliance on AI-powered decision-making could make human oversight less effective also inaccurate forecast, system failures can have direct negative impact on trading results, lending portfolios and consumer confidence.

These four fintech pillars- AI budgeting, P2P lending, neo-banks, and digital payments- are not isolated rather they are coming together to form seamless financial apps. Revolut, provides money management, stock trading, banking and payments all in a single interface. In India, Paytm integrates AI-powered expense management, P2P lending and UPI transaction processing. This transformation is backed by significant driving factors like customer demand for convenience, technical advancements and a strong regulatory structure. PWC reports that 88% of financial institutions are afraid of losing their market value to fintech firms, this is the main reason for forming alliances like JP Morgan's small business financing agreement with OnDeck (*Redrawing the Lines: FinTechs Growing Influence on Financial Services - PwC Channel Island,*).

Figure 2. Rate of revenue growth (2022-23)

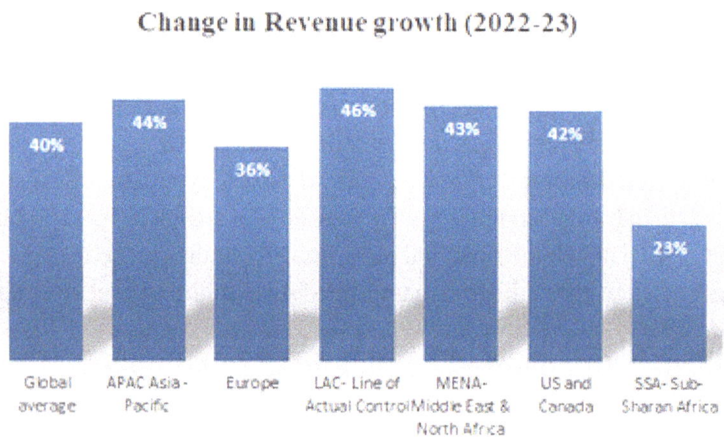

Source: Secondary Data

Figure 3. Rate of profit growth (2022-23)

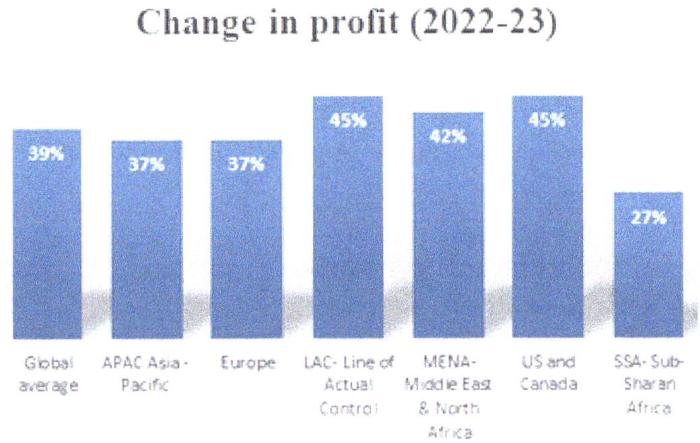

Source: Secondary Data

Fintech redefines finance with the first thought of its users rather than not just digitalizing it. The years to come will witness an even greater integration of AI, blockchain and built-in finance in routine money management, making sound financial health a default rather than a luxury. The robust sector performance and growing dependence on digital financial services for effective and ease of available solution reflected in the average revenue growth rate of 40% in 2023, figure 2. Similarly, in terms of profit, figure 3 shows that fintech industry witnessed a rapid growth rate of 39% in 2023 resulted from effective operations (*WEF_Future_of_Global_Fintech_Second_Edition_2025.Pdf*) Also, the profit raised from 9% to 12% backed by making alliances with regional banking institutions and integrating products from MSME business. The industries overall profitability proven its capacity to adjust, prosper and sustaining in an ever- changing landscape.

ADOPTION OF FINTECH: OPPORTUNITIES FOR COMMERCIAL BANKS

Commercial banks are given multiple opportunities to improve their competitiveness through the use of fintech applications. Banks may reach new customer segments, automate operations and significantly lower transaction cost via digital payments, particularly in emerging areas where tech savvy populations are prevalent. Banks are able to grow lending portfolios and reducing defaults by providing personalized financial products through the incorporation of AI and data analytics. Furthermore, banks may access futuristic business models, diversify their revenue sources, improve client experiences by integrating real-time services through fintech collaborations. Crucially, fintech platforms also help with green financing activities by allowing banks to create and track ecological investment products, green loans and risk frameworks of commercial banks. This section discusses about the multifaceted opportunities that fintech offers to commercial banks, how adoption and collaboration unlocks new avenues of growth, foster innovation and advance environmental sustainability.

Increasing financial inclusion and connecting with new clientele

Offering financial services particularly for neglected or unbanked populations in emerging economies is the finest revolutionary prospects of technology affords to commercial banks. Due to geographical, financial or infrastructural constraints, significant parts of the population in regions like Sub-Saharan Africa, Southeast Asia and portions of Latin America continue staying out of formal banking. Fintech solutions specifically digital wallets, mobile banking applications allow banks to get around these constraints at affordable prices.

In this context, mobile banking programs eliminated the necessity of branches through enabling users to open accounts, exchange money, and credit accessibility with the use of digital gadgets and network connectivity. M-Pesa of Kenya accomplished by reflecting how mobile banking could drive financial inclusion; commercial banks are now working together with equivalent networks to bring millions of new clients. Fintech enables banks to customize onboarding procedures with contactless and AI powered E-KYC norms, thereby lowering compliance expense and burden.

Operational automation through digital payments

Automation powered by fintech is transforming commercia banks back and front-end processes. For example, blockchain-based settlement networks, API integrated payment platforms and real-time payment systems like Europe's SEPA instant credit and India's UPI. AI powered chatbots offer round-the clock assistance, while Robotic Process Automation (RPA) manages repetitive tasks, reducing personnel expenses and improving service quality. According to Mckinsey, Banks that fully digitalize their payment operations can cut processing cost over 40%.

Fintech provide a springboard to move extensive financial services in developing nation that have significant mobile adoption rates and minimal banking infrastructure. In this case, customers who start utilizing a mobile wallet connected to a bank for offering P2P lending can subsequently obtain sound credit scores based on their records making them eligible for small scale business loans. As a result, fintech not only improve operational effectiveness but also foster deeper consumer interaction and opportunities for cross-selling.

Fostering innovation through strategic collaboration with fintech firms

Collaborations with fintech enables banks to react and resolve changes and to provide better product and service development (Salampasis & Mention, 2018). Fintech start-ups add flexibility, specialised knowledge and user-focused design while banks offer funding, loyal clientele and adherence to regulations. Without the high expenses and dangers of internal growth, this synergy allows for quick innovation.

There are several ways that banks can collaborate: they can start tech incubators, invest in fintech firms, engage in accelerators for incubation or use open banking API's to incorporate third-party products. For instance, BBVA was able to rapidly join the European SME banking market through its collaborations with Holvi- A digital banking platform for independent contractors i.e., freelancers (Parera & Molina, 2020). Likewise, JP Morgan Chase's partnership with OneDeck improved small business lending by utilizing the formers underwriting technologies. All these collaboration results banks in gaining access to new revenue strikes.

Green banking initiatives and sustainable finance

Fintech is essential to commercial bank ability to promote ESG goals i.e., Environmental, Social and Governance, especially through green funding. Digital applications make it easier to create, distribute and track sustainable financial services comprising of carbon credit trading, socially responsible loans and green bonds. The tendency is growing due to shareholder demand and regulatory pressure. Global programs such as the Net-zero banking alliance and the EU's Sustainable Finance Disclosure Regulation (SFDR) force banks to incorporate climate risk into their framework. According to IFC- International Finance Corporation, the global green finance market expected to reach over $30 trillion by 2030 and fintech offers the means to comply effectively while opening up new markets. (Sabilika, 2024)

According to (Murinde et al., 2022)It is also anticipated that banks also be more socially conscious in regards to inclusion, wellness, work-life harmony, sustainability and other issues. For instance, they can urge customers to behave sustainability and support environmental concerns like recycling and trash management. This can be accomplished through their fintech users and integrating some practices into their offerings like ranking their prospects according to carbon emissions statistics and include suggestions for green investing.

Supports regulatory compliance

Banks have a great chance to improve their regulatory compliance structure though incorporation of fintech applications. Banks ensures conformity to changing requirements, minimize manual errors and expedite compliance procedures by utilizing technologies like RegTech. In addition to reducing the risk of non-compliance this promotes an open and accountable culture throughout the financial system.

RegTech encompasses wide range of services powered by big-data analytics, AI, Machine Learning that enables commercial banks to follow rules and conditions stated by the regulatory bodies like RBI.

As a case example, Global Screening Service GSS a regulatory technology start-up gained $47 million funding from various investors, including the Commonwealth Bank. It specialized in approving compliance for various financial industry, aiming to speed up sanctioning process for banks and to ensure the accuracy of legal compliance.(*CBA Invests in International Transaction Screening Technology Company*, 2024) Similarly, Dotfile, a French Regtech company raised Euro 6 million to build an AI powered platforms that automates regulatory steps and protects money laundering. This platform also transfers the complex process of KYB- Know Your Business into a quick and effective task in second. (WSC, 2024)

Fintech is a strong driver of commercial banks development rather than being an obstacle to it. Its potentials are numerous and interrelated ranging from fostering sustainable financé and creating a lasting customer relationship to optimizing financial inclusion and streamlining operations.

FINTECH IMPACT ON BANKS FINANCIAL PERFORMANCES

Fintech adoption has direct and measurable impact on banks financial performances, influencing both revenue generation and cost efficiency. Fintech can enable banks to make an informed decision, risk assessment and efficient customer services results in increased banks profitability, and enhancing customer- oriented business model. This section discusses about how fintech enhanced the commercial banks financial performance with a specific focus on differentiating its impact on traditional commercial banks and modern commercial banks. Drawing on recent literatures and empirical data, the analysis underscores the effect of fintech among key financial metrics such as ROA, cost-to-income ratios, NPA management and the growth of market share.

Fintech and key financial performance measures

The two main ways that fintech adoption affects banks performance are through cost savings and enhancement of profits. Fintech gives banks the ability to provide tailored financial products, enter into underdeveloped markets and enhance cross-selling possibilities by using insights of customer records. In terms of cost, digitization, the use of cloud computing and AI-powered procedures cut down on staffing costs, optimize administrative tasks and minimize expense with acquiring and maintaining customer relationship.

A study by (Alqahtani et al., 2024) provides a strong empirical evidences that fintech adoption has statistically significant positive impact on banks Return on Asset (ROA)- a core measure of operational efficiency and profitability relates to total assets. Their cross-national analysis of more than 500 banks conducted during the year 2015 and2022 banks with great fintech adoption scores witnessed an average boost in ROA of 0.8 to 1.2% compared with their competitors, low adoption rates. However, the ROE remains the same this emphasises that fintech adoption do not always results in betterment of financial performance, some key indictors remains stable, particularly in a well-regulated landscape and that banking is capital-intensive industry.

Table 1. Comparative impact of fintech adoption: Traditional Vs Modern commercial banks

Basis	Traditional banks	Modern banks
Definition	Institutions with complex branch networks, outdated IT software.	Digital banks operating or built on cloud-based architecture, APIs and data driven ecosystem
Return on Asset (ROA)	Modest improvement: 0.8 to 1.2% due to operational efficiency and better risk control	Strong improvement: ROA consistently raised over 1.4% than global average of 0.9%
Cost efficiency	Cost-to-income ratio reduced from over 60% to 50-55% through RPA and fintech partnerships. Payment and compliance costs were lowered by up to 30%.	Highly optimized operations with cost-to-income ratios less than 45%. Similarly, DBS bank reported 42% of cost-to-income ratio in 2023. Neo-banks were operating with 70% lower expenses than their conventional peers.
NPA-Non-Performing Assets	AI- powered tracking reduces NPAs by 15-25%. State bank of India reported 22% NPA reduction during the fiscal year 2021-23. Likewise, Banco do Brazil dropped SME loan defaults over 18%. (H. Wang et al., 2023)	Minimal credit risk due to real-time scoring and adaptive underwriting. In case of modern banking NPAs ratios are typically less than 1%

continued on following page

Table 1. Continued

Basis	Traditional banks	Modern banks
Customer Acquisition Cost (CAC)	High CAC: \$200-\$400 per customer due to reliance on branches and legacy marketing	Ultra-low CAC: \$20-\$50 per customer. Chime reports \$25 CAC than compared to industry average of \$300. Resulted from applications, social referrals and embedded finance (Horváth et al., 2022)
Market share growth	Slow expansion: 1-3% annual growth in retail deposits and customers. Struggles to retain younger clients.	Robust capture: 8-12% annual growth in deposits and active users. Digitally advanced banks acquired 68% of new retail customers in developed markets (Baker et al., 2023a)
Technology integration model	Layered adoption: fintech offers integrated a top legacy key system. This involved high integration cost, slower-time to get into market and scalability limits	Internal embedding: built-on microservices, open banking and cloud platforms. This enables real-time product launching and lasting customer relationship.
Fintech strategy	Reactive partnerships: collaborations with fintech for specific use like KYC, lending.	Proactive strategy: acquire, co-develop or internally build fintech apps as a key strategy.
Impact on ROE- Return on Equity	Gained profits are reinvested in digital innovation, capital adequacy limits	Limited ROE raises despite sound operational performance, increased reinvestment and regulating capital requirements limits equity returns

Source: Primary data

The financial performance of banks is inevitably improved by the use of fintech, however the extent and operation of this impact differentiate greatly between traditional and modern commercial banks. Traditional banks, limited by obsolete structures and shorter advancement cycle turn gaining from cutting expenses, risk elimination and higher strikes in revenue. In contrast, digital banks integrate fintech into their core system of operations to achieve transformative increase in profits, scalability and its market value. As stats continuously reflects that fintech and ROA, NPA and cost effectiveness are positively correlated. Yet, in a rigid regulated banking business the lack of ROE impact highlights the struggle to convert operational efficiency into equity returns.

Finally, even if fintech offers commercial banks the chance to enhance their financial performance, the ultimate impact will rely on banks adapt to technology advancements and larger financial environment in which they function. Those who successfully use it will not exist but also prosper in an increasing intense and customer-focused landscape in this 21st century.

CURRENT CHALLENGES AND RISK TOWARDS FINTECH ADOPTION IN COMMERCIAL BANKS

Fintech adoption still has certain hinderances among its users, rural areas are backed in adopting these digital financial systems due to complex regulatory procedures, less network coverage and access to android phones. Apart from this, digital literacy and a strong rooted belief in traditional way of handling transaction resisting the population of rural areas towards fintech adoption. Tech savvy generations are facing challenges related to cyber-attacks, data privacy, taxation and various other criteria. Adding to this, infrastructure facilities for developing fintech and fintech awareness programs are being limited and challenging to adopt fintech in developing nations. Commercial banks run the danger of losing their conventional customer due to their increasing presence of fintech rivalries, especially in payment and lending segments results in lowering their market share and revenues. Customer trust and regulatory compliance of banks may be affected by cyber-attacks, data privacy and system outages. AI based decision making might result in improper evaluation of credit risk and sale of unmatched financial products. Let discuss in detail about all these challenges of commercial banks;

Erosion of core revenue stream and market share

Commercial banks are witnessing a consistent decline in their market dominance, specifically in two crucial segments i.e., payments and lending. Fintech companies have benefited from digital apps to provide quicker, less expensive and easier-to-use option since they are not constrained by regulatory weakness or old systems. Digital wallets like M-Pesa of Kenya, Paytm of India and Alipay of China familiarized by offering easy, instant payments, even without need a bank account. Similarly, fintech lenders aided by AI and customer records for quick sanction of loans for rural clients, gig workers, small business and street vendors who are excluded by traditional banks due to high initial investment.

This transition not only affects banks fee-income but also direct rapport that existed in conventional way of offering services turn affects cross-selling and tailored services. Evidence from (Klapper et al., 2025) in developing nations the significant digital payments were operating via non-banking institutions; 57% of adults used mobile gadgets to make digital payments or for accessing fintech services rather than approaching a banks, insisting a systemic revolution of banking industry that threatens traditional revenue streams of commercial banks.

Decline in customer loyalty and trust

Fintech apps' ease of use, openness and expediency are changing what consumers expect from banks. Fintech platforms offer 24/7 service in contrast to traditional banks' intricate fee structure and delayed services. Banks' brand trust is lower among younger or tech savvy generation (Gen Z and millennials) as they are more inclined to move with novel digital services. Banks with high profile cybersecurity incidents further weakens their brand image turn impacts clients trust.

Financial institutions are facing a growing number of cyber threats usually occurs through insecure third- party providers rather than just direct attacks. A striking example was in 2023, when hackers gained access to millions of user records by breaching over 2600 institutions worldwide, such as commercial banks, payment gateways and trading firms using a zero-day bug in MOVE it files transfer program. This was described as a critical point by the European Union Agency for Cybersecurity (European Union Agency for Cybersecurity., 2023), demonstrating the extent of fintech's landscape interconnectedness and volatility. Adding to the decline in customer loyalty and trust it results in fines, clean-up expenses turn increase the expenses of bank at this crisis situation profitability also gets affected.

Outdated technologies and organizational complexity

Commercial banks dependence on conventional vital banking infrastructure is a major structural disadvantage. Rather than being a built for real-time, API driven digital landscapes, these centralized, modular networks were intended for branch-driven functions. As a result, commercial banks find it difficult to incorporate novel technologies. Product development cycles are severely slowed down by the need for significant scrutiny, adherence to regulations and synchronization across global legacy systems for upgradation.

While some multinational banks have started long-term digital revolution projects such as replacing their crore systems with modular ones and migrating to the cloud, these initiatives are expensive, complex in nature and sometimes prevented by internal opposition to shift. Due to its scarce resource rural and community-based commercial banks facing even more difficult time for competing and are more prone to failures.

Risk of algorithm-based decision making and AI

Banks face significant operational and legal obstacles as they use AI more and more for detecting suspicious activities, credit scoring and customized financial advice. Unfair loan offerings resulted from AI since they were trained on traditional banking records unintentionally forcing or strengthening societal views, such as inequality based on race, gender or geography. According to (Bartlett et al., 2019) algorithm based lending system in U.S harmed younger borrowers and low income customers furthermore, many AI systems "black box" design makes it challenging to defend unfavourable judgements to customers, against the ideas of fairness and openness.

Additionally, there is increasing risk that AI-based product or service offering platforms can violate legal obligations by favouring increased commission for financial instruments above that are most aligned with their own risk standards or financial goals. Banks run the danger of fines, legal actions if they don't have strong governing mechanism for algorithm- based banking business.

Strategic dilemmas: Rival, acquire or collaborate?

Commercial banks face a strategic challenge in the face of lasting fintech competition: should banks compete on their own, buy out pioneers or form alliances? It takes a lot of resources and cultural sensitivity to develop internal digital competencies. Fintech start-up acquisitions are costly and frequently result in setting up failures because of conflicting industry cultures.

Although collaborations like banking-as-a-service (BaaS) and built-in finance agreements might foster innovation, they run the risk of standardizing the banks function and turning it into a compliance layer or discrete balance sheet where fintech control the user interface and branding. Due to this partnership, banks may no longer be the main point of contact for customers throughout their financial process which cause them to significantly re-evaluate their market value.

Gaps in talent and cultural barriers.

Finally, commercial banks are facing ongoing deficit of talent in vital digital ecosystems. Fintech's and other tech-based firms were acquiring top engineers, data analyst, product designer with ever changing industries. In contrast traditional banks operating with linear structure of decision-making, risk averse motive and outdated human resource that hold back digital talents without a cultural transform toward flexible demonstration and customer acquisition, banks will remain reluctant to build and retain sustainable financial performance through innovation.

FINTECH IN POLICY AND REGULATORY CONSIDERATION

Strong legislative regulatory frameworks are required for the incorporation of fintech into commercial banks, so as to guarantee that innovation is in line with consumer protection and financial stability. In order to maintain balance between innovation and supervision, regulators are implementing strategies like digital banking licenses, directives for open banking and regulatory platforms that allows banks to test fintech applications. Reg-tech solutions are being used to make automated reporting and compliance procedures, results in reduced cost of compliance and increased transparency. Despite all these well-structured regulatory frameworks banks are facing challenges while expanding their fintech products and services internationally due to complex and diverse regulatory frameworks across nations and dynamic data governance regulations. Therefore, policymakers are crucial in determining how fintech and banks will work together in future by promoting uniform regulations, guaranteeing fair competition among fintech companies and traditional banks and encouraging sustainable development without risking the soundness and credibility of the financial system.

Regulatory innovation: Sandbox, license and open banking.

The regulatory ***Sandbox***, a well-regulated setting where banks and fintech companies can test new products or services within a regulators oversight frequently with short-term relief, is one of the most important regulatory advancements for the last few years. Over 70 nations including Singapore, Australia and UAE have adopted well-structured frameworks, since they were first introduced by the UKs Financial Conduct Authority (FCA) in 2016 (*FCA*, 2025). These platforms give authorities early access to information about new risk, expedite the entry time into market, and cut legal expenses during the stage of testing.

The next regulatory innovation is the introduction of a ***Digital banking license***. Conventional banking can entail operational and capital constraints that are unsuited for business model, solely digital. Regions including Singapore, Hong Kong and UK have established specific licensing categories for digital banks. For example, in 2020 Grab – Singtel consortium and sea limited were among the four digital full bank licenses granted by the Monetary Authority of Singapore (MAS). Subject to strict cybersecurity, AML and capital adequacy criteria, these licenses enable non-bank entities to provide a comprehensive range of banking services excluding physical branches. This strategy emphasis regulatory protections from the beginning while fostering innovation. (*MAS Announces Successful Applicants of Licences to Operate New Digital Banks in Singapore*, 2020).

Open banking, a regulatory system that requires banks to share client-approved monetary information with third-party vendors via encrypted APIs, s growing in popularity in parallel with digital banking licenses. In 2019, the European Union implemented the Revised Payment Services Directive (PSD2), banks must grant access to client account information and payment initiation services to third-party providers (TPPs), including fintech companies so far with the customer approval.

The raise of RegTech: Automated compliance and enhanced transparency

As regulatory requirements get more complex, RegTech- the use of technology to expedite compliance processes is becoming more and more popular among commercial banks and fintech firms. Blockchain, AI and machine learning are used by RegTech solutions to automate processes including regulatory reporting, KYC validation and transaction tracking. This improves reliability and accountability in addition to lowering operating costs.

For instance, CoiN (contract intelligence) app from JPMorgan Chase, which analyses legal papers and extracts important information in seconds using Natural Language Processing. This procedure used to require 360,000 people hours per year. Similar to this, HSBC and the RegTech company Quantexa have teamed up to use AI-powered network analytics for AML adherence, which has improved the detection of complex money laundering schemes and reduced error rates by 40%. (Arnold, 2018)

The policymakers mandate: A global harmonization

Encouraging statutory reform: while non-binding guidelines on fintech risks have been released by international organizations such as Financial Stability Board (FSB) and the Basel Committee on Banking Supervision (BCBS) legally binding standards are still required. The 2020 G20 cross-border transactions, aims to lower costs and increase speed through accessible infrastructure and uniform messaging norms. Similarly, the Asian Framework on Digital Banking (2022) aims to standardize licensing and oversight throughout southeast Asia, allowing digital banks to expand regionally.

Creating an equitable environment: regulators need to stop the practice of fintech's operating under relaxed norms than banks. This is addressed by the EUs Digital Operational Resilience Act (DORA) which goes into force in 2025 and places the same technology risk management obligations on banks and their outside suppliers. This witness that innovation doesn't compromise systemic resilience.

Encouraging sustainable innovation: legislations ought to provide incentives for fintech products that promote green finance and financial inclusion. In 2020 the Pix rapid payment system was introduced by Brazil's central Bank and currently serves over 120 million customers, unbanked populations. In order to guarantee that innovation benefited society as a whole, rather than serving tech-savvy urban areas resulted from regulated costs and mandated seamless integration. (*Ar2023e*, 2023.).

As long as it is proactive, risk appropriate and cooperative, regulation can foster innovation rather than hinder it. (Wolters & Jacobs, 2019) Over the course of the next ten years, It will be determined if regulators can break down national boundaries and create a digital financial system that is inclusive, universal and resilient.

FUTURE PATHWAYS

Looking ahead the future of fintech, increased customer choice and cross-sector financial products will be made possible by open banking systems powered by APIs. Block chain will reshape trade finance and cross boarder payments, while big data analytics and AI will enhance tailored products and risk management. Fintech enables banks to offer and monitor green loans and ESG focused investment products. Commercial banks need to adapt flexible banking system, improve cyber security measures and to collaborate with regulators to create standardized international regulatory frameworks that results in long-term financial sustainability.

CONCLUSION

Fintech is assisting commercial banks in becoming more sustainable and efficient, two objectives that are closely related. Banks may save expenses, improve customer service and make more informed decisions by utilizing digital tools like AI, data analytics and online applications. Fintech also promotes sustainability by assisting banks with green loan offering monitoring ESG performance and complying with new rules.

As a summary, the future of banking is not about deciding between doing good and generating sound financial returns. Fintech demonstrates that banks are capable of doing both by acting responsibly and functioning more efficiently.

REFERENCES

AlBenJasim, S., Dargahi, T., Takruri, H., & Al-Zaidi, R. (2024). FinTech Cybersecurity Challenges and Regulations: Bahrain Case Study. *Journal of Computer Information Systems*, *64*(6), 835–851. DOI: 10.1080/08874417.2023.2251455

Alqahtani, H. A., Alqubaysi, R., Musa, A. M. H., & Boreik, D. A. S. (2024). The effect of financial technology on the financial performance of national Saudi banks. *International Journal of Data and Network Science*, *8*(3), 1399–1404. DOI: 10.5267/j.ijdns.2024.4.003

Anderloni, L., Petukhina, A., & Tanda, A. (2024). Peer-to-peer lending: Exploring borrowers' motivations and expectations. *Journal of Small Business Management*. Advance online publication. DOI: 10.1080/00472778.2024.2431232

Anne-Laure, M. (2019). The Future of Fintech. *Research Technology Management*, *62*(4), 59–63. DOI: 10.1080/08956308.2019.1613123

Arner, D. W., Barberis, J. N., & Buckley, R. P. (2015). The Evolution of Fintech: A New Post-Crisis Paradigm? SSRN *Electronic Journal*. DOI: 10.2139/ssrn.2676553

Arnold, M. (2018, April 8). HSBC brings in AI to help spot money laundering. *Financial Times*.

Baker, H., Kaddumi, T. A., Nassar, M. D., & Muqattash, R. S. (2023a). Impact of Financial Technology on Improvement of Banks' Financial Performance. *Journal of Risk and Financial Management*, *16*(4), 230. DOI: 10.3390/jrfm16040230

Baker, H., Kaddumi, T., Nassar, M., & Muqattash, R. (2023b). Impact of Financial Technology on Improvement of Banks' Financial Performance. *Journal of Risk and Financial Management*, *16*(4), 230. Advance online publication. DOI: 10.3390/jrfm16040230

Bartlett, R., Morse, A., Stanton, R., & Wallace, N. (2019). *Consumer-Lending Discrimination in the FinTech Era*.

Basha, S. A., Elgammal, M. M., & Abuzayed, B. M. (2021). Online peer-to-peer lending: A review of the literature. *Electronic Commerce Research and Applications*, *48*, 101069.

CBA invests in international transaction screening technology company. (2024, March 2). https://www.commbank.com.au/articles/newsroom/2024/03/global-screening-services.html

Chauhan, Y., & Sharma, P. (2024). A Systematic Literature Review of Digital Payments. *Metamorphosis*, *23*(2), 173–187. DOI: 10.1177/09726225241257730

Chen, P. (2024). Risk Challenges and Regulatory Approaches in Fintech Data Application Regulation. *Frontiers in Business, Economics and Management*, *16*(3), 85–91. Advance online publication. DOI: 10.54097/ypg61745

Chen, X., Zhang, H., & Teng, L. (2022). Technology risk management in fintech: Underlying mechanisms and challenges. *Journal of Operational Risk*. DOI: 10.21314/JOP.2022.022

Chime Investor Presentation. (2025).

European Union Agency for Cybersecurity. (2023). *ENISA threat landscape 2023: July 2022 to June 2023.* Publications Office. https://data.europa.eu/doi/10.2824/782573

FCA. (2025, September 30). FCA. https://www.fca.org.uk/

Gomber, P., Koch, J.-A., & Siering, M. (2017). Digital Finance and FinTech: Current research and future research directions. *Journal of Business Economics*, *87*(5), 537–580. DOI: 10.1007/s11573-017-0852-x

Gorai, S. K., & A. (2025). Artificial Intelligence In Personal Finance Management: Opportunities And Challenges. *IOSR Journal of Computer Engineering, 27*(1), 07–17. DOI: 10.9790/0661-2701010717

Horváth, D., Kerényi, Á., & Szabó, R. Z. (2022). Intended benefits and challenges of cooperation between FinTechs and commercial banks. *Acta Oeconomica*, *72*(3), 289–308. DOI: 10.1556/032.2022.00023

I.B, C., & M B, S. (2025). The Intersection of Fintech and Green Banking: Opportunities, Challenges, and Future Prospects. *IOSR Journal of Business and Management, 14th*(15th), 35–41. DOI: 10.9790/487X-conf3541

Investor Relations | Bank of America Corporation (BAC). (n.d.). Retrieved September 27, 2025, from https://investor.bankofamerica.com/

Investor Relations | JPMorganChase. (n.d.). Retrieved September 27, 2025, from https://www.jpmorganchase.com/ir

K, M. S. R., & B K, D. S. (2025, February). Neo-Banks in India -Challenges and Expansion in Future. *IOSR Journal of Business and Management, 14th*(15th), 18–22. Advance online publication. DOI: 10.9790/487X-conf1822

K, S. (2025). Evolution of Neo Banking in India – A Paradigm shift in the banking industry. *International Journal on Science and Technology*. DOI: 10.71097/IJSAT.v16.i1.1774

Kapliar, K. (2023). NEOBANKS IN THE AGE OF DIGITAL TRANSFORMATION. *International Scientific Conference Modern Science: Global Trends, Technologies and Innovations*. DOI: 10.30525/978-9934-26-354-5-2

Kapoor, N., Kapoor, T., Sisodiya, D., & Sushma, J. (2024). Impact of Fintech: Revolution in Banking and Financial Industry. *2024 IEEE 4th International Conference on ICT in Business Industry & Government (ICTBIG)*, 1–6. DOI: 10.1109/ICTBIG64922.2024.10911635

Kavitha, S., & Krishnan, S. (2025). AI-based Personal Financial Management: Opportunities and Challenges. *ComFin Research, 13*(S1-i2), 68–73. DOI: 10.34293/commerce.v13iS1-i2.8737

Klapper, L., Singer, D., & Starita, L. (2025). *The Global Findex Database 2025: Connectivity and Financial Inclusion in the Digital Economy*.

Königstorfer, F., & Thalmann, S. (2020). Applications of Artificial Intelligence in commercial banks – A research agenda for behavioral finance. *Journal of Behavioral and Experimental Finance*, *27*, 100352. DOI: 10.1016/j.jbef.2020.100352

LendingClub Reports Fourth Quarter and Full Year 2023 Results. (n.d.). Retrieved September 26, 2025, from https://ir.lendingclub.com/news/news-details/2024/LendingClub-Reports-Fourth-Quarter-and-Full-Year-2023-Results/default.aspx

Lenz, R. (2016). Peer-to-Peer Lending: Opportunities and Risks. *European Journal of Risk Regulation*, *7*(4), 688–700. DOI: 10.1017/S1867299X00010126

Li, C., He, S., Tian, Y., Sun, S., & Ning, L. (2022). Does the bank's FinTech innovation reduce its risk-taking? Evidence from China's banking industry. *Journal of Innovation & Knowledge*, *7*(3), 100219. DOI: 10.1016/j.jik.2022.100219

M, D. K. (2025). An analysis of unified payments interface (UPI): Payer and payee PSP performance, UPI apps, and P2P and P2M transaction trends in India. *ICTACT Journal on Management Studies*. DOI: 10.21917/ijms.2025.0318

MAS Announces Successful Applicants of Licences to Operate New Digital Banks in Singapore. (2020). https://www.mas.gov.sg/news/media-releases/2020/mas-announces-successful-applicants-of-licences-to-operate-new-digital-banks-in-singapore

Mhlanga, D. (2020). Industry 4.0 in Finance: The Impact of Artificial Intelligence (AI) on Digital Financial Inclusion. *International Journal of Financial Studies.* DOI: 10.3390/ijfs8030045

Murinde, V., Rizopoulos, E., & Zachariadis, M. (2022). The impact of the FinTech revolution on the future of banking: Opportunities and risks. *International Review of Financial Analysis*, *81*, 102103. DOI: 10.1016/j.irfa.2022.102103

Parboteeah, P. (2016). *LICENCE CC BY-NC-ND 4.0 REPOSITORY RECORD.*

Parera, M. P., & Molina, E. B. (2020). *BBVA Case Study: The effect of financial performance on shareholders wealth before and after Fintech acquisition.*

Peer-to-Peer Lending Market Size, Share & Growth | 2032. (n.d.). Retrieved September 26, 2025, from https://www.alliedmarketresearch.com/peer-to-peer-lending-market

Rane, N., Choudhary, S., & Rane, J. (2023). Blockchain and Artificial Intelligence (AI) integration for revolutionizing security and transparency in finance. SSRN *Electronic Journal.* DOI: 10.2139/ssrn.4644253

Redrawing the lines: FinTechs growing influence on Financial Services—PwC Channel Island. (n.d.). Retrieved September 27, 2025, from https://www.pwc.com/jg/en/publications/fintech-growing-influence-financial-services.html

RGHL_Annual Report 31 Dec 2024-2025-04-22-17-42. (n.d.). Retrieved September 26, 2025, from https://assets.revolut.com/pdf/annualreport2024.pdf

Sabilika, K. (2024). *Green Fintech Market Review.*

Salampasis, D., & Mention, A.-L. (2018). FinTech: Harnessing Innovation for Financial Inclusion. In Lee Kuo Chuen, D., & Deng, R. (Eds.), *Handbook of Blockchain, Digital Finance, and Inclusion* (Vol. 2, pp. 451–461). Academic Press., DOI: 10.1016/B978-0-12-812282-2.00018-8

Sardar, S., & Anjaria, K. (2023). *The future of banking: How neo banks are changing the industry.* 2(2).

Saroy, R., Jain, P., Awasthy, S., & Dhal, S. (2023). Impact of digital payment adoption on Indian banking sector efficiency. *Journal of Banking and Financial Technology*, 1–13. DOI: 10.1007/s42786-023-00047-2

Shah, M. A., Harish, K., Shradha, Hansda, K., Chowdhury, D., & Yadav, S. (2024). Beyond Mobile Payments: Exploring the Evolution and Future of Fintech (BY IJISRT). *International Journal of Innovative Science and Research Technology (IJISRT).* DOI: 10.38124/ijisrt/IJISRT24APR259

Subanidja, S., Sorongan, F., & Legowo, M. (2022). Leveraging Financial Technology Entity into Sustainable Bank Performance through a Competitive Advantage. *Emerging Science Journal*, *6*(1), 53–63. Advance online publication. DOI: 10.28991/ESJ-2022-06-01-04

Tamraparani, V. (2022). Ethical Implications of Implementing AI in Wealth Management for Personalized Investment Strategies. [IJSR]. *International Journal of Science and Research (Raipur, India)*, *11*(3), 1625–1633. DOI: 10.21275/SR220309091129

Temelkov, Z. (2020). OVERVIEW OF NEOBANKS MODEL AND ITS IMPLICATIONS FOR TRADITIONAL BANKING. *CHALLENGES OF TOURISM AND BUSINESS LOGISTICS IN THE 21ST CENTURY. ISCTBL*, *2020*, 156–165. Advance online publication. DOI: 10.46763/YFNTS2031156t

Voshchak, O. (2024). THEORETICAL FOUNDATIONS OF NEOBANKS DEVELOPMENT. *Scientific Opinion: Economics and Management*. DOI: 10.32782/2521-666X/2024-88-13

Wang, H., Mao, K., Wu, W., & Luo, H. (2023). Fintech inputs, non-performing loans risk reduction and bank performance improvement. *International Review of Financial Analysis*, *90*, 102849. DOI: 10.1016/j.irfa.2023.102849

Wang, Y., Xiuping, S., & Zhang, Q. (2021). Can fintech improve the efficiency of commercial banks?—An analysis based on big data. *Research in International Business and Finance*, *55*, 101338. DOI: 10.1016/j.ribaf.2020.101338

WEF_Future_of_Global_Fintech_Second_Edition_2025.pdf. (n.d.). Retrieved October 22, 2025, from https://reports.weforum.org/docs/WEF_Future_of_Global_Fintech_Second_Edition_2025

Wolters, P. T. J., & Jacobs, B. P. F. (2019). The security of access to accounts under the PSD2. *Computer Law & Security Review*, *35*(1), 29–41. DOI: 10.1016/j.clsr.2018.10.005

WSC. S. (2024, September 23). Seaya Ventures leads a €6 million round in Dotfile to automate regulatory compliance with AI. *Seaya*. https://seaya.vc/seaya-ventures-leads-a-e6-million-round-in-dotfile-to-automate-regulatory-compliance-with-ai/

Yaramolu, L. S. K. G. (2025). AI-Powered Portfolio Management: Transforming Wealth Management Through Intelligent Automation. *Journal of Computer Science and Technology Studies*, *7*(3), 14–23. DOI: 10.32996/jcsts.2025.7.3.3

Zhang, Y., Ye, S., Liu, J., & Du, L. (2023). Impact of the development of FinTech by commercial banks on bank credit risk. *Finance Research Letters*, *55*, 103857. DOI: 10.1016/j.frl.2023.103857

KEY TERMS AND DEFINITIONS

Digital Banking: It is the use of digital platforms like websites and mobile apps to execute banking operations by minimising the need to visit a physical branch office

Digital Payments: It is a type of transaction carried out by transferring money electronically between two parties through a tech-based interface, like online banking and mobile applications

Financial Inclusion: It refers to the access to affordable financial services or products for all individuals and businesses, particularly for those who have been excluded from the formal financial system.

Financial Performance: It refers to a measure of the overall financial health of a company or institution that reflects how it generates revenue and controls its assets, liabilities, and costs to turn profits.

Market Share: Market share is a measure of a company's size relative to its rivals and its market by analysing its sales to the overall sales of the specific industry

Neo-Banks: Neo-banks are digital-only bank that operates exclusively online through mobile apps and websites, eliminating the need for physical branches.

Non-Performing Asset: NPA refers to a loan or advance where the borrower has failed to repay interest or the principal amount for 90 days, as it stops the flow of income for the banks.

Sustainability: Sustainability refers to the capacity to sustain or uphold social, environmental or economic activities over an extended period of time without consuming natural resources

Chapter 4
Non-Bank to Bank-Based FinTech Determinants and Banks' Financial Performance

Abid Ali
http://orcid.org/0009-0000-7988-7887
University of Hull. UK

Muhammad Zahid
http://orcid.org/0000-0001-5790-7998
Muscat University, Oman

Muhammad Naeem Shahid
http://orcid.org/0000-0001-7167-8386
School of Accounting and Finance, Faculty of Business and Law, Taylor's University, Malaysia

Sumaira Aslam
University of Derby, UK

ABSTRACT

In recent times, Fintech has been a revolutionary force that connects finance with innovative technologies. Fintech has introduced new business model innovations, innovative banking products/services, and processes, creating a landscape that has completely transformed the financial industry. FinTech-oriented banks work in a dynamic environment where FinTech firms compete with them. Moreover, the adoption of FinTech by banks is complex due to regulatory, governance, and operational environments. Therefore, it is important to understand the adoption of FinTech and its

DOI: 10.4018/979-8-3373-6244-1.ch004

impact on banks' financial performance. The chapter examines the determinants of FinTech adoption, ranging from non-banking to bank-based components of FinTech. The chapter offers nine components that can best measure FinTech adoption in banks. The chapter also addresses the banks' FinTech adoption and financial performance from the perspectives of regulatory, governance, and stability. It has been observed that FinTech adoption enhances a bank's financial performance.

BACKGROUND

Since the last decade, unparalleled advancements in FinTech have made it the talk of the town. The year 2021 ended with a USD 210 billion investment in the Global Fintech industry (KPMG, 2021). The Global Fintech Industry experienced a 667% growth from 2017 (with USD 31 billion in investment) to 2021, with an annual growth rate of 169%. FinTech offers various digitalised solutions, including online payment, mobile banking, AI-powered customer interfaces, Blockchain-oriented transactions, robo-advisory services, and peer-to-peer lending. FinTech is improving convenience, efficiency, and accessibility to financial services and credit facilities (Claessens et al., 2018; Carb et al., 2021). Moreover, FinTech has disrupted the financial industry via innovative solutions and challenged the conventional banking models (Romanova & Kudinska, 2016; Navaretti et al., 2017; Vives, 2017; Elsinger et al., 2018; Elsinger et al., 2018; Molnar, 2018; Merton & Thakor, 2019; Thakor, 2020; Vucinic, 2020; Cumming et al., 2022; Murinde et al., 2022). Many benefits and hazards are associated with the adoption of FinTech in banks. FinTech adoption in banks presents various opportunities, including cost reduction, improved efficiency, and enhanced customer experiences (Fiordelisi et al., 2020). However, as a dark side, FinTech adoption exposes Banks to many challenges like systemic risks, regulatory compliance, and cybersecurity threats. Moreover, FinTech innovations have a dynamic nature, which has raised potential concerns for the stability of the banking sector. Furthermore, FinTech adoption in banks is facing severe competition from FinTech startups.

Previous studies exhibit mixed evidence regarding whether FinTech enhances or substitutes for the credit access offered by conventional banks. Some studies suggest that Fintech offers credit and financial access comparable to that of conventional banks' financial services (Fuster et al., 2019), while other researchers find that traditional banks' financial services are more significant (Jagtiani & Lemieux, 2019; Tang, 2019). An efficient and well-functioning financial system significantly nurtures growth by increasing credit and effectively channels funds across the business community (Adrian & Liang, 2018; Ahamed et al., 2021; Cornelli et al., 2023; Hikida & Perry, 2020). However, there are insufficient studies on FinTech adoption in banks which have tried to uncover the favourable and unfavourable consequences of FinTech adoption for banks' financial performance and financial stability.

The FinTech regulatory sandbox plays a significant role in the nexus of FinTech adoption, financial performance, and financial stability. However, ample empirical studies in this field are lacking due to the difficulty in quantifying FinTech advancements. Few studies have uncovered such connections. For example, Askitas and Zimmermann (2009) use text mining techniques to measure the extent of FinTech adoption's connection with Financial stability and performance. From a Chinese perspective, studies find FinTech adoption lessens credit risk (see Cheng & Qu, 2020; Liem, Son et al., 2022). On the other hand, studies (see Wang et al., 2021) find a U-shaped nexus between FinTech innovations and banks' risk-taking ability, and FinTech adoption destabilises the banks (see Nguyen, 2022). Moreover, Daud et al. (2022) identify a significant favourable influence of Fintech adoption on Banks' financial concerns in 63 economies. Nevertheless, these studies present inconclusive findings.

Although Fintech constitutes a narrow portion of the entire financial system, FinTech (Financial Technology) has arisen as the most significant form of financial advancement in IT and Finance (Zavolokina et al., 2016; Gomber et al., 2017; Haddad & Hornuf, 2019). Recent researchers show that FinTech is becoming economically significant and experiencing significant growth in different economies (Frost et al., 2019; Bazarbash & Beaton, 2020; Berg et al., 2020). FinTech utilises new operating platforms via emerging technologies to enable credit transactions (Claessens et al., 2018; Cornelli et al., 2023). FinTech is advancing swiftly across regional and national economies with erratic growth rates. Financial services via FinTech adoption by Banks can reduce the information asymmetry, facilitate risk allocation, enhance market competition, cut agency costs, and improve the capital market allocation efficiency, thus subsidising the economic advancements (Fuster et al., 2019). FinTech Innovations are inherent in advanced and streamlined processes; therefore, such innovations are driven by scale economics and lower operating costs, enhancing convenience, transparency, and broader access to financial services. (Jagtiani and Lemieux, 2019). Economic Theories suggest that economic conditions have a positive influence on credit demands. For example, Firm investment and consumer spending increase during economic expansion eras while falling during economic recessions (Claessens et al., 2018; Cornelli et al., 2023). Moreover, Bank theorists believe that the banking system has frictions, i.e., flaws in supervision (Buchak et al., 2018; Frost, 2020; Cornelli et al., 2023), competition (Claessens et al., 2018; Frost et al., 2019) and some other aspects, which could either smooth or hamper the Fintech advancements in Banks. FinTech Adoption and FinTech credit can augment Banks' performance. However, none of the previous studies have investigated the influence of FinTech adoption on Banks' financial performance. This chapter highlights how such adoption enhances the banks' financial performance. The subsequent segment elaborates on how FinTech determinants evolve from nonbank to banking components of FinTech.

Understanding the channels, drivers, components, and deterrents of FinTech is essential for researchers, policymakers, and financial participants. This understanding helps them to grasp recent advancements, promotions and expansions in FinTech as well as supports them to make informed decisions,

The chapter uncovers the evolution of FinTech indices and offers a comprehensive FinTech index. It also sheds light on Banks' financial performance and stability by exploring the FinTech adoption under Governance and regulatory perspectives.

The chapter contributes to the prevailing frame of Knowledge on Financial Technology and its determinants in many ways. 1) It investigates an area which is comparatively new and understudied, 2) it offers determinants of FinTech that can impede or facilitate the measurement, working and expansion of FinTech, where scholars (Claessens et al., 2018; Branzoli & Supino, 2020; Cornelli et al., 2023) have provided micro-level determinants; however, this chapter provides a macro-level perspective of determinants of FinTech, 3) Development and understanding of a comprehensive FinTech index or its determinants helps to contribute to prevailing issues/gaps in FinTech related research, its policy formulation and regulation

Evolution from non-bank to bank-based components of FinTech

The FinTech determinants are actually the potential complement or substitution of FinTech for banking services. Many scholars define FinTech credit. They argue that *crowdfunding* and *peer-to-peer (p2p) lending* are the main pillars of non-bank FinTech credit. Financial Institutions without the interference of conventional financial intermediaries operate the online lending platforms, i.e., P2P lending (Chen et al., 2013). As far as P2P lending is concerned, it offers borrowers (small-to medium-sized enterprises and households) financial services with lower credit ratings. Such platforms primarily operate across low-credit market segments; however, their expansion influences the banking risks.

Conversely, the thresholds of entrepreneurial financing are significantly reduced with the introduction of crowdfunding. Nevertheless, crowdfunding platforms are exposed to numerous risks, ranging from vendor relationships to legal, quality intellectual property, cognitive skills, project management, and operational risks. Before 2020, China was the global leader in the P2P lending market. However, P2P lending services were significantly restricted after implementing regulatory measures in 2020. In contrast to China, the US has emerged as a crowdfunding market leader, gaining swift growth in the last decade.

As the early scholars have defined, FinTech has the following main components of non-bank FinTech credit:

1) *Crowdfunding*
2) *Peer-to-peer (p2p) lending*

Claessens et al. (2018) argued that FinTech pillars are

1) Aggregate of invoice trading
2) Crowdfunding
3) P2P lending

Cornelli et al. (2023) adopted a broader definition and argued that the following are the main components of FinTech credit

1) Invoice Trading
2) P2P lending
3) Securities
4) Balance Sheet Lending

Wang et al. (2023) focus on non-bank-based funding sources, as defined by the Global Alternative Finance Market Benchmarking Report (GAFMBR), and define FinTech as an aggregate of the following GAFMBR-based components.

1. P2P/Marketplace Lending
    1.1. Customer Lending

Institutional and/or Individual creditor offers credit to a borrower (customer).

1.2. Business Lending

Institutional and/or Individual creditor offers credit to a borrower (business).

1.3. Property Lending

Institutional and/or Individual creditor offers a credit (secured against a property) to a borrower (Customer or Business).

2. Balance Sheet Lending
    2.1. Consumer Lending

Direct loan by a platform entity to a consumer (borrower).

2.2. Business Lending

Direct loan by a platform entity to a Business (borrower).

2.3. Property Lending

Direct loan (Mortgage) to a borrower (Business or customer) by a platform entity.

3. Invoice Trading

Funders (Institutional or Individual) purchase receivables or invoices from a business at a discount.

4. Securities
   4.1. Debt-Based Securities

Funders (Institutional or Individual) purchase debt-based fixed interest-bearing securities, i.e., a debenture or bond.

4.2. Mini-Bonds

Institutions or Individuals acquire an unsecured bond known as a "mini-bond". Mini bonds are issued in smaller sizes than traditional bonds in financial markets.

5. Crowdfunding
   5.1. Equity-based Crowdfunding

Funders (Institutions or individuals) acquire equity securities issued by a Firm.

5.2. Real Estate Crowdfunding

Funders (Institutions or Individuals) offer subordinated debt or equity financing for real estate.

5.3. Profit Sharing

Institutions or Individuals invest in equities (i.e., shares) issued by a company and share returns or business royalties.

5.4. Reward-based Crowdfunding

Backers fund companies, projects, or individuals, in exchange for products or non-monetary rewards.

5.5. Donation-based Crowdfunding

Donors fund companies, projects, or individuals for civic or philanthropic motivations without expecting material or monetary rewards.

6. Others

The volumes of funds raised via different alternative finance models. Research teams record these alternatives and include crowd-led micro finance, pension-led fundings, community shares, and other models different from the prevailing taxonomy.

It is very challenging to quantify or define FinTech adoption as it encompasses various business models and technologies. Moreover, it is challenging to create a standardised measure due to Fintech's evolving and diverse nature. Furthermore, the quality and availability of FinTech data across regional and national boundaries are inconsistent, constraining the precise assessment of FinTech.

FinTech adoption combines new and old technologies, so it is difficult to differentiate the determinants of traditional and Fintech-enabled banking services. The varying pace of financial technology adoption across banking companies creates a hurdle when comparing FinTech advancements. Furthermore, varying consumer preferences and behaviours are the reasons behind the development of appropriate FinTech Indicators to measure FinTech adoption in Banks.

Despite all these limitations, Khan et al. (2023) define and propose the determinants of FinTech adoption in the banking sector. The authors use "the word frequency statistics from text mining" to construct an index for FinTech adoption in the Banking industry (Bank-based FinTech). The authors follow the procedure adopted by researchers (see Gao & Wang, 2016; Cheng & Qu, 2020) to construct a fintech adoption index, follow the studies of (Romanova & Kudinska, 2016; Navaretti et al., 2017; Vives, 2017; Arner et al., 2017; Molnar, 2018; Claessens et al., 2018; Tang, 2019; Merton & Thakor, 2019; Thakor, 2020; Carbo-Valverde et al., 2021; Murinde et al., 2022) and identify the nine attributes Fintech adoption in Banking sector. These traits are aligned with the management of banking operations. Furthermore, these attributes contribute to the financial performance and stability of the banking industry.

1. Banks' Digital Presence

Banks with a solid digital presence have adopted FinTech. Such banks also offer user-friendly mobile apps and websites that enable consumers to access and perform banking transactions and services. This demonstrates banks' commitment to providing access to financial products/services, digital consumer support, and online account management. In the banking landscape, the robustness of digitalisation is crucial and the prime gauge of FinTech adoption in banks.

2. Mobile Banking Capabilities

The banks that adopt FinTech provide robust mobile banking services, such as bill payments, fund transfers, check deposits, and personalised notifications. Moreover, such banks integrate innovative technologies, i.e., fingerprint or facial recognition, for biometric authentication. Such services have become the principal channel for many customers' banking services. If a bank offers secure and seamless mobile banking services/experiences, it exhibits its ability to adapt to FinTech

3. Support for Open APIs

Open APIs empower banks' interoperability and alliances with FinTech Firms. They facilitate the growth of advanced financial products/services, enhance customer experience, and integrate with outside FinTech programs, enhancing innovative services and improving the overall consumer experience.

4. Fintech Partnerships

Fintech-oriented banks recurrently collaborate with established FinTech firms and also try to establish partnerships with newly launched FinTech ventures. Such partnerships and collaborations facilitate banks' use of technology and expertise to improve their products/services, augment competitiveness, enhance customer experiences, and improve operational efficiency. In the recent era, such collaborations have become very common.

5. Digital Payment Solutions

FinTech-oriented banks focus on delivering advanced digital transaction options beyond conventional methods. The Fintech Credit is becoming a complementary resource instead of an alternative to conventional bank credit. Advanced digital transactions include contactless payments, mobile wallets, peer-to-peer payments, and integrating their system with digital platforms, i.e., Apple Pay or PayPal.

6. Automation and Artificial Intelligence Integration

Banks pursuing FinTech must enhance customer services and streamline their processes using AI (Artificial Intelligence) and automation technologies. For example, they may utilise "AI chatbots" for consumer services, an algorithm based on machine-learning to detect fraudulent activities, and data analytics to provide custom-made financial endorsements. These are examples of significant FinTech advancements that cater to changing customer preferences.

7. Innovation Initiatives

FinTech-oriented banks vigorously engage with AI technologies, a culture of innovativeness, and constant upgrading to enhance security and personal financial services and streamline processes. Such banks participate in Fintech-oriented conferences, invest more in R&D, innovative programs, and state-of-the-art labs, and uncover emerging technologies in financial systems.

8. User Experience Focus

Banks pursuing FinTech, invest more in designing user-oriented, personalised, efficient, and intuitive banking services to deliver incomparable user experiences. Such services include easy-to-use interfaces and simplified onboarding processes. Their assurance to innovation significantly exhibits their willingness to familiarise themselves with the FinTech landscape.

9. Embracing New Technologies

FinTech-oriented Banks explore and stay current with new technologies like digital landing platforms, robo-advisory, cryptocurrencies, and blockchains to enhance their potential to offer improved banking services. Banks that aggressively uncover and adapt to digitalisation can offer novel services and gain a competitive advantage.

COMPARATIVE ANALYSIS

Khan et al.'s (2023) above nine-factor model differs from the other models prevalent in the literature (see Hou et al., 2016; Cheng & Qu, 2020) in different aspects. For example, Khan et al. (2023) define FinTech by identifying and adopting attributes significantly aligned with the banking sector, while Hou et al. (2016) and Cheng and Qu (2020) identify and adopt more generic and primary attributes of FinTech.

Moreover, Khan et al. (2023) verify whether the particular bank is initiated to a service corresponding to a specific fintech attribute. Their index is a more direct and significant calculation of fintech adoption.

FinTech adoption and financial performance of Banks under operational aspects

The literature widely acknowledges that innovative technologies have potentially transformed the landscape of financial services (Begenau et al., 2018; Chen et al., 2019; Chiu & Koeppl, 2019; Fuster et al., 2019), specifically in the banking ecosystem (Navaretti et al., 2018; Yao et al., 2018; Li et al., 2020). Researchers have focused on FinTech-based credit and uncovered the particular subcategories of Financial Technology (Agrawal et al., 2015; Heimer, 2016; Narayan et al., 2019) or scrutinised its components, i.e., technological advancement (CGFS-FSB, 2017), banking rivalry (Buchak et al., 2018), and strength of banking regulation (Frost et al., 2019; Frost, 2020; Cornelli et al., 2023). Banks' Fintech adoption is essential because FinTech credit issued by FinTech startups is currently complementing the banks' retail services, thus reducing the reliance on traditional bank credit (Demertzis et al., 2018; Bertsch & Rosenvinge, 2019). Therefore, banks are currently willing to adopt the FinTech based product and services.

FinTech adoption impacts the profitability of financial institutions, especially Banks, in many ways. A primary channel is the efficiency enhancement of function mechanics through which FinTech adoption enhances the profitability of Banks and Financial institutions. Financial institutions utilise digital platforms to augment transaction processes and other administrative tasks (Tanchangya et al., 2025). Such operational efficiencies optimise the resource allocations, accelerate processing speed, and minimise errors. Nevertheless, there should be a trade-off between the benefits of FinTech adoption and its adoption costs (i.e., initial investment, future maintenance costs related to FinTech adoption, and technological infrastructure).

Secondly, FinTech adoption via its digitalised methodologies surges the market expenditure, enhancing the banks' and financial institutions' performance. Online platforms and mobile applications are the leading digital solutions through which FinTech adoption enhances the client base of banks demographically and geographically. Such mechanics minimise rather than eliminate physical infrastructure requirements and provide improved service delivery in unreachable or deprived regions. Nevertheless, these mechanisms' efficacy depends on the target population's digital readiness and the provision of satisfactory technological infrastructure. Moreover, the profitability of Financial institutions and banks depends on substantial investment in marketing initiatives and successful market expansion.

On the other hand, using cutting-edge credit assessment capabilities and sophisticated data analytics techniques enhances the risk management mechanisms of FinTech-oriented banks (Ashta & Herrmann, 2021; Widarwati et al., 2023). Such mechanisms operate via two different networks: better portfolio management and improved risk assessment of credit applicants. Loan portfolios can be optimised, and banks can identify borrowers with potentially low default risk. The effectiveness of such mechanisms is determined by their analytical capabilities, data quality, sufficient investment in human capital development, and technological infrastructures. However, all positive outcomes of FinTech adoption face several aspects that hamper the financial performance of financial institutions. For example, the Bank's Financial performance is vulnerable to cybersecurity threats. Cybersecurity vulnerabilities are affected by fraudulent activities, system disruptions, and potential data breaches. Such vulnerabilities lead to substantial financial losses due to the accuracy of violations, thus requiring extensive and enduring investments in security infrastructure (Corbet & Gurdgiev, 2017). The profitability of FinTech-oriented banks is reduced due to potential regulatory penalties and reputational damages. Such deteriorated financial performance increases costs and adds complexity to mechanisms. The privacy protections and data governance necessitate significant investments in compliance infrastructure (Bakhoum et al., 2024). Potential high costs and penalties for non-compliance have adversely affected the financial performance of FinTech-oriented banks.

An intense competitive pressure has emerged due to changes in the financial services industry landscape. A significant competitive challenge has emerged for banks and traditional financial institutions due to the entry of FinTech and other technology companies (Mdluli & Staschen, 2022). Such a competitive challenge operates through an imperative for incessant innovation to survive, market share erosion, and price pressures. Hence, an arbitrage occurs because unregulated entities exploit the regulated entities by offering similar services at low cost; thus, financial institutions and banks operate with reduced margins. Studies have reflected the impact and interaction of these complex mechanics, where recent studies are evidencing both favourable and unfavourable impacts on operational efficiency and financial performance of FinTech-oriented financial institutions (Fersi et al., 2023).

FinTech adoption and financial performance of Banks under Banking Regulations and Governance

FinTech has brought new business model innovations, innovative banking products, services, processes, and a landscape that has completely transformed the financial industry. FinTech firms and banks work in a dynamic environment of high competition, regulatory complexity, and technological advancements. Such challenges present different threats to financial performance and stability; hence, there is a need to understand and monitor the emerging risks associated with FinTech adoption.

Regulatory requirements are dynamic, require continuous process and system updates and create long-term financial pressure, thus affecting the financial performance of banks. Moreover, FinTech adoption in banks is often subject to banking regulations because such regulatory requirements affect strategic decision-making (Frost, 2020). After the financial crisis 2008, "the Basel Committee" presented firmer liquidity and capital rules under Basel III. These regulations have prompted banks to bolster their capitalisation, augment the capital adequacy ratios, adjust the balance sheet structure to comply with the regulatory canons and reduce the default risk (Lin, 2007). However, banks' ability to expand their loan portfolios may be impeded by the requirement of higher capital adequacy (Cortina-Lorente & Schmukler, 2018). In such a scenario, Fintech platforms enhance alternative financial services very effectively, offering financing services without credit rating or history, thus endorsing financial inclusion (Philippon, 2019; Arner et al., 2020). However, the sterner regulatory requirements hinder the entry of big tech and fintech companies. The availability of alternative credit facilities may hinder the performance of FinTech oriented banks.

According to "The revised G20/OECD Principles of Corporate Governance", FinTech and digitalisation have reorganised the traditional financial ecosystem; however, both have introduced different challenges for the corporate governance structure. The intergovernmental organisation requires financial institutions and Fintech companies to implement active governance structures to respond to a changing environment effectively. Fintech firms have pursued this objective to enhance their profits (Financial Performance) by reducing risk vulnerability and by launching coalitions with obligatory listed companies and banks (Hornuf et al., 2021). The collaborations between incumbent banks/Financial institutions and FinTech companies are growing rapidly; therefore, the ensured implementation of an efficient governance system is crucial to safeguarding shareholders' rights and protecting the banking ecosystem from emergent risks

Regulatory authorities and policymakers aim to enhance the benefits of FinTech adoption for financial institutions while minimising the probable risks by promoting products/services and governance practices. Similarly, bank regulatory authorities are paying close attention to governance issues for Fintech-oriented banks to warrant risk management, financial stability, financial performance, financial innovations, and development. Credit guidelines on Financial Technology governance issued by the ECB (the European Central Bank) ensure that FinTech governance complies with the European Commission's technological neutrality principle (2018) to augment the financial performance of banking/financial institutions. In this regard, the ECB has also collaborated with the "FinTech Board of Directors" to define the

FinTech structure, its responsibilities, and its functions in agreement with them. Furthermore, the basic principles of corporate governance advise that Financial technology-oriented companies/institutions should disclose the responsibilities and roles of board members (BODs) and the CEO. The board members should have excellent management and monitoring abilities to foresee the CEO's activities. On the other hand, the CEO's responsibility is to set the company's overall direction, which can range from operational to innovations. In this regard, fintech-oriented financial institutions should pay appropriate attention to BODs and CEOs' governance characteristics, including gender, age (Sannino et al., 2020), cultural backgrounds and areas of specialisation.

The prevailing literature shows that the cooperative behaviour of the CEO and BODs, operated by their respective principles and personal traits (Berson et al., 2008), plays a vital role in determining and supervising organisational philosophy, influencing effective decision-making, enhancing managerial strategies, and finally improving financial performance. The chapter also focuses on the Governance characteristics of FinTech adoption in banks and its influence on their financial performance. It analyses the theoretical aspects of "Upper Echelons Theory (Hambrick & Mason, 1984)" and the "Resource-Based View (Wernerfelt, 1984)". The literature on corporate governance and firms' performance relates these theories to the current agenda of this chapter, i.e., fintech adoption and banks' financial performance. In this regard, literature links the governance aspects with banks' financial performance (e.g., Srivastav and Hagendorff, 2016; Martín-Oliver et al., 2017) by uncovering the influence of board size (Grove, 2011), educational training and gender diversity of BODs (Issa, 2021) on financial performance. Ujunwa (2012) uncovers that directors' specialisation positively impacts firms' financial performance. Skała and Weill (2018) argue that female CEOs have a favourable impact on firms' risk exposure, and Bhatia and Gulati (2021) find that large board size enhances the firm's performance. Such governance issues are significant to consider while a bank adopts FinTech. Therefore, the chapter uncovers that governance aspects can enhance/improve banks' financial performance and stability. For example, the roles and responsibilities of BODs and CEOs substantially influence the Risk portfolios, operational, and financial performance of banks that could potentially adopt FinTech. FinTech-oriented banks operate in a highly dynamic environment where other financial institutions are adapting to FinTech. Moreover, the innovative and BigTech firms are creating competitive and regulatory challenges for Banks as they operate in complex financial system. In such a challengeing environment, governance mechanics are essential to ensure the risk management, propmote innovation, ensure the regulatory compliance, enhance the financial performance. When banks become strategic partners with FinTech companies, the Bank's risk and FinTech governance have significant implications for financial performance. Suppose well-known banks seek a strategic partnership with a FinTech firm. In that case, the mutual efficiency of banks and FinTech firms can reduce the inherent risk and potential vulnerabilities while ensuring better operational and financial performance. Moreover, the robust governance structure of FinTech partners enhances service continuity, buffers operational inefficiencies, and sustains stakeholders' trust. A comprehensive governance mechanism for FinTech adoption in banks facilitates the stability of the financial ecosystem and supports strategic decision-making.

Fintech Adoption and financial performance of banks under Stability perspectives

FinTech enhances the economic sustainability in different countries (Li et al, 2024a,b & c). Fung et al. (2020) argue that Financial technology adoption augments financial solidity in developing economies while destabilising developed markets. Using Fintech credit data from different economies, Liem et al. (2022) and Cornelli et al. (2023) find that FinTech development enhances financial stability in 73 economies and promotes financial performance. However, there are different ways in which the adoption of Financial Technology enhances banks' financial stability and performance.

1. In FinTech adoption, novel and multifaceted technologies integrate with banking operations which are unfamiliar with regular and conventional operations. Such unfamiliar technological innovations may expose banks' stability and financial performance to risks like data breaches, cyberattacks, and system failures. Thus, it is essential to manage Fintech adoption effectively.
2. FinTech-oriented digitalisation and automation can improve operational efficiency, reduce transaction costs, and enhance profitability in banks and financial institutions. Nevertheless, it also has some dark sides. Because, the dynamic and fast technological changes initiate different implementation challenges, e.g., if banks fail to adapt to dynamic technological changes, they may experience substandard efficiency and profitability.
3. FinTech company competes with conventional banks by offering novel financial products and services. This can affect conventional banks' financial performance or stability because such competitive FinTech services reduce banks' market share and profits. In this regard, banks should successfully adopt and integrate FinTech to gain and maintain a competitive edge.
4. Traditional banks use stricter credit assessments before advancing a loan. FinTech adoption in banks may efficiently capture risk assessments through innovative and cutting-edge data analytics and algorithms. Thus, FinTech adoption can enhance the profitability and stability of banks. However, such adoption may

also hinder banks' performance if FinTech algorithms do not calibrate risk assessment properly, thus resulting in substandard profitability

5. FinTech-oriented banks must fulfil the governing requirements associated with data security and technology, and non-compliance and regulatory penalties may affect their profitability and stability. Nevertheless, banks can enhance their stability and performance by adopting FinTech and proactively addressing regulatory concerns.
6. FinTech adoption changes consumer expectations and behaviours, influencing banks' business models. Banks may lose their stability, financial performance, and market share if they fail to incorporate changing consumer preferences. However, FinTech-oriented banks can sustain their prosperity by aligning their products and services with dynamic consumer demands.
7. In banks, FinTech adoption enhances liquidity management via digital wallets and a real-time payment system. However, enhanced liquidity may introduce risks that lead to lower profitability and financial sustainability.
8. Moreover, in the FinTech ecosystem, banks' FinTech adoption is interconnected with many other financial institutions. Any disruption or failure in a FinTech entity can adversely affect other entities in the financial ecosystem, potentially disabling banks' operational and financial efficiency.
9. Higher bank competition and Fintech advancements have minimised the hostile impressions of FinTech adoption on banks' financial performance and stability.

CONCLUSION

Banks operate in a dynamic environment where FinTech firms are there to provide fast, cheap and easily accessible financial services. Therefore, Banks are adopting FinTech to compete with FinTech firms and stay competitive. However, due to different challenges like regulatory complexitics, high compctition, and technological advancements, banks' financial performance has been exposed to different threats. The chapter explores the adoption of FinTech and its impact on banks' financial performance. The chapter also offers the best components to measure the FinTech adoption in banks, which leads to better financial performance. The chapter uncovers that FinTech components range from non-bank components (crowdfunding and peer-to-peer (p2p) lending) to bank-based determinants of FinTech. It is observed that the determinants of FinTech discovered by Khan et al. (2023) are the bank-based components of FinTech adoption. These pillars are Banks' Digital Presence, Mobile Banking Capabilities, Support for Open APIs, Fintech Partnerships, Digital Payment Solutions, Automation and Artificial Intelligence Integration, Innovation Initiatives, User Experience Focus, and Embracing New Technologies. These components can best measure the FinTech adoption in banks. These traits are aligned with the management of banking operations. Furthermore, these attributes contribute to the financial performance and stability of the banking industry. It is further observed that Different governance and regulatory challenges hinder the banks' adoption of FinTech, where these pillars augment transaction processes, monitor administrative tasks, enhance operational efficiencies, optimise resource allocations, accelerate processing speed, and minimise errors. It is concluded that these components can best measure the FinTech adoption in banks and such factors can enhance their financial performance. Future studies can use these determinants to measure FinTech adoption in public, private, conventional and Islamic banks.

REFERENCES

Adrian, T., & Liang, N. (2018). Monetary policy, financial conditions, and financial stability. *52nd Issue (January 2018) of the International Journal of Central Banking*.

Agrawal, A., Catalini, C., & Goldfarb, A. (2015). Crowdfunding: Geography, social networks, and the timing of investment decisions. *Journal of Economics & Management Strategy*, *24*(2), 253–274. DOI: 10.1111/jems.12093

Ahamed, M. M., Ho, S. J., Mallick, S. K., & Matousek, R. (2021). Inclusive banking, financial regulation and bank performance: Cross-country evidence. *Journal of Banking & Finance*, *124*, 106055. DOI: 10.1016/j.jbankfin.2021.106055

Arner, D. W., Buckley, R. P., Zetzsche, D. A., & Veidt, R. (2020). Sustainability, FinTech and financial inclusion. *European Business Organization Law Review*, *21*(1), 7–35. DOI: 10.1007/s40804-020-00183-y

Arner, D. W., Zetzsche, D. A., Buckley, R. P., & Barberis, J. N. (2017). FinTech and RegTech: Enabling innovation while preserving financial stability. *Georgetown Journal of International Affairs*, 47-58.

Ashta, A., & Herrmann, H. (2021). Artificial intelligence and fintech: An overview of opportunities and risks for banking, investments, and microfinance. *Strategic Change*, *30*(3), 211–222. DOI: 10.1002/jsc.2404

Askitas, N., & Zimmermann, K. F. (2009). Google econometrics and unemployment forecasting. *Applied Economics Quarterly*, *55*(2), 107–120. DOI: 10.3790/aeq.55.2.107

Bakhoum, M., Gonzalez Otero, B., Hoffmann, J., & Sarr, M. (2024). Data Governance in Emerging Economies to Achieve the Sustainable Development Goals Senegal Country Report Based on the Workshop Shaping Data Sharing Policies in the Agricultural and the Financial Services Sector (Dakar, March 16-17, 2022).

Barba Navaretti, G., & Calzolari, G. (2017). FinTech and Banks Friends and Foes. *European Economy, 2017*(2).

Bazarbash, M., Beaton, K., & Eriksson, U. (2020). Filling the gap: Digital credit and financial inclusion.

Begenau, J., Farboodi, M., & Veldkamp, L. (2018). Big data in finance and the growth of large firms. *Journal of Monetary Economics*, *97*, 71–87. DOI: 10.1016/j.jmoneco.2018.05.013

Berg, T., Burg, V., Gombović, A., & Puri, M. (2020). On the rise of fintechs: Credit scoring using digital footprints. *Review of Financial Studies*, *33*(7), 2845–2897. DOI: 10.1093/rfs/hhz099

Berson, Y., Oreg, S., & Dvir, T. (2008). CEO values, organizational culture and firm outcomes. *Journal of Organizational Behavior: The International Journal of Industrial. Journal of Organizational Behavior*, *29*(5), 615–633. DOI: 10.1002/job.499

Bertsch, C., & Rosenvinge, C. J. (2019). FinTech credit: Online lending platforms in Sweden and beyond. *Sveriges Riksbank Economic Review*, *2*, 42–70.

Bhatia, M., & Gulati, R. (2021). Board governance and bank performance: A meta-analysis. *Research in International Business and Finance*, *58*, 101425. DOI: 10.1016/j.ribaf.2021.101425

Branzoli, N., & Supino, I. (2020). Fintech credit: A critical review of empirical research literature. *Bank of Italy Occasional Paper*, (549).

Buchak, G., Matvos, G., Piskorski, T., & Seru, A. (2018). Fintech, regulatory arbitrage, and the rise of shadow banks. *Journal of Financial Economics*, *130*(3), 453–483. DOI: 10.1016/j.jfineco.2018.03.011

Carbó-Valverde, S., Cuadros-Solas, P. J., & Rodríguez-Fernández, F. (2021). FinTech and banking: an evolving relationship. In *Disruptive technology in banking and finance: An international perspective on FinTech* (pp. 161–194). Springer International Publishing. DOI: 10.1007/978-3-030-81835-7_6

Chen, M. A., Wu, Q., & Yang, B. (2019). How valuable is FinTech innovation? *Review of Financial Studies*, *32*(5), 2062–2106. DOI: 10.1093/rfs/hhy130

Chen, X., Yang, L., Wang, P., & Yue, W. (2013). An Effective Interval-Valued Intuitionistic Fuzzy Entropy to Evaluate Entrepreneurship Orientation of Online P2P Lending Platforms. *Advances in Mathematical Physics*, *2013*(1), 467215. DOI: 10.1155/2013/467215

Cheng, M., & Qu, Y. (2020). Does bank FinTech reduce credit risk? Evidence from China. *Pacific-Basin Finance Journal*, *63*, 101398. DOI: 10.1016/j.pacfin.2020.101398

Chiu, J., & Koeppl, T. V. (2019). Blockchain-based settlement for asset trading. *Review of Financial Studies*, *32*(5), 1716–1753. DOI: 10.1093/rfs/hhy122

Claessens, S., Frost, J., Turner, G., & Zhu, F. (2018). *Fintech credit markets around the world: size, drivers and policy issues*. BIS Quarterly Review September.

Corbet, S., & Gurdgiev, C. (2017). Financial digital disruptors and cyber-security risks: Paired and systemic. *Forthcoming in Journal of Terrorism & Cyber Insurance, 1*(2).

Cornelli, G., Frost, J., Gambacorta, L., Rau, P. R., Wardrop, R., & Ziegler, T. (2023). Fintech and big tech credit: Drivers of the growth of digital lending. *Journal of Banking & Finance, 148*, 106742. DOI: 10.1016/j.jbankfin.2022.106742

Cortina Lorente, J. J., & Schmukler, S. L. (2018). The Fintech revolution: a threat to global banking?. *World Bank Research and Policy Briefs*, (125038).

Cumming, D., Farag, H., Johan, S., & McGowan, D. (2022). The digital credit divide: Marketplace lending and entrepreneurship. *Journal of Financial and Quantitative Analysis, 57*(7), 2659–2692. DOI: 10.1017/S0022109022000357

Daud, S. N. M., Khalid, A., & Azman-Saini, W. N. W. (2022). FinTech and financial stability: Threat or opportunity? *Finance Research Letters, 47*, 102667. DOI: 10.1016/j.frl.2021.102667

Demertzis, M., Merler, S., & Wolff, G. B. (2018). Capital markets union and the fintech opportunity. *Journal of financial regulation, 4*(1), 157-165.

Elsinger, H., Fessler, P., Feyrer, J., Richter, K., Silgoner, M. A., & Timel, A. (2018). Digitalization in financial services and household finance: Fintech, financial literacy and financial stability. *Financial Stability Report*, (35), 50–58.

Fersi, M., Boujelbéne, M., & Arous, F. (2023). Microfinance's digital transformation for sustainable inclusion. *European journal of management and business economics, 32*(5), 525-559.

Fiordelisi, F., Girardone, C., Minnucci, F., & Ricci, O. (2020). On the nexus between sovereign risk and banking crises. *Journal of Corporate Finance, 65*, 101717. DOI: 10.1016/j.jcorpfin.2020.101717

Frost, J. (2020). The economic forces driving fintech adoption across countries. *The technological revolution in financial services: how banks, fintechs, and customers win together, 838*(II), 70-89.

Frost, J., Gambacorta, L., Huang, Y., Shin, H. S., & Zbinden, P. (2019). BigTech and the changing structure of financial intermediation. *Economic Policy, 34*(100), 761–799. DOI: 10.1093/epolic/eiaa003

Fung, D. W., Lee, W. Y., Yeh, J. J., & Yuen, F. L. (2020). Friend or foe: The divergent effects of FinTech on financial stability. *Emerging Markets Review, 45*, 100727. DOI: 10.1016/j.ememar.2020.100727

Fuster, A., Plosser, M., Schnabl, P., & Vickery, J. (2019). The role of technology in mortgage lending. *Review of Financial Studies, 32*(5), 1854–1899. DOI: 10.1093/rfs/hhz018

Gomber, P., Koch, J. A., & Siering, M. (2017). Digital Finance and FinTech: Current research and future research directions. *Journal of Business Economics, 87*(5), 537–580. DOI: 10.1007/s11573-017-0852-x

Grove, H., Patelli, L., Victoravich, L. M., & Xu, P. (2011). Corporate governance and performance in the wake of the financial crisis: Evidence from US commercial banks. *Corporate Governance, 19*(5), 418–436. DOI: 10.1111/j.1467-8683.2011.00882.x

Haddad, C., & Hornuf, L. (2019). The emergence of the global fintech market: Economic and technological determinants. *Small Business Economics, 53*(1), 81–105. DOI: 10.1007/s11187-018-9991-x

Hambrick, D. C., & Mason, P. A. (1984). Upper echelons: The organization as a reflection of its top managers. *Academy of Management Review, 9*(2), 193–206. DOI: 10.2307/258434

Heimer, R. Z. (2016). Peer pressure: Social interaction and the disposition effect. *Review of Financial Studies, 29*(11), 3177–3209. DOI: 10.1093/rfs/hhw063

Hikida, R., & Perry, J. (2020). Fintech trends in the united states: Implications for household finance. *Public Policy Research, 16*(4), 1–32.

Hornuf, L., Klus, M. F., Lohwasser, T. S., & Schwienbacher, A. (2021). How do banks interact with fintech startups? *Small Business Economics, 57*(3), 1505–1526. DOI: 10.1007/s11187-020-00359-3

Hou, X., Gao, Z., & Wang, Q. (2016). Internet finance development and banking market discipline: Evidence from China. *Journal of Financial Stability, 22*, 88–100. DOI: 10.1016/j.jfs.2016.01.001

Issa, A., Yousef, H., Bakry, A., Hanaysha, J. R., & Sahyouni, A. (2021). Does the board diversity impact bank performance in the MENA countries? A multilevel study. *Corporate Governance (Bradford), 21*(5), 865–891. DOI: 10.1108/CG-06-2020-0222

Jagtiani, J., & Lemieux, C. (2019). The roles of alternative data and machine learning in fintech lending: Evidence from the LendingClub consumer platform. *Financial Management, 48*(4), 1009–1029. DOI: 10.1111/fima.12295

Khan, H. H., Khan, S., & Ghafoor, A. (2023). Fintech adoption, the regulatory environment and bank stability: An empirical investigation from GCC economies. *Borsa Istanbul Review, 23*(6), 1263–1281. DOI: 10.1016/j.bir.2023.10.010

Li, J., Li, J., Zhu, X., Yao, Y., & Casu, B. (2020). Risk spillovers between FinTech and traditional financial institutions: Evidence from the US. *International Review of Financial Analysis, 71*, 101544. DOI: 10.1016/j.irfa.2020.101544

Liem, N. T., Son, T. H., Tin, H. H., & Canh, N. T. (2022). Fintech credit, credit information sharing and bank stability: Some international evidence. *Cogent Business & Management, 9*(1), 2112527. DOI: 10.1080/23311975.2022.2112527

Lin, S. L. (2007). Risk management of banking industry in Taiwan. *International Journal of Services Technology and Management, 8*(4-5), 421–451. DOI: 10.1504/IJSTM.2007.013928

Martín-Oliver, A., Ruano, S., & Salas-Fumás, V. (2017). The fall of Spanish cajas: Lessons of ownership and governance for banks. *Journal of Financial Stability, 33*, 244–260. DOI: 10.1016/j.jfs.2017.02.004

Mdluli, G., & Staschen, S. (2022). Pitfalls in MFI digitization: Overlooking the regulatory environment. CGAP Blog. https://www.cgap.org/blog/pitfalls-in-mfi-digitization-o verlooking-regulatory-environment

Merton, R. C., & Thakor, R. T. (2019). Customers and investors: A framework for understanding the evolution of financial institutions. *Journal of Financial Intermediation, 39*, 4–18. DOI: 10.1016/j.jfi.2018.06.002

Molnár, J. (2018). What does financial intermediation theory tell us about fintechs? *Vezetéstudomány-Budapest Management Review, 49*(5), 38–46. DOI: 10.14267/VEZTUD.2018.05.04

Murinde, V., Rizopoulos, E., & Zachariadis, M. (2022). The impact of the FinTech revolution on the future of banking: Opportunities and risks. *International Review of Financial Analysis, 81*, 102103. DOI: 10.1016/j.irfa.2022.102103

Narayan, P. K., Narayan, S., Rahman, R. E., & Setiawan, I. (2019). Bitcoin price growth and Indonesia's monetary system. *Emerging Markets Review, 38*, 364–376. DOI: 10.1016/j.ememar.2018.11.005

Navaretti, G. B., Calzolari, G., Mansilla-Fernandez, J. M., & Pozzolo, A. F. (2018). *Fintech and banking. Friends or foes?* Friends or Foes. DOI: 10.2139/ssrn.3099337

Nguyen, Q. K. (2022). The effect of FinTech development on financial stability in an emerging market: The role of market discipline. *Research in Globalization, 5*, 100105. DOI: 10.1016/j.resglo.2022.100105

Philippon, T. (2019). *On fintech and financial inclusion* (No. w26330). National Bureau of Economic Research.

Sannino, G., Di Carlo, F., & Lucchese, M. (2020). CEO characteristics and sustainability business model in financial technologies firms: Primary evidence from the utilization of innovative platforms. *Management Decision*, *58*(8), 1779–1799. DOI: 10.1108/MD-10-2019-1360

Skała, D., & Weill, L. (2018). Does CEO gender matter for bank risk? *Economic Systems*, *42*(1), 64–74. DOI: 10.1016/j.ecosys.2017.08.005

Srivastav, A., & Hagendorff, J. (2016). Corporate governance and bank risk-taking. *Corporate Governance*, *24*(3), 334–345. DOI: 10.1111/corg.12133

Tanchangya, T., Islam, N., Naher, K., Mia, M. R., Chowdhury, S., Sarker, S. R., & Rashid, F. (2025). Financial technology-enabled sustainable finance for small-and medium-sized enterprises. *Environment. Innovation and Management*, *1*, 2550006.

Tang, H. (2019). Peer-to-peer lenders versus banks: Substitutes or complements? *Review of Financial Studies*, *32*(5), 1900–1938. DOI: 10.1093/rfs/hhy137

Thakor, A. V. (2020). Fintech and banking: What do we know? *Journal of Financial Intermediation*, *41*, 100833. DOI: 10.1016/j.jfi.2019.100833

Ujunwa, A. (2012). Board characteristics and the financial performance of Nigerian quoted firms. *Corporate Governance (Bradford)*, *12*(5), 656–674. DOI: 10.1108/14720701211275587

Vives, X. (2017). The impact of FinTech on banking. *European Economy*, (2), 97–105.

Wang, R., Liu, J., & Luo, H. (2021). Fintech development and bank risk taking in China. *European Journal of Finance*, *27*(4-5), 397–418. DOI: 10.1080/1351847X.2020.1805782

Wang, X., Hou, S., Kyaw, K., Xue, X., & Liu, X. (2023). Exploring the determinants of Fintech Credit: A comprehensive analysis. *Economic Modelling*, *126*, 106422. DOI: 10.1016/j.econmod.2023.106422

Wang, Y., Xiuping, S., & Zhang, Q. (2021). Can fintech improve the efficiency of commercial banks?—An analysis based on big data. *Research in International Business and Finance*, *55*, 101338. DOI: 10.1016/j.ribaf.2020.101338

Wernerfelt, B. (1984). A resource-based view of the firm. *Strategic Management Journal*, *5*(2), 171–180. DOI: 10.1002/smj.4250050207

Widarwati, E., Fajar, I. Y., Nurmalasari, N., & Wityasminingsih, E. (2023). Digital Finance and Microfinance Risk Level. In *10th International Conference on Management and Muamalah.*

Yao, M., Di, H., Zheng, X., & Xu, X. (2018). Impact of payment technology innovations on the traditional financial industry: A focus on China. *Technological Forecasting and Social Change*, *135*, 199–207. DOI: 10.1016/j.techfore.2017.12.023

Zavolokina, L., Dolata, M., & Schwabe, G. (2016). The FinTech phenomenon: Antecedents of financial innovation perceived by the popular press. *Financial Innovation*, *2*(1), 16. DOI: 10.1186/s40854-016-0036-7

KEY TERMS AND DEFINITIONS

FinTech Fintech refers to using technology to deliver financial products/services efficiently: cheaply, faster, improved, and automated.

FinTech Adoption When businesses or individuals start using technological means to deliver financial products/services: such as robo-advisors, peer-to-peer lending, digital wallets or mobile banking.

FinTech Determinants FinTech determinants are those aspects that lead to the adoption of technology to leverage financial products/services: such as regulatory conditions, individual/institutional characteristics, and technological infrastructure.

Financial Performance The degree to which a firm generates revenues: profits and shareholder wealth by efficiently using the company's Assets.

Financial Stability The degree to which a firm efficiently allocates resources: assesses and manages risks, absorbs economic shocks, operates efficiently, avoids disruptions and ensures confidence among customers and investors.

Chapter 5
Financial Cybercrime, FinTech Adoption, and Bank Performance in an Interconnected Indian Economy:
Typologies, Networks, and Systemic Implications

Priyakrushna Mohanty
http://orcid.org/0000-0001-6933-2757
Christ University, Bengaluru, India

Rashi Modi
http://orcid.org/0009-0006-8069-7849
Christ University, Bengaluru, India

Aaleyah Behera
http://orcid.org/0009-0000-3230-2087
Christ University, Bengaluru, India

ABSTRACT

India's rapid expansion of digital finance has transformed payment systems while heightening exposure to financial cybercrime. Real-time payments, platform-based services, and fintech integration have created risk pathways that extend beyond isolated fraud incidents. This study analyses financial cybercrime in India through a systemic lens, mapping evolving fraud typologies, payment-rail vulnerabilities,

DOI: 10.4018/979-8-3373-6244-1.ch005

organised criminal networks, and behavioural asymmetries. It also examines the capacity of regulatory, infrastructural, and enforcement mechanisms to manage these risks under real-time operational constraints. Drawing on a structured synthesis of academic and policy sources, the paper develops the Systemic Cybercrime Mitigation Framework for Digital Finance (SCMF-DF), which integrates prevention, detection, containment, recovery, and adaptive learning to address cybercrime as a financial stability concern.

1. INTRODUCTION

India has transformed the financial environment with respect to the quick introduction of digital payment systems, building one of the largest digital finance environments in the world (Migozzi et al., 2024). Digital payments over the last years have taken over the economic transactions with the digital form having nearly 99.8 percent of total transaction volume in first half of 2025 as per Reserve Bank of India statistics, meaning an overwhelming shift towards cash to cashless forms (Economic Times, 2025). The Unified Payments Interface (UPI) that contributed over 80 percent of digital payments and led to exponential growth in transaction volumes and values has been at the center of this transition and made India a real-time payment leader in the global context (PwC, 2025; NPCI, 2025). Such proliferation has brought about socioeconomic gains such as an increase in financial inclusion, efficiency, and increased access both in urban and rural settings (Mishra et al., 2024). Nevertheless, the network effects facilitating the high-speed value transfer have similarly increased the vulnerabilities, with digital payment systems becoming the large attack surfaces that cybercriminals can exploit to gain money using increasingly sophisticated schemes (Shaji et al., 2024).

Alongside the rapid escalation of financial cybercrime, India's banking sector has undergone a profound transformation driven by FinTech adoption, platform-based service delivery, and real-time payment infrastructures. Innovations such as interoperable payment rails, API-enabled partnerships, and digital-first customer acquisition have reshaped bank performance by expanding transaction volumes, improving cost efficiencies, and accelerating market reach. At the same time, these performance gains are increasingly entangled with heightened exposure to cyber-enabled financial crime, as speed, scale, and system interoperability compress detection and recovery windows. This chapter therefore situates financial cybercrime not only as a security concern, but also as an unintended consequence of performance-oriented digitalisation in banking, where FinTech adoption simultaneously enhances operational efficiency and amplifies systemic financial risk.

The growth of financial cybercrime in India is witnessed in the official statistics and the recent coverage (Chandra, 2025; Datta et al., 2020). National systems reported more than twice the number of cybersecurity incidents in two years, with reported cases growing between 1,029,000 in 2022 and 2,268,000 in 2024, indicating the presence of threats in the digital domain (PIB, 2025a). At the same time, the National Cyber Crime Reporting Portal (NCRP) registered losses to cyber fraud in tens of thousands of crores of Indian rupees, which highlights the increasing economic cost of these activities (PIB, 2025b). The statistics related to UPI fraud also demonstrate this tendency: in FY 2023-24, approximately 6.32 lakh cases of UPI fraud-related transactions were reported, which means hundreds of crores of financial loss, and fraud rates increased significantly in the current fiscal year, in comparison with the last one (CyberPeace, 2024). In addition, according to recent reporting, the Indian system of cybercrime reporting registered an approximate 3.6 million cases of fraud in 2024 alone, and cumulative losses totaled over 22,845 crore of money, more than 200 percent higher than in the previous year (Times of India, 2025). Such statistics highlight the magnitude and sophistication of financial crimes that are enabled by cyber-criminals in an ecosystem that is characterized by high volumes of transactions and widespread connectivity.

Although the body of existing empirical data on the increasing use of cyber security is rich, the academic and policy discourse contains long-term gaps in conceptualising and responding to these threats (Levi et al., 2017). Much of the current body of literature lists or reviews particular incidents or studies a particular technical vulnerability, but little attempts to systematise such phenomena into a systemic risk framework reflecting interdependences between payment rails, regulatory architecture, fintech interoperability, and user behaviour (Sottet et al., 2018; Sujatha et al., 2025; von Horn and Kudic, 2025). Specifically, the models that cut across the analytic gap between empirical mapping of typologies of fraud and evaluative diagnosis of institutional responses are lacking (Sujatha et al., 2025). This disjuncture is normative in the sense that the divided comprehensions may lead to reactive efforts and siloed ability to develop mitigation efforts that cannot be aligned with wider governance demands and financial stability issues. The more holistic analytical prism is needed in the environment of real-time settlement systems, where the speed of transactions and irreversibility are increasing the effects of fraudulent behaviour, to anticipate systemic exposure and not individual instances of it.

The given paper outlines three related research objectives that lead to the solution through diagnosis. The former is intended to investigate the evolving pattern and typologies of financial cybercrime in the digital financial landscape in India, which involves behavioral and technology-related mechanisms that are involved in fraud production. This mapping would be considering how fraudsters exploit the nature of payment systems and presentation interfaces to acquire monetary advantage.

The second objective assesses the institutional and infrastructural provisions in the event of such risks as regulatory controls, payment infrastructure regulation, fraud reporting and redress, enforcement co-ordination, and technological competence. This is a judgmental prism that gauges the mediation of the processes of present-day governance in the situation of cyber threats and the domains of operational gaps. The third aim produces a mitigation framework, Systemic Cybercrime Mitigation Framework for Digital Finance (SCMF-DF) which will form the derivatives of diagnostic insights into a consistent framework of architecture that would enhance strength within the digital finance ecosystem prevention, detection, containment and recovery. When such objectives are seen, it suggests progress on the path of evaluative diagnosis and framework development that is not only analytical in character, but one of policy concerns.

The applicability of the research is that it tries to repackage financial cybercrime as a structural risk that is diffused within the framework of digital payments and not a set of individual frauds. Certainly, increased accessibility has been made with fintech innovations and real-time payment networks all with interdependence, feedback and attack vectors that traditional risk management models may not be suitably designed to manage. The research aligns with more typical academic requirements of a systemic paradigm of cybercrime governance by considering technological, behavioral, and institutional elements of risk. This introduction is particularly applicable to India where digitalization has already outpaced the relative pace of cyber literacy and other institutional preparedness means, a breach of which creates free loopholes in regulatory and enforcement and user protection infrastructures, which are readily followed by cybercriminals.

The paper has the following progression. Section 2 explores the methods and methodology of this paper, and the third section gives an empirically based mapping of financial cybercrime trends and vulnerabilities based on official statistics, case reports, and typological inspection to elicit structural sources of risk. Section 4 focuses on institutional and infrastructural reactions, forming asymmetries, fragmentation, and capacity constraints of the prevailing governance structures. In the fifth section, based on these analyses, the authors present the SCMF-DF, its elements, and rationale as an overarching systemic cyber risk mitigation architecture. The concluding section makes an assessment on policy implications, future of adaptive governance and future research directions. In this arrangement, the research study informs both academic and policy debates in achieving digital finance security in unstable cyber threats and institutional dilemmas.

2. METHODS AND METHODOLOGY

This paper is a conceptual and integrative research study that focuses on summarizing scattered evidence on financial cybercrime into a logical analysis and solution-based model. Considering the dynamic and interdisciplinarity of financial cybercrime in digital finance ecosystems, the methodological paradigm is not based on the primary data collection, but rather, systematically developed on the background of the existing scholarly, regulatory, and policy-oriented knowledge. Aggregation of findings in and of itself is the goal, but rather organization of the interpretation where theoretical integration may be achieved across criminology, digital finance, cybersecurity governance, and financial stability literature.

The reviewed literature is within the period of the past 10-12 years (2013-2025), which is associated with the fast growth of digital payments and real-time systems of settlement in India. The corpus will contain peer-reviewed scholarly papers, official documents of regulatory and international financial bodies, and some chosen policy and industry reports, in which the academic evidence is insufficient.

The initial part of the methodology was a systematic literature search in Scopus and Google Scholar, which was chosen due to the mutual possibilities. The main database was Scopus, providing the possibility to locate peer-reviewed journal articles, conference proceedings, and review papers that comprise the financial cybercrime, digital payments, fintech risks, payment system vulnerabilities, and institutional cybersecurity governance. The search strategy had keywords representing finance, information systems, law and public policy to prevent disciplinary silos. This was followed by the search in Google scholarly in order to expand coverage at least to include working papers, policy papers, and interdisciplinary research that might not be covered by Scopus, but which have already served to inform modern debates. This two-database strategy was used to guarantee both academic rigour and conceptual breadth.

The study knows financial cybercrime is a fast-changing phenomenon and therefore uses grey literature as an additional source of evidence (Adams et al., 2016). These covered reports and publications by regulatory bodies, central banks, payment system operators and law enforcement agencies, international financial bodies, consultancy firms and credible media outlets. Grey literature was particularly critical in being able to obtain current statistics, institutional practices, supervisory outlooks and operational issues that are generally poorly represented in academic publications because of time lags (Benzies et al., 2006). The inclusion of this material enabled the study to be anchored on the real-world developments but at the same time be analytical in terms of triangulation with peer-reviewed materials.

A corpus-building process based on relevance, thematic harmony and conceptual contribution was used to filter all identified documents. The corpus featured those studies which directly covered such areas as financial fraud, cyber-enabled crime, digital payment system, real-time settlement risk, integration of fintech, regulatory frameworks, enforcement mechanisms and institutional capacity. Paperwork that only considered the technical design of cryptography and was not related to the financial systems was screened out or papers that discussed cybercrime outside a financial setting. It was the outcome of this that became the basis of analysis upon which thematic exploration and the building of frameworks proceeded.

Thematic data analysis was the fundamental analytical methodology used, which was applied in the form of repetitive reading, coding, and synthesis of the data corpus (Altameemi and Altamimi, 2023). Instead of using a preset coding scheme, the themes were entitled to emerge inductively by recurring patterns noted in the literature. The preliminary open coding was based on the identification of the recurrent ideas, including typologies of frauds, behavioural exploitation, payment-rail, institutional fragmentation, recovery limitations, and technology-induced risks. Those codes were further narrowed down to higher order thematic categories that enhanced structural relationships and not solitary observations. The identified systemic connections between digital finance structures and cybercrime dynamics were made possible by this approach.

The study also used the conceptual level of keyword mapping and clustering in order to enhance the level of analytical clarity. Keywords and phrases that were commonly observed throughout the corpus were determined and put into groups based on common analytical issues. An example is that keyword phishing, social engineering, and user manipulation are clustering around behavioural vulnerability whereas (UPI), real-time payments, irreversibility and velocity of transaction were clustering around payment-rail exposure. Likewise, the mentioning of mule accounts, laundering routes, and transfers across platforms was also a specific cluster linked to organised financial crime channels. These clusters were not seen as such ends but also as tools of analysis to visualise the relationship and overlaps between themes.

The clustering exercise demonstrated that there were major overlaps in thematic areas particularly on the point of technological design decisions that cut across institutional and regulatory constraints. Such overlaps caused the shift in descriptive mapping towards interpretive synthesis. This is where authorial interpretation was given at a centre stage. The identified themes helped the authors to identify the impacts of digital finance and financial governance on financial ecosystem layers based on the domain knowledge. This interpretation was critical in moving beyond the listing of risks, to understanding the mechanisms, in how they interact with each other, and how the processes of feedback and amplification occur in the system.

The final constituent of the methodology involved using thematic insights in developing the Systemic Cybercrime Mitigation Framework to Digital Finance (SCMF-DF). Thematic analysis resulted in the three analytic layers which were logically synthesized into the structure of sources of generation of risk related to cybercrimes, institutional and infrastructural mechanisms of response, and integrated mitigation pathways. It was conceptual argumentation that enabled them to achieve the links between these layers rather than statistical inference, and such structure enabled them to be flexible and policy relevant. Preventive, detective, containment and recovery dimensions were particularly introduced based on gaps and constraints that have been surfacing through literature.

Overall, this theoretical approach to the research makes it possible to create a systematic yet flexible approach to the insight into financial cybercrime as a system phenomenon. The systematic literature search, corpus building, themes analysis, as well as key-word-based clustering and interpretation synthesis provide the study with a structure founded on the available evidence, but with an integrative value of its originality. This research approach particularly fits dynamic and complex areas where the amount of empirical data may not be sufficient to monitor the instability of institutional dynamics and new threats to digital financial systems.

3. FINANCIAL CYBERCRIME PATTERNS IN INDIA

Such speed of digitalization of the Indian financial ecosystem has provided a unique economic inclusion and efficiency that has increased to bring a sophisticated and dynamic environment of financial cybercrime. By critically mapping, analyzing and theorizing the fluctuating patterns of financial cybercrime in India not as individual instances but as emergent systemic financial-risk vectors as an inseparable part and parcel of the rapidly changing digital environment in the country, this chapter is very meticulously done. In India, financial cybercrime has been growing consistently well since 2018.

3.1 Growth Trajectory of Financial Cybercrime in India

Financial cyber fraud cases in India have been rapidly increasing during the last few years, which is closely related to the increased use of digital technologies and the growth of an internet network, as well as the popularity of real-time payment systems (Tripathy, 2025). This is a worrying rise in government figures. The Reserve Bank of India states that the amount of money used in banking frauds in FY 2022-23 is 30,252 crore (Mehta, 2024), and the National Crime Records Bureau reported that the number of cybercrime cases constantly increased, and one of the leading cases reported is online financial scam (Chakraborty and Tiwari, 2025).

To add to these findings, a 2024 study also demonstrated that there is a distinct connection between digital convenience and economic vulnerability, with the development of digital payment infrastructures, in terms of volume and value, providing new opportunities to commit fraud (Sharma et al., 2024). The criminals have abandoned the old, physical approach and adopted more complex, digitally mediated approaches to commit financial crimes using technological innovations to expand the scope of attacks (Mehta, 2024; Tripathy, 2025).

Recent national datasets also indicate the extent of the problem. India documented more than 36.3 lakh financial fraud cases in 2024 using NCRP and CFCFRMS, which is 206 percent higher in the loss value of about 22,845 crores than the 7,465 crores in 2023 (The Times of India). Cases of financial cybercrime have been on the increase every year. Also, according to the data provided by the Indian Cyber Crime Coordination Centre (I4C), during the period between January and April 2024 alone, more than 7.4 lakh complaints were registered, and the estimated loss was 1750 crore, of which almost 85 percent of the cases were related to online financial frauds (The Economic Times). Taking together, these trends are a strong indication that along with the increased convenience and economic efficacy, digital transformation also resulted in greater susceptibility to financial fraud, moving the crime across a fast-paced, highly connected digital field and requiring more effective national systems to withstand any cyber- attacks.

3.2 Dominant Fraud Typologies in the Digital Finance Ecosystem

Several crucial typologies have arisen to prevail the financial cyber-crime situation in India; these not only relate to technological misuse, but also behavioral misuse. Phishing and social-engineering fraud are common, and they usually use tricks like pretending to be a bank or a government establishment to gain access to sensitive financial information (Manjunath and S, 2024). Cyber-attacks that are based on social engineering also utilize the trust of the user, leveraging the UPI Collect Request option along with the phishing, vishing (voice phishing), or smishing (Kaur et al., 2023). These attacks are mainly based on the trust and ignorance of users instead of the vulnerability of the system (Kaur et al., 2023). Remote-access-based and screen-sharing-based frauds are often represented as tech-support, hence allowing fraudsters to remotely control victim machines in real-time to cause immediate financial damage (Manjunath & S, 2024). There has also emerged a booming sphere of fake investment, trading, and crypto-related frauds with lucrative returns and further with intricate schemes including Ponzi schemes (Bhadra and Singh, 2024). These typologies are still common in the Indian domain because of differences in digital literacy and consumer risk perceptions, especially between nascent digital users who can only differentiate authentic and unauthentic outreach with some difficulty, which makes them more vulnerable to exploitation (Saxena et al., 2024;

Shah and Agarwal, 2020). Table 1 below describes key issues about the various types of financial cyber frauds in India.

Table 1. Dominant Financial Cybercrime Typologies, Operational Channels, and Systemic Implications in India

Fraud Type	Primary Channel	Typical Modus Operandi	Systemic Implication
Phishing/Vishing	Email, SMS, Phone Calls, UPI	Impersonation (bank, government), deceptive links/requests	Erosion of trust in digital communication and financial services
Social Engineering	Mobile Apps, social media, UPI	Manipulation of user actions (e.g., "Collect Request")	Compromised user agency, rapid illicit fund transfers
Remote Access Fraud	Mobile/Desktop Apps	Coercing victims to install screen-sharing software	Direct financial loss, data breach, identity compromise
Fake Investment	Online Platforms, social media	High-return promises, fictitious schemes	Significant capital loss, market integrity concerns
Mule Account Facilitation	Banks, Wallets, Fintech Apps	Laundering illicit funds via unsuspecting third-party accounts	Obfuscation of illicit money flows, aiding organized crime

Source: Authors' Own Compilation

3.3 Payment-Rail Vulnerabilities and Product-Level Exposure

Digital payment systems that include UPI, IMPS, cards, and internet banking have become the main objects of financial cybercrime (Sharma et al., 2024). Real-time payment rails like UPI and IMPS are structurally vulnerable due to their velocity and irreversibility (Mayo et al., 2024). Although instant settlements are vital to the contemporary business environment, they also pose a very serious problem: once a fraudulent transaction is initiated, it is incredibly hard to undo it, and the financial losses are irreversible and sometimes irrecoverable (Mayo et al., 2024). This is also exacerbated by user-side asymmetry where cybercriminals have more technical skills and manipulative abilities than the common user, which makes the abuse of digital payment systems even more efficient (Kaur et al., 2023). According to RBI data, the number of digital payment frauds with amounts of 1 lakh and more has grown almost 11 times since 202021, and the financial amount has grown approximately 12 times, which demonstrates the growing systemic exposure of real-time payments. (Indiaspend). Since such transactions are fast and final, quick identification and response becomes central.

The Financial ecosystem has disparities in the exposure to products. Real-time payments also require very aggressive and sophisticated fraud-detection schemes because they are real-time in nature and the opposite of instruments that are batch-settled, where a longer post-transmission inspection and defense can be pursued (Mayo et al., 2024). These are an increasing number of exposures points due to the growth of new financial services, including digital lending, Buy-Now-Pay-Later (BNPL) programs and app-based credit services, which are all being targeted by scammers (Dasari, 2025). The application of instant loans has generated fears on predatory lending, high-interest rates, and invasion of privacy (Lekshmi et al., 2024). This type of product, characterized by a fast onboarding and disbursement cycle, can be exposed to identity theft and loan application fraud because verification procedures are not as strict as in the traditional banking partners. Ideally, the concentration of exposures can be observed in the rapidly growing segments of the digital economy, where the rate of technological adoption is significantly higher in comparison with the rate of developing strong security infrastructure, awareness of consumers, and regulation, thus becoming an explicit target of cybercriminals (Lonkar et al., 2024; Sharma et al., 2024).

3.4 Organised Fraud Networks and Mule-Account Proliferation

The complexity and magnitude of financial cybercrime in India is highly enhanced by the spread of organised fraud networks and the high use of mule accounts. Money mules are the key participants who are hired by criminal networks to hide the flow of illicit funds and anonymize their activities (Rani et al., 2023; Raza et al., 2020). More than 24 lakh suspected mules accounts have been flagged by authorities and programs like Suspect Registry by I4C have been reported to have blocked an estimated 4,631 crore in possible fraud losses (Times of India). The socio-economic disadvantages of unemployment, financial burden, or online illiteracy are exploited by recruitment systems, which aim to attract and exploit youth (often by promising them allegedly well-paying jobs with disregard to the job descriptions or the lack of random selection) or courses of dubious online nature (Raza et al., 2020; Vedamanikam et al., 2020). These processes use psychological control and economic pressure, thus turning unknown people into accomplices against will (Raza et al., 2020). Illegal proceeds are then usually washed or laundered by using multilayered processes with multiple financial structures, such as transfers between mule accounts using traditional banking systems, digital wallets, fintech platforms, sometimes cryptocurrency exchanges, and so on, therefore, obscuring the trail of transactions (Sirawongphatsara et al., 2023). The cross-institutional and cross-platform overlays are a major hurdle to the integrity of financial institutions and efficient prevention of crimes since they significantly undermine the ability of law-enforcement agencies and financial institutions to trace and recover the information (Esoimeme, 2021). Mule networks provide anonymity that is the basis of organised financial crime and makes it particularly difficult to recover funds (Esoimeme, 2021).

3.5 Fintech Integration and Emerging Risk Modalities

Not only has fintech integration, both transformative and API-driven, including account aggregators, Payment Service Providers, and third-party vendors, redefined the modalities of the financial service delivery, but also created new and emergent risk paradigms (Kamal et al., 2025). Application Programming Interfaces both enable smooth integration and provide better user experience but also are a significant security risk (Ranjan & Haider, 2024). Lack of proper access controls, weak authentication mechanisms, and architecture can trigger a critical data breach that can compromise the privacy of the users and their financial safety (Ranjan and Haider, 2024). One of the most urgent issues that the fintech industry faces is the risk of a data breach (Rathi et al., 2024).

This default interoperability provides so-called weakest-link dynamics, where the security state of the entire financial ecosystem has been endangered by either a weak element or a poorly secured third-party vendor. Even though account aggregators claim that they can provide users with a more robust level of control over their financial data, it would require an exceptionally robust data-protection framework that would provide the necessary level of security. The upsurge in the growth of the fintech sector simultaneously poses regulatory voids and opens the possibility of new-fangled fraud, thus forcing the necessity to constantly regulate and consolidate regulatory frameworks (Shekhar and Sanjogita, 2025). The specified tendencies support the necessity to have high information-security standards and active, joint control over the security of sensitive financial information and systemic stability especially when the country does not have a national data-protection system (Kharbanda and Arora, 2022; Nalluri and Chen, 2024). Technology is a direct operational risk to banks, as well as increasing credit and market risks (D'Souza, 2017).

3.6 FinTech Adoption and Financial Performance of the Banking Sector

The fast-paced adoption of financial technology (FinTech) in the changing digital landscape of the Indian financial ecosystem is one of the most crucial shifts in the operations and strategic context of the banking industry and is the key to the fundamental restructuring of the provision and consumption of financial services (Bhasin and Rajesh, 2021; Singh, 2025). India can now be considered one of the fastest-growing FinTech markets in the world, with notably more success pushing it forward through government-driven digital infrastructure programs like India Stack and broad-based digital transactions (Datta, 2023; Singh, 2025). Available evidence indicates that FinTech adoption has played a very crucial role in ensuring better financial inclusivity, customer experience, cost efficiency, and increase in revenue to banks. Nevertheless, they also come with a list of new challenges connected with the systemic risk and financial stability (Panda et al., 2023; Ravirajan and Shanmugam, 2023). In this line, this part will analyze the effect of FinTech adoption in improving the financial performance of a bank in terms of its efficiency and profitability, as well as co-ordinating with the competitive forces, the development of revenue structures and trade-offs of risk (Singh et al., 2021; Syed et al., 2024). It is also discussed that the positive performance provided by FinTech is associated with the introduction of system-wide consequences, as despite the enhancement of operational efficiencies and robustness through digitalization, there is a risk that the systemic frailty of the banking sector could also be exacerbated by digitalization, which increases operational and cyber risks (Chouhan et al., 2023; Elekdag et al., 2025).

3.6.1 FinTech Adoption and Bank Efficiency and Profitability

The cost efficiency, volume of transactions, fee-based earnings as well as operating margins are greatly influenced by the implementation of financial technology (FinTech) in the Indian banking sector. The growth of online channels, automation of processes, and payment systems built on the platform, that is, the Unified Payments Interface (UPI) in the first place, have simplified banking activities and helped to decrease the cost-to-income ratio (Saroy et al., 2023; Singh et al., 2021). Several studies record that FinTech adoption and bank profitability have been in a positive fashion due to personalized digital services, greater customer engagement, and an expanded reach to financial services (Singh et al., 2021; Syed et al., 2024). Nevertheless, the literature also includes the opposite evidence and indicators, that is, more active competition by FinTech companies along with other digital natives can not only squeeze the profit margin of traditional banks but also cause an expansion of operational and technological risk (Syed et al., 2024). Noteworthy, the size of these impacts differs between institutions. Smaller and cooperative banks can attain relatively greater benefits of efficiency and profitability related to their agility in the organizational context and accelerated access to technological innovation but have an increased susceptibility to greater vulnerability because of the paucity of financial and technological resources than bigger banks, which are also systemically relevant (Ky et al., 2025).

3.6.2 Competitive Dynamics, Revenue Models, and Risk Trade-offs

The application of FinTech has fundamentally changed the competitive dynamics in the Indian banking sector by putting additional pressure on newcomers in the market and digital-first financial solutions that impact customer acquisition, pricing schemes, and differentiation of services (Chouhan et al., 2023; Syed et al., 2024).

This dynamic environment has catalyzed a structural transformation in response to this movement by the shift to less conventional interest-based income and more transaction-based and platform-linked compensation systems with banks becoming more and more partners with FinTech companies to provide more customer-focused and technology-enabled products (Chouhan et al., 2023; Karthika et al., 2022; Venkatachalam, 2020). Although such strategic realignment improves competitiveness and revenue diversification, it brings about invaluable risk trade-offs. It increases the operational risks, fraud risks, and reliance on third-party financial technology vendors in banks as new hybrid operations, speed, and digital scalability agendas are sought after (Syed et al., 2024). In turn, when successful integration of FinTech could enhance the competitive stance of banks, it also brings a problem where they have more difficulty maintaining financial stability during the rapid technological change and changing anticipations of the market (Chouhan et al., 2023).

3.6.3 System-Level Financial Performance and Stability Implications

The performance gains brought about by FinTech improvements at the bank level imply critical systematic impacts, especially in improving financial inclusion, scalability and resilience across the Indian financial ecosystem (Abouraia and Morsey, 2020; Kamal et al., 2025; Kushwaha and Malpani, 2025). The advocacy of digital payment, the growth of mobile financial structure penetration and the growth of FinTech-enabled infrastructure has enabled a significant enhancement of access to formal financial services particularly in rural and underserved areas as well as forming a part of the diminution of structural inequality like the gender gap in financial inclusion (Kushwaha & Malpani, 2025). These efficiency and outreach benefits are, however, accompanied by amplified systemic susceptibilities, in the first place, measures of augmented operational and cyber risks (D'Souza, 2017). Increased interconnectedness and dependence on digital platforms are the key components of performance improvement but posts hoc, increase the exposure of the financial system to cyber threats and technology shocks. This binary argument supports the overarching point that the chapter puts forward that digitalization in banking is simultaneously increasing efficiency and inclusion, increasing systemic risk and vulnerability.

3.7 Regional and Corridor-Based Clustering of Financial Cybercrime

The tendency towards financial cybercrime being concentrated in regions can also be seen in India, as it is practiced in the states and in the urban centres where the digitalisation process is advancing faster than ever before, seemingly exceeding the awareness of cybersecurity and the development of the infrastructure. State-specific granular, region-level data on concentrations of financial fraud are scarce in official threat reports as well as in popular media; however, studies also reveal an absence of state-specific differences in digital access, capacity, and ability to facilitate digitalisation (Parsheera, 2022). These inequalities indicate that the areas that have different levels of digital preparedness, including Tier 2 and Tier 3 urban centers and developed digital hubs are an excellent opportunity to scammers. Such locations are also vulnerable to direct attacks and exploitation where small traders and informal businesses are more susceptible to the loss of the digital payment system because of the lack of cybersecurity tools and education (Baradwaj, 2023). Moreover, the prevalence and increased exposure to cybercrime of people and organisations have been made worse by the extensive use of e-commerce and online payment systems (Tripathy, 2025). An example of this is that Karnataka alone documented over 8,600 cases of cybercrime, in the first seven months of 2025, highlighting the fact that regional disparities in the use of these digital tools have a direct impact on the formation of local clusters of risks (Times of India).

3.8 From Transactional Fraud to Systemic Financial Risk: Operational Indicators

One of the conceptual revaluations of financial cybercrime has been salient in understanding it as a channel of systemic financial risk as opposed to being a combination of disaggregated transactional frauds. Cyber-attacks are not merely a single event anymore, as they can quickly spread throughout the interconnected financial system, hence creating the risk of contagion (Ros, 2020). Systemic cyber risk is particularly severe in situations of increased financial stress when already existing vulnerabilities are increased (Kumar & Rao, 2024). Under such dynamics, the threat to financial stability is high, and it can result in insolvency cascades and extreme market shocks (Ali, 2020; Bhattacharya, 2024).

This theoretical shift is also connected with the evolution of the hacker strategies; hackers now are not just primitive brute-force attacks, but better behavioural attacks and platform-specific system of fraud (Kodali, 2025). This tendency is indicated by an increase in the popularity of social engineering attacks, phishing, and ransomware in India, which can be viewed as a sign of transition to less technical and more human-psychological adventures, as well as platform design as an exploitation platform (Dahiya, 2023; Tripathy, 2025). The scope of attack vectors is more focused, and multifaceted with the rising rate of digital adoption and needs to be responded to in an adaptive, sophisticated, and proactive manner (Bhattacharya, 2024; Mehta, 2024).

Financial cybercrime is one of the long-term risks besides the direct loss of funds as it compromises the trust of the users towards the authenticity of online transactions and payment systems while even questioning the credibility of financial institutions (Khan et al., 2023). This loss of trust may affect investment behaviour and reduce consumer confidence and eventually disrupt the macroeconomic equilibrium (Khan et al., 2023; Parmar, 2024). In line with this, cybersecurity is no longer a technical issue of concern but a macro-prudential need to ensure the financial reliability, systemic stability, and sustainability of the Indian digital economy in the long run (Chakraborty and Tiwari, 2025; Sharma et al., 2024).

a) Velocity–Detection Mismatch Indicators

Real-time payment systems frequently have a faster processing rate than fraud detection systems (Mayo, 2024; Sebastian, 2025). Velocitydetection indicators look at the difference between the wholeness of the moment of transaction completion and the lapse time needed to detect and respond to institutional fraud. A large ratio of the speed of transactions to detection latency indicates an increased systemic exposure because a fraudulent transaction can be processed, and the money is inaccessible to control. This discrepancy makes it easy to steal funds quickly and avoid the use of post hoc security, which presents a considerable problem of containing losses and preventing contagion.

b) Network Contagion and Correlation Indicators

Systemic cyber risk is a factual issue associated with the connectivity of the digital payment ecosystem. Network contagion and correlation measure targets the relationship between incident correlation of inter-payment service providers. This involves the detection of concomitant spikes in fraud detection across different banks or UPI apps, or shared mule account recurrence across bank accounts. These types of correlated failures indicate that they are common vulnerabilities, shared attackers, or coherent criminal campaigns that can spread sandwiches in the digital payments network within a short time (Awiszus et al., 2023; Hillairet et al., 2022).

c) Mule-Network Density Proxies

Mule networks constitute the important backbone of financial cybercrime by facilitating the laundering and disguising of illegal finance. The density of mule-networks is measured using mule-network density proxies. Such crucial proxies as the number of intermediary accounts used in a regular fraud event, and the average hop length, which is the number of transfers that money made before it was forced outside of the trackable financial system, are examples. Highly interconnected mule networks greatly hamper the processes of recovery and enforcement by adding several layers of obfuscation and therefore complicate tracing and freezing as well as find money processes (Shadrooh and Norevik, 2024; Tariq and Hassani, 2023).

d) Recovery and Containment Effectiveness Indicators

Systemic resilience primarily rests on the ability of the financial system to bounce back and limit cyber-attacks. Indicators on recovery and containment effectively monitor the conceptual parameters of time-to-freeze illicit funds, potential to recover qualitatively, and time-to-resolve complaints. The recurrent sutility of delayed freeze, low recovery opportunities, or staying with the resolved dispute are all persistent signatures of weakness in the system eroding public confidence and are harbingers of structural vulnerability of shock-absorbing and shock-recovering capacity (Ross et al., 2019).

e) User–System Stress Signals

In addition to technical indicators, user behavior and sentiment are some of the crucial signals of stress within the system. Stress indicators (that a user is under stress alert) to the system involve customer complaint increases that do not correlate with the amount or frequency of transactions. Such indicators of behavior are an indication of fading belief and confidence in the digital payment ecosystem, and there may be systemic effects. The reduction in adoption, movement toward less efficient payment mechanisms and overall contraction of the digital economy (negative effects when applied by financial inclusion and stability targets) may occur as users feel less secure and less trusting in payment systems and incur lower costs, leading to decreased use, lower efficiency, and reduced payability rates (Alamoudi et al., 2025; Armantier et al., 2021; Bijlsma et al., 2022)

These indicators classes are not meant to be prescriptive metrics of a specific number limit, but rather diagnostic and supervisory tools to be used in interpreting the shape of systemic cyber risk in digital payment systems. They will help regulators, payment system operators and other stakeholders understand latent systemic vulnerabilities to co-ordinate institutional responses to the increasing resilience of the digitizing payments environment in India.

4. FINANCIAL CYBERSECURITY ARCHITECTURE AND INSTITUTIONAL CAPACITY IN INDIA

The fast pace of the Indian digital financial ecosystem development demands the robust and multi-layered cybersecurity infrastructures. They are accompanied with the robust institutional capability to safeguard financial stability and deal with the systemic risk. This part puts the financial cybersecurity of India in perspective not simply as a technical IT challenge, but a financial stability/systemic risk challenge. This is how regulatory framework, operational processes, and technological investments of the nation are all integrated to explain the resilience of the Indian digital financial system.

4.1 Regulatory and Supervisory Scaffolding

The Reserve Bank of India is central in the creation of the cybersecurity and fraud-risk management framework of the Indian financial industry. It has a mandate on commercial banks, non-banking financial companies, and payment system operators (Rajput, 2024). The RBI has been shifting its cybersecurity policy to a more system-wide risk-containment approach, which has been developed not as a compliance model, but as an entity-level approach, acknowledging cyber threats as one of the significant operational risks to the payment system with potential systemic consequences on financial stability (Iglesias-Rodriguez, 2025; Resano, 2022).

This regulatory culture is clearly demonstrated in the supervisory communications of RBI, which are increasingly categorizing cyber incidents as operational risk with systemic spillover potential, and not as isolated compliance violations. According to RBI Financial Stability Reports, repeatedly, the cyber risks to payment systems, unless addressed, may impair the market confidence and interfere with financial intermediation, especially in real-time digital payment settings (Reserve Bank of India, 2023; Reserve Bank of India, 2024).

The most significant regulatory interventions would be the release of extensive fraud-risk management guidelines and the enhancement of awareness efforts that would educate users on the best practices of digital-banking to reduce user-side vulnerabilities (Chakraborty and Tiwari, 2025). Multi-factor authentication and transaction limits are authentication requirements that are required to enhance the security of digital payments. Indicatively, the Master Directions on Cyber Resilience and Digital Payment Security Controls to Non-bank Payment System Operators, issued by the RBI on July 30, 2024, under Section 18 of the Payment and Settlement Systems Act, 2007 (Reserve Bank of India, 2024), provide a sound Business Continuity Planning framework to maintain the critical functions even in the unfavorable operation conditions (Rajput, 2024). This resilience and continuity focus is based on the transition to protecting the integrity of the whole ecosystem instead of the individual entities in isolation (Bhattacharya, 2024). An overview of the key regulatory frameworks and supervisory directives shaping financial cybersecurity in India is presented in Table 2.

Table 2. Key Regulatory Frameworks and Directives Governing Financial Cybersecurity in India

RBI Directive/Framework	Issuing Authority	Primary Focus	Objective/Impact
Master Directions on Cyber Resilience and Digital Payment Security Controls of Non-Bank Payment System Operators.	RBI	Fraud risk and comprehensive cyber-security of payment system operators.	Increase cyber resilience, business continuity, and critical payment functionality, which is a transition to system-wide risk containment (Rajput, 2024).
Guidelines on Limiting Liability of Customer in Unauthorized Electronic Banking Transactions.	RBI	Electronic transactions, customer protection and liability allocation	Establish the liability of the customer in situations of unauthorized transactions and, thus, build trust in digital payments and assign the responsibility to the banks in some cases of fraud (D'Souza, 2017).
Fraud Risk Management Framework in Regulated Entities	RBI	Digital payment frauds proactive identification, prevention, detection, and reporting.	Enhance the financial entities security stance against the changing typologies of frauds, minimize financial losses, and facilitate a safe digital payment environment (D'Souza, 2017).
Authentication Norms (e.g., Multi-Factor Authentication)	RBI	Requirement of increased security measures in online transactions	Protect customer purchases, ensure unauthorized access to accounts, and minimize the level of fraud in different digital platforms, which is often in line with a multi-level authentication strategy (Hussain & Rafi, 2023).

Source: Authors' Own Compilation of various Sources

4.2 Role of National Payment Infrastructure Operators

National Payments Corporation of India (NPCI) is the foundation of the Indian digital payment system, with such vital platforms as UPI, IMPS, and RuPay existing there (Kumari, 2025; Ramesh et al., 2020). The cybersecurity threat posed by NPCI is severe, considering that real-time payment systems have an implicit trade-off between speed and security. Despite its convenience and efficiency in real-time, this very feature leaves users vulnerable to fast and in most cases irrevocable fraud (Kaur et al., 2023; Sharma et al., 2024).

UPI architecture security research indicates that the most common vulnerability is user behaviour-based vulnerability, especially social-engineering vulnerability, rather than systemic vulnerability (Kaur et al., 2023; Kumar et al., 2020). The risk centralization of these critical payment rails implies that any successful attack or system vulnerability would have a far-reaching effect on the financial stability of the country. Considering that NPCI systems form the basis of the payment infrastructure in India, their high level of availability, security, and integrity are the top priorities, and the cybersecurity position of NPCI is identified as a national financial security need (Ramesh et al., 2020).

4.3 Institutional Layers of Fraud Reporting and Redressal

India has set up multi-level institutional framework of the reporting and redressing of fraud; however, the operational efficiency is yet to be achieved fully. At the lowest level, banking institutions must have formal grievance-redressal through the clientele. Moreover, there exists the National Cyber Crime Reporting Portal (https://cybercrimegov.in), a centralised site where the citizens can report cybercrimes, including financial frauds (Asness et al., 2015; Tripathy, 2025). In addition, dedicated centres like the Cyber Fraud Coordination Centre or the Indian Cybercrime Coordination Centre (I4C) are essential in the coordination of the national response, facilitate investigations, and study the new trends in cybercrime (D'Souza, 2017). The distribution of roles and responsibilities across regulatory, infrastructural, institutional, and enforcement actors is outlined in Table 3.

Table 3. Institutional Roles in India's Financial Cybersecurity Architecture

Institution	Primary Role in Cybersecurity Architecture	Functional Responsibilities	Key Activities
Reserve Bank of India	Regulator & Supervisor	sets the policy, guidelines and standards of fraud prevention, cyber-security, and the resilience of financial entities	sets the master directions, conducts audit, sets authenticity norms and provides systemic regulation
NPCI	National Payment Infrastructure Operator	operates and maintains important payment rails, real-time transaction processing	fraud detection algorithms, infrastructure security and dispute management on a network level
Commercial Banks / NBFCs	Entity-level Enforcement & First Response	Before approving RBI guidelines, facilitating fraud detection, handling and addressing customer complaints and reporting their findings to the National Cyber Crime Reporting Portal (NCRP) or RBI	oversee transactions, authenticating customers, responding to incidents, and conducting fraud investigations

continued on following page

Table 3. Continued

Institution	Primary Role in Cybersecurity Architecture	Functional Responsibilities	Key Activities
Law Enforcement Agencies	Investigation & Prosecution	investigate cybercrimes, arrest suspects, conduct forensic tests, interact with financial institutions	file FIRs, collect intelligence, provide multijurisdictional cooperation and convict criminals
NCRP / I4C	National Coordination & Reporting	Single point of reporting on cybercrime, intelligence sharing and inter-agency coordination.	Accepting complaints from the people, data collection and coordinating inter-agency communication.

Source: Authors' Own Compilation of various Sources

4.4 Legal and Liability Constraints in Cyber Fraud Mitigation

The fast growth of real time digital payment systems in India especially UPI has enhanced the risks of cyber fraud which is further exacerbated by the current legal and liability frameworks. Technical detection capabilities have increased, but procedural and legal friction can slow down the process of containment, recovery and inter-institutional coordination, thus increasing systemic cyber risk.

Delay in Settling Liabilities and Resolving Liabilities

On the policy level, the Reserve Bank of India has provided instructions to standardize liability distribution, customer protection and turnaround time of unauthorized transactions in digital payments (D'Souza, 2017; Kumar et al., 2022). But in reality, it is still time consuming when it comes to establishing liability among various banks and intermediaries. Although the mechanisms of online dispute resolutions are in place and the turnaround time limits are set, the resolution of the grievances may take several weeks before it gets out of control and reaches the Ombudsman level. Such time lag between the actual payment of funds in real-time and the slow process of liability adjudication permits the relocation of fraudulent funds to be permanently done before corrective measures can be implemented.

Enforcement and Jurisdictional Frictions

Procedural delays and jurisdictional ambiguity pinch the enforcement of cyber fraud in India. The system of reporting is still not unified on both local police stations and cybercrime cells, which fosters underreporting and late investigation

(Rao, 2019). Cases of cybercrime also cut across numerous legal structures, such as the Information Technology Act, 2000, and the Criminal Procedure Code, 1973, making coordination of enforcement difficult (Jain, and Sonowal, 2025). Such legal procedures are run on schedules that are radically outpaced by the pace and irreversibility of real-time digital payments, disabling recovery opportunities.

Restriction of Data-Sharing and Legal Ambiguity

Cyber risk mitigation by systemic means needs prompt inter-institutional data sharing, which is limited by privacy regulations and no explicit safe-harbor provisions in proactive information sharing. Finance Financial institutions tend to share data conservatively because of the fear of regulatory and legal vulnerabilities, despite the potentially more effective security of the system-wide cooperation (Awosika et al., 2024; Chatzigiannis et al., 2023). This ambiguity in the law gives precedence to compliance over speedy containment, and undermines group defences against organized fraud.

Altogether, the Indian legal and liability system is supposed to protect the users of digital payments, but the inability to promptly resolve liability issues, the bottlenecks of enforcement, and the lack of a data sharing system slow the systemic response to cyber fraud. Such frictions allow the localized incidences to trigger system-wide vulnerabilities, which are eroding trust and the resilience of the digital payment ecosystem.

4.5 Challenges in Forensic Integration and Payment-Data Analysis

Financial cybercrime on the Internet presents unique investigative issues, especially combining digital-forensics equipment with transactional information and determining the flow of cross-platform funds. A good example of the complexities is the development of Fintech forensics as a sub-discipline (Nikkel, 2020). Table 4 below summarizes the major operational and institutional challenges constraining effective mitigation of financial cybercrimes.

Table 4. Operational and Institutional Challenges in Financial Cyberfraud Mitigation

Challenge Area	Description	Contributing Factors	Systemic Implication
Limited Reversal Windows	Real-time payment systems provide minimal or no time to reverse fraudulent transactions.	Real-time and finality of payment and payment rail design to settle instantly.	Reduced recovery rates among the victims, higher financial loss, and loss of confidence in the digital payment systems (Mayo et al., 2024).
Coordination Failures	Absence of smooth information exchange and action among different actors (originating/receiving banks, PSPs, fintechs).	Fragmented financial ecosystem, differing protocols, lack of standardized data exchange mechanisms, commercial sensitivities.	Slow reaction to fraud and inability to freeze/recall funds in an efficient way, which leads to a quick drainage of funds (Sharma et al., 2024).
Jurisdictional Overlaps	The uncertainties in the roles and responsibilities of various law enforcement and regulatory agencies.	Complex regulatory landscape, absence of demarcation of authority and the dynamic nature of cybercrime.	Ineffective investigations, prosecution issues, delays in justice and the possibility of cases going through loopholes (Gupta & Gupta, 2025).
Data-Sharing Constraints	Legal, technical, and commercial obstacles to the sharing of vital data to help in fraud detection and prevention.	Privacy policies (which are misunderstood most of the time), technical incompatibilities, competition, and distrust between parties.	Incomplete intelligence picture, difficulty in tracing cross-platform fund movements, hindering forensic analysis (Khan et al., 2023)
Asymmetric Capabilities	High technological infrastructure differences, cyber-security skills, and funds among institutions (large banks vs. small co-ops/ fintechs).	Disparity in the ability to invest, different levels of regulatory compliance, and the lack of resources among smaller players.	Weaknesses in the ecosystem and unequal security of the consumer, thus, taking advantage of less secure entities (Oduro et al., 2025).

Source: Authors' Own Compilation of Sources

5. SYSTEMIC CYBERCRIME MITIGATION FRAMEWORK FOR DIGITAL FINANCE (SCMF-DF)

5.1 Creation and Structure of SCMF-DF

The Systemic Cybercrime Mitigation Framework for Digital Finance (SCMF-DF) is proposed as a structured response to the patterns of financial cybercrime and institutional constraints identified in the earlier sections of this study. The framework is developed through an integrative analytical process that draws on the empirical mapping of fraud typologies, payment-rail vulnerabilities, organised network dynamics, and regional asymmetries discussed in Section 3, alongside the evaluation of regulatory, infrastructural, and enforcement capacities examined in

Section 4. It is developed to relate the sources of cyber risk generation with the current institutional response. It can also deal with the identified gap in prevention, real-time detection, containment, and recovery. The SCMF-DF, as shown in Figure 1 below, is the means of bringing together fragmented cybersecurity initiatives to the coherent, layered structure that would reinforce the resilience in the real-time digital finance ecosystem in India.

Figure 1. SYSTEMIC CYBERCRIME MITIGATION FRAMEWORK FOR DIGITAL FINANCE (SCMF-DF)

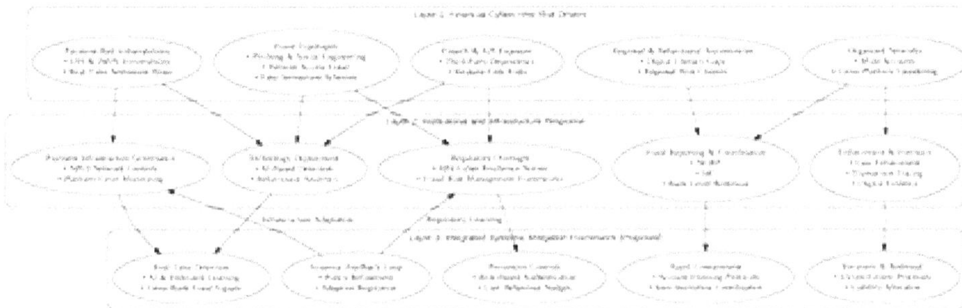

Source: Authors' Ideation

The SCMF-DF Framework suggested is a solution-based reaction to the structural and institutional issues that define the Indian digital financial ecosystem. Instead of perceiving financial cybercrime as a series of individualized fraudulent occurrences, the framework is based on the argument of cyber threats working as longstanding risk vectors, within interdependent payment systems, platform-based financial services, and behavioural interfaces. This stance is indicative of an emerging academic agreement that real time digital finance increases efficiency and vulnerability and needs governance processes that transcend the compliance at the entity level. The framework hence incorporates the source of risks, institutional reactions, and mitigation trails into a single structure that harmonises the goals of operational security and financial stability.

The initial level of the framework entails the main risk factors of financial cybercrime. These are changing types of fraud, real-time payment rail vulnerabilities, organised criminal networks, fintech interoperability exposures, and regional and behavioural asymmetries. The various elements are indicative of a separate but connected location of systemic exposure. Types of fraudulent activities, including phishing, social engineering and remote-access attacks, also deploy the behaviour of users instead of technical systems weaknesses, whereas payment rail vulnerabilities exist due to transaction velocity and irreversibility. These mule networks also increase risk, as they promote the risk of off the record transactions being trailed across platforms, whereas the integration of fintech creates weakest-link dynamics through third-party dependencies. Regional and behavioural asymmetries point to the ways that unequal digital literacy and readiness generate spatial concentrations of vulnerability. All these layers point to the fact that the creation of risks in the digital finance is a multidimensional phenomenon that cannot be dealt with by limited technical actions only.

The second layer is concerned with institutional and infrastructural responses that mediate these risks at present. The foundation of the cybersecurity architecture in India is regulatory control directing the Reserve Bank of India, governance by national payment infrastructure operators, institutional reporting, enforcement, and forensic processes, and the use of technology. Nonetheless, the framework acknowledges the fact that such responses work within the structural limitations. Cyber risk is slowly emerging as a systemic risk in regulatory frameworks, but there is operational fragmentation between institutions. Payment infrastructure governance is more focused on the availability and scale commonly at the expense of recoverability. The reporting systems of fraud are still reactive, and the enforcement and forensic tools are also not executing the money flows in real-time and cross-platform laundering. When applied to detection, the use of technology and AI, in particular, has potentials that are yet to be realised by the institutions. This layer thus introduces the issue of conflict between the intention of regulations and reality of operations, the determiner of success of cyber risk management.

The third level will be the basic value addition of the framework since it would provide a coordinated mitigation framework. The first one is referred to as preventive controls and it is concerned with risk-based authentication, user focus design intervention and behavioural nudge that causes an individual less susceptible to manipulation. This is preceded by real-time detection systems which are grounded on advanced analytics, machine learning and federated models that facilitate cross-institutional threat intelligence without tampering with data confidentiality. Rapid containment strategies address the time pressure of the digital fraud that is urgent due to the fact that the coordinated account freeze and transaction control across the banks and payment systems can be implemented. Recovery and redressal mechanisms are put as imperative in order to win back the lost trust, victim-centric process, and get a deeper insight into the distribution of liability. All these factors can turn cybersecurity into a more aggressive stance as opposed to a defensive stance.

The other significant feature of the framework is that it possesses a systemic feedback loop, which links the outcomes of mitigation with regulatory and infrastructural adjustment. This form of feedback is indicative of the realization that financial cybercrime is changing at a higher rate than fixed policy tools. The experience of detection failures, bottlenecks in the recovery, and enforcement difficulties contribute to the regulation optimisation and infrastructure redesign. An adaptive loop like this one assists in sustaining learning within institutions and aligning the priorities of supervisors with the patterns of emerging threats. The model incorporates feedback mechanism to respond to the environment in a non-prescriptive fashion by facilitating an iterative improvement process. This is especially applicable in a setting where there is rapid technological change and adaptive behaviour by perpetrators of fraud.

In general, the framework promotes a change in the conceptualisation of the prevention of financial cybercrime in digital economies. It shifts the discussion of the management of reactive fraud to the management of systemic resilience which acknowledges that technology, institutions and user behaviour all are co-producers of trust, stability and sustainability of digital finance. To the policymakers, the framework provides a systematic prism through which to synchronize regulation, infrastructure regulation and enforcement coordination. In the case of financial institutions, it gives them a guide on how to incorporate prevention, detection, and recovery in real time operational constraints. On a larger scale, the structure makes cybersecurity a financial security activity, which supports the point of view that the security of digital payments cannot be discussed outside the context of the integrity of the broader economic system.

5.2 Operationalizing SCMF-DF With Roles and Responsibilities, Implementation Steps, and Measurable KPIs

To respond to calls for practical applicability, the SCMF-DF framework is further operationalised by specifying institutional roles, phased implementation steps, and measurable performance indicators. Rather than prescribing a rigid execution model, this operational layer is intended to guide regulators, financial institutions, and payment ecosystem actors in translating the framework into practice. The operationalisation clarifies accountability, sequencing, and evaluation mechanisms, thereby enhancing the framework's relevance for policy design, supervisory oversight, and organisational adoption within India's digital financial ecosystem.

Table 5. Operationalisation of the SCMF-DF Framework

Framework Component	Key Actors & Responsibilities	Implementation Steps	Illustrative KPIs
Financial cybercrime pattern monitoring	Regulators monitor trends; banks and PSPs report incidents; payment operators aggregate transaction data	Standardise fraud reporting formats, integrate complaint and transaction datasets, periodic pattern analysis	Fraud incidence rate, value of losses per channel, time to fraud detection
Institutional control mechanisms	Banks and fintechs implement controls; regulators supervise compliance; payment networks enforce standards	Upgrade authentication rules, deploy real-time monitoring, conduct periodic control audits	False-positive rate, authentication success rate, compliance audit scores
Exposure and concentration management	Regulators assess systemic exposure; institutions map product and partner risks	Identify high-risk products and partners, set exposure thresholds, conduct stress scenarios	Concentration index, exposure per product, recovery ratio
Incident response and recovery	Banks execute response; PSPs coordinate reversals; regulators oversee systemic events	Define escalation protocols, improve rollback windows, simulate cyber-fraud drills	Mean time to resolution, recovery percentage, customer grievance closure time

Source: Authors' Own Conceptualization

6. DISCUSSION AND IMPLICATIONS

6.1 Discussion

The results of the current paper confirm that financial cybercriminals in India could no longer be represented sufficiently in terms of individual fraud incidents or an occasional security malfunction (Balabantaray, 2024). Rather, it is indicative of an institutionalised risk environment caused by the interplay between real-time payment systems, platform-based financial services, behavioural vulnerabilities and piecemeal organisational reactions (George, 2024). As the empirical patterns that were mapped out in the previous section expose, speed, scale, and interoperability as the attributes that make the digital finance ecosystem in India efficient are also the factors that increase the susceptibility to cyber-enabled financial crime (Balabantaray, 2024). This supports the claims regarding the general literature on digital financial innovation, which suggests that it tends to move faster than the development of the related governance and risk-management frameworks (Datta et al., 2020).

One of the main implications of the analysis is the role of behavioural exploitation in the modern financial cybercrime. Although technical risks are present, the prevailing types of frauds are based on social engineering, manipulation of trust, and cognitive differences between users and attackers (Wang et al., 2021). This changes the analytical focus on a more technological protection toward a more socio-technical concept of risk. The problem of payment systems like UPI is not that they are not secure, but the nature of their design combines with the human decision-making process under time pressure, a lack of information, and perceived authority (Pal et al., 2020). The result of this interaction is systemic exposure which cannot be addressed only by stepwise technical solutions.

The institutional analysis also shows that the regulatory acceptance of the cyber risk as a systemic risk has been better enhanced than their coordination in the working sector of the financial ecosystem (Ng and Kwok, 2017; Peihani, 2022). Although the supervisory frameworks still redefine cybersecurity as an operational and financial stability issue, recovery, reversal, and enforcement still have practical constraints (Peihani, 2022). The structures of real-time settlement restrain the possibilities of intervening after the transaction and institutional fragmentation restrains the possibilities to disseminate information promptly and act as a coherent force. The existence of such gaps provides room within which the fraud losses can barely be recouped, further reinforcing the distrust towards the digital finance. One of such challenges is that the mule-account networks persist, and they exploit the institutional and jurisdictional discontinuities to obscure the illicit transfers of money.

It is on this basis that the suggested Systemic Cybercrime Mitigation Framework of Digital Finance (SCMF-DF) offers a structured remedy, which is the best in terms of development of risks and institutional capacity and remedial avenues. The stratification of the framework is an empirical specificity of the fact that the dangers of cybercrime are realized concurrently on various levels and, therefore, there is a need to treat them as a complex. Going by the fact that a feedback loop is involved, cybercrime mitigation is an adaptive response, and not a pre-policies effect. This is a direct response to the evolutional form of digital frauds which the thieves keep varying their strategies, owing to regulatory and technological interference. SCMF-DF supports a resilience approach within the framework through incorporating learning and changeability into fast-evolving digital payment environments.

6.2 Implications

The key academic and practical implications derived from the study's findings and the proposed framework are summarised in Table 6 below.

Table 6. Academic and Practical Implications of the Study

Dimension	Implications
Academic Implications	• Moves financial cybercrime from the balance sheet as pervasive and structural risks within digital finance systems as opposed to incidental phrases. • Combines knowledge of cybersecurity, digital payments, financial regulation, and institutional governance and overcomes the lack of fragmentation in the current literature. • Shows conceptual and thematic synthesis as valuable in analyzing swiftly changing digital threats where only primary data are accessible. • Places less emphasis on technologies in explanation and more emphasis on socio-technical and behavioral aspects of cybercrime. • Makes a conceptual foundation of comparative and cross-country studies of the systemic cyber risks of digital payment systems.
Practical Implications	• It illuminates the necessity of regulators to conform cybersecurity regulations to financial stability and payment systems regulation. • urges financial institutions and payment service providers to build prevention, detection, containment and recovery controls into a real-time operation setting. • Focusses on behavioral risk control such as user-facing controls and risk-based authentication as a fundamental part of cybersecurity policy. • Assist law enforcers and regulatory authorities to deal with mule-account networks and cross-platform transfer of funds via coordinated institutional initiatives. • Makes the significance of adaptive regulation and lifelong institutional learning to address a changing cybercrime specification.

Source: Authors' Own Ideation

7. CONCLUSION AND SCOPE FOR FUTURE WORK

The key idea of the paper is that the topic of financial cybercrime should be discussed as the issue of governance, which is the result of co-evolution of technology, institutions, and user behaviour. The example of India shows that the rapid digital growth could transform the time of decision-making into a shorter period, redistribute the responsibility between different participants, and blur the established boundaries between the threats to the operations, consumer protection, and financial security. The use of cybercrime within such a setting does not merely exploit the infirmities but goes out of its way to recast the conditions whereby the market of trust, accountability and legitimacy within the financial systems will be constructed in the premises of the weaknesses. To be socially viable and institutionally sound, it is imperative for digital finance to be cognizant of this change.

The most important input to this work is the revitalization of the perception of mitigation as a dynamic ability, rather than regulated controls. The SCM-DF paradigm proposed by this study implicitly points out at the fault of the linear approaches to risk management that assume the predictability of threats and that have articulated institutional roles. Instead, it results in logic of governance in which prevention, response, and learning is continuously reformulated according to the current trends of fraud practices. It is not just impacting cybersecurity. It hypothesizes that digital financial systems progressively become within a more reflexive regime and therefore become shock resistant and they can re-tune rules and redistribute responsibilities without undermining usability or inclusion. This perspective would give cybersecurity its place in overall conversation of resilience, versatility, and managing the systemic systems of complex socio-technical systems.

Various research potentials are available in future research. One of the avenues is an empirical study of the organizational alignment between institutional arrangements and the success of systemic mitigation of cybercrime. Comparative studies of cross-country or payment systems in different countries or regions might aid in illuminating the relationship between regulatory coordination, payment architecture design or emphasis of enforcement approaches and resilience. The other trend is of behavioral aspect of digital fraud. Additional participation in behavioral economics and cognitive psychology would benefit the information regarding risk perception of users in digital context, authority displays and urgency perception in digital context, and definition of more effective intervention development. Moreover, the accessibility of the data will also possibly give opportunity to other researchers in future to model dynamics in transactions at transaction level and simulate the occurrence of contagion and stress conditions in the real time payment networks.

Systemic cybersecurity normative and ethical considerations may also receive further study in additional research. As the financial institutions are increasingly interested in automated surveillance, behavioral analytics as well as artificial intelligence, transparency, accountability, and proportionality become questioned. An important follow-up of this work is to explore how the objectives of security can be complemented with the objectives of privacy, fairness and autonomy of users. Finally, any scholar can always take a chance to examine the progress of adaptive structures such as the one proposed here, particularly the influence of feedback process on learning of regulation and the institutional reform over time. All these presuppose that research of financial cybercrime ought to continue moving beyond incident studies to a deeper study of governance, behaviour, and system design in mediated economies using digital tools.

REFERENCES

Abouraia, M. K., & Al Morsey, R. M. (2020). Analyzing the impact of fintech adoption on financial inclusion and economic development: A data-driven approach. [TURCOMAT]. *Turkish Journal of Computer and Mathematics Education, 11*(1), 973–984. DOI: 10.61841/turcomat.v11i1.14257

Adams, J., Hillier-Brown, F. C., Moore, H. J., Lake, A. A., Araujo-Soares, V., White, M., & Summerbell, C. (2016). Searching and synthesising 'grey literature' and 'grey information' in public health: Critical reflections on three case studies. *Systematic Reviews, 5*(1), 164. DOI: 10.1186/s13643-016-0337-y

Alamoudi, H., Glavee-Geo, R., Alharthi, M., Doszhan, R., & Suyunchaliyeva, M. M. (2025). Exploring trust and outcome expectancy in FinTech digital payments: Insights from the stimulus-organism-response model. *International Journal of Bank Marketing, 43*(4), 897–919. DOI: 10.1108/IJBM-04-2024-0252

Ali, S. E. A., Lai, F.-W., & Hassan, R. (2020). Socio-economic factors on sector-wide systematic risk of information security breaches: Conceptual framework. In Othman, N. S., Jaaffar, A. H. B., Harun, N. H. B., Buniamin, S. B., Mohamad, N. E. A. B., Ali, I. B. M., Razali, N. H. B. A., & Hashim, S. L. B. M. (Eds.), *Driving sustainability through business-technology synergy. European Proceedings of Social and Behavioural Sciences (EpSBS).*, DOI: 10.15405/epsbs.2020.12.05.54

Altameemi, Y., & Altamimi, M. (2023). Thematic Analysis: A Corpus-Based Method for Understanding Themes/Topics of a Corpus through a Classification Process Using Long Short-Term Memory (LSTM). *Applied Sciences (Basel, Switzerland), 13*(5), 3308. DOI: 10.3390/app13053308

Armantier, O., Doerr, S., Frost, J., Fuster, A., & Shue, K. (2021). Whom do consumers trust with their data? *US survey evidence* (No. 42). Bank for International Settlements.

Asness, C. S., Frazzini, A., Israel, R., & Moskowitz, T. J. (2015). Fact, fiction, and value investing. *Journal of Portfolio Management, 42*(1), 34–52. Advance online publication. DOI: 10.3905/jpm.2015.42.1.034

Awiszus, K., Knispel, T., Penner, I., Svindland, G., Voß, A., & Weber, S. (2023). Modeling and pricing cyber insurance: Idiosyncratic, systematic, and systemic risks. *European Actuarial Journal, 13*(1), 1–53. DOI: 10.1007/s13385-023-00341-9

Awosika, T., Shukla, R. M., & Pranggono, B. (2024). Transparency and privacy: The role of explainable ai and federated learning in financial fraud detection. *IEEE Access : Practical Innovations, Open Solutions*, *12*, 64551–64560. DOI: 10.1109/ACCESS.2024.3394528

Balabantaray, S. R. (2024). Examining the Impact of Cyber Fraud on Indian Society: An Assessment of the Potential Damage. In Kaur, G., Dalei, N. N., Mahapatra, S. K., & Kandpal, V. (Eds.), *Cybersecurity, Law, and Economics* (pp. 38–50). Routledge. DOI: 10.4324/9781003517290-5

Baradwaj, V. (2023). *UPI adoption and usage patterns by small merchants: A study*. Research Archive of Rising Scholars., DOI: 10.58445/rars.545

Benzies, K. M., Premji, S., Hayden, K. A., & Serrett, K. (2006). State-of-the-Evidence Reviews: Advantages and Challenges of Including Grey Literature. *Worldviews on Evidence-Based Nursing*, *3*(2), 55–61. DOI: 10.1111/j.1741-6787.2006.00051.x

Bhadra, S., & Singh, K. N. (2024). Ponzi scheme like investment schemes in India–causes, impact and solution. *Journal of Money Laundering Control*, *27*(2), 348–362. DOI: 10.1108/JMLC-02-2023-0040

Bhasin, N. K., & Rajesh, A. (2021). Impact of E-collaboration between Indian banks and fintech companies for digital banking and new emerging technologies. [IJeC]. *International Journal of e-Collaboration*, *17*(1), 15–35. DOI: 10.4018/IJeC.2021010102

Bhattacharya, S. (2024). Enhancing Cyber Defenses in Indian Banking Industry. *Available at SSRN* 4924267. https://doi.org/DOI: 10.53739/samvad/2024/v28/173776

Bijlsma, M., van der Cruijsen, C., & Koldijk, J. (2022). Determinants of trust in banks' payment services during COVID: An exploration using daily data. *De Economist*, *170*(2), 231–256. DOI: 10.1007/s10645-022-09405-9

Chakraborty, A., & Tiwari, S. (2025). An analytical study on challenges and gaps in India's cyber security framework. https://doi.org/DOI: 10.22271/27899497.2025.v5.i1a.110

Chandra, D. (2025). Examining the Contours and Challenges of National Cybercrime Reporting Portal in Countering Digital Financial Frauds. *Journal of Victimology and Victim Justice*, *8*(1), 65–83. DOI: 10.1177/25166069241306546

Chatzigiannis, P., Gu, W. C., Raghuraman, S., Rindal, P., & Zamani, M. (2023). Privacy-enhancing technologies for financial data sharing. *arXiv preprint arXiv:2306.10200*. https://doi.org//arXiv.2306.10200DOI: 10.48550

Chouhan, V., Ali, S., Sharma, R. B., & Sharma, A. (2023). The effect of financial technology (Fin-tech) on the conventional banking industry in India. *International Journal of Innovative Research and Scientific Studies*, *6*(3), 538–544. DOI: 10.53894/ijirss.v6i3.1578

CyberPeace. (2024, December 2). *Domestic UPI frauds: Finance Ministry presented data in Lok Sabha*. https://www.cyberpeace.org/resources/blogs/domestic-upi-frauds-finance-ministry-presented-data-in-loksabha cyberpeace.org

D'Souza, E. (2017). Reserve Bank of India: The way forward. In Kapur, D., Mehta, P. B., & Vaishnav, M. (Eds.), *Rethinking public institutions in India*. Oxford University Press., DOI: 10.1093/oso/9780199474370.003.0005

Dahiya, K. (2023). Trends in cyber crime in India. *International Journal for Research in Applied Science and Engineering Technology*, *11*(5), 6393–6406. DOI: 10.22214/ijraset.2023.53073

Dasari, P. (2025). Digital Lending in India: Harassment, Settlements, and the Rise of Financial Exploitation. *Settlements, and the Rise of Financial Exploitation*. https://dx.doi.org/DOI: 10.2139/ssrn.5092390

Datta, D. (2023). The future of financial inclusion through FinTech: A conceptual study in post pandemic India. *Sachetas*, *2*(1), 11–17. DOI: 10.55955/210002

Datta, P., Panda, S. N., Tanwar, S., & Kaushal, R. K. (2020). A Technical Review Report on Cyber Crimes in India. *2020 International Conference on Emerging Smart Computing and Informatics (ESCI)* DOI: 10.1109/ESCI48226.2020.9167567

Economic Times. (2025, April 23). *Digital payments comprise 99.8 percent of total transactions volume in H1 2025: RBI. The Economic Times*. https://m.economictimes.com/news/economy/finance/digital-payments-comprise-99-8-of-total-transactions-volume-in-h1-2025-upi-transactions-rbi/articleshow/124760861.cms The Economic Times

Elekdag, S., Emrullahu, D., & Naceur, S. B. (2025). Does FinTech Increase Bank Risk-taking? *Journal of Financial Stability*, *76*, 101360. DOI: 10.1016/j.jfs.2024.101360

Esoimeme, E. E. (2021). Identifying and reducing the money laundering risks posed by individuals who have been unknowingly recruited as money mules. *Journal of Money Laundering Control*, *24*(1), 201–212. DOI: 10.1108/JMLC-05-2020-0053

George, A. S. (2024). Finance 4.0: The transformation of financial services in the digital age. *Partners Universal Innovative Research Publication, 2*(3), 104-125. https://doi.org/https://doi.org/10.5281/zenodo.11666694

George, A. S., Baskar, T., & Srikaanth, P. B. (2024). Cyber Threats to Critical Infrastructure: Assessing Vulnerabilities Across Key Sectors. *Partners Universal International Innovation Journal*, *2*(1), 51–75. DOI: 10.5281/zenodo.10639463

Gupta, M., & Gupta, A. (2025). Cyber security legal framework in India – overlaps, problems and challenges. *Journal of Business Management and Information Systems*, *12*(1), 11–20. DOI: 10.48001/jbmis.1201002

Hillairet, C., Lopez, O., d'Oultremont, L., & Spoorenberg, B. (2022). Cyber contagion: Impact of the network structure on the losses of an insurance portfolio. *Insurance, Mathematics & Economics*. Advance online publication. DOI: 10.1016/j.insmatheco.2022.08.002

Hussain, B. M. I., & Rafi, M. (2023). Online Financial Transactions in India: A Study of Its-Significance, Frauds and Security Models to Counter Frauds. *International Journal of Intelligent Engineering and Systems*, *16*(3), 455–469. DOI: 10.22266/ijies2023.0630.36

Iglesias-Rodríguez, P. (2025). The future of instant payments in the EU: bank ownership, market contracting costs, and the accomplishment of financial regulation objectives: P. Iglesias-Rodríguez. *Journal of Banking Regulation*, 1-21. https://doi.org/DOI: 10.1057/s41261-025-00296-9

Indian Press Information Bureau. (2025, March 11). *Digital payment transactions surge with over 18,000 crore transactions in 2024–25*. https://www.pib.gov.in/PressReleaseIframePage.aspx?PRID=2110405 Press Information Bureau

Indian Press Information Bureau. (2025, October 8). *Curbing cyber frauds in digital India*. https://www.pib.gov.in/PressNoteDetails.aspx?ModuleId=3&NoteId=155384 Press Information Bureau

Jain, R., & Sonowal, B. (2025). Analyzing the Procedure for Investigation in Cybercrime and Admissibility of Electronic Evidence. In *Cybercrime Unveiled: Technologies for Analysing Legal Complexity* (pp. 265-289). Cham: Springer Nature Switzerland. https://doi.org/DOI: 10.1007/978-3-031-80557-8_12

Kamal, M., Rahmani, S., & Alam, M. R. (2025). Beyond traditional banking: How FinTech is reshaping financial access in India. *Available at SSRN* 5122110. https://dx.doi.org/DOI: 10.2139/ssrn.5122110

Karthika, M., Neethu, K., & Lakshmi, P. (2022). Impact of fintech on the banking sector. *Integrated Journal for Research in Arts and Humanities*, *2*(4), 109–112. DOI: 10.55544/ijrah.2.4.66

Kaur, S., Mishra, H., & Goyal, A. (2023). Cyber-security in UPI payments. *International Journal for Research in Applied Science and Engineering Technology, 11*(5), 4955–4960. DOI: 10.22214/ijraset.2023.52175

Khan, N. F., Ikram, N., & Saleem, S. (2023). Effects of socioeconomic and digital inequalities on cybersecurity in a developing country. *Security Journal, 1*. Advance online publication. DOI: 10.1057/s41284-023-00375-4

Kharbanda, V., & Arora, C. (2022). Guidelines to build robust security standards for the financial technology sector in India. *Indian Journal of Law and Technology, 18*(1), 4. Advance online publication. DOI: 10.55496/VMVA2405

Kodali, P. (2025). The evolving threat landscape: Examining predominant cyber fraud methodologies in e-commerce ecosystems. *World Journal of Advanced Research and Reviews, 26*(1), 2552–2560. DOI: 10.30574/wjarr.2025.26.1.1308

Kumar, A., Choudhary, R. K., Mishra, S. K., Kar, S. K., & Bansal, R. (2022). The growth trajectory of UPI-based mobile payments in India: Enablers and inhibitors. *Indian Journal of Finance and Banking, 11*(1), 45–59.

Kumar, S., & Rao, A. (2024). Assessing And Mitigating The Impact Of Geopolitical Risk Uncertainty On The Indian Financial Sector: A Policy Perspective. *Bulletin of Monetary Economics and Banking, 27*(3), 483–526. DOI: 10.59091/2460-9196.2278

Kumari, S. (2025). Rise of UPI and its impact on traditional payment systems in India: A digital transformation analysis. *International Journal of Research Publication and Reviews, 6*(6), 6403–6408. DOI: 10.55248/gengpi.6.0625.2216

Kushwaha, D., & Malpani, D. (2025). The Impact of Fintech on Financial Inclusion in India: An Empirical Analysis of Digital Payment Adoption and Banking Access. *International Journal of Environmental Sciences, 11*(12s), 218–227. DOI: 10.64252/g845vb32

Ky, S. S., Rugemintwari, C., & Sauviat, A. (2025). Is fintech good for bank performance? The case of mobile money in the East African Community. *International Journal of Finance & Economics, 30*(4), 3918–3949. DOI: 10.1002/ijfe.3100

Lekshmi, A., Atul, J., Pillai, A. J., Dhanya, M., & Kaladharan, S. (2024, August). Risks in Instant Loan Apps: Analyzing User Perceptions Using Machine Learning Approach. In *International Conference on ICT for Sustainable Development* (pp. 461-471). Singapore: Springer Nature Singapore. https://doi.org/DOI: 10.1007/978-981-97-8602-2_41

Levi, M., Doig, A., Gundur, R., Wall, D., & Williams, M. (2017). Cyberfraud and the implications for effective risk-based responses: Themes from UK research. *Crime, Law, and Social Change*, *67*(1), 77–96. DOI: 10.1007/s10611-016-9648-0

Manjunath, M., & Selvi, S. (2024). A study on cyber frauds post digitalization in India. *International Journal for Research in Applied Science and Engineering Technology*, *12*(IV), 60191. Advance online publication. DOI: 10.22214/ijraset.2024.60191

Martínez Resano, J. R. (2022). Digital resilience and financial stability. The quest for policy tools in the financial sector. *The Quest For Policy Tools In The Financial Sector*. https://dx.doi.org/DOI: 10.2139/ssrn.4336381

Mayo, K., Grabill, N., & Wellman, M. P. (2024, January). Fraud risk mitigation in real-time payments: A strategic agent-based analysis. In *33rd International Joint Conference on Artificial Intelligence* (pp. 157-165). https://doi.org/DOI: 10.24963/ijcai.2024/18

Mehta, A. (2024). Impact of technological advancements on banking frauds: A case study of Indian banks. *emergence*, 11. https://doi.org/DOI: 10.33545/26175754.2024.v7.i1c.308

Migozzi, J., Urban, M., & Wojcik, D. (2024). "You should do what India does": FinTech ecosystems in India reshaping the geography of finance. *Geoforum*, *151*, 103720. DOI: 10.1016/j.geoforum.2023.103720

Mishra, D., Kandpal, V., Agarwal, N., & Srivastava, B. (2024). Financial Inclusion and Its Ripple Effects on Socio-Economic Development: A Comprehensive Review. *Journal of Risk and Financial Management*, *17*(3), 105. https://www.mdpi.com/1911-8074/17/3/105. DOI: 10.3390/jrfm17030105

Nalluri, V., & Chen, L. S. (2024). Modelling the FinTech adoption barriers in the context of emerging economies—An integrated Fuzzy hybrid approach. *Technological Forecasting and Social Change*, *199*, 123049. DOI: 10.1016/j.techfore.2023.123049

National Payments Corporation of India. (2025). *Unified Payments Interface (UPI) product statistics*. https://www.npci.org.in/product/upi/product-statistics NPCI

Ng, A. W., & Kwok, B. K. B. (2017). Emergence of Fintech and cybersecurity in a global financial centre: Strategic approach by a regulator. *Journal of Financial Regulation and Compliance*, *25*(4), 422–434. DOI: 10.1108/JFRC-01-2017-0013

Nikkel, B. J. (2020). Fintech forensics: Criminal investigation and digital evidence in financial technologies. *Forensic Science International Digital Investigation*, *33*, 200908. Advance online publication. DOI: 10.1016/j.fsidi.2020.200908

Oduro, D. A., Okolo, J. N., Bello, A. D., Ajibade, A. T., & Muritala, A. (2025). AI-powered fraud detection in digital banking: Enhancing security through machine learning. https://doi.org/DOI: 10.30574/ijsra.2025.14.3.0854

Pal, A., De', R., & Herath, T. (2020). The Role of Mobile Payment Technology in Sustainable and Human-Centric Development: Evidence from the Post-Demonetization Period in India. *Information Systems Frontiers*, *22*(3), 607–631. DOI: 10.1007/s10796-020-09982-7

Panda, K., Sahoo, A., & Kumar, A. (2023). From the Margins to Mainstream: Fintech's Quest for Financial Inclusion in Emerging Markets. *European Economic Letters*, *13*(5), 341–361. DOI: 10.52783/eel.v13i5.762

Parmar, M. (2024). The Impact of Cybercrime on Consumer Trust in E-Commerce. *Available at SSRN* 4843094. https://dx.doi.org/DOI: 10.2139/ssrn.4843094

Parsheera, S. (2022). Understanding state-level variations in India's digital transformation. *The African Journal of Information and Communication*, *2022*(30), 1–9. DOI: 10.23962/ajic.i30.15082

Peihani, M. (2022). Regulation of Cyber Risk in the Banking System: A Canadian Case Study. *Journal of Financial Regulation*, *8*(2), 139–161. DOI: 10.1093/jfr/fjac006

Rajput, S. (2024). Building Robust Securities in PSO'S: Adopting RBI's Baseline Controls for Business continuity. *Planning (Chicago, Ill.)*, *ii*. Advance online publication. DOI: 10.2139/ssrn.4947696

Rao, H. S. (2019). Cyber crime in banking sector. *International Journal of Research-Granthaalayah*, *7*(1), 148–161. DOI: 10.29121/granthaalayah.v7.i1.2019.1043

Rathi, C., Varshney, A. K., Chaudhary, S., Prakash, V., & Garg, A. (2024). A paradigm shifts in fintech and rural inclusion challenges in India. *International Journal of Science and Research Archive*, *12*(1), 299–311. DOI: 10.30574/ijsra.2024.12.1.0763

Ravirajan, K., & Shanmugam, K. R. (2023). *Determinants of Efficiency of Commercial Banks in India After Global Crises*. Madras School of Economics., DOI: 10.33423/jaf.v23i4.6456

Raza, M. S., Zhan, Q., & Rubab, S. (2020). Role of money mules in money laundering and financial crimes a discussion through case studies. *Journal of Financial Crime*, *27*(3), 911–931. DOI: 10.1108/JFC-02-2020-0028

Ross, R., Pillitteri, V., Graubart, R., Bodeau, D., & McQuaid, R. (2019). *Developing cyber resilient systems: a systems security engineering approach* (No. NIST Special Publication (SP) 800-160 Vol. 2 (Draft)). National Institute of Standards and Technology.

Saroy, R., Jain, P., Awasthy, S., & Dhal, S. C. (2023). Impact of digital payment adoption on Indian banking sector efficiency. *Journal of Banking and Financial Technology*, *7*(1), 1–13. DOI: 10.1007/s42786-023-00047-2

Saxena, R., Budki, A., & Gupta, A. (2024). A Study on the Consumer Risk Perceptions for FinTech Platforms in India. *Advances in Economics and Business*, *12*(3), 33–41. DOI: 10.13189/aeb.2024.120302

Sebastian, D. (2025). Modernizing Credit Risk with Data Mesh: A Large Bank's Transformation to Real-Time Credit Intelligence. *Journal of Computer Science and Technology Studies*, *7*(10), 650–664. DOI: 10.32996/jcsts.2025.7.10.65

Shadrooh, S., & Nørvåg, K. (2024). SMoTeF: Smurf money laundering detection using temporal order and flow analysis. *Applied Intelligence*, *54*(15), 7461–7478. DOI: 10.1007/s10489-024-05545-4

Shah, P., & Agarwal, A. (2020). Cybersecurity behaviour of smartphone users in India: An empirical analysis. *Information and Computer Security*, *28*(2), 293–318. DOI: 10.1108/ICS-04-2019-0041

Sharma, P., Gallani, V., & Maheria, S. (2024). Digital payments and fraud connection: Insights from the Indian economy. *International Journal of Management. Economics and Commerce*, *1*(2), 102–111. DOI: 10.62737/spqxve67

Shekhar, V., & R, S. (2025). Navigating the dark side of fintech: A developer perspective. *Management Practice Insights*, *3*(Sp1, SI1), 58–64. DOI: 10.59571/mpi.v3si1.10

Singh, A. (2025). Generational Perspectives on Fintech Adoption: Challenges, Demographics, and Digital Inclusion. *Mercados y negocios, 26*(56). https://doi.org/ DOI: 10.32870/myn.vi56.7827

Singh, R., Malik, G., & Jain, V. (2021). FinTech effect: Measuring impact of FinTech adoption on banks' profitability. *International Journal of Management Practice*, *14*(4), 411–427. DOI: 10.1504/IJMP.2021.116587

Sirawongphatsara, P., Pornpongtechavanich, P., Sriamorntrakul, P., & Daengsi, T. (2023). Analyzing Bank Account Information of Nominees and Scammers. *arXiv preprint arXiv:2308.01586*. https://doi.org//arXiv.2308.01586DOI: 10.48550

Sottet, J. S., Grandry, E., & Bjeković, M. (2018). Managing regulatory system with megamodelling. Proceeding - 2018 20th IEEE International Conference on Business Informatics, CBI 2018

Sujatha, D., Sudheer, A. K., & Balasundaram, E. (2025). Black swan dynamics: A network-based framework for systemic risk detection and mitigation [Article]. *Risk Management, 27*(4), 24. Advance online publication. DOI: 10.1057/s41283-025-00177-5

Syed, A. A., Grima, S., & Sood, K. (2024). Assessing the Role of the Fintech Era on the Banking Stability of an Emerging Economy: Interaction Analysis of the Indian Banking Industry. *Folia Oeconomica Stetinensia*, *24*(1), 182–202. DOI: 10.2478/foli-2024-0011

Tariq, H., & Hassani, M. (2023, September). Topology-agnostic detection of temporal money laundering flows in billion-scale transactions. In *Joint European Conference on Machine Learning and Knowledge Discovery in Databases* (pp. 402-419). Cham: Springer Nature Switzerland.

Tripathy, S. S. (2025). A comprehensive survey of cybercrimes in India over the last decade. *arXiv preprint arXiv:2505.23770*. http://dx.doi.org/DOI: 10.2139/ssrn.5048282

Venkatachalam, P. (2020, December). Influence of FinTech companies on banking landscape an exploratory study in Indian context. In *International Working Conference on Transfer and Diffusion of IT* (pp. 523-528). Cham: Springer International Publishing. https://doi.org/DOI: 10.1007/978-3-030-64849-7_46

von Horn, R., & Kudic, M. (2025). Systemic risk in the fintech-banking system: Assessing instabilities and vulnerabilities in Central Europe [Article]. *The Quarterly Review of Economics and Finance*, *104*, 102071. Advance online publication. DOI: 10.1016/j.qref.2025.102071

Wang, Z., Zhu, H., & Sun, L. (2021). Social Engineering in Cybersecurity: Effect Mechanisms, Human Vulnerabilities and Attack Methods. *IEEE Access : Practical Innovations, Open Solutions*, *9*, 11895–11910. DOI: 10.1109/ACCESS.2021.3051633

KEY TERMS AND DEFINITIONS

Analytical Orientation of Typologies: Concentrates on institutional, structural, and behavioral elements that enable fraud instead of technical procedure and legal systems.

Cyber-Dependent Financial Crime: Offenses that can only be committed through cyberspace and have a direct threat on digital hardware, networks, or data, such as hacking attacks and malware attacks.

Cyber-Enabled Financial Crime: Conventional financial offenses, like fraud, which are enhanced by means of digital platforms and can become quicker, bigger, and more convenient, but remain attainable, even without digital infrastructure.

Financial Cybercrime: Is defined as illegal financial work that is carried out through, or basically dependent on, digital technologies. It encompasses, in general, cyber-enabled crimes as well as cyber-dependent crimes.

Fraud Typologies: Analytical compilations of the prevalent fraud methods such as social engineering frauds, remote-access fraud, fake investment scheme, and mule-account facilitation.

Systemic Cyber Risk: The risk of a localized cyber-attack spreading to the integrated financial systems causing a widespread effect, characterized by discontinuity and financial instability.

Chapter 6
Measuring FinTech Adoption in Banking:
Constructing Indices and Assessing Impacts on Profitability, Stability, and Institutional Diversity

R. N. Ravikumar
http://orcid.org/0009-0009-3705-1681
Marwadi University, Rajkot, India

S. Aarthi
http://orcid.org/0009-0006-9064-2091
Marwadi University, Rajkot, India

ABSTRACT

The chapter explores the measurement and impact of FinTech adoption within the banking industry, presenting a structured methodology for constructing a FinTech Adoption Index (FAI) that integrates multiple dimensions such as digital presence, automation, open APIs, artificial intelligence, and FinTech partnerships. It examines how these digital innovations influence banks' profitability, operational stability, and institutional diversity across conventional, Islamic, foreign, and digital-only models. Empirical results demonstrate that higher FinTech maturity enhances efficiency and competitiveness but introduces governance and cybersecurity challenges. Through real-world cases from DBS Bank and the State Bank of India, the study validates the transformative potential of data-driven innovation in achieving sustainable financial performance and inclusive digital growth.

DOI: 10.4018/979-8-3373-6244-1.ch006

1. INTRODUCTION

Financial Technology (FinTech) represents an extreme transformation that is rocking the banking sector redefining the process of delivering, receiving, and experiencing financial services. Digitalization of banking, automation, Artificial Intelligence (AI), and blockchain technology have revolutionized the traditional banking mode to lead to the greater efficiency, transparency, and customer-centric innovation. It has brought its own set of complications to the task of defining the level and quality of FinTech implementation in different banking organizations as well (Shmuratko and S. A. Sheludko, 2021). This chapter aims at the creation of a comprehensive analytical model of evaluating the magnitude of FinTech acceptance, its connection with the profitability and stability of banks and its connection with institutional variety. It comes up with technological innovation, digital engagement, and operational automation indices, which enable comparative and empirical observation in the banking segments. The theoretical and data-driven knowledge expressed by the study is added to the process of understanding the role of the digital transformation in the financial performance, market position, and the resilience (Darji et al., 2025). This chapter is a roadmap that may be applied by policy makers and other interested practitioners to evidence-based approaches to assessing and optimizing plans to adopt FinTech.

1.1. Evolution of FinTech in the Banking Landscape

FinTech is not in the margins of the financial system anymore, but a component of the banking system. The first steps in ele-transactions and online banking have aided to bring new hi-tech necessities such as artificial intelligence credit ratings, blockchain settlement systems, and fully online neobanks. Convergent trend that takes place between technology and finance also marks this transformation that redefines what is expected by the customers and the market competition. To produce real-time analytics and make auto decisions, banks have left their ancient systems to develop agile and data-driven systems (Le et al., 2024). In addition, the co-innovation culture has been established through FinTech partnerships, such as open banking APIs, strategic alliances, and regulatory sandboxes. Mobile usage and the application of digital wallets is one of the fast-growing adoptions of technologies that transform access to financial services into a democratic one. FinTech innovation is, hence, a structural change, rather than a technological change, which has impacted the governance, business models, and risk structures. This evolution needs to be known in order to place the reasoning on which the strength of adoption is gauged among banks and what it means in the financial performance (Basdekis et al., 2022). The figure 1 demonstrates the aspect of FinTech adoption dimensions (digital presence, automation, AI, and open APIs) that are combined with each other to form a composite index that defines profitability, stability, and institutional diversity within the banking ecosystem.

Figure 1. Conceptual Framework for Measuring FinTech Adoption and Its Impact on Bank Performance

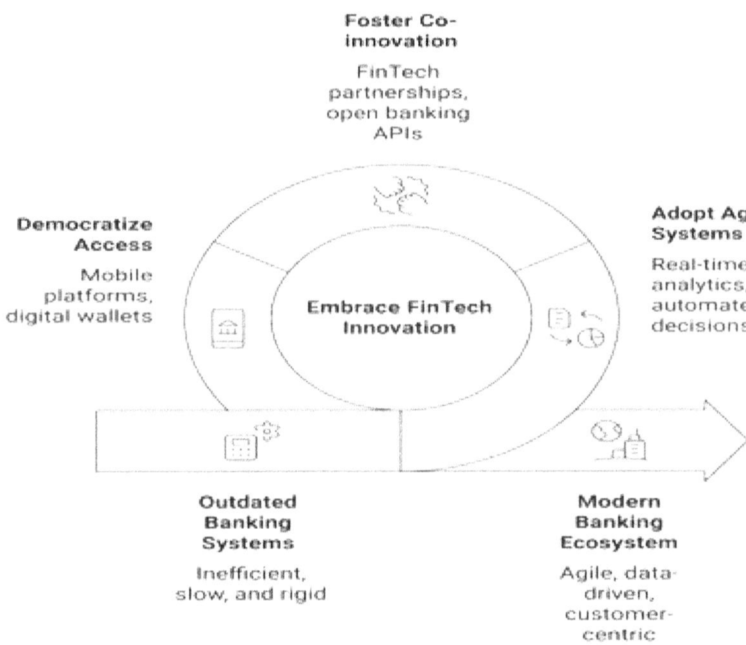

1.2. Importance of Measuring FinTech Adoption

In spite of a high level of digital technology integration, however, there exists no standardized measures required to determine the level of FinTech adoption in banking organizations. Adoption measurement is a key element to assess the digital maturity, strategic gaps, and connect technology investments to the financial performance. In the absence of clear indicators, comparisons between banks or markets cannot be consistent to restrict strategic decision-making, and academic analysis (Qiang, 2024). Building a measurement framework that is structured will allow the stakeholders to evaluate the impact of digital tools on the important variables, including the operational efficiency, customer experience, and risk management. Besides, the quantification of adoption can assist regulating entities to learn more about systemic impacts of technological change, including cybersecurity resilience or market concentration. The chapter highlights that measurement should not be confined to the surface of the digital action, but should encompass the following areas: integration of AI, automation of processes, open APIs as well as collaborations with FinTech (Khuan, 2024). Through the establishment of an empirical index of FinTech adoption provides a gap between theory and practice, and it is thus viable to quantitatively determine the influence of it on profitability, stability, and institutional diversity in banking segments.

1.3. Scope, Significance, and Structure of the Chapter

The conceptualization, measurement, and the impact assessment of the level of FinTech adoption in the banking ecosystem is addressed in this chapter. It integrates theoretical and empirical approaches to create a FinTech Adoption Index to apply it in various banking environments. This significance of the study is that it adds to the work on digital finance as the multidimensional tool to gauge the technological transformation process. It is also of practical use since it offers practical information that can be implemented by policymakers, regulators, and banking executives. The chapter has been subdivided into ten big segments, the first of them being the contextual background and research objectives, followed by the conceptual model, methodology, literature review, results and implications. The information in each section is progressive to a full understanding of the inferences brought by adoption of FinTech on the financial and institutional performance of banks. The conclusion sections are aimed at the research directions and implications in the future to the managers, which supports the overall objective, which is to develop a robust and innovation-driven banking ecosystem to withstand a digital transformation.

2. BACKGROUND TO THE STUDY

Among the most important transformations in the history of the modern banking business, the pace of digitalization of the financial sector is especially important. The FinTech innovations (such as automation, data analytics, AI, blockchain and open banking) are changing the new mode of doing things and re-design the customer interaction mode. The scope and degree of technological penetration is different between institutions, markets and regulatory environments. This segment comprises the contextual background to the research because, it responds to the environment of digital transformation, the challenge of measuring the technological integration, and the readiness of the banking segments. The dynamics is critical in understanding actual levels of technological maturity, as compared to being superficially digitalized, and it is therefore important to build valid measurement indices grounded on the dynamics (Serdarušician et al., 2024). Interdependence between the adoption of FinTechs, competitive advantage, and the systemic stability is also visible in the background. Giving FinTech a contextual backdrop in the broader conceptualization of financial modernization, this section solidifies the necessity of having an integrated framework that may encompass both technological penetration and flexibility of institutions within the conventional, Islamic, as well as hybrid banking systems.

2.1. Digital Transformation in the Financial Sector

The digitalization of banking is far beyond the deployment of new technologies but is a cultural and strategic re-balancing of business processes on data-driven and customer-centric processes. To enhance efficiency, banks are doing predictive analytics by means of Artificial Intelligence, detecting fraud with machine learning, and robotically processing automation. Secure and scalable infrastructure that is capable of supporting global operations is now possible through the application of cloud computing and distributed ledger technologies. Also, the Internet as well as mobile banking, chatbots, and other digital solutions have changed the interaction of consumers with financial institutions at the most basic level (Gekhaeva et al., 2023). This revolution facilitates and simplifies it but introduces such an issue as cybersecurity, data management and talent acquisition. This digital shift which was caused by the pandemic also required even traditional banks to lay a heavy focus on remote transactions and the delivery of digital services. The scale of integration and maintenance of digital ecosystems is being established as a source of competitiveness as it grows (Ravikumar et al., 2025). In this way, digital transformation is the basis in which FinTech adoption index could be developed and measured systematically (Mhlanga, 2024). This figure 2 demonstrates the analysis pathway according to which the FinTech Adoption Index mediates the effect on the key financial performance outcomes, including profitability, operational stability, and institutional diversity.

Figure 2. Analytical Model Linking FinTech Adoption with Profitability, Stability, and Diversity

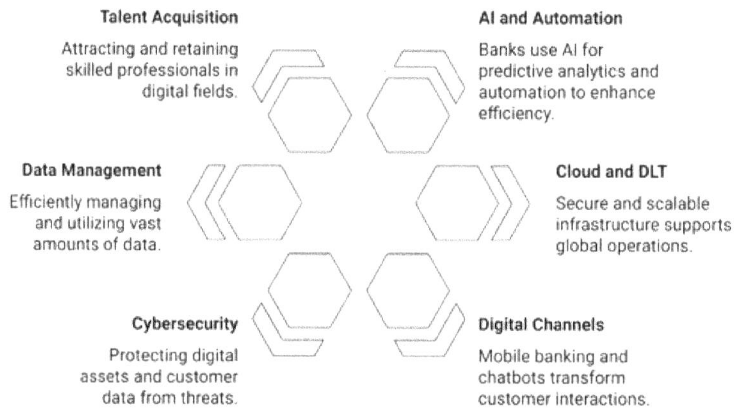

2.2. Challenges in Quantifying Technological Integration

The measurement of technological integration in banking is still a complex practice because of the variety of innovations and lack of a common set of standards. Banks vary in terms of their level of technological investments, internal capacity, and regulatory exposure and measurement is extremely context-specific. Among the major issues is that it is difficult to find credible measures that can be used to track both qualitative and quantitative aspects of FinTech adoption, or the use of mobile app sophistication on the one hand, and AI-based credit systems on the other. Another weakness is the availability of data because most banks also share only part of the information concerning their digital endeavors (Abedalrhman, 2025). Moreover, technological integration is a dynamic activity, metrics should allow the cycles of continuous innovations and obsolescence. Conventional financial metrics do not consider non-physical digital assets or efficiency driven benefits due to innovations. Therefore, to create a FinTech Adoption Index, a combination of various data sources and criteria weighting and normalization are necessary to capture a real picture of digital maturity. These problems need to be tackled in order to generate strong, comparative, and policy-relevant information between institutions (Ranković et al., 2023).

2.3. Overview of Banking Segments and Technological Readiness

The world banking environment is diverse, comprising of traditional, Islamic, cooperative or digital-only banks, with different technology directions. The larger commercial banks tend to have more resources and infrastructure to implement at least the more advanced solutions of FinTech, whereas smaller regionals or cooperative banks are likely to have limited capital and skills. Islamic banks are regulated by Sharia compliant rules and therefore are using technology in a different manner, focusing on ethical finance, transparency and partnership-based models. Emerging markets have different rates of digital preparedness and regulatory assistance that have to be adjusted to by the foreign banks (Niroula & Adhikari, 2024). The technological preparedness is therefore pegged on the availability of IT infrastructure, employee skill base, regulatory conditions, and customer digital literacy. Inter-segmental comparison of these segments indicates not only differences in adoption but also a possibility of interventions targeting these segments. Such differences would necessitate the insights in the development of an inclusive FinTech Adoption Index that would not just manifest the technological potentials but rather the institutional heterogeneity, which, in the long run, would result in the balanced digital transformation and equitable financial innovation across the banking ecosystem.

3. RESEARCH OBJECTIVES

The increased overlap between banking and FinTech requires the systematic method to quantify, examine, and synthesize the level of technological adoption and its consequences on institutional performance. The purpose of the chapter is to offer an overarching model to connect FinTech adoption and profitability, operational stability, and institutional diversity. The goals are planned to lead the theoretical exploration and empirical analysis to guarantee that the acquired FinTech Adoption Index will be relevant, scalable, and applicable in a variety of banking situations. The Main Objectives of the Chapter are:

- To create a universal FinTech Adoption Index (FAI): Build an empirically-based, multidimensional index of digital presence, innovation capacity, automation and AI integration in the banks.
- To examine the effect of the adoption of FinTech on financial performance: Test the effects of the different levels of digital transformation on the profitability, the return on assets (ROA), and the cost efficiency of banks.

- In order to determine the correlation between FinTech adoption and financial stability: Explore the issue of how high technological integration enhances or destabilizes the operational resilience and risk exposure.
- Comparing the patterns of adoption in institutional types: Compare the conventional, Islamic, foreign, and domestic banks in terms of their digital readiness and innovation behavior.
- To offer strategic information to policy and management: Present operational implications to regulators and bank leaders on how to achieve an inclusive, safe and sustainable integration of FinTech.

4. CONCEPTUAL MODEL

The conceptual model is a systematic prism in terms of which the multidimensionality of the FinTech adoption in banking can be considered. It combines theoretical frameworks of innovation diffusion, technology adoption and institutional theory to elaborate how technological transformation impacts financial performance. The model connects the internal strengths of the banks, including the digital infrastructure, human capital, and strategic orientation, with the external forces such as competition, customer demand, and regulation incentives (Shanti et al., 2023). These interconnections lie on a causal link between investment in technology to quantifiable performance outcomes in terms of profitability, stability and diversity. These relations enable the creation of an operational value systemic assessment of the value creation of the FinTech usage by creating relationships and balance of the operational risks by the conceptual model. It also adds emphasis on the feedback loops indicating the fact that its successful adoption may be exploited to reinforce the culture of innovation and future behavior of investment and create a sustainable loop of digital competitiveness in the banking ecosystem.

4.1. Framework for FinTech Adoption Measurement

The FinTech adoption measurement framework is a progression of a multidimensional construct which encompasses the technological, organizational, and strategic measures. It does not merely conceive the adoption of FinTech as the presence of digital tools but as an evolving capacity to integrate digital infrastructure, innovation partnerships and data-driven capabilities. The framework divides indicators into seven core dimensions, i.e., digital presence, mobile banking functionality, open API integration, FinTech collaboration, digital payment innovation, automation intensity, and the use of Artificial Intelligence. Every dimension is a quantifiable proxy of digital maturity and can be compared to other institutions and analyzed through time (Qi et al., 2024a). The framework promotes the use of composite scoring system that has undergone normalization and weighting to offer a comparative score between banks of different magnitude and operational environment. It, therefore, converts qualitative technological features into quantifiable data that can be summed up into the FinTech Adoption Index (FAI). It is an empirical validation that is based on a structured measurement model, which would in turn be the theoretical basis to assess objective technological transformation and its resultant financial implications in the banking industry (Qi et al., 2024b). The figure 3 compares FinTech adoption strategies between traditional, Islamic, foreign, and digital-only banks and has shown dissimilarity in technological focus, intensity of innovation and regulatory fit.

Figure 3. Comparative Framework of FinTech Adoption Across Banking Models

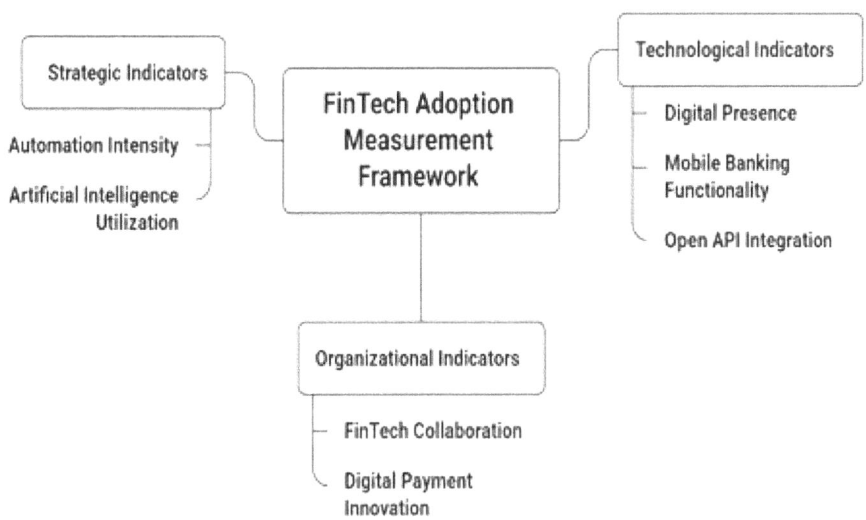

4.2. Theoretical Linkages: Innovation Diffusion and Technology Adoption Models

The theoretical basis of conceptual model is based on two major theoretical premises, the Diffusion of Innovations (DOI) theory and the Technology Adoption

Model (TAM). DOI describes the mechanisms of spreading of innovations in the organization and includes the steps of awareness, interest, evaluation and implementation with the focus on the influence of organizational culture and perceived relative advantage. This is supplemented by TAM which dwells on acceptance by the users especially the constructs of usefulness and ease of use which determine the intent of adoption in the institutions (Zhao et al., 2022). These models in total can be beneficial in the banking domain context in explaining the rate and extent of FinTech integration on technological complexity, compatibility and observability. DOI, combined with TAM, provides the opportunity to conduct a multi-level analysis according to which managerial choices, institutional features, and market specifics are related to adoption behavior. This theoretical combination enhances the explanatory capacity of the conceptual model, which gives an analytical connection between the individual-level acceptance processes and the organizational-level change outcomes that are caused by the FinTech diffusion.

4.3. Conceptual Pathways: From Adoption to Performance Outcomes

The conceptual pathways will show how the adoption of FinTech will be transformed into financial and institutional results via interconnected processes. Efficiency is both achieved through technological integration lowering the cost of transactions, automating the processes, and increasing the level of accuracy of data, all of which increase profitability measures like ROA and ROE. Meanwhile, enhanced data analytics and AI-related risk management enhance financial stability as it reduces credit, liquidity, and operational risks. Institutional diversity has such advantages as different models of banks, including conventional, Islamic, or digital-only, have different approaches to the innovation process, depending on how they are governed and which customers they target (Arena et al., 2023). The pathways are also conscious of the potential trade-offs; accelerated digitalization may introduce layers into the operations and expose them to cybercrimes. The model therefore incorporates such mediating variables as regulatory setting, market competitive forces and organizational responsiveness. All these paths provide a hypothetical road map within which the various stages of FinTech use can be experimented in the multidimensional performance of banks in various circumstances and business models.

5. RESEARCH METHODOLOGY

The research methodology offers the conceptual outline upon which the study follows in order to arrive at the FinTech Adoption Index (FAI) and its effect on the financial performance of banks. It is a mixed research study; it is a combination of quantitative modeling analysis and qualitative validation. This is achieved through the use of primary and secondary data in order to be robust and statistical data analysis such as correlation, regression and structural equation modeling in order to have empirical testing. The representative type will be used as the sample will consist of a different number of banks depending on their size, ownership and area of operation. It also utilizes the methods of normalization and sensitivity analysis to increase reliability and cross-country comparability (Duan et al., 2023a). The process is guided by ethical considerations that consider confidentiality of data. The methodology helps to establish a descriptive and inferential analysis of measurement index relating to profitability, stability, and diversity measures. It is a structured design that can be replicated and applied in policies which are contributing to the academic rigor and practical relevance in measuring the adoption of FinTech in banking sector.

5.1. Data Sources and Sampling Framework

The paper deploys both primary and secondary data to develop the FinTech Adoption Index and performance outcomes. The secondary information will be obtained in the annual reports of banks, regulatory reports, financial statements, and other digital disclosure services that capture technological initiatives. The complementary primary data can consist of survey results and assessments of the maturity of innovation in banks conducted by experts. Sampling structure follows a stratified method to take care of representation in different categories conventional, Islamic, domestic, foreign and digital-only banks (Li, 2023). The inclusion criteria focus on operations continuity, data accessibility, and disclosure of digital activities of at least three years. This type of design is a longitudinal design that permits a trend analysis and impact assessment over time. The interdependence of data is also ensured with the help of cross-checking with various sources, including the records of central banks and financial databases. The aim of the framework is to develop a well-balanced set of data which is both technologically heterogeneous and statistically viable to make comparative and causal inferences in the context of FinTech adoptions (Oladipo et al., 2024). The figure 4 shows how bank executives, regulators, and policymakers interact and engage with each other in order to make FinTech adoption in the banking ecosystem responsible, inclusive, and sustainable.

Figure 4. Managerial and Policy Framework for Sustainable FinTech Integration

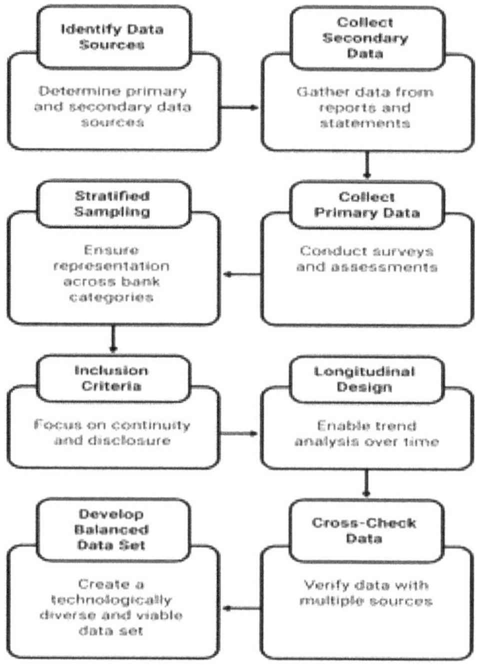

5.2. Construction of FinTech Adoption Index (FAI)

The FinTech Adoption Index (FAI) is created in a multi-stage way that includes selecting indicators, normalizing them, weighting them and aggregating the results. The indicators that will be used are based on the conceptual framework and include the seven dimensions, namely, digital presence, mobile and internet banking, the use of open API, collaboration with FinTech, digital payments innovation, automation intensity, and the use of AI. All indicators undergo min max normalization in a way that they are based on a scale of 0 to 1 in comparison to other banks. The weight-assigning process is implemented through both expert judgment and data statistical techniques such as the Principal Component Analysis (PCA) to eliminate subjectivity (Arora et al., 2023). The weighted indicators are then aggregated according to composite index formula which gives a single score that represents the extent of adoption of the FinTech by an individual bank. The sensitivity and correlation tests to the financial performance measures also affirm the strength of the index. The FAI that has resulted out of it is a holistic scaling tool of digital maturity and technological advances within the banking sector. The most significant dimensions and measurable indicators, which were employed to design FinTech Adoption Index (FAI), are given in the table 1.

Table 1. Dimensions and Indicators of the FinTech Adoption Index (FAI)

Dimension	Indicator Examples	Measurement Criteria	Expected Impact on Bank Performance
Digital Presence	Website functionality, digital product portfolio	Scored 0–1 based on completeness and interactivity	Enhances customer accessibility
Mobile Banking Capability	Mobile app features, digital onboarding	App store metrics, service range	Improves service convenience and retention
Open API Integration	API availability, third-party partnerships	Number and type of APIs published	Encourages innovation and data sharing
FinTech Collaboration	Joint ventures, startup investments	Number of partnerships or incubators	Drives co-innovation and product agility
Digital Payments	UPI, QR, contactless, wallets	Share of transactions via digital channels	Increases transaction efficiency
Automation & AI	Chatbots, RPA, predictive models	Presence and functionality of AI systems	Reduces costs, boosts accuracy

5.3. Analytical Models for Assessing Profitability, Stability, and Diversity

To determine the impact of the adoption of FinTech on the performance of banks, a number of analytical models are employed. An analysis of the profitability is done through regression models and it compares FAI scores and related financial ratios such as Return on Assets (ROA) and Net Interest Margin (NIM). The financial stability is considered through the prism of such indicators as Z-score and Non-Performing Loan (NPL) ratio, indicating whether digital transformation reduces the level of systemic risk. The cluster analysis and the discriminant analysis are used to find the patterns of technological differentiation between various types of banks and ownership structures (Gao, 2023). The methods used to ensure the control of the temporal and institutional variations are panel data techniques and the fixed-effects models. Heteroskedasticity and multicollinearity tests are diagnostic tests that provide model validity. All these analytical frameworks form the empirical basis of associating the degree of FinTech adoption with quantifiable financial success, offering not only strategic policy-making but also scholarly discussion elements of digital banking performance (Kumar et al., 2023). The following table 2 connects the main financial indicators and the anticipated effects of the adoption of the FinTech that serve as the foundation of the empirical results of the regression models.

Table 2. Hypothetical Relationship Between FinTech Adoption and Financial Performance Metrics

Performance Indicator	Model Variable	Expected Relationship	Rationale
Return on Assets (ROA)	Profitability (Dependent Variable)	Positive	FinTech increases operational efficiency
Return on Equity (ROE)	Profitability (Dependent Variable)	Positive	Digital innovation enhances returns to shareholders
Z-Score	Stability (Dependent Variable)	Positive	AI-based analytics reduce default risks
Non-Performing Loans (NPLs)	Risk Indicator	Negative	Improved digital monitoring reduces loan defaults
Net Interest Margin (NIM)	Profitability Proxy	Positive	Digital platforms optimize revenue channels

6. LITERATURE REVIEW

The scholarly sources on the adoption of FinTech in banking indicate the fast transformation of the conceptual and empirical frameworks. It has been noted by scholars that digital transformation is not an operational upgrade, but a strategic reorientation that has an impact on competitiveness, risk, and sustainability. The initial research was concerned with the factors of technology adoption, and the recent publications discuss the consequences, including profitability, efficiency, and stability of the system (Zuhroh, 2021). The advent of open banking, Artificial Intelligence, and blockchain has added another prism into the analytical framework, as digital innovation is connected with regulatory compliance and customer experience. A number of models such as the Diffusion of Innovation, Technology Acceptance and Resource-Based View models have been used to explain the difference in adoption in different institutions and regions. Nevertheless, empirical studies on the relationship between FinTech adoption and long-term resilience and financial inclusion are still at a low level of empirical agreement (Master USA. et al., 2025). This sub-section is a literature review that will allow finding out the gaps in theoretical and empirical research and build a multidimensional FinTech Adoption Index, as well as discuss its implications on profitability, risk management, and institutional diversity in the banking industry.

6.1. Empirical Studies on FinTech Adoption in Banking

Empirical research of the FinTech adoption indicates varying approaches and results of worldwide banking systems. The panel data analysis and composite indices are common in quantitative studies that aim to identify the level of digitalization and its impact on performance metrics. Results show that banks that are more digitally mature are more cost effective, capable of innovation and more interested in customers. There is also the presence of empirical evidence which highlights the influences of organizational culture, governance structures and regulatory environments on adoption trajectories (Kalai & Toukabri, 2024). Research in the emerging markets highlights how FinTech alliances and digital payment networks are being used to catalyze the inclusion and competition. On the other hand, in developed economies, the use has been instigated by data analytics, cloud computing, and integration of Artificial Intelligence. Multiple scholars point to the two-way causality between technological investment and profitability, as technological investment improves performance, and better-performing banks also invest more in it (Banerjee et al., 2022). Regardless of these observations, cross-country comparability is still not up to the mark, as different metrics are used, and it is important to have a single measurement framework like the FinTech Adoption Index suggested in the current chapter.

6.2. Impact of Digitalization on Profitability and Risk Management

The process of digitalization has significantly changed the way banks generate value, the cost management and the management of risks. Research on profitability has indicated that the digital technologies enable the efficiency of the processes, transaction cost reduction, and the increase of the revenue streams based on the enhanced product personalization. Mobile and internet banking, such as that, can help banks to have more customers with less physical infrastructure (Mellyana et al., 2024). Besides, data analytics and Artificial Intelligence-driven decision systems are associated with the high quality of loan underwriting, preventing fraud, and predictive risk modeling, leading to increased credit quality. The literature however also warns of excessive dependence on digital systems since productivity gains may be counterbalanced by operational and cyber risks. According to some studies, a fast adoption of technology may also result in the integration problems and temporary decrease in profits. Others find the relationship between the digital intensity and performance is U-shaped with moderate digitalization producing the best efficiency and then falling returns set in (Ben Bouheni et al., 2023). Overall, the evidence confirms that digitalization is the addition in profitability and stability in the situation of its strategic coordination with governance, security frameworks, and organizational versatility.

6.3. Comparative Studies Across Conventional, Islamic, And Foreign Banks

Comparative analyses reveal that there are different patterns of FinTech adoption in the models of banking. Traditional banks focus on automation and integration of AI to reduce efficiency; Islamic banks focus on transparency and ethical compliance by the use of blockchain and digital audit; and foreign banks use the worldwide digital ecosystem to harmonize services. The level of technological preparedness is dependent on the size, ownership and the regulatory environment (Agustin, 2023). These differences allow policy makers to create specific policies of digital transformation that will promote inclusive innovation in all sectors of the banking industry. The following table 3 contrasts the priorities to the adoption of FinTech using the example of the various types of banking models, such as conventional, Islamic, foreign and digital-only, identifying their core areas of technological focus and operational features.

Table 3. Comparative FinTech Adoption Patterns Across Banking Types

Bank Type	Primary Focus in FinTech Adoption	Key Characteristics
Conventional Banks	Automation, AI, digital payments	Profit-driven innovation, efficiency optimization
Islamic Banks	Blockchain, ethical finance tools	Sharia compliance, transparency, partnership-based systems
Foreign Banks	Global digital integration	Cross-border operations, standardized platforms
Digital-Only Banks	AI-driven customer engagement	Cloud-native systems, high agility, low-cost delivery

7. RESULTS / DISCUSSION

Findings of the built FinTech Adoption Index (FAI) show that the technological maturity in the banking institutions is quite different. The adoption scores tend to be higher when it comes to large commercial banks and foreign banks, which have greater capacity to invest, and a better digital infrastructure. The level of adoption is moderate in Islamic and cooperative banks, but the focus is on technologies that are ethically motivated and transparency-driven. The results affirm that the use of

FinTech is positively related to profitability and operational efficiency, but the level of association depends on the context. Regression tests show advanced economies have a greater advantage in terms of regulatory preparedness and market sophistication to the benefit of the banks (Engineering & Doroshenko, 2023). Another point of the discussion is that the rise of technological integration is not only a predeterminer of performance but also risk behavior because the more digitally exposed institutions have the high cybersecurity and data-management demands. The lessons argue in favor of the necessity of promoting digital change in a moderate manner in other words raising innovation and competitiveness and securing financial resilience and institutional diversity within the banking ecosystem.

7.1. Index Outcomes and Bank Categorization

The FinTech Adoption Index uses composite scores across seven categories of digital capability in classifying banks into three levels, namely, high, moderate, and low adopters. The most developed digital ecosystems in high adopters, which are usually large private and foreign banks, include AI-led analytics, open APIs, and real-time payment systems. The moderate adopters consist of regional banks and Islamic banks that have been selective with the adoption of digital tools, paying special attention to mobile banking and automation of processes (Banna & Alam, 2021). The low adopters are usually small cooperative banks that have low digital presence and rely a lot on the traditional systems. The index results also indicate the existence of a digital divide based on ownership and geographic levels, where urban based institutions use it at a higher rate compared to rural based institutions. In addition, expert interviews are a method of qualitative validation which accompanies the quantitative results and indicates that organizational culture, commitment of the management, and the alignment of the regulatory models play a significant role in establishing the readiness to adopt. Through these categorizations, policymakers and researchers are able to determine the technology leaders, laggards and the transitional institutions which form the foundation of comparative and developmental analyses across the sector.

7.2. Relationship Between FinTech Adoption and Financial Indicators

The empirical investigation confirms the existence of statistically significant positive correlation between the level of FinTech adoption and such key financial metrics as Return on Assets (ROA), Return on Equity (ROE), and Net Interest Margin (NIM). Banks that score higher on FAI always show better cost efficiency and diversification of revenue, which is explained by the auto-processing and spread of digital services. Nevertheless, it does not have a linear relationship, and above a certain level, excessive digital investments without strategic alignment can decrease short-term profitability as a result of implementation and cybersecurity expenses (Kaddumi et al., 2023). Stability indicators like the Z-score reveal that in most cases, digitalized banks are more immune to market shocks, due to the improved risk analytics and early warning systems. Nevertheless, the institutions with high-adoption also add that operation complexity and technological risk exposure are more. The discussion suggests that the digitalization process must be balanced through good governance, cybersecurity measures and continuous growth of the human capital which will be sustainable in profitability and institutional stability in the dynamic financial landscape.

7.3. Cross-Institutional and Cross-Regional Insights

With the help of cross-institutional analysis, it can also be observed that FinTech adoption is contingent on external ecosystem maturity and internal strategy. The developed region banks, through their strong regulatory frameworks and policy that favor fintech, are quickly going through digital transformation faster than emerging markets. The careful and ethical digitalization with an emphasis on transparency are also exercised by the Islamic banks, and the foreign banks rely on the global technology relationships to maintain the operational standardizing (Nguyen et al., 2022). The comparisons in the regions also indicate that customer digital literacy level and the presence of infrastructure is a significant determinant of the adoption outcomes. The findings drive the point that one-fits-all approaches are ineffective; tailored approaches running on the institutional objectives, culture, and regulatory benchmarks are required. These remarks confirm the dynamic and contextual nature of FinTech adoption, in which macro trends of technology are mixed with local institutional facts. The institutional diversity is revealed in the table 4 that gives a comparison of adoption, strength and constraint of FinTech in major banking segments.

Table 4. Comparative FinTech Adoption Across Banking Segments

Bank Type	FinTech Focus Areas	Strengths	Challenges
Conventional Banks	Automation, AI, mobile apps	High resources, digital infrastructure	Integration with legacy systems
Islamic Banks	Blockchain for transparency	Sharia-compliant innovation	Limited vendor ecosystem
Foreign Banks	Global API standards	Cross-border digitalization	Regulatory divergence

continued on following page

Table 4. Continued

Bank Type	FinTech Focus Areas	Strengths	Challenges
Digital-Only Banks	Cloud-native architecture	Cost efficiency, scalability	Cyber risk exposure
Cooperative / Regional Banks	Digital payments, process automation	Local customer trust	Low digital literacy, resource limits

8. CASE STUDY ANALYSIS

The practicality of FinTech implementation can be more justified by practical examples, which can allow to realize how digital transformation can result in a more efficient and profitable work and resilience. The subsequent case studies outline some recent trends of the global and regional banking institutions that have managed to use data-driven and AI-driven financial technologies successfully. These examples illustrate the physical advantages of going digital, both in automating the process and integrating open banking, as well as in sustainable innovation, but also discusses the issues of cybersecurity, data control, and customer loyalty (Chan et al., 2022). In combination, they provide empirical data to support the FinTech Adoption Index (FAI) framework suggested in this chapter, which strengthens the relationship between technological capability and financial performance.

8.1 Case Study 1: DBS Bank – AI-Driven Digital Transformation in Singapore (2023–2024)

DBS Bank is a digitally advanced financial institution in Asia and has been cited to have an extensive FinTech integration strategy. In the year 2023-2024, the bank launched an AI-driven analytics platform Customer Intelligence Platform (CIP), which allows making hyper-personalized recommendations in 30 million digital touchpoints each month. Combined with real-time transaction information, this initiative enhanced the efficiency of cross-selling by 28% and digital contribution to retail revenue to 74% of the total retail revenue. Another example of how DBS applied AI in its IT infrastructure is the predictive maintenance model that was launched in the IT infrastructure, which used machine learning to decrease the number of system downtimes by 40% and enhance the accuracy of risk monitoring (Sarfraz et al., 2022). The FinTech adoption index of DBS would be in the top category as it is mature in AI, open API and digital payment. The case highlights how sound digital investments guided by data ethics and governance can bring quantifiable gains in terms of profitability, customer satisfaction and resilience in the system. The figure 5 illustrates the main digital transformation outcomes of DBS Bank, including cross-sell efficiency, digital revenue share, and reduction in downtimes giving an idea of the quantifiable effect of the use of FinTech in the process of innovating.

Figure 5. DBS Bank: FinTech Adoption Outcomes (2023–2024)

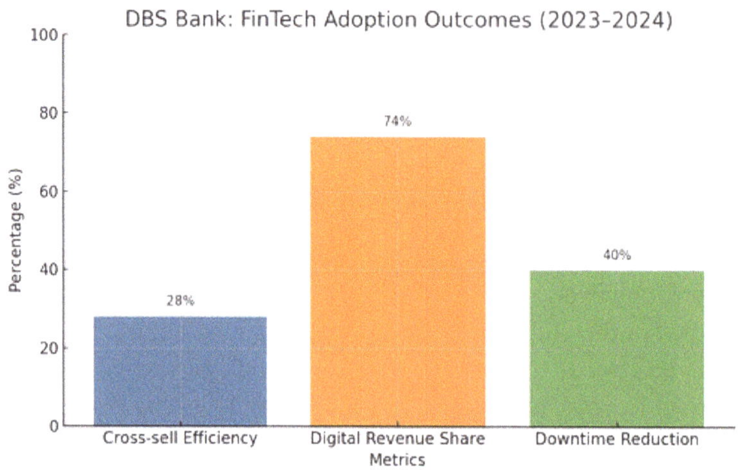

8.2 CASE STUDY 2: STATE BANK OF INDIA (SBI) – FINTECH COLLABORATION AND FINANCIAL INCLUSION IN INDIA (2024–2025)

The State Bank of India has accelerated FinTech partnerships through its "YONO 2.0" platform, launched in 2024 to strengthen digital inclusion and financial accessibility. Working with Indian startups in the areas of blockchain, regtech and digital payments, SBI increased the number of open banking ecosystems to more than 500 third-party APIs. The effort facilitated over 90 million monthly active users to receive combined services including digital loans, insurance and e-commerce via a unified interface. The bank also implemented AI-powered fraud analytics and real-time credit risk scores, which resulted in the bank cutting loan processing by 35% and reducing fraud by 25% (M. Anwarul Islam and, 2024). The case shows that a hybrid FinTech collaboration model has the potential to improve financial inclusion and efficiency in a large public sector bank. SBI example is very close to the principles of institutional diversity and demonstrates how old institutions can effectively transform into data-driven and customer-oriented digital processes. The figure 6 demonstrates that the impact of the digital transformation of SBI can be observed in terms of an increase in API, the number of users, and operational efficiency obtained through the collaboration with FinTech.

Figure 6. SBI: FinTech Collaboration & Inclusion Outcomes (2024–2025)

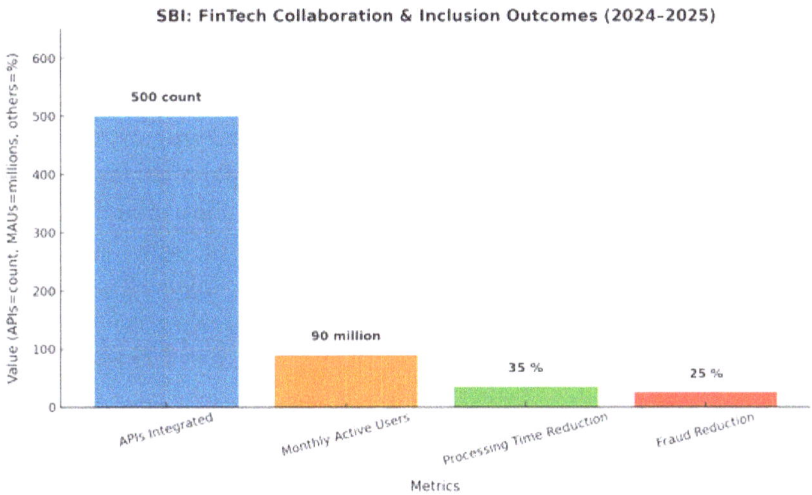

9. FUTURE RESEARCH

Further studies of the FinTech adoption process should not be focused on profitability but covered the socio-economic and sustainability aspects of the digital transformation. A holistic view of digital responsibility can be achieved through the combination of Environmental, Social, And Governance (ESG) measures with FinTech measures. It is also important to conduct comparative studies on the countries, ownership structures, and regulatory environments in order to reflect the best practices and the points of convergence of policies (Zebari & Al Musalhi, 2025). New frontiers like blockchain interoperability, quantum finance and AI-based risk models are exciting prospective new areas. Methodologically, the longitudinal and causal inference methods should be used in future research to investigate the effects of adoption of FinTech on institutional resilience with time. Theoretical foundation can be further improved by expanding the interdisciplinary perspectives, i.e., the emergence of economics, data science, and behavioral finance. Following these guidelines, researchers will be able to assist in developing a comprehensive evidence base that would inform sustainable and inclusive digitalization of the banking systems of the globe.

9.1. Integrating ESG and Sustainability Dimensions in FinTech Adoption

The FinTech and sustainability intersection offer new responsible innovation in the banking industry. The addition of the ESG dimensions to the FinTech adoption models allows the institutions to reconcile the technological progress with the environmental sustainability and social interaction. An example of this is green digital finance platforms, carbon-tracking payment systems, and inclusive credit algorithms, which are examples of ways to use technology to advance the wider developmental agenda. It is suggested that further research is necessary to evaluate the effect of ESG oriented digital solutions to the allocation of capital, customer trust and compliance (Naz et al., 2023). In addition to this, sustainability-related performance indicators can be incorporated into the FinTech Adoption Index to determine the quality of innovation in terms of ethics and environment. The awareness of the crossroads of FinTech and ESG could serve to guide banks towards sustainable competitiveness in such a way that the digital innovation becomes a profitable method of making the bank profitable but also equitable economic development and climate resiliency. It is such integration that has propelled FinTech towards ensuring that global sustainability objectives in the financial ecosystem are achieved.

9.2. Expanding to Cross-Country Comparative Analysis

International comparative research is necessary to derive generalized knowledge about the evidences of the various patterns of FinTech adoption that have been provided based on institutional, cultural, and regulatory environments. Inequality in the digital infrastructure, consumer trust and enabling policies is a significant factor in adoption trends. The new study should also look into the regulatory sandbox variations, open-banking conditions, and cybersecurity laws and the impact they have on innovation in different regions. Global data can be contrasted in search of convergent and divergent tendencies in digital maturity, efficiency and resilience (Varma et al., 2022). Also, the localized adaptation strategies are available in the regional case studies of Asia, Europe, and the Middle East that may be applied to obtain granular information. The generalizability of FinTech Adoption Index is favorable because of the expansion of the comparative research and the knowledge sharing of the new market with the existing markets. Lastly, such analysis will result in harmonization of digital finance policies, which will enable cross-border interoperability, increased inclusiveness and sustainable competitive advantage within the global financial ecosystem.

9.3. Exploring AI, Blockchain, and Quantum Finance Applications

The new generation of FinTech development is based on artificial intelligence, blockchain, and quantum computing, which are the emerging technologies that are transforming them. AI augments predictive analytics, fraud detection, and personalization of the customer, and blockchain removes any visibility or immutability in transactions. Quantum finance is an emergent discipline that has the potential to have the ability to optimize portfolios and risk assessment at an exponential rate. In the future, research should also be carried out in relation to the possibilities of using these technologies synergistically to achieve maximum efficiency, security, and scalability of financial systems (Elrefae & Nuseir, 2022). Empirical models are required in strategic investment decisions to analyze their readiness to adopt, the cost implication of adoption and the governance aspect. In addition to that, AI and blockchain hybrids can change the credit checks, compliance checks, and international payments. The studies on these new frontiers will provide a futuristic view on how convergence of technologies will lead to resilience and innovation to make quantum-ready and intelligent and decentralized banking ecosystems in the future.

10. MANAGERIAL IMPLICATIONS

The findings of this chapter have practical implications on the banking executives, policymakers and regulators. FinTech implementation is to be viewed as a strategic investment in which one should strike a balance between innovation and caution. It is also advised that managers ought to develop consistent digital roadmaps concentrating on data governance, cybersecurity, and reskilling of its employees. The regulators should come up with regulatory sandboxes that encourage experimentation and also ensure financial stability. Technological investments need to be integrated in the risk management operations, and ESG to be resilient in the long run, institutionally (Harmadi et al., 2022). FinTech Adoption Index is a diagnostic tool, and it is possible to utilize it to assess the degree of advances and identify gaps in pinpointing the capabilities. All these suggestions support the argument that the digital transformation is not a typically occurring event, but a process of constant learning, adjustment, and regulation. Strategic alignment, institutional agility and cross-sector collaboration are the three enablers to achieve sustainable growth in FinTech-embarked modern banking systems. The following table 5 presents the main managerial and regulatory recommendations to make the FinTech adoption in the banking industry responsible, inclusive, and sustainable.

Table 5. Managerial and Policy Implications for Sustainable FinTech Integration

Stakeholder	Key Recommendation	Strategic Objective	Outcome
Bank Executives	Develop digital transformation roadmap	Align technology with business goals	Improved competitiveness
Regulators	Implement adaptive regulatory sandboxes	Balance innovation and stability	Safe innovation environment
IT Managers	Strengthen cybersecurity and data governance	Ensure secure and ethical digitalization	Risk mitigation
Human Resource Units	Upskill employees in AI and analytics	Build internal digital capabilities	Workforce readiness
Policy Makers	Promote financial inclusion via FinTech	Support underserved regions	Equitable digital access

10.1. Strategic Recommendations for Bank Executives

Bank leaders ought to give top priority to the implementation of FinTech as a fundamental strategic operation incorporated in the organizational planning and investment activities. An effective digital transformation planning strategy should have set milestones, which can guarantee the cohesive nature of technological initiative and corporate goals. Ongoing education of employees on the digital literacy, data analytics, and cybersecurity issues enhances internal capabilities and creates a culture of innovativeness. It is also the responsibility of the executives to incorporate the use of balanced scorecards that connect digital performance with both financial and non-financial performance in order to hold the parties accountable. Technological risks can be shared by forming strategic alliances with FinTech companies, startups, and educational institutions to speed up innovation (Wang, 2024). Ethical AI, customer-centric design, and transparent data practices by the leadership are additional beliefs that promote reputation and trust. It is recommended that executives should incorporate the FinTech Adoption Index as a performance benchmarking instrument to track the level of digital maturity and make evidence-based decisions. With responsible and active leadership, banks will be able to make digital adoption a sustainable competitive advantage.

10.2. Policy and Regulatory Implications for Fintech Integration

FinTech policy frameworks are important in empowering or limiting the innovation. Regulators have to reconcile between the overall financial stability and innovation promotion by setting up dynamic, risk-based principles. Other programs like open-banking standards, digital identity schemes, and regulatory sandboxes have been effective to enhance innovation besides protecting consumers. Interoperability can be achieved through standardization of cross-border laws and it can also enhance foreign investment in digital banking infrastructure. Moreover, the problem of cybersecurity, data privacy, and AI ethics must have an unceasing regulation to reduce the system risks (Duan et al., 2023b). The other policy area that the policymakers should address to ensure is equitable access to technology that is most likely to boost digital inclusion of small banks and underserved regions. Frequent evaluation of the FinTech adoption, based on the standardized indexes, can be used to support evidence-based policymaking and timely recognition of risks. To achieve a sustainable financial industry, regulators could balance innovation stimulation and prudential control and establish a healthy and inclusive FinTech ecosystem that will support sustainable financial development.

10.3. Operational Guidelines for Enhancing Digital Maturity

Enhancing the digital maturity requires management operational plans that are engaged in technology, people, and processes. Banks must adopt the modular IT models in order to facilitate the process of expansion and interoperability between systems. The cloud infrastructure, API-based connection and real-time analytics will enable the creation of products in a more agile manner and giving customers personal experiences. Effective cybersecurity tactics and the regular evaluation should also be part of automation of the processes (Wahga et al., 2023). The promotion of the culture of innovation through continuous learning, the ability to work in teams regardless of functional boundaries, and the incentive based on the innovative problem-solving is also essential. Predictive analytics and digital twins can also enhance operational efficiency through optimization of the workflow, along with, resource use. Regular self-assessment using the FinTech Adoption Index will help the institutions gauge their level of advancement, areas of weakness, and resources. Ultimately, digital maturity is a strategic vision, a functional skill, and a human capability in a flexible futuristic company structure, rather than just a technology issue.

11. CONCLUSION

The article concludes that the use of FinTech has proven to be an inevitable wave of transformation in the global banking system which in essence redefines efficiency, competitiveness and stability. The chapter gives a good structure with which to quantify and evaluate the multidimensionality of digital transformation, such as automation, Artificial Intelligence, open banking, and digital payments and strategic FinTech relationships with a much more detailed framework of FinTech adoption by developing a comprehensive index of FinTech adoption (FAI). The empirical results show that the rate of adoption is positively related to the rates of profitability, efficiency of operations, and financial stability, however, the over digitalization in the absence of a strategic orientation can lead to augmented cyber vulnerabilities and huddles in the integration process. The findings highlight the fact that the impact of FinTech implementation is not uniform among the institutions: big commercial and foreign banks are in the first place of the field of innovation, but small and Islamic banks have biased but ethically-driven adoption policies. It is based on this heterogeneity that contextual strategies of aligning technology to institutional capacity and regulatory maturity is critical.

Theoretically, the chapter merely closes the gap between the view of diffusion of innovation and technology adoption since it displays the interplay between organizational readiness, perceived usefulness, and regulatory structures in the establishment of organizational digital transformation orientations. It helps to indicate that the acceptance of FinTech is not a unidirectional process but a process of continuous changes and feedback that determines the long-term performance and short-term performance. Practically speaking, a FinTech Adoption Index is a diagnostic and benchmarking tool to policymakers, regulators, and banking executives so as to make evidence-related choices, evaluate performance, and formulate policies. Most of the weaknesses of the study are linked to the availability of data and time frame meaning that in subsequent research longitudinal analysis and cross-country analysis ought to be employed to capture the transformation in digital trend. Overall, the chapter makes it clear that to achieve a digitally resilient banking ecosystem, there must be a strike between innovation and governance. Cybersecurity, ethical AI, and ESG should be part of the digital strategy of the banks, and the regulators should encourage testing and diversity. FinTech may be implemented strategically so as to improve financial performance and systemic trust and sustainability. The way forward is to ensure that you possess symbiotic ecologies at the point at which technology and regulation are intertwined with human capital to create adaptive, open and futuristic financial institutions.

REFERENCES

Abedalrhman, K. (2025). Integrative analysis of FinTech innovations in industry: Enhancements and challenges. SSRN Electronic Journal. DOI: 10.2139/ssrn.5074495

Agustin, G. (2023). The rise of financial technology and its credit risk in Indonesia. *International Journal of Accounting & Finance in Asia Pasific*, *6*(2), 98–109. DOI: 10.32535/ijafap.v6i2.2318

M., , & Anwarul Islam, , K., & Saifuddin Khan, M. (2024). The role of financial literacy, digital literacy, and financial self-efficacy in FinTech adoption. *Investment Management and Financial Innovations*, *21*(2), 370–380. DOI: 10.21511/imfi.21(2).2024.30

Arena, C., Catuogno, S., & Naciti, V. (2023). Governing FinTech for performance: The monitoring role of female independent directors. *European Journal of Innovation Management*, *26*(7), 591–610. DOI: 10.1108/EJIM-11-2022-0621

Arora, A., Gupta, S., Devi, C., & Walia, N. (2023). Customer experiences in the era of artificial intelligence (AI) in context to FinTech: A fuzzy AHP approach. *Benchmarking*, *30*(10), 4342–4369. DOI: 10.1108/BIJ-10-2021-0621

Banerjee, R., Majumdar, S., & Albastaki, M. (2022). Ideal self-congruence: Neo-banking by traditional banks and the impact on market share - A case of uae banks. *International Journal of Professional Business Review*, *7*(4), e0779. DOI: 10.26668/businessreview/2022.v7i4.e779

Banna, H., & Alam, M. R. (2021). Does digital financial inclusion matter for bank risk-taking? Evidence from the dual-banking system. *Journal of Islamic Monetary Economics and Finance*, *7*(2), 401–430. DOI: 10.21098/jimf.v7i2.1320

Basdekis, C., Christopoulos, A., Katsampoxakis, I., & Vlachou, A. (2022). FinTech's rapid growth and its effect on the banking sector. *Journal of Banking and Financial Technology*, *6*(2), 159–176. DOI: 10.1007/s42786-022-00045-w

Ben Bouheni, F., Tewari, M., Sidaoui, M., & Hasnaoui, A. (2023). An econometric understanding of Fintech and operating performance. *Review of Accounting and Finance*, *22*(3), 329–352. DOI: 10.1108/RAF-10-2022-0290

Chan, R., Troshani, I., Rao Hill, S., & Hoffmann, A. (2022). Towards an understanding of consumers' FinTech adoption: The case of Open Banking. *International Journal of Bank Marketing*, *40*(4), 886–917. DOI: 10.1108/IJBM-08-2021-0397

Darji, D. A., Parikh, S. M., Patel, A. M., Patel, K. D., & Suthar, A. B. (2025). Measuring the impact of AI key metrics and KPIs in Financial Services. In *Intersecting Natural Language Processing and FinTech Innovations in Service Marketing* (pp. 337–370). IGI Global., DOI: 10.4018/979-8-3693-9944-6.ch018

Duan, C., Mao, M., & Tang, L. (2023a). Research on the evaluation of core competitiveness of commercial banks: Based on the perspective of digital transformation. Advances in Economics. *Management and Political Sciences*, *52*(1), 91–99. DOI: 10.54254/2754-1169/52/20230701

Duan, C., Mao, M., & Tang, L. (2023b). Research on the evaluation of core competitiveness of commercial banks: Based on the perspective of digital transformation. Advances in Economics. *Management and Political Sciences*, *52*(1), 91–99. DOI: 10.54254/2754-1169/52/20230701

Elrefae, G., & Nuseir, M. T. (2022). Blockchain in global finance make-over: Exploring the mediating role of supply chain flexibility. *Uncertain Supply Chain Management*, *10*(3), 983–992. DOI: 10.5267/j.uscm.2022.2.015

Engineering, N. U. (2023). Formation of the fintech sector: Opportunities and risks in the conditions of the digital economy. *Aktual'ni Problemi Ekonomìki*, *1*(259), 24–34. DOI: 10.32752/1993-6788-2022-1-259-24-34

Gao, P. (2023). Analysis of the impact of digital currency on traditional banking and financial stability. *Advances in Economics and Management Research*, *8*(1), 326. DOI: 10.56028/aemr.8.1.326.2023

Gekhaeva, P., Bolotkhanov, E., & Ismoilova, S. (2023). Global Digital Transformation Trends: Financial-Economic Sector. SHS Web of Conferences, 172, 02025. DOI: 10.1051/shsconf/202317202025

Harmadi, U. W., Trinugroho, I., & Atmaji. (2022). The effect of fintech on conventional bank performance and bank risk. In Advances in Economics, Business and Management Research (pp. 140–152). Atlantis Press International BV. DOI: 10.2991/978-94-6463-066-4_13

Kaddumi, T. A., Baker, H., Nassar, M. D., & A-Kilani, Q. (2023). Does financial technology adoption influence bank's financial performance: The case of Jordan. *Journal of Risk and Financial Management*, *16*(9), 413. DOI: 10.3390/jrfm16090413

Kalai, L., & Toukabri, M. (2024). Risks, regulations, and impacts of FinTech adoption on commercial banks in the United States and Canada: A comparative analysis. *Thunderbird International Business Review*, *66*(6), 609–641. Advance online publication. DOI: 10.1002/tie.22404

Khuan, H. (2024). Fintech and the future of banking: Collaboration and innovation for better financial services. [DEMAND]. *Economics Studies and Banking Journal, 1*(2), 75–93. DOI: 10.62207/c0y42z81

Kumar, S., Lim, W. M., Sivarajah, U., & Kaur, J. (2023). Artificial intelligence and blockchain integration in business: Trends from a bibliometric-content analysis. Information Systems Frontiers: A Journal of Research and Innovation, 25(2), 871–896. DOI: 10.1007/s10796-022-10279-0

Le, T., Ngo, T., Nguyen, D. T., & Do, T. T. M. (2024). Fintech and banking: Friends or foes? Evidence from bank–fintech cooperation. *International Journal of Bank Marketing, 42*(7), 1513–1535. DOI: 10.1108/IJBM-09-2023-0525

Li, L. (2023). The digital transformation of the banking industry in the era of big data. Advances in Economics. *Management and Political Sciences, 39*(1), 24–30. DOI: 10.54254/2754-1169/39/20231929

Mellyana, D., & Hasan Basri, M. (2024). Business solution for profit optimization at PBS clinic. *International Journal of Current Science Research and Review, 07*(08). Advance online publication. DOI: 10.47191/ijcsrr/V7-i8-03

Mhlanga, D. (2024). The role of big data in financial technology toward financial inclusion. *Frontiers in Big Data, 7*, 1184444. DOI: 10.3389/fdata.2024.1184444

Naz, S., Asif, M., & Hameed, S. (2023). Fintech's role in sustainable banking performance: Are green banking policies driving sustainability in Pakistan's banking system? *Gomal University Journal of Research, 39*(03), 294–312. DOI: 10.51380/gujr-39-03-04

Nguyen, L., Tran, S., & Ho, T. (2022). Fintech credit, bank regulations and bank performance: A cross-country analysis. *Asia-Pacific Journal of Business Administration, 14*(4), 445–466. DOI: 10.1108/APJBA-05-2021-0196

Niroula, A., & Adhikari, S. (2024). Machine learning, banking, industry, digitalization, innovation. *American Journal of Finance and Business Management, 3*(1), 62–72. DOI: 10.58425/ajfbm.v3i1.286

Oladipo, J. O., Okoye, C. C., Elufioye, O. A., Falaiye, T., & Nwankwo, E. E. (2024). Human factors in cybersecurity: Navigating the fintech landscape. *International Journal of Science and Research Archive, 11*(1), 1959–1967. DOI: 10.30574/ijsra.2024.11.1.0258

Qi, J., Chatterjee, S., Worthy, S., Herndon, K., & Wojdynski, B. (2024a). Using an extended post-acceptance framework to examine consumer adoption of fintech. *International Journal of Bank Marketing*, *42*(3), 642–668. DOI: 10.1108/IJBM-10-2022-0448

Qi, J., Chatterjee, S., Worthy, S., Herndon, K., & Wojdynski, B. (2024b). Using an extended post-acceptance framework to examine consumer adoption of fintech. *International Journal of Bank Marketing*, *42*(3), 642–668. DOI: 10.1108/IJBM-10-2022-0448

Qiang, X. (2024). Digital transformation in the financial sector through FinTech. Advances in Economics. *Management and Political Sciences*, *76*(1), 226–234. DOI: 10.54254/2754-1169/76/20241656

Ranković, M., Gurgu, E., Martins, O. M. D., & Vukasović, M. (2023). Artificial intelligence and the evolution of finance: Opportunities, challenges and ethical considerations. *EdTech Journal*, *3*(1), 20–23. DOI: 10.18485/edtech.2023.3.1.2

Ravikumar, A. S., & Mamadiyarov, Z. (2025). Mitigating risks through AI-powered fraud detection systems in digital banking. In Innovating Cost-Efficient and Scalable Business Models in the Digital Era (pp. 343–376). IGI Global Scientific Publishing. DOI: 10.4018/979-8-3373-2120-2.ch011

Sarfraz, M., Ye, Z., Banciu, D., Dragan, F., & Ivascu, L. (2022). Intertwining digitalization and sustainable performance via the mediating role of digital transformation and the moderating role of FinTech behavior adoption. *Studies in Informatics and Control*, *31*(4), 35–44. DOI: 10.24846/v31i4y202204

Shanti, R., Siregar, H., Zulbainarni, N., & Tony, . (2023). Role of digital transformation on digital business model banks. *Sustainability (Basel)*, *15*(23), 16293. DOI: 10.3390/su152316293

Shmuratko, Y. A., & Sheludko, S. A.Ya. A. ShmuratkoS. A. Sheludko. (2021). Financial technologies' impact on the development of banking. *Financial and Credit Activity Problems of Theory and Practice*, *4*(31), 61–69. DOI: 10.18371/fcaptp.v4i31.190792

Varma, P., Nijjer, S., Sood, K., Grima, S., & Rupeika-Apoga, R. (2022). Thematic analysis of financial technology (Fintech) influence on the banking industry. *Risks*, *10*(10), 186. DOI: 10.3390/risks10100186

Wahga, A. I., Majid, S., Ahmad, N., Aftab, I., & Awais, M. (2023). FinTech and Pakistan's banking industry: An exploratory study. *Journal of Policy Research*, *12*(4), 19–28. DOI: 10.61506/02.00122

Wang, L. (2024). Impact of FinTech on Commercial Banks. Advances in Economics. *Management and Political Sciences*, *72*(1), 211–216. DOI: 10.54254/2754-1169/72/20240699

Zebari, G. M., & Al Musalhi, N. (2025). A comprehensive review of integrating AI and blockchain security: Innovations, challenges, and future directions. *Security and Privacy*, *8*(5), e70094. Advance online publication. DOI: 10.1002/spy2.70094

Zhao, X., Sun, X., Zhao, L., & Xing, Y. (2022). Can the digital transformation of manufacturing enterprises promote enterprise innovation? *Business Process Management Journal*, *28*(4), 960–982. DOI: 10.1108/BPMJ-01-2022-0018

Zuhroh, I. (2021). The impact of Fintech on Islamic banking and the collaboration model: A systematic review studies in Indonesia. *Jurnal Perspektif Pembiayaan Dan Pembangunan Daerah*, *9*(4), 302–312. DOI: 10.22437/ppd.v9i4.12054

13. KEY TERMS AND DEFINITIONS

Artificial Intelligence (AI) in Banking: The application of intelligent algorithms for predictive analytics, fraud detection, credit scoring, and personalized financial services.

Blockchain Technology: A distributed ledger system ensuring transparency, immutability, and traceability of financial transactions within digital banking ecosystems.

Cybersecurity: The practice of protecting financial systems, networks, and data from digital threats, ensuring confidentiality, integrity, and availability.

Digital Maturity: The extent to which a banking institution has integrated, optimized, and institutionalized digital technologies within its strategic and operational processes.

Digital Transformation: The process of reengineering banking operations, products, and services using digital tools to improve efficiency, agility, and customer engagement.

ESG Integration (Environmental, Social, Governance): The incorporation of sustainability and ethical responsibility within FinTech strategies to promote green and inclusive finance.

Financial Stability: The resilience of banking institutions to withstand market fluctuations, credit risks, and operational disruptions while maintaining performance continuity.

FinTech (Financial Technology): The integration of advanced digital technologies such as AI, blockchain, and data analytics into financial services to enhance efficiency, innovation, and customer experience.

FinTech Adoption Index (FAI): A composite measurement framework developed to quantify the degree of FinTech integration across banks based on multiple dimensions including digital presence, automation, AI, and open APIs.

Institutional Diversity: The coexistence of various banking models conventional, Islamic, foreign, and digital-only each adapting differently to technological change.

Open Banking: A financial system that allows third-party developers to build services around banks through secure API integrations, promoting transparency and competition.

Operational Efficiency: The optimization of banking processes and resource utilization through automation and data-driven decision-making.

Profitability Indicators: Financial measures such as Return on Assets (ROA) and Return on Equity (ROE) used to assess the impact of digital transformation on financial performance.

Quantum Finance: An emerging field utilizing quantum computing to optimize risk management, portfolio analysis, and complex financial simulations in digital banking.

Regulatory Sandbox: A controlled framework provided by regulators that allows banks and FinTech startups to test innovative products under relaxed compliance conditions.

Chapter 7
Designing a FinTech Adoption Index:
A Strategic Framework for Measuring Digital Transformation in Asian Banks

V. Lava Kumar
http://orcid.org/0000-0002-3539-9280
GITAM (Deemed to be) University, India

Santhapalli Gautami
http://orcid.org/0000-0002-5667-1343
Sri Venkateswara College of Engineering, India

E. Gnanaprasuna
http://orcid.org/0000-0001-5648-7004
Madanapalle Institute of Technology & Science (Deemed to be University), India

N. Sathyanarayana
http://orcid.org/0000-0002-4185-7751
Jain (Deemed to be) University, India

D. Srikanth Reddy
http://orcid.org/0009-0005-7308-924X
REVA University, India

ABSTRACT

The emergence of Financial Technology (FinTech) as an accelerated phenomenon is reshaping the banking industry, particularly in regions such as Asia, where insti-

DOI: 10.4018/979-8-3373-6244-1.ch007

tutional varieties and regulatory regimes present both opportunities and challenges to digital transformation. The chapter presents a map of the FinTech Adoption Index (FAI), a comprehensive framework developed to measure the level of FinTech adoption among various banking organisations. The FAI measures various dimensions of adoption, including customer experience, regulatory compliance, technological infrastructure, and strategic alliances. The index provides banks, regulatory authorities, and policymakers with a crucial tool that helps measure progress, identify shortcomings, and inform future decision-making in digital projects. Although the adoption of FinTech has significant potential, the remnants of past systems, regulatory challenges, and concerns about consumer trust are among the graver obstacles that must be overcome.

1 INTRODUCTION

Financial services are being reinvented due to the widespread application of financial technology. The AI-driven risk models, blockchain-based compliance architecture and digital-only customer interfaces are transforming banking processes, competitiveness, risk risk management, and customer interaction (Omarini, 2018; Rahim et al., 2023). The Banking systems in Asia are institutionally heterogeneous and must be forced to absorb new technologies and work in the complex regulatory environment, which causes fast modernisation (Banna et al., 2021). The commercial banks in the area must adopt FinTech solutions since the consumer demands of digital services are ever increasing and new regulatory structures are open (Setiawan et al., 2021).

The entrepreneurship of FinTech implies a range of advantages, such as efficiency, enhanced customer experience, and the coverage of a greater number of customers in terms of financial services. Nevertheless, it is yet to be discovered to what extent the adoption is adopted and how it affects various banking institutions (Yan et al., 2022). The main challenge is in assessing the FinTech acceptance in the context of the typology of various banks, banks of different sizes, and the regulatory environment (Ali et al., 2021). The digital-first, state-owned and regional institutions (regardless of being digital-first) are encountering singular FinTech adoption issues and opportunities in the Asian banks (Bajwa et al., 2022). Regulators and policymakers need to pay closer attention to subtle appreciation of the digital transformation and the implementation of the relevant evaluation frameworks by banks, therefore.

The empirical research on the adoption of FinTech is often done at the level of the technology or type of institutions, like digital payments or blockchain applications, without offering a generalized and systematic method of evaluating the adoption of FinTech in the bigger picture (Banna et al., 2021). The existing literature tends to be specialised, such as financial inclusion measures or econometric effects of technology, which leaves a blank of comprehensive indices that can be used to measure the impact of FinTech in different institutional contexts (Setiawan et al., 2021). These inadequacies underscore the need for a more holistic paradigm that acknowledges the multidimensional nature of FinTech integration within the banking industry (Morgan and Long, 2020).

To address this gap, the paper presents the FinTech Adoption Index (FAI)- a conceptual and practical framework of the measurement of FinTech adoption among Asian banking institutions. Instead of using econometric models to analyse the correlations, the suggested framework develops a holistic index to evaluate the strategic, institutional, and regulatory integration of FinTech (Siddik et al., 2023). Researchers interested in knowing the dynamics of FinTech adoption use the tool, regulators require solutions to evaluate the effectiveness of their policies once more, and the makers of banking strategies require intelligence that would allow them to take action in their digital transformation (Yan et al., 2022).

The Financial Adoption Index (FAI) is a rating system that ranks financial institutions based on their readiness to adopt new technologies, compliance with legal documents, and the novelty of services provided to customers (Yan et al.,, 2022). The index measures the heterogeneity of the Asian banking sector, incorporating additional variables such as the institution's scale, market share, and regulatory framework (Zainal et al., 2021). This, in its turn, will allow stakeholders to see how various regional banks are tackling FinTech issues and how they can use new opportunities through the comparative institutional lens of the index (Ali et al., 2021).

According to Siddik and Rahman (2023), the framework is flexible to the new trends and market forces in FinTech. It gives information on forecast trends on the future and details the possible improvements, in addition to estimating the current usage (Yan et al., 2022). The FAI emphasises technological infrastructure, customer-oriented innovation, legislative environment, and institutional readiness to change as the main aspects that determine an institution's readiness to adopt FinTech (Ali et al., 2021).

Bajwa et al. (2022), the Financial Analytics Initiative can be used to shed light on the process of bank embedding FinTech and other areas where the resources can be justified. In addition to protecting innovation and financial sustainability, the programme helps regulators develop an opinion on how much of the current regulations contribute to or obstruct the use of FinTech (Siddik et al., 2023). The FAI allows conducting a structured inquiry into the implications of FinTech adoption on financial performance, inclusivity, and sustainability in the Asian banking sector by providing a formalised structure (Banna et al., 2021).

2 BACKGROUND AND CONTEXT

2.1 The Necessity of FinTech Adoption

The financial world today is evolving rapidly, which emphasises the idea that the fintech shift is no longer a competitive advantage but a precondition of the existence and maintenance of banking companies. With the ecstatic transformation of financial services increasingly becoming more digital, to keep afloat, banks must adopt new digital technologies, which are increasingly emerging, specifically artificial intelligence, blockchain, and mobile banking (Omarini, 2018). These technologies would cease being discretionary, but systemic processes which drive financial institutions to emerge in an ecosystem that is becoming increasingly more digitised. Any reluctance to adopt such technologies will expose banks to a loss of market share and the threat of being outdone by more innovative banks.

2.2 Regulatory Support and Policy Frameworks in Asia.

As governments in Asia have responded to the accelerating rate of digital innovation, various governments, including the Reserve Bank of India, the Monetary Authority of Singapore (MAS), and Bank Negara Malaysia, have enacted policy frameworks to facilitate the adoption of FinTech. These authorities have implemented policies that stimulate innovation, alongside other measures that enhance financial sustainability and consumer protection, including open APIs, innovation hubs, and digital banking charters, to foster innovation (Buckley et al., 2020). As an example, MAS has developed an enabling FinTech development capacity in its regulatory sandbox, where new financial products and services can be tested in a regulated environment. Similarly, the digital banking of the Bank Negara Malaysia provisions is also a self-introduction where it has put or prescribed a platform that enables both traditional and digital-only banks to have a play-level field. These types of regulation can enable more people to adopt FinTech in the Asian continent.

2.3 Inequalities in adoption among Banks.

The distribution of FinTech solutions within the Banking environment in Asia is highly heterogeneous, as all the regulatory advances have been implemented over the last few years. Such disparity is justified by a string of determinants, including the inequality in resource endowments, the constraints of old infrastructures, and institutions susceptible to risk (Setiawan et al., 2021). Namely, the implementation of new technologies, such as artificial intelligence or robotic process automation, is crucially faced by the financial institutions of the emerging markets, partially because they have an archaic information-technology infrastructure that is ill-equipped to adopt the emerging technologies (Zainal et al., 2021). These pre-digital platforms have posed a massive challenge to the companies who would rather deploy solutions that will invariably involve scaling, dynamicism and assimilation by the already existing ecosystems. Comparatively, the banks that have moved already far in the digital spectrum might be too busy with their regulatory needs and building customer confidence to enact the most recent technology, particularly the one that employs a distributed ledger system or electronic money.

2.4 The Impact of Institutional Models on FinTech Adoption

The kind of institution greatly determines the adoption of the FinTech in Asian banking ecosystem of heterogeneous institutions. The state-owned banks fall into the crossfire of bureaucracy and burdensome regulation regimes, where the advancement of technologies is harshly stifled (Banna et al., 2021). New barriers to the work of Islamic banks, controlled by the Sharia law, also exist because it is difficult to adopt the systems of interest or blockchain technologies that do not correspond to the principles of religion (Rahim et al., 2023). All these controls and cultural constraints are obstacles to the digital transformation agenda of such institutions. On the other hand, digital-only banks, which are not restricted by the legacy systems, develop the implementation of the FinTech solutions at a faster rate; however, they face the challenge of customer confidence and regulatory ambiguity, especially where digital banking legislation is not well-developed on the jurisdiction level (Setiawan et al., 2021). Based on this, FinTech implementation has to be carefully customized according to the institutional structures and business conditions typical of regional banks.

2.5 Technological Readiness and Regulatory Agility

The technological readiness of banks and the rate at which regulatory frameworks keep up bring about a big obstacle to implementing FinTech solutions. Application of artificial intelligence, machine learning and automation is particularly difficult with institutions whose legacy infrastructure and limited resources are not adapted to such innovations (Zainal et al., 2021). The innovations can require enormous realisation of hardware, software and specialised knowledge that most banks lack. Besides, successful AI systems are built with large amounts of data to train algorithms and improve the performance, which is often out of the scope of traditional banks that have archaic data-management structures.

On the other hand, even banks that have successfully implemented these innovative technologies often struggle to balance their technical advantages with the ever-changing regulatory environment (Buckley et al., 2020). This flexibility in rapidly changing regulatory compliance mechanisms, which can be referred to as regulatory agility, is necessary to help institutions smoothly incorporate new solutions into the workflow. Although flexible instruments, like regulatory sand-boxes implemented by different bodies, like the Monetary Authority of Singapore, have been introduced, a significant percentage of banks still avoid innovation because of fears raised over compliance issues (Arner et al., 2019).

2.6 The Proposed FinTech Adoption Index (FAI)

Taking everything into consideration, it is obvious that banks do lack a sound diagnostic tool to measure their digital maturity and monitor progress. FinTech Adoption Index (FAI) is an inclusive model aimed at assessing the level of digitalization among banking organisations. It reviews all the relevant aspects, including the preparedness and compliance stance of an organisation and the congruence of strategic goals with fintech needs to ensure that it goes beyond the naive view of mobile banking apps or even digital alliances (Omarini, 2018). The FAI allows tracing a logical path of a bank digitally by mapping its evolution in a variety of dimensions, thus identifying possible areas of enhancement to speed up access to a new stage of progress. In practise, the FAI will permit banks to undertake a self-evaluation of its digital maturity, which will provide comparative knowledge against other Asian banks. These benchmarking offer regulatory agencies information on how to identify underperforming institutions, as well as to develop specific legal or policy interventions to help more to adopt them (Yan et al., 2022). Bank managers also use the index to develop custom transformation roadmaps that are sensitive to both the organisational environment and to the unique challenges they are facing.

Comparative takeaway: Across Asian markets, banks face the same broad drivers (customer expectations, regulatory change, and technology availability), but adoption pathways diverge by institutional model—private and larger banks typically move faster due to capital and governance agility, while public/development and smaller institutions often require modular, risk-aware adoption with stronger regulatory alignment. The FAI is designed to make these differences visible and comparable.

3 GAP IN THE LITERATURE

Researchers take a significant interest in the adoption of fintech; however, most of their research focuses on either grand-level policy issues or on small-scale deployments of technologies, such as AI, blockchain, or mobile banking (Omarini, 2018). The existing literature illuminates on the individual technologies or the regulatory milieus, but it is silent on a multi-layered approach that may explain why banks adopt fintech as boards. The presence of a mobile application or online collaboration is just a superficial examination (Banna et al., 2021). Even though these observations are relevant to the comprehension of adoption, it does not go deep enough to talk about how fintech could be incorporated into the regular banking activities, strategic decision-making, and compliance models. This superficial outlook is a good effort to de-aggregate the phenomenon and hide the details regarding how even the implementation of these technologies happens.

The other dimension that is usually disregarded is connected with the heterogeneity of the regions and institutions that characterize the Asian banking industry (Siddik et al., 2023). All the abovementioned developmental banks, Islamic finance institutions, and state-owned entities possess certain challenges and opportunities to implement fintech into the Asian market (Setiawan et al., 2021). Even though the fintech boom remains salient in the field, theoretical treatments do not pay due attention to these institutional settings resulting in the thinness of the way in which fintech could take shape in the diverse banking environment of Asia (Zainal et al., 2021). Consequently, we do not get an insight into the subtleties of the way banks manage the fintech and in which situations the technology integration will become a genuine competitive advantage. Though the literature on Islamic fintech and financial inclusion includes a small number of studies on the topic (Rahim et al., 2023), comparatively few studies investigate the issue of how Asian-based Islamic banks negotiate their regulatory and cultural landscapes (Ali et al., 2021). Banks owned by the state and under increased regulation are even more complex in implementing fintechs; these banks experience specialised regulatory issues that hinder the implementation of technology. How such banks could effectively overcome these obstacles is not discussed in the literature, which clearly shows a significant gap in our knowledge of policy-making and technological innovation in the Asian banking sector (Bajwa et al., 2022).

In many cases, the frameworks of FinTech adoption rely on econometric modeling or address specific tech solutions, without regard to how they map with the overall strategy of a bank or regulatory requirements (Yan et al., 2022). The implementation path by a bank is to be considered in relation to an implementation strategy, corporate governance, and compliance arrangements (Siddik & Rahman, 2023). It is difficult to see how the digital transformation is actually taking place across banks because of the absence of a smooth, all-in-one framework that reflects the many faces of FinTech adoption.

Differences across regions lead to difficulty in developing a framework that is universally applicable. The banks of Southeast Asia typically engage in vague FinTech regulation and policy frameworks (Setiawan et al., 2021). East Asian state-owned or development banks might encounter various regulatory hassles, in particular, state-sponsored digital money or blockchain technology (Zainal et al., 2021). Since regulations, finance and market maturity vary throughout the region, we require a multi-dimensional framework that can be adapted to numerous national and institutional settings.

An integrated, unified index to assess the adoption of FinTech by banks in various locations does not exist (Bajwa et al., 2022). Single case studies or regional snapshots are the preferred method of current research, which makes comparison of adoption between institutions or countries a genuine pain. An index such as the one that we are suggesting in this chapter can represent a benchmarking instrument to assess the FinTech adoption in each bank, cross-rate between bank types, and provide a strong understanding of the regulatory forces at work (Siddik & Rahman, 2023). Such an index would also be useful in designing policies and strategies on Asian banking industry.

To address these gaps in a standardised, customisable and regionally contextualised FinTech Adoption Index (FAI) is being proposed in this chapter. The index will be used to gauge adoption of FinTech by a combination of Asian institutions in different dimensions. It will examine the technology itself, the role of the banks in aligning the technology with the strategy, keeping pace with the regulations and institutional preparedness. The index will be used to describe the way FinTech is transforming the Asian banking by incorporating the regional and institutional specifics. It will also address the lack of a complete framework that scholars, strategists and policy makers are longing to have (Setiawan et al., 2021).

In such a way, the proposed FinTech Adoption Index completes the gaps in the literature by assessing the adoption in terms of tech, strategy, regulatory, and institutional aspects. The chapter contributes to the growing literature on the topic of digital transformation in banking, providing a comprehensive practical perspective that may be applied in various institutional contexts and provide a point of reference in the regional research and policy making.

3.1 Integrative synthesis and analytical positioning

Across the FinTech adoption literature, two complementary strands dominate. A performance-driven strand treats adoption as a capability investment—aimed at improving efficiency, customer retention, and risk outcomes—often measured via profitability and cost metrics (Xu, Kasperskaya, & Sagarra, 2025; Lin, Zhang, & Zachariadis, 2025). A governance- and ethics-driven strand emphasises responsible AI, explainability, model risk management, and regulatory compliance as preconditions for sustainable adoption, especially in high-stakes domains like fraud detection, credit, and AML (Arner et al., 2019; Bajwa et al., 2022).

This chapter positions the FinTech Adoption Index (FAI) at the intersection of these strands: it evaluates observable adoption signals while explicitly incorporating strategic alignment and regulatory-tech readiness as core dimensions. Doing so allows a structured comparison of how banks translate digital capabilities into performance (e.g., improved service quality and reduced operational frictions) without ignoring governance constraints that shape what can be automated, what must remain human-in-the-loop, and how risk and compliance responsibilities are allocated (Liu, Li, & Li, 2024; Rafiq & Sohail, 2025).

Comparative takeaway: Commercial and larger private banks often pursue performance-led scaling of AI and APIs, whereas public/development and mandate-driven institutions tend to prioritise control, auditability, and decision-support models. The FAI is designed to surface these trade-offs through a common scoring lens, enabling both peer benchmarking and context-sensitive interpretation.

4 FINTECH ADOPTION INDEX (FAI) — 12 BANKS ACROSS SINGAPORE, HONG KONG, INDIA, MALAYSIA & INDONESIA

4.1 Index Design and Methodological Framework

The adoption of a multi-dimensional approach to the design of the FinTech Adoption Index (FAI) is informed by the fact that the levels of digital transformation in banking establishments in Asia differ. Instead of concentrating on econometric correlations, the FAI centres a qualitative comparative approach, which analyzes the main indicators of the adoption of FinTech using a narrative-based classification system. The method is highly applicable in order to reflect the intricate and heterogeneous character of FinTech integration in various forms of banking organizations, all of which possess different operational size, regulatory limits, and clientele categories (Setiawan et al., 2021).

The FAI is composed of five dimensions that are considered to be core and characterized by the adoption of FinTech among institutions. Each of the dimensions comprises a list of indicators that represent key elements of FinTech integration, including the underlying infrastructure to facilitate digital transformation and the strategic partnerships and regulatory frameworks that will allow sustainable adoption (Yan et al., 2022).

4.2 Methods & Replicability

1. **Scope and unit of analysis:** We evaluated 12 regulated retail banks across five Asian markets: Singapore (DBS, OCBC, UOB), Hong Kong (HSBC HK, Standard Chartered HK, Hang Seng), India (HDFC, ICICI, Axis), Indonesia (BCA, BRI) and Malaysia (Maybank).
2. **Indicator set (six pillars):** (i) Open Banking & API readiness (public developer portals or national open-API schemes); (ii) Digital customer experience (CX) proxied by Google Play/App Store star ratings (0–5) rescaled to 0–100; (iii) AI/GenAI initiatives (bank-announced programmes or regulator sandboxes); (iv) Core modernisation (named public cloud/modern architecture cases); (v) RegTech & cyber (public bank-level initiatives; scored conservatively if unclear); (vi) Ecosystem (participation in national instant-payment/open-API rails and/or partner ecosystems).
3. **Scoring and weights:** Composite FAI = 0.30·Open APIs + 0.30·Digital CX + 0.20·AI + 0.10·Core + 0.10·RegTech/Ecosystem. Binary indicators are mapped to {0,100}; Digital CX = (stars ÷ 5) × 100. Pillar values and FAI are reproducible from the CSV packaged with this document.
4. **Data capture and audit trail:** Evidence derives from public, citable sources. Store-rating snapshots were recorded on September 20, 2025 (IST). See Source Notes for clickable links corresponding to each pillar.

Figure 1. FinTech Adoption Index (FAI) — Pillar Heatmap

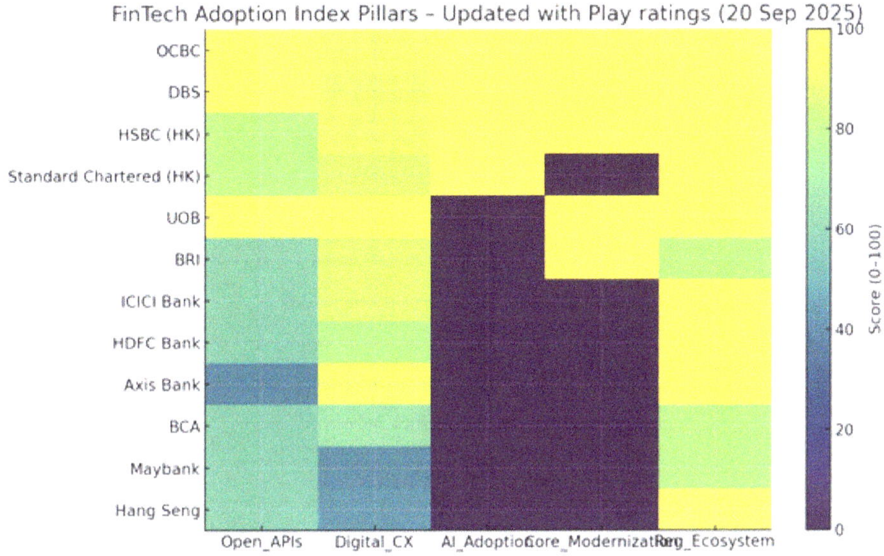

Source: Authors' contributions

Note: *Heatmap shows pillar scores on a 0–100 scale: Open APIs, Digital CX (store ratings rescaled), AI/GenAI initiatives, Core modernisation, and RegTech/Ecosystem. Weights: 30/30/20/10/10 (see Scoring and Weights).*

The heat map (Figure 1) indicates a tiered capability landscape: a small leader group exhibits uniformly high scores across pillars, a larger mid-tier shows selective strengths alongside a single constraining weakness, and a residual group displays fragmented maturity. Dispersion is greatest in Digital Customer Experience, suggesting that front-end quality is highly sensitive to release cadence, UX governance, and incident response, whereas Open Banking/API tends to cluster at high values in regulator-led markets and thus discriminates less. By contrast, AI and Core modernisation emerge as structural differentiators: banks with documented AI programmes anchored on modernised platforms display consistently stronger adjacent capabilities, evidencing complementarities among data governance, deployment pipelines, and product iteration. Mid-tier banks typically face a binding constraint—either Core or AI—that depresses the overall profile, implying that targeted remediation of the bottleneck would yield outsized gains relative to diffuse investment. Overall, balanced progress across pillars—not excellence in any single domain—best predicts higher composite readiness.

Table 1. FinTech Adoption Index (FAI) Rank Table — 12 Banks

Rank	Bank	Market	Open APIs	Digital CX	AI	Core	Reg/ Ecosys	FAI
1	OCBC	Singapore	100.0	92.0	100.0	100.0	100.0	97.6
2	DBS	Singapore	100.0	90.8	100.0	100.0	100.0	97.24
3	HSBC (HK)	Hong Kong	80.0	91.0	100.0	100.0	100.0	91.3
4	Standard Chartered (HK)	Hong Kong	80.0	88.0	100.0	0.0	100.0	80.4
5	UOB	Singapore	100.0	95.2	0.0	100.0	100.0	78.56
6	BRI	Indonesia	60.0	88.2	0.0	100.0	80.0	62.46
7	ICICI Bank	India	60.0	88.0	0.0	0.0	100.0	54.4
8	HDFC Bank	India	60.0	80.0	0.0	0.0	100.0	52.0
9	Axis Bank	India	40.0	94.0	0.0	0.0	100.0	50.2
10	BCA	Indonesia	60.0	68.0	0.0	0.0	80.0	46.4
11	Hang Seng	Hong Kong	60.0	44.0	0.0	0.0	100.0	41.2
12	Maybank	Malaysia	60.0	42.0	0.0	0.0	80.0	38.6

Source: Author's contributions

Note: Digital CX values are derived from Google Play/App Store ratings rescaled to 0–100; *all other indicators use publicly verifiable evidence as described in Methods.*

The ranks (Table 1) show a clear three-tier profile of FinTech adoption across the 12 banks. OCBC and DBS (both Singapore) lead with near-perfect composites (97.6 and 97.24), reflecting uniformly strong scores across Open APIs, Digital CX, AI, Core, and Reg/Ecosystem, while HSBC (HK) (91.3) tops Hong Kong with similarly balanced capability. A second tier—Standard Chartered (HK) (80.4) and UOB (78.56)—illustrates "single-bottleneck" effects: StanChart's Core = 0 and UOB's AI = 0 materially depress their otherwise strong profiles. Below these, scores fall sharply, led by BRI (62.46) and India's ICICI (54.4), HDFC (52.0), and Axis (50.2): despite high Digital CX (e.g., Axis 94.0) and full Reg/Ecosystem participation (100.0), the absence of publicly evidenced AI/Core keeps their composites low; Axis is further constrained by weaker Open APIs (40.0). BCA (46.4), Hang Seng (41.2), and Maybank (38.6) round out the table, with the last two weighed down primarily by Digital CX (≤44.0). Overall, the pattern confirms that while rails and APIs are necessary (and often high), institutionalised AI and modernised core platforms are the decisive differentiators: a single zero in either pillar can pull otherwise competitive banks out of the leadership band.

Table 2. Google Play ratings

Bank	Rating ( )	Date	Source type
Axis Bank	4.70	02-Sep-2025	Google Play
ICICI Bank (iMobile)	4.40	02-Sep-2025	Google Play
HDFC Bank	4.00	02-Sep-2025	Google Play
Hang Seng (HK)	2.20	02-Sep-2025	Google Play
Standard Chartered (HK)	4.40	02-Sep-2025	Similar web (Play rating reflection)
HSBC (HK)	4.55	02-Sep-2025	Android Rank snapshot
DBS (SG)	4.54	02-Sep-2025	Android Rank snapshot
OCBC (SG)	4.60	02-Sep-2025	Google Play (localized)
UOB (SG)	4.76	02-Sep-2025	Android Rank snapshot
BCA (ID)	3.40	02-Sep-2025	Android Rank snapshot
BRI (BRImo, ID)	4.41	02-Sep-2025	Android Rank snapshot
Maybank (MAE, MY)	2.10	02-Sep-2025	Google Play

Source: Author's contributions

Note: Play ratings fluctuate by locale and time; figures above reflect snapshots on 02 Sep 2025 (IST). Where Play's static page did not render the numeric rating, a reputable tracker (AndroidRank/Similarweb/AppFollow) was used and is cited.

Table 2 reveals the snapshot of mobile-app ratings (02-Sep-2025, IST) indicates a clear CX gradient across institutions: Singaporean incumbents and two Hong Kong majors cluster at the upper end (UOB 4.76★; OCBC 4.6★; DBS 4.54★; HSBC (HK) 4.55★; Standard Chartered (HK) 4.4★), while India's leading private banks sit in a competitive middle band (Axis 4.7★; ICICI 4.4★; HDFC 4.0★). Indonesian banks are more dispersed (BRI 4.41★ vs. BCA 3.4★), and the lowest outliers are Hang Seng (HK) 2.2★ and Maybank (MAE) 2.1★, signalling acute user-perceived issues in stability, usability, or recent incident handling. Interpreted as a CX proxy, these ratings suggest that high performers combine mature mobile journeys and release practices with effective incident response, whereas laggards likely face friction in authentication, performance, or feature completeness. The reliance on Google Play versus tracker snapshots (AndroidRank/Similarweb) for a few entries should be noted: although both reflect Play's underlying rating, locale rendering and scrape timing can introduce minor measurement noise, which does not alter the rank-order pattern. Overall, variance at the tails (≥4.6★ vs. ≤2.2★) is large enough to be practically meaningful, implying that banks in the lower decile would see the greatest uplift from focused remediation and that mid-band institutions could differentiate by tightening release cadence, crash rates, and UX polish to approach the leader cluster.

5 DIMENSIONS OF THE FINTECH ADOPTION INDEX

5.1 Digital Infrastructure

The dimension can be used to assess the level to which a bank has digitised the main banking platform, applied application programming interfaces and the complexity of the mobile platform. An effective digital infrastructure will enable the seamless integration of FinTech solutions hence operational efficiency. Additionally, it allows banks to interact with customers online, thus increasing the use of FinTech.

1. **Core Banking System Digitisation:** This indicator quantifies the share of core banking services in a bank that has been digitised into digital core banking services. Banks need central systems to manage their accounts, process transactions and govern the client data. The process of digitising these systems makes data accessible and compatible with more complex digital applications, like mobile banking, payment systems, AI-driven analytics, and so on, which makes it an invaluable asset to banks that wish to adopt the FinTech innovation (Banna et al., 2021).
2. **API Deployment:** Application Programming Interfaces (APIs) is a way that banks can share information with third-party applications such as FinTech startups, regulatory bodies, and other banks, which involves connecting internal and external systems. The implementation of API is a key component of open banking and digital partner ecosystems. High API adoption rate means that a bank is open and cooperates with other technological actors in their ecosystem, thus, increasing the ability to be innovative and able to rapidly respond to the market (Ali et al., 2021).
3. **Sophistication of Mobile Platform:** Mobile banking is a crucial digital communication with the client in the digital era. The indicator measures the mobile platform of a bank regarding design, usability and the range of application offerings. More advanced solutions allow customized solutions, secure transactions, and incorporation with other supplementary digital solutions, which enhance user experience and FinTech adoption, overall (Setiawan et al., 2021).

5.2 Strategic Alliances

Strategic alliances involve dating banks with third parties such as FinTech startups, regulating authorities and open banking projects. Such relations result in the innovation and the acceleration of adopting new technologies; the experience of such contracts enables banks to create their Internet service and to become more competitive in the market.

1. **FinTech Startup engagement:** It is essential that banks engage with FinTech startups in order to access new technologies and become competitive. The indicator measures the intensity between banks and new FinTech companies. These partnerships may lead to co-invention of new products, services or technologies that can improve customer experiences or operating efficiencies. Such collaborations informative of the capacity and speed at which a bank is evolving to outside innovation (Rahim et al., 2023).
2. **Inclusion in Regulatory Sandboxes:** Regulatory sandboxes are spaces that are regulated by regulatory authorities to allow financial institutions to test new technologies and business models under softer regulation. The measure indicates that a bank is willing to adopt new FinTech solutions without refusing to comply with the relevant regulations. A regulatory sandbox is a good sign of proactive innovation and the desire of a bank to navigate the regulatory environment safely and launch FinTech (Bajwa et al., 2022).
3. **Open Banking:** Open banking involves banks making their information available to third-party developers, with the consent of the customer, to develop new financial products or services based on the information. The indicator is used to quantify the presence of open banking protocols in a bank, which enables increased competition and consumer choice in the financial sector. Open banking is another part of the adoption of FinTech that leads to innovation in digital payments, personal finances management, and lending (Yan et al., 2022).

5.3 Technological Integration

The dimension measures the pace at which banks roll out innovations into their systems as better technologies, such as AI/ML, blockchain, and cloud-based operations, thrive. Technologies can be integrated, which enhances efficiency, risk management, and support in the decision-making process based on data. It demonstrates that a bank can be innovative and scale in an online economy.

5.3.1 Decision-support vs decision-automation in AI-enabled fraud/AML controls

Decision-support: models surface risk signals, explainable features, and recommended actions; a human reviewer makes the final decision (human-in-the-loop).

Decision-automation: models trigger or execute actions automatically (e.g., real-time transaction blocks, auto-freezes), usually with post-event monitoring and audit trails.

Practical implication for bank types: mandate-driven public/development banks typically emphasise decision-support to preserve accountability and reduce model-risk exposure, while large commercial banks may automate narrow, well-governed use cases where latency matters (e.g., card fraud) and controls are mature.

1. **AI/ML (Artificial Intelligence / Machine Learning):** AI and machine learning are applied across numerous applications in banking, including predictive analytics, customer fraud detection, risk management, and customer service automation. The indicator assesses the extent to which AI and ML technologies have been integrated into a bank's operations, with a particular focus on how these technologies can be leveraged to support decision-making and customer communications. The adoption of AI/ML embodies the transition into less human-centered, more automated and intelligent processes within a bank (Siddik et al., 2023).
2. **Blockchain Pilots:** Blockchain technology facilitates decentralised, transparent and secure record keeping and applications are useful in payment systems, smart contracts and identity management. The indicator evaluates the extent to which a bank is considering the application of blockchain into pilot projects, which are often precursors to more widespread application. The blockchain pilots may assist the banks to determine the viability and effect of the introduction of blockchain in their operations especially on improving security and decreasing operational expenses (Yan et al., 2022).
3. **Cloud-Native Operations:** The transition to cloud-native operations implies the use of scalable and flexible cloud-based technologies that enable banks to scale up or down their IT infrastructure accordingly. This indicator evaluates the shift of a bank to the cloud, based on the data storage, application execution, and support of digital services stored and executed in the cloud. Cloud-native processes can play a vital role when banks are interested in growing their FinTech solutions and improving their efficiency in a short period of time (Setiawan et al., 2021).
4. **Process Automation:** Process automation refers to the substitution of manual processes and functions by digital means to enhance efficiency, correctness, and cost-efficiency. This indicator is used to gauge the levels at which a bank has automated its business operations like account management, customer services or the regulators. Automation is a highly important part of the digital transformation, as well as an essential aspect of implementing FinTech solutions to reduce the human error and increase the efficiency of operations (Siddik et al., 2023).

5.4 Customer Experience Design

Customer experience design is dedicated to the experiences established by banks online, including online onboarding, personalised UI/UX designs, and customer offerings. An elegant online experience leads to customer satisfaction and loyalty, which encourages them to utilize FinTech solutions. It indicates the capability of a bank to live up to the current expectations of customers.

1. **Digital Onboarding:** Digital onboarding is a feature that enables customers to open accounts and receive services virtually without having to visit the physically. This indicator measures the level at which a bank has digitalised its onboarding process and thus customer engagement with the bank has been made easier and faster. Efficient customer onboarding is an essential part of customer satisfaction and a sign of a high FinTech adoption (Ali et al., 2021).
2. **UI/UX Customisation:** Bank design of online platforms has a major impact on customer interaction with online services. The indicator assesses the extent to which a bank has tailored its digital offerings to be intuitive, user friendly and smooth. The more advanced UI/UX shows that a bank aims at developing the positive customer experience and using FinTech to improve the interaction (Yan et al., 2022).
3. **Customised Products:** Personalisation refers to the act of designing products and services to suit individual customers. The indicator measures how far a bank goes to leverage customer data and sophisticated algorithms to provide personalised banking services, including personalised offers, recommendations, or tailored pricing. Personalised offerings are another important signifier of the adoption of FinTech since they are based on the utilisation of data-based decision-making and technology to increase customer satisfaction (Setiawan et al., 2021).

5.5 Regulatory-Tech Alignment

Regulatory-Tech alignment gauges how well the digital infrastructure of a given bank meets the modern regulatory requirements, specifically, it considers the automation of compliance, the maturity of cybersecurity, and the use of RegTech. With a strong alignment, banks can maintain compliance as innovative technologies are integrated. This kind of alignment is also used to mitigate risks and to build trust in online financial services.

Actionable governance practices (indicative):

Define clear model/accountability roles: model owner (business), model developer (data/AI), independent validator (second line), and internal audit (third line).
Maintain end-to-end documentation and an audit trail: data lineage, feature definitions, training/validation logs, and decision rationale for high-impact cases.
Establish control mechanisms: pre-deployment model risk assessment, approval gates, periodic performance monitoring (drift/bias), and incident playbooks.
Ensure human-in-the-loop escalation rules for exceptions and adverse actions, especially for AML/KYC and customer-impacting decisions.
Align cybersecurity and privacy controls with RegTech tooling (access control, encryption, secure MLOps, and vendor risk management for third-party models).

1. **Compliance Automation**: As used in the banking industry, compliance automation refers to the implementation of technological services that are aimed at mechanising and automating the regulatory compliance processes. The indicator identifies the degree of professionalism with which an organisation embraces digital devices to impose adherence to national and international laws, such as anti-money laundering (AML), know-your-customer (KYC), and data-protection rules. Institutions can automate compliance processes, reduce manual labour, minimise risk exposure, and enhance the accuracy of regulatory reporting (Banna et al., 2021).
2. **Cybersecurity Maturity.** Considering that more banks are turning to digital platforms, robust cyber-security policies are paramount when it comes to safeguarding sensitive customer information and financial dealings. This index assesses the maturity of institution-level cyber-architecture, which involves data encryption, threat detection, and incident response aspects. A greater level of cybersecurity maturity implies an organisation's devotion to ensuring its digital ecosystems and maintaining client trust (Zainal et al., 2021).
3. **RegTech Adoption**: Regulatory technology or RegTech is the digital technology that assists financial institutions in meeting regulatory needs in a more efficient and less costly way. The indicator assesses the degree to which banks have deployed RegTech solutions to automate the compliance reporting, fraud detection and risk governance process. RegTech implementation is central to the attempts by institutions to streamline the compliance process and stay up-to-date with the evolving regulatory requirements (Bajwa et al., 2022).

4. **Comparative takeaway:** Among the FAI dimensions, customer-facing experience and open APIs often improve first because they are visible and regulator-supported, while AI maturity and core modernisation tend to be the binding constraints that separate leaders from mid-tier adopters. RegTech/cyber/ecosystem readiness is the "safety and trust" layer that determines whether advanced capabilities can be scaled responsibly across bank types.

6 DIGITAL PROFILES AND BANK-TYPE COMPARISON

The FinTech Adoption Index (FAI) framework categorises each bank as a low, moderate or high adopter, combining them to develop a robust taxonomy. This theoretical category enables a delicate comparison between material banking differences, thereby pinpointing inter-institutional differences. With this purpose, the analysis below will focus on the implementation of FinTech by major, public, and Islamic banks, with the focus on explaining how institutional and governance-related factors and market strategies predetermined the way FinTech will be adopted.

6.1 Islamic vs. Conventional Banks: Ethical Finance and Alternative Credit Platforms

Comparative evaluation of Islamic and conventional banking institutions will indicate how adoption of FinTech will impact ethical finance and other credit systems. Islamic banks that are Sharia-compliant are advocates of ethical finance, avoiding the use of interest in their dealings and encouraging equity and profit-sharing agreements. Conventional banks, in turn, create shareholder value by applying models that are based on interest lending, which is largely free of ethical issues (Alam et al., 2019).

Alternative credit platforms represent the biggest gap in the FinTech adoption of these banking paradigms. FinTech platforms, such as crowdfunding and peer-to-peer lending, are a type of ethical Islamic banking that implements interest-free financial modalities. On these platforms, Sharia-compliant investing and borrowing platforms are offered (Irfan et al., 2023). By contrast, traditional banks use credit rating and interest-based lending algorithms to estimate risk and issue credit.

Islamic banks also use blockchain technology to increase the transparency, safety, and efficiency of smart contracts in carrying out Sharia-compliant transactions (Alam et al., 2019). In this case, blockchain can be considered specifically relevant as it allows decentralisation platforms that comply with the Islamic law, which in turn eliminates fraud and contributes to higher investor confidence. On the other hand, traditional banks use blockchain to realise operational efficiencies and regulation policies; operations with blockchain are linked to cross-border payments and settlement systems but not morality (Alam et al., 2019).

6.2 Public and Private Sector Banks: Governance Models, Digital agility, and Constraints to innovation

The use of FinTech in the further comparison between the public and the private sector banks is quite different because they vary in terms of their different governance systems, the degree of digitalisation and their ability to innovate. Policies and regulators generally directly affect the work of state banks, especially in emerging economies, which may limit the implementation of FinTech programmes. They are characterised by the presence of bureaucratic management, long processing of decisions and the focus on financial stability and innovation is not prioritised (Aspal and Dhawan, 2016). Therefore, they are likely to be slow adopting FinTech and rather focus on the traditional banking alternatives instead of innovative solutions.

Conversely, private banks are less regulated and more digitally nimble. They have the capability to make fast decisions and adopt new technologies to improve productivity, customers and risk management (Alam, Zainuddin, and Rizvi, 2019). This flexibility gives private banks the chance to test FinTech ideas, such as AI-based risk management, blockchain-based compliance and funding systems and open-banking infrastructure. Such developments enhance the personalisation of services, reduction of costs and positioning in a fast-changing market.

Regulatory frameworks also affect the FinTech adoption of both the public and the private institutions. The regulatory environment of public banks is stricter and has the potential to slow down or hinder the implementation of technology (Alam et al., 2019). Conversely, banks in the private sector have the advantage of having a more relaxed regulatory environment that is faster in adopting technology. For instance, Singapore and Hong Kong's regulatory sandboxes enable private banks to pilot FinTech solutions within a regulated environment, thereby providing them with a competitive edge over their public competitors (Aspal & Dhawan, 2016).

6.3 Commercial vs. Development Banks: Mandates, risk appetite, and human-in-the-loop adoption

Although the empirical illustration in this chapter uses regulated retail banks, the comparative logic of the FAI also applies to public development banks whose mandates prioritise financial inclusion, sectoral lending, and long-term resilience.

These institutions often face tighter public accountability and political constraints, which shapes both the pace of adoption and the acceptable level of automation.

In practice, development banks are more likely to adopt AI for decision-support (portfolio monitoring, anomaly detection, and risk triage) rather than fully automated adverse actions, especially in credit and AML contexts. This makes governance, explainability, and auditability central adoption determinants: a high AI score in the FAI should be interpreted alongside Regulatory-Tech Alignment to indicate whether the institution can scale AI safely.

Comparative takeaway: Commercial banks may convert higher digital maturity into faster revenue growth and cost efficiency through scaled automation, whereas development banks often pursue capability building that improves risk controls and service reach while retaining human oversight—implying different optimal "paths" through the same FAI pillars.

6.4 Large vs. Small Banks: Scale Advantages and Digital Modularity

The third divergence in FinTech adoption occurs in a unique way with large organisations and small organisations in the banking sector, where the structural differences associated with the large and small organisation size give latitude and constraint to the digital transformation agenda. Big banks usually take advantage of economies of scale and thus allow them to make major capital investments in sophisticated, state-of-the-art technologies that make their businesses more efficient and their relationships with customers more effective. Indeed, AI-driven analytics, machine-learning algorithms, and state-of-the-art cybersecurity are significantly more likely to be used in such institutions, as they have a large resource base and need to handle a large and multi-regional business (Irfan et al., 2023). As such, megabanks have strong structural infrastructure that easily supports the integration of sophisticated digital platforms, including core banking systems that support real-time data analytics and the delivery of omni-channel services.

Conspicuously, the smaller banks have to face prohibitive upfront costs, which are linked to the above technologies. As such, they will tend to develop a modular digital integration strategy to integrate with FinTech solutions that cannot be implemented with large-scale investments, though can be extended in phases over time (Alam, Zainuddin, and Rizvi, 2019). By way of example, these facilities may be interested in the integration of digital payment services or cloud-based solutions, which are more susceptible and scalable and demand a significantly smaller investment. This modular stance allows small banks to remain competitive by being able to keep pace with certain elements of the technology, such as customer relationship management (CRM) or the digital wallet without having to undergo a wholesale, end-to-end digitalisation.

Small banks, however, face a series of challenges in integrating FinTech, including limited access to capital, a lack of specialised knowledge, and a limited market presence. The challenges usually prompt a requirement to resort to third-party vendors, thereby compromising operational control and may cause loss of customer experience. Thus, big banks can invest in specific FinTech systems that can be integrated into their established systems almost perfectly well, but small institutions tend to use off-the-shelf products that might not be on a perfect fit with the requirements.

Nevertheless, despite these difficulties, the modular approach allows small banks to have the freedom to selectively adopt the most pertinent FinTech solutions that can also be attractive to their strategic ambitions. A case in point, a local bank may adopt a peer-to-peer (P2P) system of lending or an automated underwriting system and, therefore, compete with larger players on selected market niches without having to make large infrastructure upgrades (Aspal and Dhawan, 2016).

Comparative takeaway: Across bank types, the same FinTech building blocks yield different adoption profiles—Islamic banks use FinTech to reinforce ethical transparency (e.g., smart contracts), private banks often lead in speed and experimentation, and smaller banks typically adopt modularly via partners. Interpreting FAI scores through institutional constraints (mandate, governance agility, and capital) helps explain why similar technologies are implemented as either scalable automation or controlled decision-support.

7 STRATEGIC AND POLICY IMPLICATION

This robust current trend of FinTech development is essentially changing the landscape of the financial services industry, both compelling both financial institutions and regulators to question their current paradigm and regulatory framework. The high learning curve of the FinTech industry necessitates that the two industries simplify their strategic areas of focus in order to sustain a competitive advantage, maintain a high degree of security, and foster financial inclusion. The FinTech Adoption Index (FAI) is a highly organised measurement tool that provides banks with a structured approach to assessing how far they have progressed in achieving a digital transformation, while also providing regulators with an instrument to ensure that the adoption path leads to the benefit of all. The discussion below outlines the strategic and policy implications of the FAI on both the banking institutions and the regulating agencies.

7.1 For Banks

7.1.1 Linking FAI pillars to bank financial performance (expected channels)

To align the index more directly with bank strategy, each FAI pillar can be interpreted as influencing performance through specific (but context-dependent) channels (Xu, Kasperskaya, & Sagarra, 2025; Lin, Zhang, & Zachariadis, 2025).

Open APIs / Open banking: new fee-income opportunities via partnerships, faster product launches, and improved customer stickiness—especially in platform markets.
Digital CX: higher retention and cross-sell, fewer service failures, and reduced servicing costs through self-service journeys and better UX.
AI/GenAI: fraud-loss reduction, improved risk selection/monitoring, and productivity gains (automation of investigation triage and customer support) when governance is mature.
Core modernisation: lower change and run costs, faster time-to-market, improved resilience, and a foundation for scalable data/AI capabilities.
RegTech/Cyber/Ecosystem readiness: lower compliance cost and operational risk, fewer regulatory incidents, stronger trust, and safer scaling of automation (Rafiq & Sohail, 2025).

7.1.2 Enables Internal Benchmarking and the Identification of Priority Transformation Areas

An introduction of a FinTech Adoption Index provides banks with the ability to conduct hard internal benchmarking, thus letting banks to assess their technological position in comparison with peers and competitors. This benchmarking is essential to banks that aim to develop efficient digital transformation plans because it will provide insights into the operational aspects that need to be improved and innovated (Coetzee, 2018). Banks can use the index results to prioritize transformation focus areas, especially in areas with high-impact, such as the use of AI in risk management and blockchain integration and mobile banking solutions.

As an example, a bank that has a low score in customer-facing technologies (mobile apps or digital wallets) could use such segments to supplement customer interaction and service provision. On the same note, organisations with low scores in data analytics or automation technologies might invest in transforming their internal systems to enhance operational effectiveness and reduce expenditures (Banna et al., 2021). This concentration of change reduces inefficiencies allowing banks to deploy resources in a strategically accurate way.

The comparison with the competitors also gives a competitive advantage as it highlights the areas on which they can improve their performance. Banks will be able to meet the expectations of customers better through the identification and correction of the gaps in adoption and improvement of operations and compliance with progressively complex regulatory frameworks (Setiawan et al., 2021). With the ongoing digital transformation of the banking industry, it is highly important to capitalize on the knowledge offered by the FinTech Adoption Index to stay on top of the market.

7.1.3 Supports Digital Strategy Planning and Board-Level Innovation Oversight

In addition to enabling internal benchmarking, the FinTech Adoption Index plays a crucial role in supporting digital strategy planning and guiding board-level oversight of innovation. The digitalisation of banking services requires banks to shift their focus from traditional banking models to more technologically driven business strategies (Ali et al., 2021). The FAI helps senior management and boards of directors understand the stages at which various technologies are being adopted and integrated into the bank's operations.

The index should enable leadership teams to determine how good their current digital strategies are by providing a detailed summary of the adoption of FinTech in the diverse business units. Furthermore, it provides useful data on new technologies and areas to focus on to improve so that boards can set realistic and data-driven targets for their digital transformation path (Siddik et al., 2023). This evidence-based decision-making will help in enhancing the fact that the banks are not just going along with the trend of technology, but they have ventured into the digital innovations which are related to their overall strategic goals.

Additionally, the modular approach to technology adoption, as disclosed by the index, enables the board of directors and executives to focus on targeted technologies that will produce the most value in terms of operational efficiency and client satisfaction. As an example, a bank would make a decision to first invest in improving its digital payment system, and then launch AI-based fraud detection technologies as a part of a staged change strategy.

7.1.4 Encourages Modular Innovation Through a Visualisation of Adoption Gaps

The ability to visualise the gaps in the adoption of various technological areas is one of the main strengths of the FinTech Adoption Index. By clearly showing in which areas a bank is behind in its own digital transformation, the index encourages modular innovation, meaning that a bank can make changes step-by-step instead of making a massive transformation that disrupts its whole structure. Such a modular innovation allows implementing more minor and manageable technological upgrades with minimal risk and making sure that every technological addition can be integrated easily into the existing systems (Setiawan et al., 2021).

Another benefit of modular innovation is the ability to respond to emerging technology changes with flexibility. In case a bank realises that there is a certain technology, which can enhance its business (e.g., an identity verification system based on blockchain) that it can explore, it will not be forced to redesign its whole operational framework (Banna et al., 2021). Such a focused strategy allows banks to engage in innovations, with less of a financial cost and the operational disruption that can potentially result from wide-scale changes.

Furthermore, the customer-first innovation is encouraged by this visualisation of gaps. By determining which technologies have the greatest potential impact on improving customer experience, i.e. mobile banking apps, chatbots, or bespoke financial services, banks can focus on them, and thus make sure that the needs of the clients are at the core of their innovation efforts.

7.2 For Regulators

7.2.1 Offers a Framework to Structure Regulatory Sandboxes and Innovation Grants

FinTech Adoption Index provides a platform through which regulators can structure regulatory sandboxes and innovation grants in order to provide a clear roadmap on how they can effectively enforce policies. Special-purpose environments, called regulatory sandboxes, are where FinTech startups and banks can test their digital products and services, with no maximum regulatory costs imposed by the traditional financial markets. With the FinTech Adoption Index to measure the digital maturity of institutions, regulators will be better-positioned to determine the innovations that need to be tested in sandboxes (Tsang, 2019).

Regulators can also use the index to make specific grants to banks that are improving their adoption of new technologies. This is how regulators can focus on grants and incentives to institutions that are either leading in technological adoption or need additional help with technological adoption. A bank that demonstrates the need to invest in AI-based fraud detection would then have an opportunity to be funded or sponsored to use this specific technology (Siddik et al., 2023). Such grants would stimulate innovation, but would ensure that the balance of the regulatory environment and financial stability would not be disrupted.

Furthermore, the regulated character of the FinTech Adoption Index ensures that the regulatory authorities can guide the banks to the technologies that support a wider policy aim, such as financial inclusivity or cybersecurity.

7.2.2 Supports Oversight of Digital Systemic Risk Through Structured Mapping of Digital Maturity

The other significant implication on the regulator side is that they can manage digital systemic risk by mapping digital maturity systematically. As more financial institutions switch to digital solutions, the risk of cyberattack, system outages, or data breaches is bound to continue growing. The FinTech Adoption Index offers a framework allowing financial institutions and regulators to understand the digital resilience of financial institutions, as well as which banks may be more vulnerable to such risks due to the low level of digital adoption (Siddik et al., 2023).

By the time regulators can see the digital maturity of financial institutions, they can predict potential risks to the financial system and take action before these risks become systemic issues. As an example, the index can sound alarms at a bank that is not making progress in cybersecurity use or data encryption, and the index may force the bank to modernise its infrastructure or supply additional oversight (Tsang, 2019). Regulators have the opportunity to stabilise and secure the financial system by tracking and plotting digital maturity, and still ensure that banks can modernise their practices in stages.

7.3 Enhances Financial Inclusion Efforts by Identifying Low-Adoption Institutions for Targeted Support

One of the most significant impacts on regulators' activity regarding the index is that it can be used to promote financial inclusion. Recent literature suggests that access to financial services remains a barrier in many underserved or underbanked communities, as digital infrastructure is not available in all banks or locations (Banna et al., 2021). Recognising low-adoption institutions will enable regulators to focus their resources and attention on helping those banks enhance their technological capabilities, and, as a result, make financial services accessible to everyone.

The targeted support can take various forms, such as investments, regulatory relief, or collaboration with FinTech firms to promote the online offerings of banks in distress. Regulators will make sure that the sector develops inclusively by making sure that none of the institutions that still lag behind in embracing the latest technology are left behind in the wave of digital transformation.

In addition, regulators can give rural or geographically remote populations, who have been hitherto denied access to physical bank facilities, a chance to access services by promoting the adoption of digital-only banking (Banna et al., 2021). In doing so, the FinTech Adoption Index will serve as an effective tool by which regulators can monitor and accelerate the adoption of digital technologies in underserved areas, ultimately bringing financial inclusion to everyone.

Comparative takeaway: For banks, FAI-based benchmarking is most valuable when translated into a sequenced investment plan (fix the binding constraint—often core, AI, or cyber—before scaling customer-facing innovation). For regulators, the same lens supports proportional oversight and targeted enablement (sandboxes, incentives) that account for institutional diversity and systemic-risk exposure.

8 CHALLENGES AND FUTURE DIRECTIONS

There are numerous challenges that FinTech implementation in the banking industry is experiencing in Asia that must be overcome in order to realize sustainable growth and transformational change. These are technological, regulatory and institutional barriers, but their removal will have a significant impact on the future of digital banking.

1. **Technological Obstacles:** A major cause of the unwillingness to adopt FinTech is the presence of out-of-date technology in the majority of banks. The majority of them, particularly those in the emerging markets, still use legacy systems, and implementing new technologies such as artificial intelligence and blockchain is a challenging undertaking. The digital tools needed in modern banking facilities are of the large capacity, which is not always as scalable and flexible in current infrastructure. The switch to cloud-based solutions will be time-consuming and resource-intensive. Another problem is that stringent laws on cybersecurity are necessary to be implemented. As banks are digitised, the vulnerability to cyberattacks, invasion of privacy, and fraud increases and as such, the primary countermeasures are the implementation of strong and extendable security solutions.
2. **Regulatory Hurdles:** Despite the positive encouragement of regulatory authorities on the adoption of FinTech in Asia through sandbox platforms and open banking systems, the issue of regulatory risk is structural. The absence of a common system of regulations across jurisdictions presents a thorny puzzle

that banks in need of FinTech solutions should address. A coherent cross-border regulatory infrastructure is lacking, which restricts the capacity of most regions to participate in the market. Enforceors have to find a delicate balance between encouraging innovation, financial stability and consumer protection. It is not an easy task because creating laws that can easily adapt to technological change and still be trusted by the people is a challenging endeavour.

3. **Institutional Diversity:** The Asian region is typified by a complicated institutional framework with various levels of development, government and fiscal autonomy. Digital transformation agenda of state-owned, commercial and online-only banks is different. The state-owned banks are more likely to be compared to bureaucratic inertia, which renders change processes hard. Private banks must compete in the market, even as they oversee their regulatory mandates, which is a dynamic environment. Each of these institutions needs a paradigm background, which will lead to positive and universal adoption of FinTech. Smaller banks that have few resources would not be able to tap the capital and technical expertise to go digital.
4. **Consumer Trust and Adoption:** The problem of consumer trust is one of the key ones. Internet based financial services are popular but people are not convinced about its security and reliability. The security of personal information is among the privacy issues. The use of mobile banking and electronic wallets is also increasing in urban centres; however, there is a fear that the rural population will be left behind, as they will not be able to access the internet and are digitally illiterate. Based on some consumer-education strategies and trust-building, these problems can be overcome and the digital solutions made available and safe.
5. **Future Implications:** It is time high that the above challenges are effectively addressed in order to achieve successful adoption of FinTech in Asia. Modular integration of the emerging technologies should also be carried out in the technological support systems of the banks to manage the digital risks and enhance their postures in cybersecurity. The level of regulation should be favourable to cross-border collaboration in order to create standardised, flexible frameworks based on the evolution of FinTech. The most vital thing is the inclusion; all these tools would be available to everyone regardless of the size of the institution and would be supported with the helping hand to the digital transformation. Finally, consumer education and trust building, especially in under-served areas will be necessary to enable massive adoption.

9 CONCLUSION

In fact, the banking business in Asia is being affected by the FinTech revolution and in that case, it provides certain new opportunities to be innovative, to be more productive, to establish a customer-oriented service orientation. But even if it does not compare to a panacea. The most critical obstacles to the adoption of FinTech are the lack of standardised infrastructure, the bizarre system of regulation, and the checkerboard of inconsistencies in institutional structure. The incumbent scramble to digitise is already being realised but how fast this change is effected will be dictated by the institutional form, regulatory system and the resource endowments that dominates in every market.

A multi-dimensional and multi-purpose tool proposed to aid in the measurement of FinTech adoption by banks is FinTech Adoption Index (FAI). It provides banks, regulators, and policy-makers with the relevant information about their role in the digital transformation and explains where the further evolution is needed. Besides that, the FAI also follows the implementation of innovative technologies, adherence to rules and customer experience that will help in building a more implicated image of the digital maturity of the banks.

FinTech should be made to benefit all banks in Asia by overcoming regulatory, technological, and institutional hurdles. The regulatory collaboration among the agencies, banks, and FinTech startups will play a crucial role in introducing a novel, standardised, consumer-friendly ecosystem. The interconnection of the two will bring Asian banking to be the first to experience the digital transformation on a global scale, which will consequently trigger economic growth and bring financial inclusion to an even higher level.

REFERENCES

Alam, N., Hamid, B. A., & Tan, D. T. (2019). Does competition make banks riskier in dual banking system? *Borsa Istanbul Review*, *19*, S34–S43. DOI: 10.1016/j.bir.2018.09.002

Alam, N., Zainuddin, S. S. B., & Rizvi, S. A. R. (2019). Ramifications of varying banking regulations on performance of Islamic Banks. *Borsa Istanbul Review*, *19*(1), 49–64. DOI: 10.1016/j.bir.2018.05.005

Ali, M., Raza, S. A., Khamis, B., Puah, C. H., & Amin, H. (2021). How perceived risk, benefit and trust determine user Fintech adoption: a new dimension for Islamic finance. *foresight, 23*(4), 403-420.

Arner, D., Buckley, R., Zetzsche, D., Zhao, B., Didenko, A., Park, C. Y., & Brummer, C. (2019). *Policy and regulatory challenges of distributed ledger technology and digital assets in Asia.* Oxford Scholarship Online. DOI: 10.1093/oso/9780190077310.003.0011

Aspal, P. K., & Dhawan, S. (2016). Camels rating model for evaluating financial performance of banking sector: A theoretical perspective. *International Journal of System Modeling and Simulation*, *1*(3), 10–15.

Bajwa, I. A., Ur Rehman, S., Iqbal, A., Anwer, Z., Ashiq, M., & Khan, M. A. (2022). Past, present and future of FinTech research: A bibliometric analysis. *SAGE Open*, *12*(4), 21582440221131242. DOI: 10.1177/21582440221131242

Banna, H., Hassan, M. K., & Rashid, M. (2021). Fintech-based financial inclusion and bank risk-taking: Evidence from OIC countries. *Journal of International Financial Markets, Institutions and Money*, *75*, 101447. DOI: 10.1016/j.intfin.2021.101447

Buckley, R. P., Arner, D., Veidt, R., & Zetzsche, D. (2020). Building FinTech ecosystems: Regulatory sandboxes, innovation hubs and beyond. *Wash. UJL & Pol'y*, *61*, 55.

Coetzee, J. (2018). Strategic implications of Fintech on South African retail banks. *Suid-Afrikaanse Tydskrif vir Ekonomiese en Bestuurswetenskappe*, *21*(1), 1–11. DOI: 10.4102/sajems.v21i1.2455

Irfan, M., Kadry, S., Sharif, M., & Khan, H. U. (Eds.). (2023). *Fintech applications in Islamic finance: AI, machine learning, and blockchain techniques: AI, machine learning, and blockchain techniques*. IGI Global. DOI: 10.4018/979-8-3693-1038-0

Lin, X., Zhang, S. S., & Zachariadis, M. (2025). Open data and API adoption of U.S. banks. *Journal of Financial Intermediation*, *63*, 101162. DOI: 10.1016/j.jfi.2025.101162

Liu, Z., Li, X., & Li, Z. (2024). Inclusive FinTech, open banking, and bank performance: Evidence from China. *Financial Innovation*, *10*(1), 149. DOI: 10.1186/s40854-024-00679-3

Morgan, P. J., & Long, T. Q. (2020). Financial literacy, financial inclusion, and savings behavior in Laos. *Journal of Asian Economics*, *68*, 101197. DOI: 10.1016/j.asieco.2020.101197

Omarini, A. E. (2018). Banks and FinTechs: How to develop a digital open banking approach for the bank's future. *International Business Research*, *11*(9), 23–36. DOI: 10.5539/ibr.v11n9p23

Rafiq, M., & Sohail, M. K. (2025). Adopting regulatory technology for anti-money laundering in banking: Key enablers and barriers in a RegTech model. *Sustainable Futures : An Applied Journal of Technology, Environment and Society*, *10*, 101377. DOI: 10.1016/j.sftr.2025.101377

Rahim, N. F., Bakri, M. H., Fianto, B. A., Zainal, N., & Hussein Al Shami, S. A. (2023). Measurement and structural modelling on factors of Islamic Fintech adoption among millennials in Malaysia. *Journal of Islamic Marketing*, *14*(6), 1463–1487. DOI: 10.1108/JIMA-09-2020-0279

Setiawan, B., Nugraha, D. P., Irawan, A., Nathan, R. J., & Zoltan, Z. (2021). User innovativeness and fintech adoption in Indonesia. *Journal of Open Innovation*, *7*(3), 188. DOI: 10.3390/joitmc7030188

Siddik, A. B., Rahman, M. N., & Yong, L. (2023). Do fintech adoption and financial literacy improve corporate sustainability performance? The mediating role of access to finance. *Journal of Cleaner Production*, *421*, 137658. DOI: 10.1016/j.jclepro.2023.137658

. Tsang, C. Y. (2019). From industry sandbox to supervisory control box: rethinking the role of regulators in the era of Fintech. *U. Ill. JL Tech. & Pol'y*, 355.

Xu, F., Kasperskaya, Y., & Sagarra, M. (2025). The impact of FinTech on bank performance: A systematic literature review. *Digital Business*, *5*(2), 100131. DOI: 10.1016/j.digbus.2025.100131

Yan, C., Siddik, A. B., Yong, L., Dong, Q., Zheng, G. W., & Rahman, M. N. (2022). A two-staged SEM-artificial neural network approach to analyze the impact of FinTech adoption on the sustainability performance of banking firms: The mediating effect of green finance and innovation. *Systems*, *10*(5), 148. DOI: 10.3390/systems10050148

Zainal, N., Md Nassir, A., Kamarudin, F., & Law, S. H. (2021). Does bank regulation and supervision impedes the efficiency of microfinance institutions to eradicate poverty? Evidence from ASEAN-5 countries. *Studies in Economics and Finance*, *38*(2), 272–302. DOI: 10.1108/SEF-10-2019-0414

Chapter 8
Mobile Payment Systems: Thematic Insights, Research Gaps, and Emerging Opportunities

Veenu Madan
http://orcid.org/0000-0001-7014-1106
Chandigarh University, Mohali, India

Manjit Kour
http://orcid.org/0000-0003-1043-3187
Chandigarh University, Mohali, India & North-West University, South Africa

Md Rezaul Haque
http://orcid.org/0000-0001-5990-4918
Metropolitan University, Sylhet, Bangladesh

Asia Aman
Muscat University, Oman

ABSTRACT

Based on the data set collected from 2018 to 2022 from the Scopus database, this study represents a bibliometric and systematic evaluation analysis of the mobile payment system. In this study, literature classification based on theory and technology is done by extensive literature study by preparing a table in Excel. Bibliometric research is done by VOS viewer software.The findings of the study show that TAM is used by most of the researchers for theoretical framework and the "partial least square structure equation modelling" technique is the most prevalent. All the highly cited articles used the survey method in collecting the data. The text-based and keywords graphs cluster shows various keywords' relationships. The cluster analysis reveals that the primary emphasis of research is on how customers accept technology. It also highlights the need for more research into how consumers em-

DOI: 10.4018/979-8-3373-6244-1.ch008

ploy mobile payments and how small businesses and merchants use them. The title "Predicting the determinants of mobile payment acceptance: A hybrid SEM-neural network approach" is highly cited theme.

1. INTRODUCTION

Mobile payments can be considered a subset of electronic payments. de Bel and Ga^za (2011) defined " mobile payment as a transfer of funds in return for a good or service, where the mobile phone is involved in both the initiation and confirmation of the payment''. The ''location of the payer and supporting infrastructure is not important: he may or may not be 'mobile' or 'on the move' or at a Point of Sale (PoS)". The payment systems environment has changed dramatically in the last several years, moving from typical cash or credit card transactions to a range of mobile payment options (Madan & Kour, 2023). This transition may be attributable to several elements, such as modifications in the general economic landscape, progressions in Internet technology, the extensive impact of social media platforms, and the increasing ubiquity of mobile gadgets (de Luna et al., 2019). Mobile receipt and payments make use of cellular and other communication networks to pay for products, services, or invoices with the help of portable electronic devices (such as a cell phone, a smartphone, a handheld PC, mobile telecommunications networks, or near-field communication technology) (Dahlberg et al., 2006; Madan & Kour, 2024). The coronavirus disease 2019 (COVID-19) has impacted the majority of economies and civilizations around the world. To stop the spread of the pandemic, lockdowns were first implemented. The digital transformation of social and economic spheres accelerated as soon as people understood the importance of public health and the economy (Lim, 2021). The outbreak of the virus has reduced the number of card withdrawals and ATM cash withdrawals. People became health-conscious, and to prevent the transmission of viruses, they moved to cashless payments using their mobile phones and app-based payment methods. Now applications have become super applications with funding methods, payment features, bill payment, e-commerce, travel, and financial services, and thoroughly enter into the daily lives of users (Madan & Kour, 2023). Users can request money from others, make QR code payments, check bank account balances, and reload prepaid mobile accounts using UPI-enabled payment apps. Electricity, landline, broadband, gas, and other bills can be paid (India Mobile Payment Report, 2020). The use of technology in finance can be divided into four major categories based on their diverse business structures: financing, asset management, payments, and others. Under the umbrella of the payment segment, mobile Payments come as an alternative payment method (Dorfleitner et al., 2017). Information technology changes give consumers more options for searching for the best alternative through comparison (Nadkarni & Prügl, 2021). The government of different countries started various initiatives for boosting digital payment and UPI is one of the Initiative products that launched in 2017. Google rebranded its application Google Pay in 2018 and COVID-19 safety precautions bound people to go for mobile payment. The financial environment has changed dramatically as a result of the growing use of mobile payment systems, which provide companies and consumers alike with easy and simple means of making payments. But this industry's complexity and quick evolution demand a thorough assessment of its development and significance. As a developing field, having links and integration with new technologies and user behaviour, mobile payment requires a more holistic, in-depth outlook. In this study, the motivation for systematically reviewing the available literature on mobile payment is the changing way of payment mechanisms. The literature that was already available on mobile payments may be systematically and bibliometrically evaluated to provide important information that will guide future development and study (Teng & Khong, 2021; Wenner et al., 2018). By synthesizing the body of available information, bibliographic and systematic reviews can also contribute to the development of more comprehensive and durable theoretical frameworks for understanding mobile payment systems (Albuquerque et al., 2014). Consequently, this can direct the planning of further research projects and the execution of fruitful mobile payment mechanisms (Karjaluoto et al., 2019). This study's primary goal is to assess m-payment studies published between 2018 to 2022. The change in consumer buying habits has increased scholarly interest in the area of mobile payments over the last few years. This paper adopts a bibliometric methodology to review the extant literature on mobile payment. Unlike alternative review methods (e.g., framework, narrative/thematic), the bibliometric method is a highly objective method for reviewing the literature due to its reliance on quantitative techniques to assess the performance and map the science in the field (Donthu et al.,2021). This paper thoroughly examined the substance of the existing research on payment through mobile to enhance understanding of the current state of technology. Based on the analysis, we describe the tendencies, patterns, new inventions, gaps in the existing literature, and practical difficulties in adopting mobile payment. Recommendations and suggestions made in this study will be able to better focus on the key areas that need improvement in the adoption and acceptance of mobile payment.

The following research questions are addressed in this study:

(1) To ascertain the kinetics of research literature generation.
(2) To determine the most impactful theory and research technique in a specific field.
(3) To build and visualize collaboration patterns between writers and countries.
(4) Map the clusters of thematically related publications.

(5) To determine the research theme circulating among researchers in the field of study.
(6) To determine the intellectual structure of study in this area and the periodic progression of m-payment research.

2. REVIEW OF LITERATURE

A literature review helps academics fill in the gaps in their knowledge by highlighting areas of inquiry that still need to be thoroughly examined. The academics have employed various techniques to produce state-of-the-art literature evaluations, including scoping reviews, meta-analyses, systematic investigations, and weight analyses. The systematic literature review (SLR) and bibliometric analysis methodologies were used in this work to provide a thorough overview of the area, which in turn made it easier to identify the intellectual framework. Dahlberg et al. (2015) critically and comparatively examined mobile payment through a systematic literature review from the period 2007 to 2014 by extracting 188 articles. They found very little progress in theoretical contribution; most of the studies repeated the already-done work. Their study was mostly concerned with thematic depiction; it was devoid of other crucial components like network analysis and the use of cutting-edge instruments like Gephi and Vos viewer to look at connections between different field subjects yet they provide valuable insights for mobile payment researchers. Liu et al. (2020) analysed the factors affecting the behaviour of consumers in adopting mobile payment through a meta-analysis. Their analyses were based on 61 data sets from 2008 to 2017 extracted from the Web of Science. The findings showed that the place where people live is the most important influencing factor affecting customer behaviour. Chhonker et al. (2018) extensively reviewed the literature in the area of mobile commerce. The databases Scopus and Google Scholar were used to gather the information for this research. They analysed 86 empirical studies between 2008 and 2017 using association rule mining and community finding techniques. Abdullah and Naveen Khan (2021) conducted a bibliometric analysis by extracting the literature from 2005 to 2020 from the Scopus database. Their study was however, restricted by the small number of papers in the evaluation data set, and they discovered that quantitative research predominated in the literature and that there were few studies on merchant acceptance of mobile payments. Tounekti et al.(2022) conducted a bibliometric analysis of the electronic payment system by extracting 177 articles from the 2001 to 2021 Web of Science database. They found that China and Spain are the leading contributors to electronic payment transactions. Trust and security are the major factors affecting customer preference in adopting digital payment systems.

3. RESEARCH METHODOLOGY

Figure 1. Research design of the study

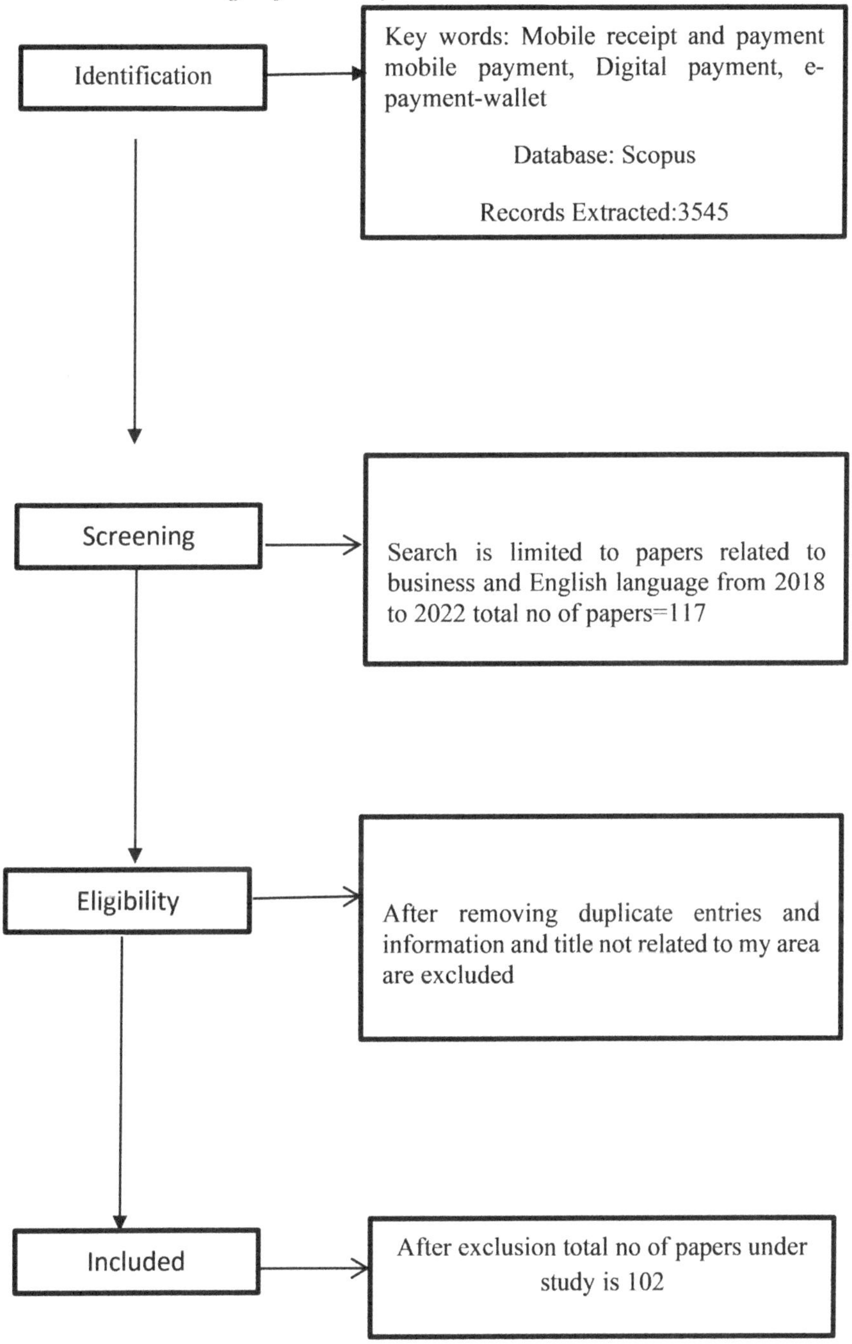

Source: The author

To find pertinent literature for this systematic search, a research plan is established. The search keywords used in the study were customised for the Scopus database using this search approach: TITLE-ABS-KEY (”mobile receipt and payment adoption” OR “mobile payment” OR “mobile wallet” OR “Digital payments” OR “e-payment” OR “M-payment”). Journal articles and review papers published in English were included in all searches, which spanned from the database's creation until 2022. The results show 3545 documents, including all domains. After that search is limited to domain business, published papers, English language and the years 2018 to 2022. A total of 117 records were extracted at this stage. Some papers were not included because of scope, and 102 articles were included in the study. The PRISMA statement served as the foundation for determining the methodology. The primary goal of this search is to map the body of research on mobile payments across social science, business, and economics. For systematic evaluation, Excel is used, and VosViewer software is used for bibliometric analysis. VOS viewer is one of the best tools for visualising bibliometric networks, such as co-authorship, co-citation, and keyword networks. It provides interactive and visually appealing representations. VOS viewer is known for its user-friendly interface, making it accessible to researchers without advanced programming skills. The tool allows for clustering and mapping, enabling users to identify and explore thematic clusters within their bibliometric data.

The methodology consists of two complementary stages:

1. Systematic Literature Review (SLR): Articles were manually reviewed and classified based on theoretical foundations, research context (consumer, merchant, institutional), and methodological design. This enabled the identification of dominant research patterns and gaps.
2. Bibliometric Analysis: Bibliometric techniques were applied using VOSviewer to analyse co-authorship networks, keyword co-occurrence, bibliographic coupling, and citation patterns. These techniques facilitate objective mapping of intellectual structures and thematic evolution within the mobile payment research domain.

The integration of systematic and bibliometric approaches enhances analytical depth by combining qualitative interpretation with quantitative mapping.

4. ANALYSIS AND FINDINGS

4.1 Classification based on the theory

The theory provides the base for research. It is comparable to the bones that the human body is constructed from. Research is only conducted to give the intended results on a theoretical foundation that has been clearly stated. By analysing the 102 literature, it was found that various researchers used different approaches to form academic research backgrounds. Figure 2 shows the graph depicting the widely used theory in adopting the mobile payment system.

Figure 2. Classification based on the theory

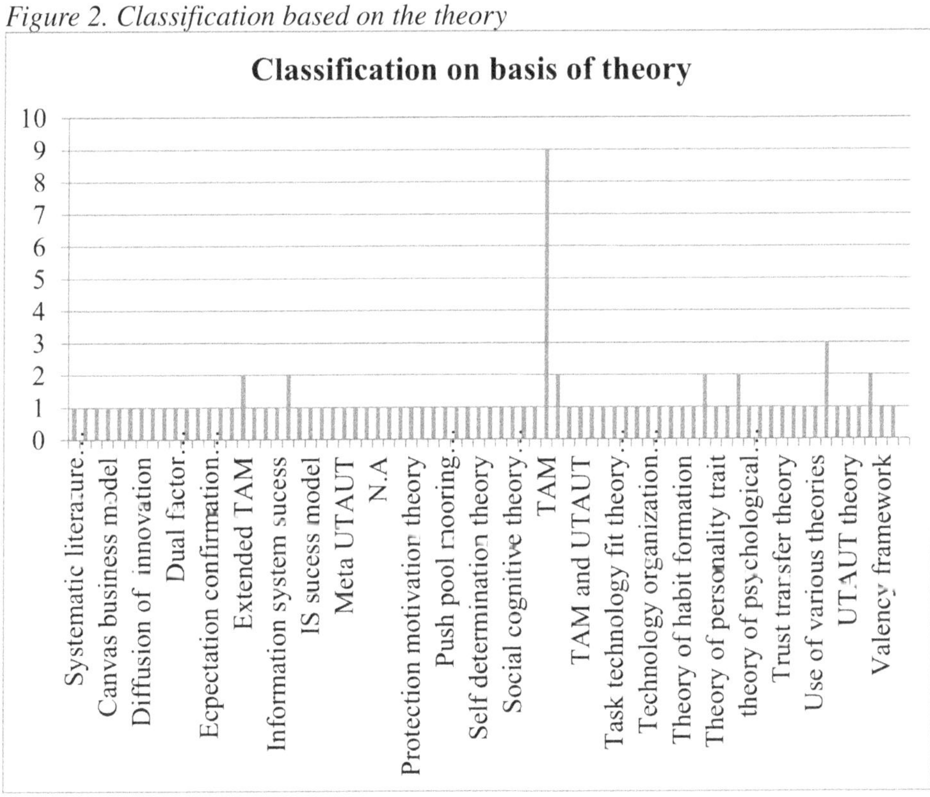

Source: Scopus data analysis by the author

Figure 2 shows that the researchers studying technology adoption have used a diverse set of theoretical concepts and models, such as the "Theory of Reasoned Action (TRA)", "Theory of Planned Behaviour (TPB)", "Task Technology Fit (TTF)", "Unified Theory of Acceptance and Use of Technology (UTAUT)", and "Technology Acceptance Model (TAM)" to analyse and predict how users will adopt a technology. "The technology Adoption Model" is the most comprehensive theory used in mobile payment. Most of the researchers in their study used the technology acceptance model to investigate the acceptance of new technology in mobile payment, e-wallets, and online shopping, web payment, QR payments, SMS, NFC (Wabma et al., 2021; Garrouch, 2021; Lew et al., 2020; Flavin et al., 2020; Schmidthuber et al., 2020; Lu & Lu, 2020; Singh et al.2020; Kalinić et al., 2019; Oentoro, 2021; Haong et al.,2020; Altounjy et al.,2020; de Luna et al., 2019; Liébana et al.2019; Qu et al.,2018; Matemba et al.,2018; Liébana et al.,2018; Su et al.2018; Salloum et al.,2018).TAM was primarily created to facilitate organizational technology adoption (Davis,1989). To expand the TAM model, the researcher designed the Unified Theory of Acceptance and Use of Technology (UTAUT), which looked at customers' intentions for using a database and computer system and their subsequent behaviour (Venkatesh, 2003). TAM was criticized for using a deterministic method and paying little attention to the unique qualities of users. Various studies in Spain, Mauritius, China and India supplemented the meta-UTAUT model with consumer-related dimensions to understand better customer behaviour, including additional variables innovativeness, stress, trust, grievance redressal, and charges (Patil et al.,2020; Singh, 2021). The availability of digital devices and cutting-edge wireless technology has stimulated the creation and implementation of value-added mobile apps and services. But still, the acceptance rate is not good in developing countries. Even in developed countries, the highest adoption rate is in China at 92%, the United States at 52%, and Mexico at 49%. So there is a great need to understand the factors that affect the adoption of technology by framing a suitable model with a sound theoretical base. UTAUT theory explains the behaviour intention of consumers more explanatory way for technology adoption by using additional variables.UTAUT theory is extended by incorporating an additional variable called UTAUT 2 theory (Venkatesh et al., 2013). This theory provides a noteworthy contribution to theory and practice (Al-Okaily et al., 2020; Chaiyasoonthorn et al., 2019).

4.2 Distribution based on techniques

A technique is a process, tool, or mechanism by which data is gathered, examined, and interpreted in research. The application of techniques helps to ensure the accuracy and precision of data collection and analysis. Methods that are well-established and validated reduce errors and increase reliability. Employing the appropriate research methods and tools when performing your research is essential. For the analysis to be successful, it is essential to have the right tools. Because research technique impacts the study, the results and interpretations may not be accurate if wrong research techniques are utilized.

Figure 3. Distribution based on techniques

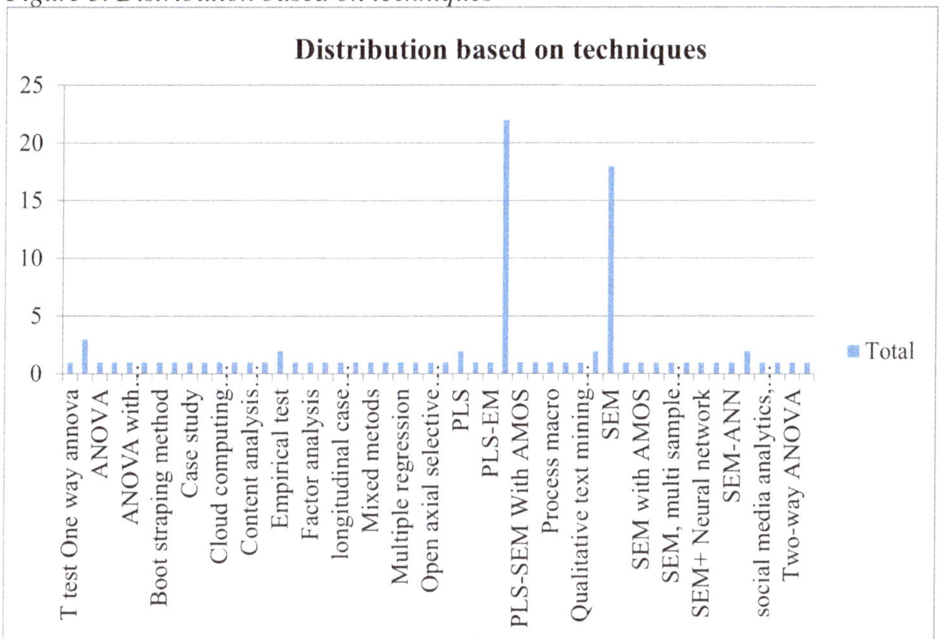

Source: Scopus data analysis by author

Figure 3 depicts that A partial least square with a structural equation modelling technique is used for data analysis by most researchers (Lian et al., 2021; Menash et al.,2021; Singh, 2021; Wabma et al.,2021; Pal et al.,2021; Liu et al.,2021; Handarkho et al.,2021; Lui et al.,2021; Lai & Liew, 2021; Wang et al.2019). Multivariate statistical analysis of structural relationships is conducted using structured equation models. A component analysis and a multiple regression analysis were used to determine the structural relationship between latent constructs and measured variables. Researchers prefer this method since it estimates several interconnected dependencies at once. This study used both endogenous and exogenous variables. As with endogenous variables, independent and dependent variables are the same. PLS-SEM is well suited to evaluating models with multiple constructs and complex associations. Also, this technique is ideal for measuring behaviour intention and actual Usage (Yoon & Barker Steege, 2013). SEM is a powerful statistical method that incorporates a simultaneous statistical test with a measurement model or confirmatory factor analysis (CFA) of the structural model (Hoe, 2008). The method assists the scholar in validating or testing a theoretical model for use in theory testing and development. It combines CFA and path analysis, and the relationship represents the researchers' hypothesis. So for testing and developing a theory, the PLS-SEM second-generation model of SEM is the best and most widely used in different countries to know the factors that affect the adoption of technology and visualise the extensive quantitative data in the simplest way.

4.3 Year and title-wise citation and analyses of the research theme

A citation can be defined as "a reference to a book, article web page or other published or unpublished item that includes sufficient details to uniquely identify that item." As observed in Figure 4, the year-wise citation was highest in 2020.

Figure 4. Year and title-wise title citations

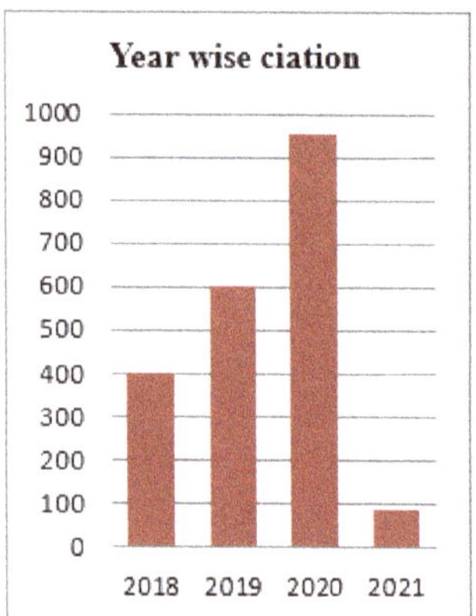

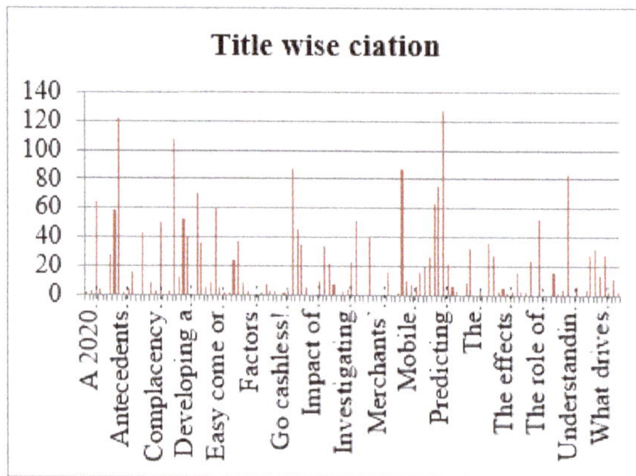

Source: Scopus data analysis by author

Figure 4 shows the sum of citations received in 2020 is 992, which is the highest, and it depicts the researcher's interest in investigating the new payment methods via technology. Technology brings change initially. Various stakeholders also resist it, but its adoption also brings convenience for users (Hueske & Guenther, 2015). Our culture's interest in mobile payments is rising as a contemporary substitute for cash, checks, and credit cards among consumers and business owners. The title "Predicting the determinants of mobile payment acceptance: A hybrid SEM-neural network approach" is a highly cited theme. The author analyses people's intentions to adopt NFC mobile payments as the primary objective. To evaluate the variables, SEM with neural network models was used. (Liébana et al., 2018; leong et al., 2020). A two-step framework was used in analysing pre-adoption factor trust and post-adoption factor satisfaction in digital payment, and all the highly cited articles used online survey method for investigation of the adoption and acceptance intention in different countries, i.e., Spain, China, gulf countries, India, Malaysia, UAE,

Indonesia (Matemba et al., 2018; Su et al.2018; Salloum et al.2018; Rizkyandy et al., 2018; Nguyen, 2018)

5. BIBLIOMETRIC ANALYSIS

5.1 Co-authorship analysis

Co-authorship analysis is a technique that looks at the links between co-authors in academic papers to investigate and analyse patterns of collaboration among scholars. This approach sheds light on the composition of academic or scientific communities, the dynamics of teamwork, and the output and influence of individual researchers.

Figure 5. Co-authorship Analysis

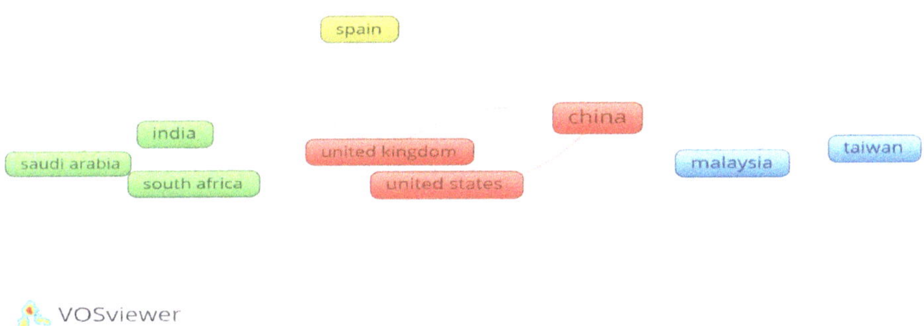

Source: Scopus data analysis by author

The graph in Figure 5 shows the co-authorship analysis country-wise and is divided into four clusters. Cluster 1, the red color indicates the collaboration between China, the United States, and the United Kingdom. Cluster 2, green color includes three co-authorship countries: India, South Arabia, and South Africa. Cluster 3, blue, consists of 2 countries, Malaysia and Taiwan, and the yellow cluster includes only a single country Spain. It means Spain's author didn't collaborate with any other country's author. The total link strength of the four clusters is 28.

5.2 Co-occurrence analysis based on keywords

A co-occurrence occurs when two terms are familiar or close together. Exact terms with different meanings but related to the same subject matter are also included in co-occurrence. The degree of co-occurrence is closely correlated with the closeness of keywords. Through the detection of clusters of keywords that occur together frequently, researchers can determine the underlying structure of knowledge domains and follow the evolution of research trends over time. These materials may be of great interest to scholars interested in gaining a better understanding of their subject matter today, identifying new directions for research, and developing interdisciplinary connections.

Figure 6. Co-occurrence Analysis

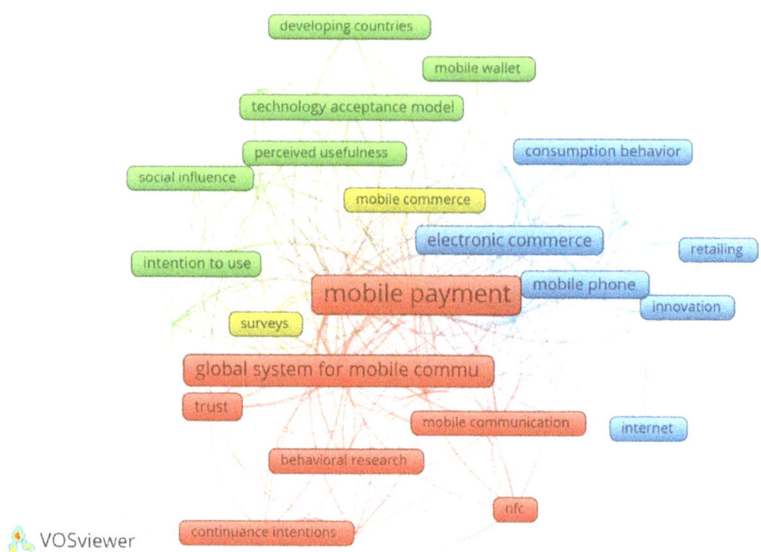

Source: Scopus data analysis by author

Figure 6 depicts a co-occurrence network developed by using keywords with the help of VOS viewer software. It represents the clusters of common keywords for analysis. The relationship between keywords "contains valuable information about the knowledge structure of the field, its relevant concepts, and their connections" (Lozano et al., 2019). The red cluster includes the relationship of keywords between behavioural research on continuance intention of mobile payment, electronic money, mobile communication, and global system for mobile communication and NFC using structural equation modelling, including variables perceived security and trust.

Cluster 2, green color includes 9 items showing the adoption and intention to use a mobile wallet in developing countries, measuring the usefulness, economic and social influence by least-square approximation, and TAM model. Cluster 3, blue, includes nine items that depict consumer behaviour regarding adopting innovative technology like e-commerce, mobile phones, and mobile payment in retailing. Cluster 4, yellow, shows the association of keywords between mobile commerce and survey.

5.3 Bibliographic coupling

Bibliographic coupling is the term used to describe how connected two items are, as determined by how many references they have in common. When a document gets more citations, the stronger their relatedness (coupling) is. It presents the topic matter parallels between the two works in the form of documents, sources, authors, organisations, and nations. The bibliographic connection used in my research is a graph based on the author.

Table 1. Top 10 Authors based on bibliographic coupling

SR.No	Document	Citations	Total link strength
1	liébana-cabanillas f. (2018)	128	356
2	Shao z. (2019)	122	215
3	Singh n. (2020)	107	401
4	de luna i. r. (2019)	87	203
5	karjaluoto h. (2019)	87	87
6	Patil p. (2020)	83	409
7	leong l.-y. (2020)	75	120
8	Kazan e. (2018)	70	46
9	kalinic z. (2019)	65	294
10	talwar s. (2020)	63	32

Source: Scopus data analysis by author

Table 1 revealed the top 10 authors based on bibliographic coupling, taking a minimum number of citations per document 10 and a list of 48 authors shown in vos viewer. Out of 44 top 10 authors list were selected, and the highest citation was received by Liebana et al. (2018), with a total link strength of 353. A model for estimating the factors influencing the decision to use mobile payment was developed through the integration of an SEM and neural network approach with a web-based survey of Spanish people who use smartphones. Privacy and utility are important considerations for other payment modes, such as SMS, quick response, and near-field communication. It's vital to keep in mind that technological advances and innovations extend beyond digital payments to any type of terminal handling "money," enabling payments to be made whenever and from anywhere in the world, hence raising the consumer's understanding of value (liébana et al.,2018; de luna et al.,2019). In China, third-party payment applications we chat with and Alipay mobility and reputation affect the male users, but females consider security factors in building trust (Shao et al., 2019). Indian consumers, while adopting a technology affected by society, risk, and psychological factors; their intention is moderated by these factors (Singh et al., 2020; Patil et al., 2020).

Figure 7. Bibliometric coupling

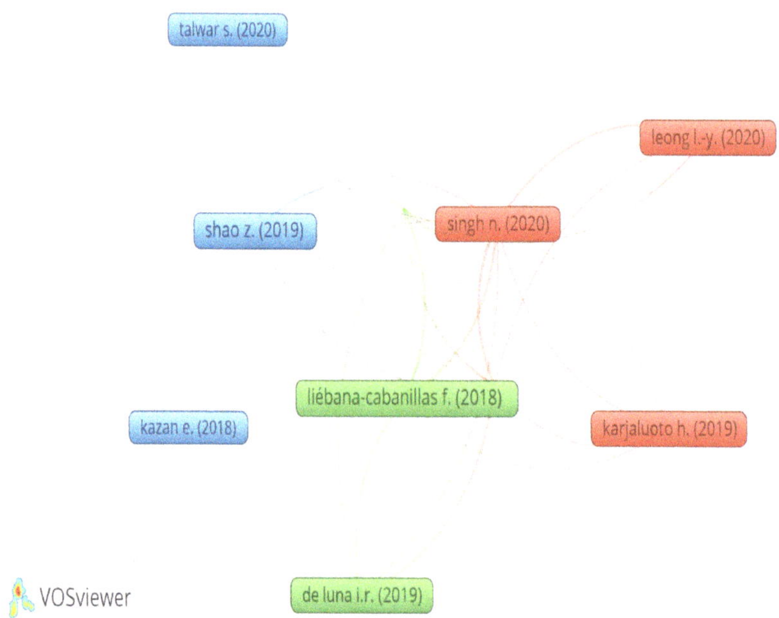

Source: Scopus data analysis by author

5.4 Text-based analysis

In bibliometric analysis, text-based analysis involves the study and interpretation of textual components found in academic publications, including full-text articles, abstracts, titles, and keywords. Text-based analysis in Figure 8 shows the network of association based on title and abstract field and various clusters in different colours and shows the association among them.

Figure 8. Text-based Analysis

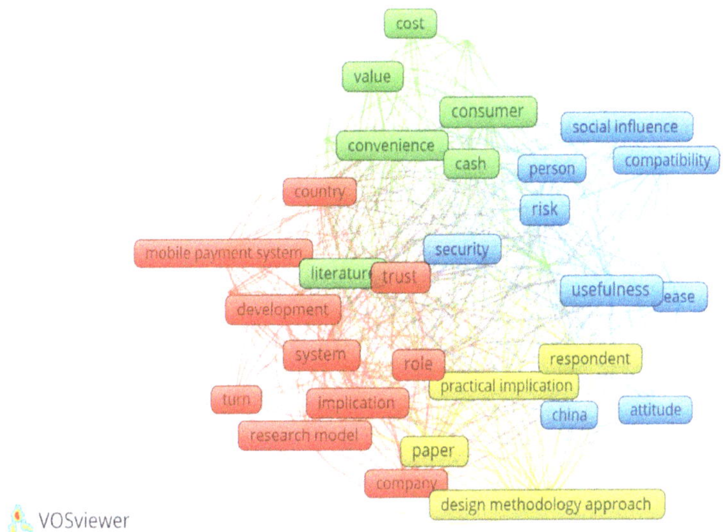

Source: Scopus data analysis by author

The text-based analysis graph in Figure 8 revealed the association of abstract and title fields in three different clusters. It included 33 items, 3 clusters, 486 links, and 1706 link strengths. Cluster 1, red color comprises 12 items that show the practical implementation of the M payment research model for a person in a country using antecedents of trust, security, and convenience through structural equation modeling. Cluster 2, green color includes 11 items showing the behaviour of the company business or merchant regarding payment using the design methodology approach. Cluster 3, blue color, consists of 10 items showing the payment attitude regarding cash and technology adoption in China using variables ease, usefulness, risk, social influence, and compatibility.

5.6 Citation country-wise

Citation country-wise describes the examination of citations within various national contexts. In bibliometrics, investigators frequently study the international citation patterns of academic publications that are associated with or originate from particular nations. This specific kind of analysis sheds light on the influence and worldwide effect of research conducted by researchers or organisations in a certain nation.

Table 2. Citation country-wise

Sr. No.	Country	Document	Citations	Total link strength
1	China	28	565	56
2	Spain	9	488	41
3	India	11	394	33
4	United States	12	354	23
5	United Kingdom	7	315	30
6	Malaysia	14	285	31
7	South Africa	7	171	29
8	South Arabia	5	137	18
9	Taiwan	10	93	28
10	Indonesia	6	30	5

Source: Scopus data analysis by the author

Figure 9. Citation country-wise

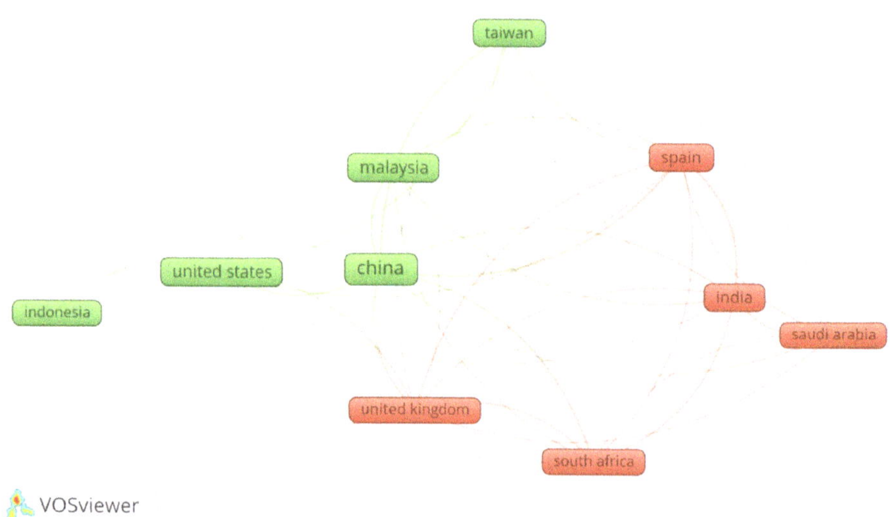

Source: Scopus data analysis by author

Figure 9 and Table 2 depict how researchers in a certain nation reference both their own and other researchers' work. The table shows the minimum number of documents and citations per country 5. Out of 39 countries, 10 countries meet the threshold. In the figure, Country-wise citation is divided into 2 clusters. Cluster 1 includes 5 countries India, South Africa, South Arabia, the United Kingdom and Spain. Cluster 2 includes China, Malaysia, the United States, Indonesia and Taiwan.

5.7 Co-citation cited references

When two or more papers are cited jointly by a third document, this is known as co-citation. It is a method of bibliometric analysis that assists in determining the linkages and intellectual connections between various authors, works, or subjects. Co-citation analysis was used to examine relationships between cited references. Figure 9 shows that "Kim, c., mirusmonov, m.lee, i.," appeared as the highest total link strength.

Figure 10. Co-citation cited references

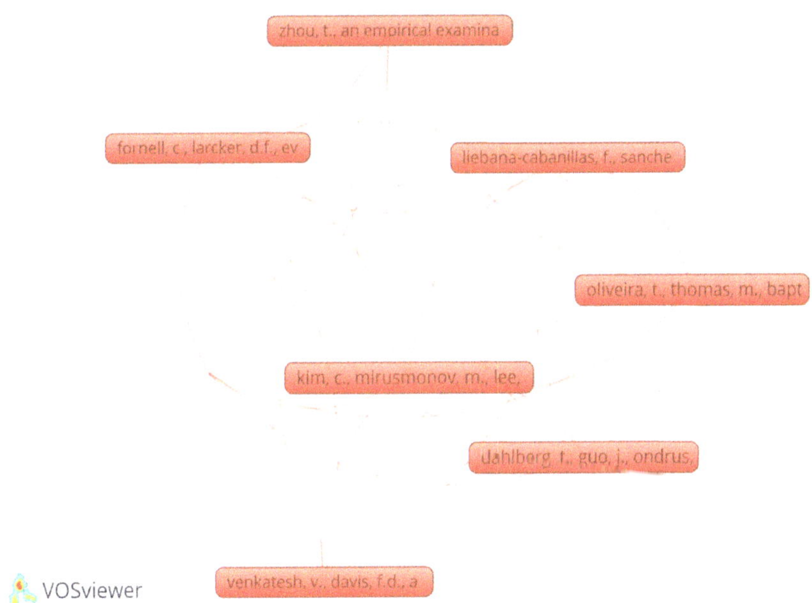

Source: Scopus data analysis by the author

6. DISCUSSION

To analyse the literature systematically, it is found that the theory most widely adopted by researchers is the technology adoption theory. The theory provides a foundation for the researcher to build a conceptual model based on theoretical constructs. TAM originated from the organisational context of adopting new technology in companies, but this model is extensively used for understanding the adoption of technology from the consumer point of view. Venkatesh et al. 2013 developed the UTAUT theory, which has more explanatory power to explain customers' intentions regarding adopting technology. Due to TAM's deterministic approach, it overlooked consumers' distinctive characteristics. China, India, Spain, Mauritius, and other countries added consumer-related dimensions to the meta-UTAUT model.

All the highly cited articles used the survey method in collecting the data. Tools and techniques employed in analysing the collected data were structural equation modelling. SEM is the best tool for exploring the relationship between various constructs. Most of the studies are empirical and identify the factors affecting mobile payments. They analysed that consumers felt a variety of risks and uneasiness when using wireless devices to make payments, thus it's important to look into the variables influencing their intention and actual use of mobile payments.

In bibliometric analysis, co-authorship analysis shows significantly less collaboration among the authors of different countries spain didn't collaborate with any other country's author.. Bibliographic coupling reveals that the highest citation received by liébana-Cabanillas f. (2018) and the research title predicts the determinates of mobile payment acceptance. The highest citation was received by China on 28 documents.

Cluster in bibliometrics shows mobile payment technologies looked to know the intention of customers, but actual use is not up to mark. Co-occurrence based on keywords shows that the TAM model is used for theoretical constructs. This model is used by researchers to analyse the behavioural intention of consumers. In developing countries, mobile payment adoption is in the initial phase. Governments can encourage mobile payment applications with a greater emphasis on creating trust through legislative initiatives and targeted campaigns to improve the credibility of mobile payment applications. Businesses might increase their efforts to engage customers and collect pertinent information from customer touch points for improved consumer involvement while setting up MPAs. Using MPAs more often can help governments drastically reduce the cost of creating and managing currency bills, freeing up taxpayer funds for social investments. For this reason, researchers are more interested in examining the variables influencing the adoption of digital payment methods.

Text-based analysis and keyword analysis show the association between keywords and texts and build the cluster to quickly find the less associated words and their relationship with other words. It gives a clear-cut path for the future scope of research. Most studies related to consumer analysis of the inclination to use mobile payment, but actual usage analysis is still under investigation. Merchant adoption, especially small retailers also affected by various factors; it is a good area of research for researchers. UTAUT theory is more effective in explaining the intention of customers. Many researchers used it, but studying moderators and mediators with primary variables is a good area of research.

7. CONCEPTUAL FRAMEWORK FOR MOBILE PAYMENT RESEARCH

This study suggests a multilayered conceptual framework for upcoming mobile payment research based on the synthesis of findings, which includes:

Technology Layer: data analytics, security architecture, usability, and interoperability
User Layer: post-adoption behaviour, behavioural intention, trust, digital literacy, and actual usage
Ecosystem Layer: FinTech collaborations, network effects, platform competition, and merchant adoption
Institutional Layer: consumer protection, inclusion policies, public digital infrastructure, and regulation

The majority of the literature now in publication focuses on the user-technology interface, but there are clear study shortages at the institutional and ecosystem levels, especially with regard to merchants and regulatory oversight.

8. EMERGING RESEARCH THEMES AND OPPORTUNITIES

The accelerating evolution of mobile payment systems, fueled by technological advances and changing consumer trends, offers many avenues for future studies. Whereas the current literature mostly employs models like the Technology Acceptance Model (TAM) and Unified Theory of Acceptance and Use of Technology (UTAUT) to study consumer adoption (Singh et al., 2020; Patil et al., 2020; Venkatesh et al., 2013), such models overwhelmingly concentrate on behaviour intention and pay little or no attention to contextual and socio-cultural variables. Therefore, future research should use broader theoretical perspectives like institutional theory and socio-technical systems theory to gain a more thorough understanding of mobile payment adoption resulting from the interaction of technology, users, organisations, and regulatory environments. Building on this basis, systemic and data-driven approaches that take into consideration platform governance, ecosystem dynamics, real usage behaviour, and changing institutional arrangements are necessary for mobile payment scholarship to go beyond traditional adoption models and established technological constructs. These integrative frameworks can provide more in-depth understanding of how social context, technology design, and regulatory frameworks all work together to influence the uptake and continued usage of mobile payment systems. Examining actual usage trends, platform switching behavior, and ecosystem lock-in requires more scholarly attention, especially in the context of multi-service super-app settings. There is still a lack of research on adoption dynamics among small and medium-sized businesses and merchants, particularly in rural and informal marketplaces where institutional and infrastructure limitations are very different from those in urban areas. Another interesting approach to comprehending cross-national differences in mobile payment spread is comparative institutional research that focuses on interoperability and digital public infrastructure.Algorithmic trust, data governance, and AI-enabled decision-making in payment systems should all be included in emerging research subjects since these factors have a growing impact on user confidence and system transparency. Increasing international cooperation and policy-focused research can improve knowledge of how institutional capacity, technology infrastructure, and regulatory frameworks influence adoption outcomes in various economies. Furthermore, future models may have far greater explanatory power if moderating and mediating variables like digital literacy, perceived security, trust, and social impact are included (Shao et al., 2019; Kalinić et al., 2019). To produce more complex and useful findings, context-sensitive field studies that are adapted to local socioeconomic and geographic settings are crucial, especially in developing economies.

Additionally, the introduction of moderating and mediating variables such as digital literacy, perceived security, trust, and social influence may further enrich the explanatory capability of these models (Shao et al., 2019; Kalinić et al., 2019). Field studies suited to individual geographic and socio-economic environments, particularly within developing economies, can also provide more useful insights.

One of the key gaps in the literature is the narrow attention paid to merchants and small firms, who are essential stakeholders in the mobile payment value chain. Consumer-side adoption has been the primary focus for most studies, with little attention given to how small merchants and informal firms interact with mobile payment systems (Abdullah & Khan, 2021). Future studies need to explore the supply-side issues like infrastructural constraints, shortage of digital literacy, transaction costs, and trust deficiency constraining adoption among traders, especially in rural and semi-urban regions. Similarly, although behavioural intention has been well-explored, actual use behaviour and post-adoption phenomena require further investigation. As noted, several of the most-cited studies are based on cross-sectional survey data (Liébana-Cabanillas et al., 2018; Su et al., 2018), which could be supplemented by longitudinal research that tracks user experiences and changes in behaviour over time based on actual transaction data.

In the context of financial inclusion, mobile payments are often touted as a means for extending services to the unbanked and underbanked. Yet, empirical evidence to support this is sparse. Subsequent studies ought to carefully examine the effect of mobile payments on financial inclusion indicators, with attention to gendered adoption trends and the digital divide (Tounekti et al., 2022). For example, while Chinese male users value mobility and reputation, female users value security as a key influence for trust-building (Shao et al., 2019). Knowledge of these differences in behaviour might assist in more inclusive financial technology design. In addition, post-adoption determinants of customer satisfaction, loyalty, repeated use, and app-switching behaviour also need more research attention, especially in competitive multi-platform settings (Leong et al., 2020).

Methodologically, the prevalence of partial least squares structural equation modelling (PLS-SEM) in the investigated studies (Lian et al., 2021; Pal et al., 2021) indicates a need for diversification. Future scholars may harness machine learning, neural networks, text mining, and social network analysis to gain deeper insights into behavior and predictive modeling. Bibliometric resources used in this research, VOSviewer, may be supplemented with other cutting-edge visualization platforms such as Gephi, CiteSpace, and HistCite to reveal refined intellectual and thematic patterns (Lozano et al., 2019). Mixed methods combining both qualitative and quantitative data would further enrich the analysis and yield more context-sensitive results.

By and large, although the existing literature has provided substantial insights into mobile payment systems, there is still a vast potential for developing theoretical frameworks further, investigating under-studied populations and situations, and utilising more advanced research tools. Developing answers to these issues will not only extend scientific knowledge but also drive the evolution of more inclusive, secure, and adaptive mobile payment environments.

9. PRACTICAL AND POLICY IMPLICATIONS

The results give enterprises, platform providers, and governments streamlined yet practical consequences. By guaranteeing legal certainty in areas like data protection, cybersecurity, and interoperability while concurrently funding digital public infrastructure and digital literacy programs, governments can promote the adoption of mobile payments. These actions are especially crucial for encouraging participation among underprivileged communities, rural consumers, and small business owners.The findings emphasize the necessity for FinTech companies and platform operators to provide top priority to merchant-oriented solutions that lower onboarding and transaction costs, clear data governance, and ensure safe system design. Mobile payment platforms can be used by businesses, particularly small and medium-sized ones, to boost customer interaction and operational insights in addition to facilitating quick transactions. Building sustainable and equitable mobile payment ecosystems requires coordinated efforts across the commercial, technological, and regulatory realms.

10. CONCLUSION

This paper dealt with a systematic literature and bibliometric analysis of mobile payment systems. This study assists academics and practitioners in understanding the factors that promote and impede the adoption of mobile payments by identifying trends, gaps in understanding, and new problems in the field. The article highlighted the relationships and collaborations between the most prominent academics, organisations, and journals. Technology's importance in financial transactions has grown. Through employing artificial intelligence and machine learning to gather and evaluate credit-related information scores, mobile payments meet the demands of small business owners and those without bank accounts. The results of our evaluation indicate that mobile payment research has been progressing in the correct direction, as scholars from a variety of institutions, disciplines, and jurisdictions have published their findings in esteemed peer-reviewed publications. So payment system using technology changes the structure of the incumbent. Research in this field is gaining momentum in co-authorship analysis, showing the Indian author is collaborating with South African and Saudi Arabian authors. Still, the Spanish author didn't cooperate with any other author. The author received the highest citation for "Predicting the determinants of mobile payment acceptance: A hybrid SEM-neural network approach." SEM is the most popular technique in analysing data by the researcher using the SEM with AMOS, PLS, and neural network approach.

Limitations of the study

The main drawback of this review paper is that the researcher exclusively utilised data from the Scopus database. This limitation may have resulted in the inclusion specific documents in this study, which would offer a more precise understanding for future research. Therefore, researchers can acquire additional papers and identify additional research voids by extracting data from additional databases, including Web of Science, JSTOR, and Research Gate. The vos-viewer has been employed as a bibliometric instrument in the current study to perform a variety of statistical analysis patterns. The current study's purview can be broadened in the future by incorporating other cutting-edge bibliometric tools, including Gephi, HistCite, and Bib Excel, to facilitate a deeper investigation and improved visualisation. In addition, prospective researchers may employ a diverse array of science mappings analysis software, including Sci2tool, SciMat, CiteNetExplore, and CiteSpace, to more effectively illustrate the relationship between various units of analysis.

Funding Declaration

No funding has been received for carrying out this research

REFERENCES

Al-Okaily, M., Lutfi, A., Alsaad, A., Taamneh, A., & Alsyouf, A. (2020). The determinants of digital payment systems' acceptance under cultural orientation differences: The case of uncertainty avoidance. *Technology in Society*, *63*, 101367. DOI: 10.1016/j.techsoc.2020.101367

Altounjy, R., Alaeddin, O., Hussain, H. I., & Sebastian, K. O. T. (2020). Moving from bricks to clicks: Merchants' acceptance of the mobile payment in Malaysia. *International Journal of eBusiness and eGovernment Studies, 12*(2), 136-150.

Chaiyasoonthorn, W., & Suksa-Ngiam, W. (2019). The diffusion and adoption of electronic payment systems in Bangkok. [IJEBR]. *International Journal of E-Business Research, 15*(2), 102–115. DOI: 10.4018/IJEBR.2019040106

Chhonker, M. S., Verma, D., Kar, A. K., & Grover, P. (2018). m-commerce technology adoption: Thematic and citation analysis of scholarly research during (2008-2017). *The Bottom Line (New York, N.Y.)*, *31*(3/4), 208–233. DOI: 10.1108/BL-04-2018-0020

Dahlberg, T., Guo, J., & Ondrus, J. (2015). A critical review of mobile payment research. *Electronic Commerce Research and Applications*, *14*(5), 265–284. DOI: 10.1016/j.elerap.2015.07.006

Dahlberg, T., Mallat, N., Ondrus, J., & Zmijewska, A. (2006).Mobile Payment Market and Research - Past, Present, and Future.Presentation at Helsinki Mobility Roundtable, Helsinki, Finland, June 1-2, 2002(January 2006), 1–16.

Davis, F. D. (1989). Perceived usefulness, perceived ease of use, and user acceptance of information technology. *Management Information Systems Quarterly*, *13*(3), 319–339. DOI: 10.2307/249008

De Bel, J., & Gâza, M. (2011). Mobile Payments 2012- My mobile, my wallet. *Director*, •••, 1–100.

de Luna, I. R., Liébana-Cabanillas, F., Sánchez-Fernández, J., & Muñoz-Leiva, F. (2019). Mobile payment is not all the same: The Adoption of mobile payment systems depending on the technology applied. *Technological Forecasting and Social Change*, *146*, 931–944. DOI: 10.1016/j.techfore.2018.09.018

Donthu, N., Kumar, S., Mukherjee, D., Pandey, N., & Lim, W. M. (2021). How to conduct a bibliometric analysis: An overview and guidelines. *Journal of Business Research*, *133*, 285–296. DOI: 10.1016/j.jbusres.2021.04.070

Garrouch, K. (2021). Does the reputation of the provider matter? A model explaining the continuance intention of mobile wallet applications. *Journal of Decision Systems*, *30*(2-3), 150–171. DOI: 10.1080/12460125.2020.1870261

Gong, X., Cheung, C. M., Zhang, K. Z., Chen, C., & Lee, M. K. (2020). Cross-side network effects, brand equity, and consumer loyalty: Evidence from mobile payment market. *International Journal of Electronic Commerce*, *24*(3), 279–304. DOI: 10.1080/10864415.2020.1767427

Gong, X., Zhang, K. Z., Chen, C., Cheung, C. M., & Lee, M. K. (2020). What drives trust transfer from web to mobile payment services? The dual effects of perceived entitativity. *Information & Management*, *57*(7), 103250. DOI: 10.1016/j.im.2019.103250

Handarkho, Y. D., Harjoseputro, Y., Samodra, J. E., & Irianto, A. B. P. (2021). Understanding proximity mobile payment continuance usage in Indonesia from a habit perspective. *Journal of Asia Business Studies*, *15*(3), 420–440. DOI: 10.1108/JABS-02-2020-0046

Hoe, S. L. (2008). Issues and procedures in adopting structural equation modelling technique. *Journal of Quantitative Methods*, *3*(1), 76.

Hueske, A. K., & Guenther, E. (2015). What hampers innovation? External stakeholders, the organization, groups and individuals: A systematic review of empirical barrier research. *Management Review Quarterly*, *65*(2), 113–148. DOI: 10.1007/s11301-014-0109-5

Kalinić, Z., Liébana-Cabanillas, F. J., Muñoz-Leiva, F., & Marinković, V. (2019). The moderating impact of gender on the acceptance of peer-to-peer mobile payment systems. *International Journal of Bank Marketing*, *38*(1), 138–158. DOI: 10.1108/IJBM-01-2019-0012

Kalinic, Z., Marinkovic, V., Molinillo, S., & Liébana-Cabanillas, F. (2019). A multi-analytical approach to peer-to-peer mobile payment acceptance prediction. *Journal of Retailing and Consumer Services*, *49*, 143–153. DOI: 10.1016/j.jretconser.2019.03.016

Karjaluoto, H., Shaikh, A. A., Saarijärvi, H., & Saraniemi, S. (2019). How perceived value drives the use of mobile financial services apps. *International Journal of Information Management*, *47*, 252–261. DOI: 10.1016/j.ijinfomgt.2018.08.014

Kazan, E., Tan, C. W., Lim, E. T., Sørensen, C., & Damsgaard, J. (2018). Disentangling digital platform competition: The case of UK mobile payment platforms. *Journal of Management Information Systems*, *35*(1), 180–219. DOI: 10.1080/07421222.2018.1440772

Lai, P. C., & Liew, E. J. (2021). Towards a Cashless Society: The Effects of Perceived Convenience and Security on Gamified Mobile Payment Platform Adoption. *AJIS. Australasian Journal of Information Systems*, *25*, 25. DOI: 10.3127/ajis.v25i0.2809

Leong, L. Y., Hew, T. S., Ooi, K. B., & Wei, J. (2020). Predicting mobile wallet resistance: A two-staged structural equation modeling-artificial neural network approach. *International Journal of Information Management*, *51*, 102047. DOI: 10.1016/j.ijinfomgt.2019.102047

Lew, S., Tan, G. W. H., Loh, X. M., Hew, J. J., & Ooi, K. B. (2020). The disruptive mobile wallet in the hospitality industry: An extended mobile technology acceptance model. *Technology in Society*, *63*, 101430. DOI: 10.1016/j.techsoc.2020.101430

Liébana-Cabanillas, F., Marinkovic, V., de Luna, I. R., & Kalinic, Z. (2018). Predicting the determinants of mobile payment acceptance: A hybrid SEM-neural network approach. *Technological Forecasting and Social Change*, *129*, 117–130. DOI: 10.1016/j.techfore.2017.12.015

Liébana-Cabanillas, F., Molinillo, S., & Ruiz-Montañez, M. (2019). To use or not to use, that is the question: Analysis of the determining factors for using NFC mobile payment systems in public transportation. *Technological Forecasting and Social Change*, *139*, 266–276. DOI: 10.1016/j.techfore.2018.11.012

Lim, W. M. (2021). Toward an agency and reactance theory of crowding: Insights from COVID-19 and the tourism industry. *Journal of Consumer Behaviour*, *20*(6), 1690–1694. DOI: 10.1002/cb.1948

Liu, J., Li, X., & Wang, S. (2020). What have we learnt from 10 years of fintech research? ascientometric analysis. *Technological Forecasting and Social Change*, *155*, 120022. DOI: 10.1016/j.techfore.2020.120022

Liu, R., Wu, J., & Yu-Buck, G. F. (2021). The influence of mobile QR code payment on payment pleasure: Evidence from China. *International Journal of Bank Marketing*, *39*(2), 337–356. DOI: 10.1108/IJBM-11-2020-0574

Lu, X., & Lu, H. (2020). Understanding Chinese Millennials' Adoption Intention Towards Third-Party Mobile Payment. [IRMJ]. *Information Resources Management Journal*, *33*(2), 40–63. DOI: 10.4018/IRMJ.2020040103

Madan, V., & Kour, M. (2023). Mobile payment usage: Systematic literature review. In *Emerging Trends and Innovations in Industries of the Developing World: A Multidisciplinary Approach* (pp. 89–93). CRC press, Taylor & Francis. DOI: 10.1201/9781003457602-16

Madan, V., & Kour, M. (2024), "Fintech and Mobile Payments in Transition: A Study of Adoption Challenges", *2024 IEEE International Conference on Interdisciplinary Approaches in Technology and Management for Social Innovation (IATMSI)*, (Vol. 2, pp. 1-6).

Matemba, E. D., & Li, G. (2018). Consumers' willingness to adopt and use WeChat wallet: An empirical study in South Africa. *Technology in Society*, *53*, 55–68. DOI: 10.1016/j.techsoc.2017.12.001

Nadkarni, S., & Prügl, R. (2021). Digital transformation: A review, synthesis and opportunities for future research. *Management Review Quarterly*, *71*(2), 233–341. DOI: 10.1007/s11301-020-00185-7

Nguyen, H. V. (2018). *Cash or cashless? Promoting consumers' adoption of mobile payments in an emerging economy*. Strategic Direction.

Oentoro, W. (2021). Mobile payment adoption process: A serial of multiple mediation and moderation analysis. *The Bottom Line (New York, N.Y.)*, *34*(3/4), 225–244. DOI: 10.1108/BL-09-2020-0059

Pal, A., Herath, T., & Rao, H. R. (2021). Why do people use mobile payment technologies and why would they continue? An examination and implications from India. *Research Policy*, *50*(6), 104228. DOI: 10.1016/j.respol.2021.104228

Patil, P., Tamilmani, K., Rana, N. P., & Raghavan, V. (2020). Understanding consumer adoption of mobile payment in India: Extending Meta-UTAUT model with personal innovativeness, anxiety, trust, and grievance redressal. *International Journal of Information Management*, *54*, 102144. DOI: 10.1016/j.ijinfomgt.2020.102144

Qu, Y., Rong, W., Chen, H., Ouyang, Y., & Xiong, Z. (2018). Influencing factors analysis for a social network web based payment service in China. *Journal of Theoretical and Applied Electronic Commerce Research*, *13*(3), 99–113. DOI: 10.4067/S0718-18762018000300106

Rizkyandy, R., Setyohadi, D. B., & Suyoto, S. (2018). What should be considered for acceptance mobile payment: An investigation of the factors affecting of the intention to use system services T-Cash. *Advances in Science, Technology and Engineering Systems Journal*, *3*(2), 257–262. DOI: 10.25046/aj030230

Salloum, S. A., & Al-Emran, M. (2018). Factors affecting the Adoption of E-payment systems by university students: Extending the TAM with Trust. *International Journal of Electronic Business*, *14*(4), 371–390. DOI: 10.1504/IJEB.2018.098130

Schmidthuber, L., Maresch, D., & Ginner, M. (2020). Disruptive technologies and abundance in the service sector-toward a refined technology acceptance model. *Technological Forecasting and Social Change*, *155*, 119328. DOI: 10.1016/j.techfore.2018.06.017

Shao, Z., Zhang, L., Li, X., & Guo, Y. (2019). Antecedents of trust and continuance intention in mobile payment platforms: The moderating effect of gender. *Electronic Commerce Research and Applications*, *33*, 100823. DOI: 10.1016/j.elerap.2018.100823

Singh, N., Sinha, N., & Liébana-Cabanillas, F. J. (2020). Determining factors in the adoption and recommendation of mobile wallet services in India: Analysis of the effect of innovativeness, stress to use and social influence. *International Journal of Information Management*, *50*, 191–205. DOI: 10.1016/j.ijinfomgt.2019.05.022

Singh, U. G. (2021). Investigating Mobile Payment Adoption in Mauritius. *African Journal of Business and Economic Research*, *16*(3), 257. DOI: 10.31920/1750-4562/2021/v16n3a13

Su, P., Wang, L., & Yan, J. (2018). How users' Internet experience affects the adoption of mobile payment: A mediation model. *Technology Analysis and Strategic Management*, *30*(2), 186–197. DOI: 10.1080/09537325.2017.1297788

Teng, S., & Khong, K. W. (2021). Examining actual consumer usage of E-wallet: A case study of big data analytics. *Computers in Human Behavior*, *121*, 106778. DOI: 10.1016/j.chb.2021.106778

Tounekti, O., Ruiz-Martínez, A., & Skarmeta Gomez, A. F. (2022). Research in electronic and mobile payment systems: A bibliometric analysis. *Sustainability (Basel)*, *14*(13), 7661. DOI: 10.3390/su14137661

Venkatesh, V., Morris, M., Davis, G., & Davis, F. (2003). User acceptance of information technology: Toward a unified view. *Management Information Systems Quarterly*, *27*(3), 425–478. DOI: 10.2307/30036540

Wang, L., Luo, X. R., Yang, X., & Qiao, Z. (2019). Easy come or easy go? Empirical evidence on switching behaviors in mobile payment applications. *Information & Management*, *56*(7), 103150. DOI: 10.1016/j.im.2019.02.005

Wenner, G., Bram, J. T., Marino, M., Obeysekare, E., & Mehta, K. (2018). Organizational models of mobile payment systems in low-resource environments. *Information Technology for Development*, *24*(4), 681–705. DOI: 10.1080/02681102.2017.1311830

Chapter 9
Revolutionizing Banking Operations With AI and ML Technologies

D. Rajeswari
http://orcid.org/0000-0002-2677-4296
Department of Data Science and Business Systems, School of Computing, College of Engineering and Technology, SRM Institute of Science and Technology, Kattankulathur, India

K. J. Amala
http://orcid.org/0009-0003-6863-2565
Department of Data Science and Business Systems, School of Computing, College of Engineering and Technology, SRM Institute of Science and Technology, Kattankulathur, India

Athish Venkatachalam
http://orcid.org/0000-0001-6258-5188
Clemson University, USA

ABSTRACT

Financial institutions can meet client demand for better, safer, and easier money management with AI and ML.AI helps the financial sector manage risk, trade with numbers, and make investment decisions more efficiently.Thus, automated solutions are predicted to transform financial services.Managers can spend less time on mundane tasks and more on strategic tasks with AI and ML.AI is taking over critical financial tasks like risk assessment, stock trading, and loan approvals.To elaborate, AI is a powerful tool for banking and insurance.The financial services business could benefit from ML and AI.It may improve internal procedures, cybersecurity, and risk management and create more personalized products and services.

DOI: 10.4018/979-8-3373-6244-1.ch009

AI speeds responses, improving customer satisfaction.AI and ML are changing how banks and financial institutions collect and use data insights.This is driving firms to develop new operational strategies, changing competitive dynamics, work methods, and risk management, and creating new problems for businesses and governments.

INTRODUCTION

Artificial intelligence and machine learning are the two big trends in the 21st century. The banking sector is always a prestigious field where security in all respects is the main concern. To improve financial services, we can use AI and ML, so customers receive better service and experience less transaction risk. The world economy and the financial services sector are the primary sectors that have benefited from AI. According to a recent study, AI could generate more than $1 trillion annually for the global banking sector by reducing costs, increasing revenue, and making customers happier (Millennium Consultants, 2022). The global financial services industry is expected to earn around USD 28.529 trillion from 2025 to 2030, at a compound annual growth rate (CAGR) of 6% (Ross, 2015). This change has already been reflected, especially after COVID-19, and we are in the era of Banking 4.0, where everything is digital, AI makes decisions, and customers can communicate beyond location and time. As adaptability is the most highlighted feature, it can meet the demands of any business regardless of the structure. In the 1960s, the ATM at Barclays Bank was a breakthrough in this domain, but since 2017, AI has been changing how processing and database management are handled. There is always a need for advanced analytics and automation solutions to prevent cyberattacks. New services are still evolving to enhance customer connections, control risks, and make the system more efficient. One study by Autonomous Next found that people worldwide saved $447 billion by using AI applications by 2023.

Neural networks, data analytics tools, natural language processing, etc., are common technologies of Artificial Intelligence in Banking that automate and improve various features of financial services. Banks use AI-backed chatbots, recommendation systems, and sentiment analysis tools to engage with consumers. They also adapt to evolving needs and provide products and services that address them. AI has the potential to create new financial products, such as flexible credit limits, tailored savings plans, and investment advice. Digital banking, mobile payments, and partnerships with fintech companies have created large, high-quality datasets for AI to use. Additionally, banks have invested in smart tracking and reporting systems to meet increasing regulatory demands to combat financial crime, protect client data, and comply with regulations. Traditional banks have had to update their technology due to tougher competition from fintech startups that can move quickly and from digital-only banks. Lastly, customers' standards are changing because they have used digital-native services in other areas. They want everything to occur quickly, be obvious, and be made just for them. This is something AI and data mining excel at.

One of the major advantages of AI in banking is its ability to detect fraud. AI has already proven its ability to recognise patterns. In certain patterns, these automated systems can spot irregularities that could indicate fraud. The fact that AI is ever-evolving and can distinguish between real and fake content is also a plus. The number of transactions that are mistakenly marked as fraudulent is high. These erroneously identified fraudulent transactions can be eradicated through AI learning (Pamarthi, 2024). AI uses biometrics, such as iris and fingerprint scanners, to verify user identity and prevent fraud across ever-growing digital banking channels. This helps limit access to private data. Falsely detected transactions are one concern with AI in fraud protection. Even as AI improves, it still causes problems for businesses and their customers.

The bank's financial efficiency shows different impacts across contexts (Kumar, 2024; Paramesha et al., 2024). Based on real-time experiences from developed markets (Bodemer, 2024) and empirical evidence from growing economies across different countries (Kaddumi et al., 2023; Hendawi et al., 2024; Hmoud et al., 2025; Abu Khalaf et al., 2025), we can understand the following matters. The combination of cloud computing with AI, rather than using AI alone, appears essential for achieving significant operational improvements. FinTech affects different dimensions of bank performance differently. While studies consistently show improvements in operational efficiency (Kaddumi et al., 2023; Hendawi et al., 2024), the impact on profitability metrics varies by bank size, capital adequacy, and market share (Abu Khalaf et al., 2025). From the above-mentioned studies, we can conclude that technology adoption, along with organisational and market conditions, is also necessary to bring about societal change. Regulatory uncertainty, talent scarcity, data quality issues, and cultural resistance are perennial challenges in the market literature (Aldboush et al., 2023; Othman, 2025). In reality, it indicates that greater attention from professionals, including researchers and practitioners, is always needed, and their contributions are an integral part.

Recently, fintech companies and digital banks have been increasingly emerging in the banking sector, rather than conventional banks with significant branch networks. It strongly shows digital transformation (Aithal, 2023). AI has become a crucial technology transforming banking operations through new solutions that improve scalability, efficiency, and the customer experience. Also, advanced data analytics, robots, embedded banking, and intelligent infrastructure are four key digital disruptors. The implementation of AI models in digital banking can be classified into three sequential tiers (Radenković et al., 2023). To identify trends and improve digital banking operations, machine learning must be used in the initial stage. Customers and employees may not even realise they are interacting with a computer because of the second level's general intelligence, which can mimic human interactions so well. AI systems that are more intelligent and capable of making decisions than human bank employees are included in the third and most advanced level.

This chapter is organised as follows: Section 2 reviews the theoretical foundations and existing literature, Section 3 presents the proposed methodology for successful AI/ML implementation in banking, Section 4 discusses results from both developed and emerging market contexts, Section 5 discusses advantages, social welfare implications, and future enhancements, and Section 6 addresses deepened risks and challenges. Section 7 concludes with practical recommendations for banking institutions pursuing AI-driven transformation.

LITERATURE SURVEY

The article by Ridzuan, N. N., et al. (2024) provides policymakers with guidance. It discusses how the ASEAN guidelines for AI development can be applied in practice at the national and regional levels. Mixed-method research can help address the theoretical vacuum by examining future research directions, a blend of extended UTAUT, change theory, and institutional theory, and the critical success element. The demographic gap can be closed by researching in a place where fintech services are expected to be less popular, like a developing or Islamic country. In short, this work uses descriptive analysis in a new way. It makes four primary contributions that make it unique: (1) how AI is used in banking and finance, (2) the pros and cons of using AI in these fields, (3) the rules and regulations that control AI right now, and (4) the types of theories that could be useful for further research.

The work on traditional banking (Kaddumi, T. A., et al., 2023) conducted on the Amman Stock Exchange (ASE) and utilising financial data from 2012 to 2020, prepared a tool. It was a questionnaire that focused on three main areas: financial inclusion (FI), alternative payment methods (APMs), and automation (Auto). 115 questionnaires were mailed to all commercial banks listed on the Amman Stock Exchange (ASE). From the analysis, all three FinTech dimensions - FI, APMs, and Auto-had a favourable and significant effect on the financial performance metrics of Jordanian commercial banks in deposits, total loans, and net profit margin. To stay competitive in the banking market, banks need to invest more in financial technology tools and apps. This will help them attract new customers and keep their current ones.

New developments in financial technology services (Bashayreh et al., 2020) have made standard financial services less useful. Using panel data, this study examines how fintech services affected the performance of 13 commercial banks in Jordan from 2012 to 2018. The study used three control factors to examine performance:

Gross Domestic Product (GDP) growth, Bank Size (BS), and financial leverage (LEV). Return on equity (ROE) was used as a proxy for performance. Some of the Fintech factors are ATMs, online and phone banking, and automatic teller machines. The study found that Fintech improved the success of Jordanian banks.

This paper (Xu et al., 2025) conducts a comprehensive bibliometric analysis of articles in the Web of Science Core Collection Database published between 2015 and July 2024 to examine how financial technology (FinTech) affects bank performance. The study examines five main questions: research trends, important writers and sources, geographical factors, interesting research clusters, and how FinTech affects different aspects of bank performance. The article suggests four areas for future research: examining different ways to measure bank success, focusing on specific locations, exploring new topics such as financial inclusion and the importance of entrepreneurship, and improving methods. This essay discusses how FinTech has changed the banking industry.

The study (Khalaf et al., 2025) demonstrates that FinTech influences the profitability of banks in the MENA region. A group of 63 banks has come together over the past 14 years (2010–2023) to form a consortium. To construct a FinTech index, text mining was applied to the annual reports of all institutions. Tobit regression to examine how the FinTech Index affects the profits of MENA banks. This study demonstrates that banks can enhance their profitability by adopting additional FinTech technologies. People think that bigger banks, banks with a lot of cash on hand, and banks with a bigger market share will do better.

The swift rise of financial technology (Fintech) has transformed the credit and equity markets, providing small enterprises with unprecedented access to financing and fostering financial inclusion (Hmoud et al., 2025). However, the impact of this financial inclusion on the efficacy of capital allocation remains unclear. This study examines the impact of Fintech on capital allocation efficiency by analysing data from Fintech firms in Jordan and Palestine from 2010 to 2020. The main point is that Fintech can make it easier to access money, but it could also make it harder to use resources effectively. Fintech companies are hindering the process, as they divert resources from people/companies who would use them for more efficient systems. This trend is evident both industry-wide and at the corporate level. Mechanism studies show this effect stems from increased competition in the loan market and simpler stock interchanges. In short, the principal cause of this inefficiency is the alterations introduced by Fintech's debt finance.

The research by Untoro et al. (2022) examines the role of Fintech in determining the performance and risk of traditional banks in Indonesia. Fintech in this study is represented by P2P lending and banks that utilise fintech technology. The research spanned five years (2017–2021). The results show that fintech and peer-to-peer financing do not significantly affect the performance or risk faced by traditional banks.

We show that banks' ownership structure magnifies the effects of P2P lending and fintech adoption on risk but has little effect on performance. This advances the risk profile of traditional institutions in P2P lending and reduces bank risk, especially for cooperative banks.

Alboush, al (2023) explores the ethical challenges presented by financial technology (fintech). It concerns privacy, big data, and artificial intelligence (AI). A systematic literature review identifies ethical, and privacy issues associated with fintech. Some of these issues involve bias, discrimination, privacy, transparency, justice, ownership and control. It's got implications for how we protect client data and uphold data protection regulations and encourage businesses to behave responsibly online." This guide is useful for organisations — it includes tips and suggestions on using encryption, making clear what data they collect and how they use it, giving customers the option to opt out of certain features related to their data, and training employees on relevant aspects of the privacy policies.

Hendawi, R. et al. (2024) addressed how financial technology impacts the efficiency of Islamic banks in Jordan. From these banks, they selected a sample of 130 employees. The listed distinct factors for evaluating FinTech included regulated payment systems, financial inclusion, and technology. The economic performance of Islamic banks in Jordan was the major focus of interest. The study from Othman, M. (2025) examines the potential impact of financial technology (fintech) on transforming the banking system in Jordan to enhance sustainability, financial inclusion, and customer engagement. A quantitative descriptive survey methodology was employed to collect data from 400 individuals, comprising 300 bank clients and 100 banking professionals, via a standardised multilingual questionnaire disseminated through digital media. The goal of the study is to examine how fintech innovations align with sustainable finance practices, how they help common people without access to banking services, and how they affect customer satisfaction.

Artificial intelligence is increasingly integrated into banking and finance, with the potential to significantly improve financial performance. A study across 20 countries found that AI innovation positively impacts banks' return on assets and economic growth. However, prolonged exposure can lead to diminishing returns. Non-performing loans negatively affect financial performance, emphasising the importance of asset quality. Regulatory capital and economic growth are positively associated with financial performance, whereas government regulations negatively affect financial performance (Nguyen et al., 2023).

PROPOSED METHODOLOGY

The proposed system aims to combine AI and ML to make financial jobs smarter, more automated, and more secure. So, it focuses more on data processing and algorithm accuracy, enabling services to become more reliable and customer-friendly. There are seven steps in the framework, and each depends on the others, as shown in Figure 1.

Figure 1. AI-Enabled Banking System Architecture

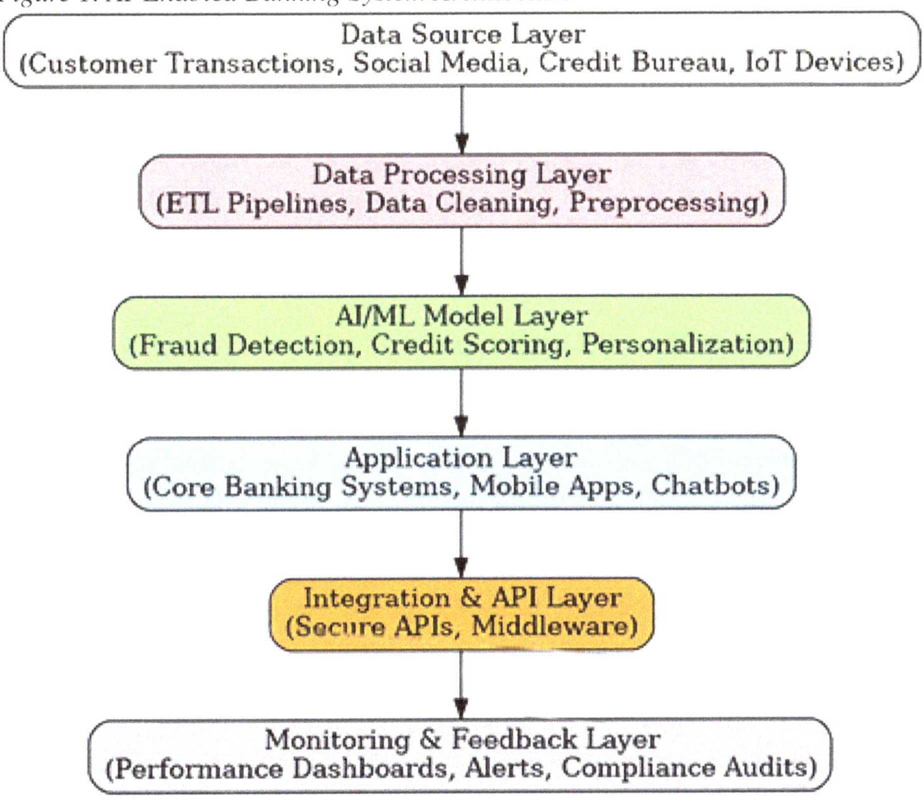

DATA COLLECTION

The datasets for banking should be large and varied to formulate an accurate framework of the financial ecosystem. Core banking provides structured data, such as loan application records, repayment schedules, credit scores, and payment histories. Unstructured data sources are chat logs for customer service, emails, voice call records, and social media conversations. It provides a qualitative context to understand the customer's state of mind and state of action. External data sources provide the dataset with more detail and allow predictive models to consider both small and large economic factors. To keep data safe and private, it is sent through encrypted and secure channels. This is done in strict accordance with global and regional privacy rules.

DATA PREPROCESSING

The bootstrap phase of AI and ML projects is data preparation, after collection. Overall, this is the most time-consuming step. Banking demands a veritable assurance of the integrity and uniformity of data as it is collected from multiple sources and in diverse formats. This can include short-changing missing values, merging existing attributes, removing features and altering raw data into a specific format.

ANALYSIS OF EXPLORATORY DATA AND FEATURE ENGINEERING

EDA (Exploratory Data Analysis) in the Banking Sector is used to understand the structure, patterns, and relationships in a dataset. Analysts frequently use classification and clustering methods to detect trends within financial data. We use descriptive statistics, data visualisation tools and correlation heatmaps to identify the most important factors. Exploratory data analysis can help identify minute errors and multicollinearity that, if left unaddressed, can compromise predictive quality. After exploratory data analysis (EDA), feature engineering identifies domain-specific, high-impact factors that improve accuracy and can be interpreted accordingly. Applying better feature extraction methods for improving model inputs. The outcome of EDA and feature engineering is a clean & enriched dataset containing quantitative and qualitative indicators that describe operational and customer behaviour. This dataset will serve as the base for developing trustworthy AI and ML models in the banking domain.

MODEL SELECTION AND TRAINING

AI and ML, however, are more about choosing and training models. This is a crucial step, as it defines the analytical intelligence behind the automated decisions made by banks. Types of problems include classification, regression, clustering, and outlier. Key objectives are to prevent fraud, evaluate credit risk, predict remittance defaults, and offer personalised recommendations. Logistic Regression, Random Forests, Gradient Boosting Machines and Deep Neural Networks (DNNs) are commonly used tools for supervised learning to predict outcomes from labelled datasets. In unsupervised learning, methods such as K-Means clustering, Hierarchical Clustering, and Autoencoders can identify hidden patterns in unlabelled data. Reinforcement learning approaches are effective for decisions that require flexibility, such as adjusting loan interest rates or optimising a portfolio quickly. These approaches enable models to learn via continuous interaction with the surrounding environment. A common practice in training is to separate the dataset into smaller sets for development, validation and testing. This is usually achieved by splitting the data into a 70:15:15 or 80:10:10 ratio, depending on the dataset's size and diversity. Grid Search, Random Search or Bayesian Optimisation can now be used on the validation subset to find hyperparameters. The model is trained using the training subset.

MODEL EVALUATION AND VALIDATION

For an AI and ML processing system to be useful in the banking industry, its predictions should be tested and verified across different scenarios to ensure they are deterministic, accurate, and fair. The key aim of this stage is to assess how well the model can anticipate future occurrences, how effectively it can utilise what it has learned in a new context, and how successfully it adapts to changes in real-world data. Performance measurement methods differ from task to task. There exists a wide variety of methods to measure classification performance, including but not limited to accuracy, recall, F1-score, and receiver operating characteristic-Area Under the Curve (ROC-AUC) measures. This can be used for fraud detection or to inform loan approval decisions. High accuracy means that questionable items are truly questionable, while high recall indicates that few false transactions go untracked. Here are some ways to test the accuracy of regression predictions, including Mean Squared Error (MSE), Root Mean Squared Error (RMSE), and mean absolute percentage error (MAPE).

DEPLOYMENT AND SYSTEM INTEGRATION

Deployment and System Integration: This is a significant step for AI and ML models because it moves the model from a well-controlled development environment into the banking infrastructure. A detailed strategy must be put in place to integrate with the core banking, CRM applications, payment gateways, and fraud monitoring systems to ensure this step is successful.

RESULTS AND DISCUSSION

Recent studies using correlation analysis and multiple regression modelling investigated how AI and ML perform in the banking industry. Descriptive statistics are provided for the variables under consideration: knowledge of AI, perceived usefulness, perceived risk, subjective norms, awareness, and attitude toward AI. These studies are all consistent in noting that most people agree on the potential benefits of AI and machine learning. This agreement increases the likelihood of large-scale implementation in financial institutions. The correlation study demonstrated the strength and direction of the relationship between independent and dependent variables. This demonstrates that when users care about efficiency, accuracy and customer experience, they are more likely to use AI. And more knowledge about AI was positively correlated with interest in using it. How the multiple regression analysis has provided a reliable estimate of how these factors affect the dependent variable, the desire to use AI in banking. The model was statistically significant ($p < 0.01$) and possessed a sufficient coefficient of determination (R^2). The key indicator highlights the advantages of AI for average individuals. Although subjective norms were indicative at $p < 0.05$ level, their effect size was considerably small. This finding indicates that even though peers and business influence do make a difference, the person's comprehension and perception of AI applications' advantages outweigh this important topic in deciding whether to use it or not. The above results suggest that strong security systems and clear governance policies are essential to alleviate citizen concerns, as evidenced by the statistically significant negative coefficient for perceived risk.

1. Operational Efficiency Improvements

Here are some real-time examples of improving operational efficiency. According to the JPMorgan Chase report, COIN is an AI-driven platform that automates the review of legal loan documents. This modification reduced manual effort by almost 360,000 hours per year. For credit scoring, KYC verification and onboarding, ICICI Bank used AI-powered Robotic Process Automation (RPA).

2. Enhanced Fraud Detection and Risk Management

Capital One uses machine learning to evaluate millions of transactions every day. This has resulted in a significant reduction in false positives and faster fraud detection. The bank has applied AI to AML screening. That reduced false alarms by 60 per cent, improved risk scoring accuracy, and enhanced regulatory compliance.

3. Improved Customer Experience and Personalisation

AI & ML algorithms have led to significant improvements in customer satisfaction, risk management, and operational efficiency within the banking system. Bank of America's AI assistant, Erica, managed more than 50 million customer interactions within two years of its introduction. It helps with balance checks, spending insights and transaction queries. In Singapore, DBS Bank deployed AI across various segments to move towards hyper-personalisation and now generates wealth management advice that is specific to individual customer profiles resulting in double-digit growth in all key engagement metrics.

4. Financial Impact and Bank Performance Enhancement

According to McKinsey (2023), global banks that use AI strategically report up to a 20% increase in revenue through personalised cross-selling, up to a 40% reduction in operational costs through automation, and a 50–60% increase in risk modelling accuracy.

ADVANTAGES OF THE PROPOSED METHOD

1. Better customer service and customisation:

AI and machine learning could help banks and other financial institutions deliver world-class services. Consequently, customers are a lot happier and more loyal. Banks can determine what a customer requires by analysing their previous transactions, spending behaviour, and even social media contacts. They can then provide customised financial products. AI-powered chatbots can answer customer queries with no human intervention 24/7. It is a customer preference, and businesses are less pressured because of it. Internet of Things (IoT)- based virtual assistance powered by natural language processing (NLP) helps individuals make financial decisions by performing tasks such as account tracing and loan processing. Targeted marketing, personalised product recommendations, and flexible loan options attract new customers and boost sales. AI reduces friction in online interactions and streamlines services, which makes clients feel acknowledged and supported. This strategy helps banks nurture deeper, more enduring relationships with their customers. Banking customer segmentation: As well as creating specialised services beyond traditional segmentation using consumer data, behaviour patterns and real-time analytics. AI algorithms can analyse past transactions, spending habits, and even social media activity to offer specialised financial products that can improve investment strategies and provide personalised financial advice. This level of customisation establishes new benchmarks for digital banking engagements, boosting customer satisfaction and fostering loyalty. Moreover, the Internet of Things (IoT) has enabled financial institutions to collect and analyse data in unique ways. Wearables, sensors and GPS trackers are typical IoT devices that generate massive data volume for predictive modelling and improved decision-making. Datday-to-day lives allows the AIML model to give a better performance on transactions, which eventually helps fintech in launching a a collection through IoT, client data gathering, and pattern monitoring of their day to day lives allow the AIML model to give a better performance on transactions, which eventually helps fintech in launching myriad of products.

2. Enhancing Decision-Making via Data-Informed Understanding:

With predictive analytics, banks can calculate the market fluctuations, figure out investments, and find new ways to make money. Decision-making processes become increasingly precise and evidence-based. AI-powered systems also continue to learn from new data, making their predictions more accurate over time. Real-time dashboards and analytical tools that display key performance metrics and emerging hazards are helpful to executives and financial managers. Thus, management tactics are proactive instead of reactive. In a competitive financial market, banks make more money, have less risk, and are better able to bounce back.

3. More people can get access to money:

Another advantage of the proposed strategy is that it helps people get access to financial services. It helps laypeople keep official credit records much simpler, and collateral is typically excluded from traditional banking, especially in developing areas. AI and ML models solve daily chores such as using phones, paying utility bills, and posting on social media. This promotes banks and fintech companies to give loans and other services to less experienced people. People in rural and low-income areas can now access financial products that were previously out of reach, thanks to AI-driven micro-lending platforms.

4. Better data protection and hacking:

As more financial services move to digital platforms, banks have had to worry about cybersecurity. Our suggested AI-ML-based system enhances data security by continuously tracking transactions, issuing alerts for unusual login attempts, and identifying system vulnerabilities in real time. AI models become familiar with evolving cyber challenges, while traditional solutions rely on static security protocols. New techniques for identifying anomalies help guard against fraud, identity theft, and account takeovers. AI further strengthens security by simplifying biometric authentication methods such as voice and facial recognition.

5. Quicker loan approvals and more precise credit scores:

Traditional loan approval processes are time-consuming as they require manual credit checks and extensive paperwork. The AI solution approaches the process differently by incorporating algorithmic credit scoring beyond income and credit history. Machine learning systems analyse activities such as bill payments, spending habits, and purchases. When banks can approve loans in minutes rather than days, customers are happier, and businesses have more flexibility. AI-based credit ratings are more accurate and fairer than older methods, and fewer people were wrongly denied loans. By eliminating non-performing assets and loan losses, financial institutions can realise profits while making sure that all customers can exercise the same credit rights.

6. AI-Powered Risk Assessment:

People without a traditional credit history are not always fairly evaluated by traditional credit scoring systems. With AI and machine learning, banks can now rely on alternative data sources — such as utility bills, rental payments, mobile phone usage, and online shopping activity — to mitigate default risk while also deepening their relationships with underbanked communities. As AI continues to learn and adapt, these models will become better at risk assessment and decision-making. One is the Banach contraction principle, which has applications in proving the existence and uniqueness of solutions to various problems, including those in risk management. It has also been applied to develop new models and algorithms for computing risk metrics, such as projected shortfall and value-at-risk.

7. AI Ethics and Regulatory Adherence:

AI Ethics matters because it is widely used, hence so we need to regulate it). Current state of affairs: What changes will be necessary? More transparency in AI decision-making will be needed down the road — particularly in risk-profiling and lending. To comply with regulatory requirements and foster trust among stakeholders and customers, explainable AI(XAI) will be essential. It is anticipated that the authorities will create tighter guidelines for AI governance, with an emphasis on responsibility, fairness, and data protection. In an environment where responsible innovation is aligned with trust, banks that proactively pursue ethical AI will have an advantage.

8. Cost-effective monitoring of data:

The ability of machine learning to identify patterns in data, handle diverse data types, and operate autonomously enables financial institutions to detect money laundering activities in a cost-effective manner using multiple data collection tools

SOCIAL WELFARE OF THE PROPOSED SYSTEM

- Making use of AI and ML in banks is an excellent step for guaranteeing that everyone has access to financial services. AI and ML systems broaden the parameters of creditworthiness, adjusting to help at all levels of society.
- People from diverse backgrounds can improve their lives through investing in homes, small businesses and health care with access to affordable banking services. AI-based banking is revolutionizing how the rich and the poor are interacting with this domain, which ultimately facilitates easier access to money for all.
- Economic inequality is a burning issue for society, and an AI-ML banking model is one of the ways to address.
- Is Very strange things indeed: Machine learning systems judge whether you excel at creditworthiness based on factors that defy sense.
- Banks and other financial institutions could provide training programs for their employees to adapt to the new digital reality. AI-backed solutions help entrepreneurs streamline loan and investment acquisition for small businesses and startups.
- Governments and financial institutions can collaborate to provide computer and money management education. This will provide people with the abilities they need to succeed in an AI-driven economy.

- Conversational AI-powered bots and automated assistants also keep customers up to date on their payments, interest rates, and loan terms in real time.
- AI also makes banking more accountable: it destroys hidden fees, unethical practices and unfair loans.
- Institutions that are more open and honest gain trust from their clientele. This results in more people using electronic services and more people trusting financial institutions. Sound financial institutions are the cornerstones of a stable societal fabric, and AI will be a major part in making this foundation firm.
- Anti-money laundering (AML) is another potential use case which helps prevent financial crimes by detecting suspicious transactions and activities. Nonetheless, the application of advanced analytics and machine learning algorithms has significantly improved the effectiveness and efficiency of AIML programs in detecting money laundering.

POSSIBLE TREATS ON THE MACHINE LEARNING MODEL

Detection of cyber-attack is still a major challenge in banking. The time it takes to recognise intrusion activities is a significant factor behind this (Sobers, 2022). Machine learning offers a highly effective means of enhancing cyberattack detection by leveraging the massive datasets available in modern computing environments. Machine learning systems are particularly clever at detecting software vulnerabilities in giant codebases with millions of lines of code. This complicates manual analysis, leading to slow, error-prone processes. By leveraging training and automation, machine learning models can accurately detect these vulnerabilities faster than any human programmer. Machine learning systems learn and evolve with experience and data, thereby becoming better at detecting vulnerabilities. Machine learning also shows great prospects for developing new intrusion detection systems (IDSs). Different machine learning techniques, such as supervised, unsupervised, and reinforcement learning, offer distinct advantages to IDSs. Supervised learning excels at detecting known attacks with low false-positive rates, although it fails to handle unknown threats (Shaukat et al., 2020; Pinto et al., 2023). Although unsupervised learning can detect zero-day attacks, it often yields higher false-positive rates (Almalawi et al., 2020).

Reinforcement learning can adapt dynamically to evolving cyber threats, but only with sufficient training time (Nguyen & Reddi, 2023). The integration of these advanced techniques has led to notable improvements in the accuracy and responsiveness of IDSs, further advancing the field of cybersecurity. Machine learning models require a very large dataset to develop the exact model. Factors such as the time required for model development, tuning, and validation make the entire system costly. The most interesting part of this is securing sensitive information from further exploitation, as attackers often gain unauthorised access. Any attack can significantly affect entire systems and reduce their effectiveness. By analysing threat vectors in the context of attacks on machine learning, the following attack types are identified (Koball et al., 2024).

Data Extraction: The attacker attempts to uncover the data used to train the model. It becomes particularly dangerous if the model uses sensitive data.

In this attack, an attacker modifies the training dataset by inserting false samples, causing the model to provide incorrect predictions. Due to the nature of the model, even imperceptible differences in input data lead to misclassifications. Model extraction is the process of extracting information about a model's internal architecture. On the other hand, an evasion attack occurs when the attacker produces adversarial examples that cause the model to make incorrect predictions without being detected. Data poisoning and evasion attacks are categorised as affecting the outputs of machine learning, whereas data extraction and model extraction attacks are passive attacks. One notable case of data poisoning occurred at a bank, where adversaries altered the training data used to detect fraud, leading the system to incorrectly allow fraudulent transactions.

Adversarial attacks are the next widespread form of malicious manipulation in machine learning algorithms. The decision-making processes in machine learning can be affected by these attacks, leading to outcomes that favour the attacker (Goodfellow et al., 2014a; Goodfellow et al., 2014b). Neural networks classify data in a manner that is distinct from human perception, so even a minor adjustment to a few pixels can drastically change the classification result, even if the difference is imperceptible to a human (Goodfellow et al., 2014b). Moreover, altering an object's position can lead to misclassification (Alcorn et al., 2019), and Li et al. (2019) demonstrated that a facial recognition system can yield inaccurate results even with slight shifts in object position. Depending on the level of access to the machine learning model, attackers may focus on systems categorised as follows (Kobal et al., 2024). The first set of categories is Black Box. In the black box, the attacker lacks insight into the model's details but uses inputs and outputs to analyse vulnerabilities. Another set named White Box. In the white box, the attacker has complete knowledge of the model's architecture. It enables them to create precise perturbations to exploit its weaknesses. The last category is Grey Box. In the grey box, these attacks grant the attacker partial access to information, somewhere between full access in white-box attacks and the limited data available in black-box attacks. Model inversion can allow an attacker to reveal key characteristics of the underlying data used to train the system, especially if the model is trained on confidential data (Buchanan, 2021).

A machine learning model must exhibit several essential traits when considering significant societal impact. Critical features include security, model trustworthiness, robustness, and resilience (Khadka et al., 2024). Robustness refers to a model's ability to operate effectively even in times of crisis. In contrast, resilience is the system's ability to resume normal operations within a reasonable timeframe after a disruption. These attributes are vital in high-stakes domains, as their lack can lead to severe repercussions, especially in critical infrastructures. Enhancing resilience and robustness can greatly bolster trust and security within the system.

REFERENCES

Abu Khalaf, B., Al-Sharkas, A., & Sarea, A. (2025). Realising opportunities: The influence of FinTech on the success of MENA banks. *Discover Sustainability*, *6*(1), 501. DOI: 10.1007/s43621-025-01374-8

Aithal, P. S. (2023). An Analytical Study of Applications of Artificial Intelligence on Banking Practices. International Journal of Management [IJMTS]. *Technology and Social Sciences*, *8*(2), 133–144.

Alcorn, M. A., Li, Q., Gong, Z., Wang, C., Mai, L., Ku, W.-S., & Nguyen, A. (2019). Strike (With) a Pose: Neural Networks Are Easily Fooled by Strange Poses of Familiar Objects. *2019 IEEE/CVF Conference on Computer Vision and Pattern Recognition (CVPR)*, 4840–4849. DOI: 10.1109/CVPR.2019.00498

Aldboush, H. H., & Ferdous, M. (2023). Building trust in fintech: An analysis of ethical and privacy considerations in the intersection of big data, AI, and customer trust. *International Journal of Financial Studies*, *11*(3), 90. DOI: 10.3390/ijfs11030090

Almalawi, A., Fahad, A., Tari, Z., Khan, A. I., Alzahrani, N., Bakhsh, S. T., Alassafi, M. O., Alshdadi, A., & Qaiyum, S. (2020). Add-On Anomaly Threshold Technique for Improving Unsupervised Intrusion Detection on SCADA Data. *Electronics (Basel)*, *9*(6), 6. Advance online publication. DOI: 10.3390/electronics9061017

Bashayreh, A., & Wadi, R. M. A. (2020, November). The effect of Fintech on banks' performance: a case study of Jordan. In *International Conference on Business and Technology* (pp. 812–821). Springer International Publishing.

Bodemer, O. (2024). Revolutionizing finance: The impact of AI and cloud computing in the banking sector. *Unpublished manuscript.*

Buchanan, A. B. (2021). A National Security Research Agenda for Cybersecurity and Artificial Intelligence CSET. *Issue Brief.*

Consultants, M. Benefits Of Artificial Intelligence In the Banking Sector; Millennium Consultants: Kuala Lumpur, Malaysia, 2022. Available online: https://www. millenniumci.com/benefits-of-artificial-intelligence-in-the-banking-sector. (Accessed 11 September 2022).

Goodfellow, I., Pouget-Abadie, J., Mirza, M., Xu, B., Warde-Farley, D., Ozair, S., Courville, A., & Bengio, Y. (2014). Generative Adversarial Nets. Advances in Neural Information Processing Systems, 27. https://proceedings.neurips.cc/paper_files/paper/2014/hash/5ca3e9b122f61f8f06494c97b 1afccf3-Abstract.html

Goodfellow, I. J., Shlens, J., & Szegedy, C. (2014). Explaining and harnessing adversarial examples. arXiv Preprint arXiv:1412.6572.

Hendawi, R., Ineizeh, N. I., Hussein, O. J., & Alkahtani, M. (2024). The role of financial technology in improving performance in Jordanian Islamic banks. *Journal of Ecohumanism*, *3*(4), 279–290. DOI: 10.62754/joe.v3i4.3493

Hmoud, A., Magableh, F. A., Badwan, N., & Almashaqbeh, M. (2025). *Impact of FinTech on capital allocation: Empirical evidence from Jordan and Palestine*. Borsa Istanbul Review.

Kaddumi, T. A., Baker, H., Nassar, M. D., & A-Kilani, Q. (2023). Does financial technology adoption influence bank's financial performance: The case of Jordan. *Journal of Risk and Financial Management*, *16*(9), 413. DOI: 10.3390/jrfm16090413

Khadka, A., Sthapit, S., Epiphaniou, G., & Maple, C. (2024). Resilient Machine Learning: Advancement, Barriers, and Opportunities in the Nuclear Industry. *ACM Computing Surveys*, *56*(9), 1–29. DOI: 10.1145/3648608

Koball, C., Wang, Y., Rimal, B. P., & Vaidyan, V. (2024). *Machine Learning Security: Threat Model*. Attacks, and Challenges., DOI: 10.1109/MC.2024.3396357

Kumar, A. (2024). Redefining finance: The influence of Artificial Intelligence (AI) and Machine Learning (ML). *Transactions on Engineering and Computing Sciences*, *12*(4), 59–69.

Li, Y., Yang, X., Wu, B., & Lyu, S. (2019). Hiding faces in plain sight: Disrupting ai face synthesis with adversarial perturbations. arXiv Preprint arXiv:1906.09288.

D. K. Nguyen, G. Sermpinis, and C. Stasinakis, "Big data, artificial intelligence and machine learning: A transformative symbiosis in favour of financial technology, "European Financial Management, vol. 29, no. 2, pp. 517-548, 2023/03/01 2023, .DOI: 10.1111/eufm.12365

Nguyen, T. T., & Reddi, V. J. (2023). Deep Reinforcement Learning for Cyber Security. IEEE Transactions on Neural Networks and Learning Systems, 34(8), 3779–3795. *IEEE Transactions on Neural Networks and Learning Systems*. Advance online publication. DOI: 10.1109/TNNLS.2021.3121870 PMID: 34723814

Othman, M. (2025). Fintech and sustainability: Charting a new course for Jordanian banking. *Journal of Risk and Financial Management*, *18*(6), 328. DOI: 10.3390/jrfm18060328

Pamarthi, K. (2024). Analysis on opportunities and challenges of AI in the banking industry. *Journal ID*, *1232*, 1214.

Paramesha, M., Rane, N. L., & Rane, J. (2024). Artificial Intelligence, Machine Learning, Deep Learning, and Blockchain in financial and banking services: A comprehensive review. *SSRN*, *1*(2), 68–83. DOI: 10.2139/ssrn.4855893

Pinto, A., Herrera, L.-C., Donoso, Y., & Gutiérrez, J. A. (2023). Survey on Intrusion Detection Systems Based on Machine Learning Techniques for the Protection of Critical Infrastructure. *Sensors (Basel)*, *23*(5), 5. Advance online publication. DOI: 10.3390/s23052415 PMID: 36904618

Radenković, S. D., Hanić, H., & Bugarčić, M. (2023). Applying Artificial Intelligence in the Digital Transformation of the Banking Sector. *Proceedings*, *85*(1), 1. Advance online publication. DOI: 10.3390/proceedings2023085019

Ridzuan, N. N., Masri, M., Anshari, M., Fitriyani, N. L., & Syafrudin, M. (2024). AI in the financial sector: The line between innovation, regulation and ethical responsibility. *Information (Basel)*, *15*(8), 432. DOI: 10.3390/info15080432

Ross, S. What percentage of the global economy is comprised of the financial services sector? Invest 5 (2015), 2015. Available online: https://www.investopedia.com/ask/answers/030515/what-percentage-global-economy-comprised-financial-services-sector.asp

Shaukat, K., Luo, S., Varadharajan, V., Hameed, I. A., & Xu, M. (2020). A Survey on Machine Learning Techniques for Cyber Security in the Last Decade. IEEE Access, 8, 222310 222354. IEEE Access. DOI: 10.1109/ACCESS.2020.3041951

Sobers, R. (2022). Data Breach Response Times: https://www.varonis.com/blog/data-breach-response-times

Untoro, W., & Trinugroho, I. (2022, December). The effect of FinTech on conventional bank performance and bank risk. In *International Colloquium on Business and Economics (ICBE 2022)* (pp. 140–152). Atlantis Press.

Xu, F., Kasperskaya, Y., & Sagarra, M. (2025). The impact of FinTech on bank performance: A systematic literature review. *Digital Business*, *5*(2), 100131. DOI: 10.1016/j.digbus.2025.100131

KEY TERMS AND DEFINITIONS

Artificial Intelligence: A field of Computer Science that focuses on giving intelligence to the domain or object in which it is applied.

Anti-Money Laundering: A set of laws, regulations, and procedures to prevent illegal activities related to money.

Adversarial Attack: An intentional modification of input data.

Cybersecurity: The practice of protecting computer systems, networks, and data from unauthorised access, attacks, or damage.

Fintech: Financial Technology is used to improve and automate financial transactions.

Machine learning: is one of the broad branches of Computer science, focusing on learning from data by machines.

Compilation of References

Abad-Segura, E., González-Zamar, M. D., López-Meneses, E., & Vázquez-Cano, E. (2020). Financial technology: Review of trends, approaches and management. *Mathematics*, *8*(6), 951. DOI: 10.3390/math8060951

Abdul-Majid, M., Falahaty, M., & Jusoh, M. (2017). Performance of Islamic and conventional banks: A meta-frontier approach. *Research in International Business and Finance*, *42*, 1327–1335. DOI: 10.1016/j.ribaf.2017.07.069

Abedalrhman, K. (2025). Integrative analysis of FinTech innovations in industry: Enhancements and challenges. SSRN Electronic Journal. DOI: 10.2139/ssrn.5074495

Abouraia, M. K., & Al Morsey, R. M. (2020). Analyzing the impact of fintech adoption on financial inclusion and economic development: A data-driven approach. [TURCOMAT]. *Turkish Journal of Computer and Mathematics Education*, *11*(1), 973–984. DOI: 10.61841/turcomat.v11i1.14257

Abu Khalaf, B., Al-Sharkas, A., & Sarea, A. (2025). Realising opportunities: The influence of FinTech on the success of MENA banks. *Discover Sustainability*, *6*(1), 501. DOI: 10.1007/s43621-025-01374-8

Adalessossi, K. (2023). Impact of E-Banking on the Islamic bank profitability in Sub-Saharan Africa: What are the financial determinants? *Finance Research Letters*, *57*, 104188. DOI: 10.1016/j.frl.2023.104188

Adams, J., Hillier-Brown, F. C., Moore, H. J., Lake, A. A., Araujo-Soares, V., White, M., & Summerbell, C. (2016). Searching and synthesising 'grey literature' and 'grey information' in public health: Critical reflections on three case studies. *Systematic Reviews*, *5*(1), 164. DOI: 10.1186/s13643-016-0337-y

Adrian, T., & Liang, N. (2018). Monetary policy, financial conditions, and financial stability. *52nd Issue (January 2018) of the International Journal of Central Banking*.

Aggarwal, M., Nayak, K. M., & Bhatt, V. (2023). Examining the factors influencing fintech adoption behaviour of gen Y in India. *Cogent Economics & Finance, 11*(1), 2197699. DOI: 10.1080/23322039.2023.2197699

Agrawal, A., Catalini, C., & Goldfarb, A. (2015). Crowdfunding: Geography, social networks, and the timing of investment decisions. *Journal of Economics & Management Strategy, 24*(2), 253–274. DOI: 10.1111/jems.12093

Agustin, G. (2023). The rise of financial technology and its credit risk in Indonesia. *International Journal of Accounting & Finance in Asia Pasific, 6*(2), 98–109. DOI: 10.32535/ijafap.v6i2.2318

Ahamed, M. M., Ho, S. J., Mallick, S. K., & Matousek, R. (2021). Inclusive banking, financial regulation and bank performance: Cross-country evidence. *Journal of Banking & Finance, 124*, 106055. DOI: 10.1016/j.jbankfin.2021.106055

Ahmad, R., Xie, C., Wang, P., Liu, B., Zainir, F., & Mohsin, M. I. A. (2025). FinTech innovation, stability and efficiency: Evidence from Malaysian bank industry. *International Journal of Finance & Economics, 30*(1), 221–241. DOI: 10.1002/ijfe.2917

Aithal, P. S. (2023). An Analytical Study of Applications of Artificial Intelligence on Banking Practices. International Journal of Management [IJMTS]. *Technology and Social Sciences, 8*(2), 133–144.

Alam, N., Hamid, B. A., & Tan, D. T. (2019). Does competition make banks riskier in dual banking system? *Borsa Istanbul Review, 19*, S34–S43. DOI: 10.1016/j.bir.2018.09.002

Alam, N., Zainuddin, S. S. B., & Rizvi, S. A. R. (2019). Ramifications of varying banking regulations on performance of Islamic Banks. *Borsa Istanbul Review, 19*(1), 49–64. DOI: 10.1016/j.bir.2018.05.005

Alamoudi, H., Glavee-Geo, R., Alharthi, M., Doszhan, R., & Suyunchaliyeva, M. M. (2025). Exploring trust and outcome expectancy in FinTech digital payments: Insights from the stimulus-organism-response model. *International Journal of Bank Marketing, 43*(4), 897–919. DOI: 10.1108/IJBM-04-2024-0252

AlBenJasim, S., Dargahi, T., Takruri, H., & Al-Zaidi, R. (2024). FinTech Cybersecurity Challenges and Regulations: Bahrain Case Study. *Journal of Computer Information Systems, 64*(6), 835–851. DOI: 10.1080/08874417.2023.2251455

Alcorn, M. A., Li, Q., Gong, Z., Wang, C., Mai, L., Ku, W.-S., & Nguyen, A. (2019). Strike (With) a Pose: Neural Networks Are Easily Fooled by Strange Poses of Familiar Objects. *2019 IEEE/CVF Conference on Computer Vision and Pattern Recognition (CVPR)*, 4840–4849. DOI: 10.1109/CVPR.2019.00498

Aldboush, H. H., & Ferdous, M. (2023). Building trust in fintech: An analysis of ethical and privacy considerations in the intersection of big data, AI, and customer trust. *International Journal of Financial Studies, 11*(3), 90. DOI: 10.3390/ijfs11030090

Ali, M., Raza, S. A., Khamis, B., Puah, C. H., & Amin, H. (2021). How perceived risk, benefit and trust determine user Fintech adoption: a new dimension for Islamic finance. *foresight, 23*(4), 403-420.

Ali, H., Abdullah, R., & Zaini, M. Z. (2019). Fintech and its potential impact on Islamic banking and finance industry: A case study of Brunei Darussalam and Malaysia. [IJIEF]. *International Journal of Islamic Economics and Finance, 2*(1), 73–108. DOI: 10.18196/ijief.2116

Ali, S. E. A., Lai, F.-W., & Hassan, R. (2020). Socio-economic factors on sector-wide systematic risk of information security breaches: Conceptual framework. In Othman, N. S., Jaaffar, A. H. B., Harun, N. H. B., Buniamin, S. B., Mohamad, N. E. A. B., Ali, I. B. M., Razali, N. H. B. A., & Hashim, S. L. B. M. (Eds.), *Driving sustainability through business-technology synergy. European Proceedings of Social and Behavioural Sciences (EpSBS).*, DOI: 10.15405/epsbs.2020.12.05.54

Almalawi, A., Fahad, A., Tari, Z., Khan, A. I., Alzahrani, N., Bakhsh, S. T., Alassafi, M. O., Alshdadi, A., & Qaiyum, S. (2020). Add-On Anomaly Threshold Technique for Improving Unsupervised Intrusion Detection on SCADA Data. *Electronics (Basel), 9*(6), 6. Advance online publication. DOI: 10.3390/electronics9061017

Alnabulsi, Z. H., & Salameh, R. S. (2022). THE IMPACT OF LAUNCHING THE FINANCIAL INCLUSION STRATEGY ON ECONOMIC DEVELOPMENT. *Journal of Management Information & Decision Sciences, 25*(1).

Al-Okaily, M., Lutfi, A., Alsaad, A., Taamneh, A., & Alsyouf, A. (2020). The determinants of digital payment systems' acceptance under cultural orientation differences: The case of uncertainty avoidance. *Technology in Society, 63*, 101367. DOI: 10.1016/j.techsoc.2020.101367

Aloulou, M., Grati, R., Al-Qudah, A. A., & Al-Okaily, M. (2024). Does FinTech adoption increase the diffusion rate of digital financial inclusion? A study of the banking industry sector. *Journal of Financial Reporting and Accounting, 22*(2), 289–307. DOI: 10.1108/JFRA-05-2023-0224

Alqahtani, H. A., Alqubaysi, R., Musa, A. M. H., & Boreik, D. A. S. (2024). The effect of financial technology on the financial performance of national Saudi banks. *International Journal of Data and Network Science, 8*(3), 1399–1404. DOI: 10.5267/j.ijdns.2024.4.003

Alqudah, M. Z., Sierra-García, L., & Garcia-Benau, M. A. (2025). The moderating role of ESG scores on the relationship between FinTech adoption and financial performance: Evidence from Middle East banks. *Economic Change and Restructuring, 58*(6), 1–50. DOI: 10.1007/s10644-025-09927-7

Altameemi, Y., & Altamimi, M. (2023). Thematic Analysis: A Corpus-Based Method for Understanding Themes/Topics of a Corpus through a Classification Process Using Long Short-Term Memory (LSTM). *Applied Sciences (Basel, Switzerland), 13*(5), 3308. DOI: 10.3390/app13053308

Altounjy, R., Alaeddin, O., Hussain, H. I., & Sebastian, K. O. T. (2020). Moving from bricks to clicks: Merchants' acceptance of the mobile payment in Malaysia. *International Journal of eBusiness and eGovernment Studies, 12*(2), 136-150.

Anagnoste, S. (2017, July). Robotic Automation Process-The next major revolution in terms of back office operations improvement. In *Proceedings of the International Conference on Business Excellence* (Vol. 11, No. 1, pp. 676-686). Sciendo. DOI: 10.1515/picbe-2017-0072

Anderloni, L., Petukhina, A., & Tanda, A. (2024). Peer-to-peer lending: Exploring borrowers' motivations and expectations. *Journal of Small Business Management*. Advance online publication. DOI: 10.1080/00472778.2024.2431232

Anne-Laure, M. (2019). The Future of Fintech. *Research Technology Management, 62*(4), 59–63. DOI: 10.1080/08956308.2019.1613123

Arena, C., Catuogno, S., & Naciti, V. (2023). Governing FinTech for performance: The monitoring role of female independent directors. *European Journal of Innovation Management, 26*(7), 591–610. DOI: 10.1108/EJIM-11-2022-0621

Armantier, O., Doerr, S., Frost, J., Fuster, A., & Shue, K. (2021). Whom do consumers trust with their data? *US survey evidence* (No. 42). Bank for International Settlements.

Arner, D. W., Barberis, J. N., & Buckley, R. P. (2015). The Evolution of Fintech: A New Post-Crisis Paradigm? SSRN *Electronic Journal*. DOI: 10.2139/ssrn.2676553

Arner, D. W., Zetzsche, D. A., Buckley, R. P., & Barberis, J. N. (2017). FinTech and RegTech: Enabling innovation while preserving financial stability. *Georgetown Journal of International Affairs*, 47-58.

Arner, D. W., Buckley, R. P., Zetzsche, D. A., & Veidt, R. (2020). Sustainability, FinTech and financial inclusion. *European Business Organization Law Review, 21*(1), 7–35. DOI: 10.1007/s40804-020-00183-y

Arner, D., Buckley, R., Zetzsche, D., Zhao, B., Didenko, A., Park, C. Y., & Brummer, C. (2019). *Policy and regulatory challenges of distributed ledger technology and digital assets in Asia*. Oxford Scholarship Online. DOI: 10.1093/oso/9780190077310.003.0011

Arnold, M. (2018, April 8). HSBC brings in AI to help spot money laundering. *Financial Times*.

Arora, A., Gupta, S., Devi, C., & Walia, N. (2023). Customer experiences in the era of artificial intelligence (AI) in context to FinTech: A fuzzy AHP approach. *Benchmarking*, *30*(10), 4342–4369. DOI: 10.1108/BIJ-10-2021-0621

Arslanian, H., & Fischer, F. (2019). *The future of finance: The impact of FinTech, AI, and crypto on financial services*. Springer. DOI: 10.1007/978-3-030-14533-0

Ashta, A., & Herrmann, H. (2021). Artificial intelligence and fintech: An overview of opportunities and risks for banking, investments, and microfinance. *Strategic Change*, *30*(3), 211–222. DOI: 10.1002/jsc.2404

Askitas, N., & Zimmermann, K. F. (2009). Google econometrics and unemployment forecasting. *Applied Economics Quarterly*, *55*(2), 107–120. DOI: 10.3790/aeq.55.2.107

Asness, C. S., Frazzini, A., Israel, R., & Moskowitz, T. J. (2015). Fact, fiction, and value investing. *Journal of Portfolio Management*, *42*(1), 34–52. Advance online publication. DOI: 10.3905/jpm.2015.42.1.034

Aspal, P. K., & Dhawan, S. (2016). Camels rating model for evaluating financial performance of banking sector: A theoretical perspective. *International Journal of System Modeling and Simulation*, *1*(3), 10–15.

Awiszus, K., Knispel, T., Penner, I., Svindland, G., Voß, A., & Weber, S. (2023). Modeling and pricing cyber insurance: Idiosyncratic, systematic, and systemic risks. *European Actuarial Journal*, *13*(1), 1–53. DOI: 10.1007/s13385-023-00341-9

Awosika, T., Shukla, R. M., & Pranggono, B. (2024). Transparency and privacy: The role of explainable ai and federated learning in financial fraud detection. *IEEE Access : Practical Innovations, Open Solutions*, *12*, 64551–64560. DOI: 10.1109/ACCESS.2024.3394528

Bajwa, I. A., Ur Rehman, S., Iqbal, A., Anwer, Z., Ashiq, M., & Khan, M. A. (2022). Past, present and future of FinTech research: A bibliometric analysis. *SAGE Open*, *12*(4), 21582440221131242. DOI: 10.1177/21582440221131242

Baker, H., Kaddumi, T. A., Nassar, M. D., & Muqattash, R. S. (2023). Impact of financial technology on improvement of banks' financial performance. *Journal of Risk and Financial Management, 16*(4), 230. DOI: 10.3390/jrfm16040230

Bakhoum, M., Gonzalez Otero, B., Hoffmann, J., & Sarr, M. (2024). Data Governance in Emerging Economies to Achieve the Sustainable Development Goals Senegal Country Report Based on the Workshop Shaping Data Sharing Policies in the Agricultural and the Financial Services Sector (Dakar, March 16-17, 2022).

Balabantaray, S. R. (2024). Examining the Impact of Cyber Fraud on Indian Society: An Assessment of the Potential Damage. In Kaur, G., Dalei, N. N., Mahapatra, S. K., & Kandpal, V. (Eds.), *Cybersecurity, Law, and Economics* (pp. 38–50). Routledge. DOI: 10.4324/9781003517290-5

Banerjee, R., Majumdar, S., & Albastaki, M. (2022). Ideal self-congruence: Neo-banking by traditional banks and the impact on market share - A case of uae banks. *International Journal of Professional Business Review, 7*(4), e0779. DOI: 10.26668/businessreview/2022.v7i4.e779

Banik, B., & Roy, C. K. (2023). Measuring fintech-driven financial inclusion for developing countries: Comprehensive Digital Financial Inclusion Index (CDFII). *Economic Journal of Emerging Markets*, 143-159.

Banna, H., & Alam, M. R. (2021). Does digital financial inclusion matter for bank risk-taking? Evidence from the dual-banking system. *Journal of Islamic Monetary Economics and Finance, 7*(2), 401–430. DOI: 10.21098/jimf.v7i2.1320

Banna, H., Hassan, M. K., & Rashid, M. (2021). Fintech-based financial inclusion and bank risk-taking: Evidence from OIC countries. *Journal of International Financial Markets, Institutions and Money, 75*, 101447. DOI: 10.1016/j.intfin.2021.101447

Baradwaj, V. (2023). *UPI adoption and usage patterns by small merchants: A study*. Research Archive of Rising Scholars., DOI: 10.58445/rars.545

Barba Navaretti, G., & Calzolari, G. (2017). FinTech and Banks Friends and Foes. *European Economy, 2017*(2).

Barbu, C. M., Florea, D. L., Dabija, D. C., & Barbu, M. C. R. (2021). Customer experience in fintech. *Journal of Theoretical and Applied Electronic Commerce Research, 16*(5), 1415–1433. DOI: 10.3390/jtaer16050080

Bartlett, R., Morse, A., Stanton, R., & Wallace, N. (2019). *Consumer-Lending Discrimination in the FinTech Era.*

Basdekis, C., Christopoulos, A., Katsampoxakis, I., & Vlachou, A. (2022). FinTech's rapid growth and its effect on the banking sector. *Journal of Banking and Financial Technology*, *6*(2), 159–176. DOI: 10.1007/s42786-022-00045-w

Basha, S. A., Elgammal, M. M., & Abuzayed, B. M. (2021). Online peer-to-peer lending: A review of the literature. *Electronic Commerce Research and Applications*, *48*, 101069.

Bashayreh, A., & Wadi, R. M. A. (2020, November). The effect of Fintech on banks' performance: a case study of Jordan. In *International Conference on Business and Technology* (pp. 812–821). Springer International Publishing.

Bazarbash, M., Beaton, K., & Eriksson, U. (2020). Filling the gap: Digital credit and financial inclusion.

Begenau, J., Farboodi, M., & Veldkamp, L. (2018). Big data in finance and the growth of large firms. *Journal of Monetary Economics*, *97*, 71–87. DOI: 10.1016/j.jmoneco.2018.05.013

Behl, A. (2022). Antecedents to firm performance and competitiveness using the lens of big data analytics: A cross-cultural study. *Management Decision*, *60*(2), 368–398. DOI: 10.1108/MD-01-2020-0121

Ben Bouheni, F., Tewari, M., Sidaoui, M., & Hasnaoui, A. (2023). An econometric understanding of Fintech and operating performance. *Review of Accounting and Finance*, *22*(3), 329–352. DOI: 10.1108/RAF-10-2022-0290

Benzies, K. M., Premji, S., Hayden, K. A., & Serrett, K. (2006). State-of-the-Evidence Reviews: Advantages and Challenges of Including Grey Literature. *Worldviews on Evidence-Based Nursing*, *3*(2), 55–61. DOI: 10.1111/j.1741-6787.2006.00051.x

Berg, T., Burg, V., Gombović, A., & Puri, M. (2020). On the rise of fintechs: Credit scoring using digital footprints. *Review of Financial Studies*, *33*(7), 2845–2897. DOI: 10.1093/rfs/hhz099

Berson, Y., Oreg, S., & Dvir, T. (2008). CEO values, organizational culture and firm outcomes. *Journal of Organizational Behavior: The International Journal of Industrial. Journal of Organizational Behavior*, *29*(5), 615–633. DOI: 10.1002/job.499

Bertsch, C., & Rosenvinge, C. J. (2019). FinTech credit: Online lending platforms in Sweden and beyond. *Sveriges Riksbank Economic Review*, *2*, 42–70.

Bhadra, S., & Singh, K. N. (2024). Ponzi scheme like investment schemes in India–causes, impact and solution. *Journal of Money Laundering Control*, *27*(2), 348–362. DOI: 10.1108/JMLC-02-2023-0040

Bhasin, N. K., & Rajesh, A. (2021). Impact of E-collaboration between Indian banks and fintech companies for digital banking and new emerging technologies. [IJeC]. *International Journal of e-Collaboration, 17*(1), 15–35. DOI: 10.4018/IJeC.2021010102

Bhatia, M., & Gulati, R. (2021). Board governance and bank performance: A meta-analysis. *Research in International Business and Finance, 58*, 101425. DOI: 10.1016/j.ribaf.2021.101425

Bhattacharya, S. (2024). Enhancing Cyber Defenses in Indian Banking Industry. *Available at SSRN* 4924267. https://doi.org/DOI: 10.53739/samvad/2024/v28/173776

Bijlsma, M., van der Cruijsen, C., & Koldijk, J. (2022). Determinants of trust in banks' payment services during COVID: An exploration using daily data. *De Economist, 170*(2), 231–256. DOI: 10.1007/s10645-022-09405-9

Bodemer, O. (2024). Revolutionizing finance: The impact of AI and cloud computing in the banking sector. *Unpublished manuscript.*

Branzoli, N., & Supino, I. (2020). Fintech credit: A critical review of empirical research literature. *Bank of Italy Occasional Paper*, (549).

Buchak, G., Matvos, G., Piskorski, T., & Seru, A. (2018). Fintech, regulatory arbitrage, and the rise of shadow banks. *Journal of Financial Economics, 130*(3), 453–483. DOI: 10.1016/j.jfineco.2018.03.011

Buchanan, A. B. (2021). A National Security Research Agenda for Cybersecurity and Artificial Intelligence CSET. *Issue Brief.*

Buckley, R. P., Arner, D., Veidt, R., & Zetzsche, D. (2020). Building FinTech ecosystems: Regulatory sandboxes, innovation hubs and beyond. *Wash. UJL & Pol'y, 61*, 55.

Carbó-Valverde, S., Cuadros-Solas, P. J., & Rodríguez-Fernández, F. (2021). FinTech and banking: an evolving relationship. In *Disruptive technology in banking and finance: An international perspective on FinTech* (pp. 161–194). Springer International Publishing. DOI: 10.1007/978-3-030-81835-7_6

CBA invests in international transaction screening technology company. (2024, March 2). https://www.commbank.com.au/articles/newsroom/2024/03/global-screening-services.html

Chaiyasoonthorn, W., & Suksa-Ngiam, W. (2019). The diffusion and adoption of electronic payment systems in Bangkok. [IJEBR]. *International Journal of E-Business Research, 15*(2), 102–115. DOI: 10.4018/IJEBR.2019040106

Chakraborty, A., & Tiwari, S. (2025). An analytical study on challenges and gaps in India's cyber security framework. https://doi.org/DOI: 10.22271/27899497.2025.v5.i1a.110

Chandra, D. (2025). Examining the Contours and Challenges of National Cybercrime Reporting Portal in Countering Digital Financial Frauds. *Journal of Victimology and Victim Justice*, *8*(1), 65–83. DOI: 10.1177/25166069241306546

Chand, S. A., Singh, B., Narayan, K., & Chand, A. (2025). The Impact of Financial Technology (FinTech) on Bank Risk-Taking and Profitability in Small Developing Island States: A Study of Fiji. *Journal of Risk and Financial Management*, *18*(7), 366. DOI: 10.3390/jrfm18070366

Chan, R., Troshani, I., Rao Hill, S., & Hoffmann, A. (2022). Towards an understanding of consumers' FinTech adoption: The case of Open Banking. *International Journal of Bank Marketing*, *40*(4), 886–917. DOI: 10.1108/IJBM-08-2021-0397

Chatzigiannis, P., Gu, W. C., Raghuraman, S., Rindal, P., & Zamani, M. (2023). Privacy-enhancing technologies for financial data sharing. *arXiv preprint arXiv:2306.10200*. https://doi.org//arXiv.2306.10200DOI: 10.48550

Chauhan, Y., & Sharma, P. (2024). A Systematic Literature Review of Digital Payments. *Metamorphosis*, *23*(2), 173–187. DOI: 10.1177/09726225241257730

Chen, X., Zhang, H., & Teng, L. (2022). Technology risk management in fintech: Underlying mechanisms and challenges. *Journal of Operational Risk*. DOI: 10.21314/JOP.2022.022

Cheng, M., & Qu, Y. (2020). Does bank FinTech reduce credit risk? Evidence from China. *Pacific Basin Finance Journal*, *63*, 101398. DOI: 10.1016/j.pacfin.2020.101398

Chen, L., Huang, Z., & Liu, D. (2016). Pure and hybrid crowds in crowdfunding markets. *Financial Innovation*, *2*(1), 19. DOI: 10.1186/s40854-016-0038-5

Chen, M. A., Wu, Q., & Yang, B. (2019). How valuable is FinTech innovation? *Review of Financial Studies*, *32*(5), 2062–2106. DOI: 10.1093/rfs/hhy130

Chen, P. (2024). Risk Challenges and Regulatory Approaches in Fintech Data Application Regulation. *Frontiers in Business, Economics and Management*, *16*(3), 85–91. Advance online publication. DOI: 10.54097/ypg61745

Chen, T. H. (2020). Do you know your customer? Bank risk assessment based on machine learning. *Applied Soft Computing*, *86*, 105779. DOI: 10.1016/j.asoc.2019.105779

Chen, X., Yang, L., Wang, P., & Yue, W. (2013). An Effective Interval-Valued Intuitionistic Fuzzy Entropy to Evaluate Entrepreneurship Orientation of Online P2P Lending Platforms. *Advances in Mathematical Physics, 2013*(1), 467215. DOI: 10.1155/2013/467215

Chhonker, M. S., Verma, D., Kar, A. K., & Grover, P. (2018). m-commerce technology adoption: Thematic and citation analysis of scholarly research during (2008-2017). *The Bottom Line (New York, N.Y.), 31*(3/4), 208–233. DOI: 10.1108/BL-04-2018-0020

Chime Investor Presentation. (2025).

Chiu, J., & Koeppl, T. V. (2019). Blockchain-based settlement for asset trading. *Review of Financial Studies, 32*(5), 1716–1753. DOI: 10.1093/rfs/hhy122

Chouhan, V., Ali, S., Sharma, R. B., & Sharma, A. (2023). The effect of financial technology (Fin-tech) on the conventional banking industry in India. *International Journal of Innovative Research and Scientific Studies, 6*(3), 538–544. DOI: 10.53894/ijirss.v6i3.1578

Claessens, S., Frost, J., Turner, G., & Zhu, F. (2018). *Fintech credit markets around the world: size, drivers and policy issues*. BIS Quarterly Review September.

Coetzee, J. (2018). Strategic implications of Fintech on South African retail banks. *Suid-Afrikaanse Tydskrif vir Ekonomiese en Bestuurswetenskappe, 21*(1), 1–11. DOI: 10.4102/sajems.v21i1.2455

Consultants, M. Benefits Of Artificial Intelligence In the Banking Sector; Millennium Consultants: Kuala Lumpur, Malaysia, 2022. Available online: https://www. millenniumci.com/benefits-of-artificial-intelligence-in-the-banking-sector. (Accessed 11 September 2022).

Corbet, S., & Gurdgiev, C. (2017). Financial digital disruptors and cyber-security risks: Paired and systemic. *Forthcoming in Journal of Terrorism & Cyber Insurance, 1*(2).

Cornelli, G., Frost, J., Gambacorta, L., Rau, P. R., Wardrop, R., & Ziegler, T. (2023). Fintech and big tech credit: Drivers of the growth of digital lending. *Journal of Banking & Finance, 148*, 106742. DOI: 10.1016/j.jbankfin.2022.106742

Cortina Lorente, J. J., & Schmukler, S. L. (2018). The Fintech revolution: a threat to global banking?. *World Bank Research and Policy Briefs*, (125038).

Cumming, D., Farag, H., Johan, S., & McGowan, D. (2022). The digital credit divide: Marketplace lending and entrepreneurship. *Journal of Financial and Quantitative Analysis, 57*(7), 2659–2692. DOI: 10.1017/S0022109022000357

CyberPeace. (2024, December 2). *Domestic UPI frauds: Finance Ministry presented data in Lok Sabha*. https://www.cyberpeace.org/resources/blogs/domestic-upi-frauds-finance-ministry-presented-data-in-loksabha cyberpeace.org

D. K. Nguyen, G. Sermpinis, and C. Stasinakis, "Big data, artificial intelligence and machine learning: A transformative symbiosis in favour of financial technology, "European Financial Management, vol. 29, no. 2, pp. 517-548, 2023/03/01 2023, .DOI: 10.1111/eufm.12365

D'Souza, E. (2017). Reserve Bank of India: The way forward. In Kapur, D., Mehta, P. B., & Vaishnav, M. (Eds.), *Rethinking public institutions in India*. Oxford University Press., DOI: 10.1093/oso/9780199474370.003.0005

Dahiya, K. (2023). Trends in cyber crime in India. *International Journal for Research in Applied Science and Engineering Technology*, *11*(5), 6393–6406. DOI: 10.22214/ijraset.2023.53073

Dahlberg, T., Mallat, N., Ondrus, J., & Zmijewska, A. (2006).Mobile Payment Market and Research - Past, Present, and Future.Presentation at Helsinki Mobility Roundtable, Helsinki, Finland, June 1-2, 2002(January 2006), 1–16.

Dahlberg, T., Guo, J., & Ondrus, J. (2015). A critical review of mobile payment research. *Electronic Commerce Research and Applications*, *14*(5), 265–284. DOI: 10.1016/j.elerap.2015.07.006

Darji, D. A., Parikh, S. M., Patel, A. M., Patel, K. D., & Suthar, A. B. (2025). Measuring the impact of AI key metrics and KPIs in Financial Services. In *Intersecting Natural Language Processing and FinTech Innovations in Service Marketing* (pp. 337–370). IGI Global., DOI: 10.4018/979-8-3693-9944-6.ch018

Dasari, P. (2025). Digital Lending in India: Harassment, Settlements, and the Rise of Financial Exploitation. *Settlements, and the Rise of Financial Exploitation*. https://dx.doi.org/DOI: 10.2139/ssrn.5092390

Datta, D. (2023). The future of financial inclusion through FinTech: A conceptual study in post pandemic India. *Sachetas*, *2*(1), 11–17. DOI: 10.55955/210002

Datta, P., Panda, S. N., Tanwar, S., & Kaushal, R. K. (2020). A Technical Review Report on Cyber Crimes in India. *2020 International Conference on Emerging Smart Computing and Informatics (ESCI)* DOI: 10.1109/ESCI48226.2020.9167567

Daud, S. N. M., Khalid, A., & Azman-Saini, W. N. W. (2022). FinTech and financial stability: Threat or opportunity? *Finance Research Letters*, *47*, 102667. DOI: 10.1016/j.frl.2021.102667

Davis, F. D. (1989). Perceived usefulness, perceived ease of use, and user acceptance of information technology. *Management Information Systems Quarterly, 13*(3), 319–339. DOI: 10.2307/249008

De Bel, J., & Gâza, M. (2011). Mobile Payments 2012- My mobile, my wallet. *Director,* •••, 1–100.

de Luna, I. R., Liébana-Cabanillas, F., Sánchez-Fernández, J., & Muñoz-Leiva, F. (2019). Mobile payment is not all the same: The Adoption of mobile payment systems depending on the technology applied. *Technological Forecasting and Social Change, 146*, 931–944. DOI: 10.1016/j.techfore.2018.09.018

Demertzis, M., Merler, S., & Wolff, G. B. (2018). Capital markets union and the fintech opportunity. *Journal of financial regulation, 4*(1), 157-165.

Demirgüç-Kunt, A., Klapper, L., Singer, D., & Ansar, S. (2022). *The Global Findex Database 2021: Financial inclusion, digital payments, and resilience in the age of COVID-19.* World Bank Publications. DOI: 10.1596/978-1-4648-1897-4

Donthu, N., Kumar, S., Mukherjee, D., Pandey, N., & Lim, W. M. (2021). How to conduct a bibliometric analysis: An overview and guidelines. *Journal of Business Research, 133*, 285–296. DOI: 10.1016/j.jbusres.2021.04.070

Duan, C., Mao, M., & Tang, L. (2023a). Research on the evaluation of core competitiveness of commercial banks: Based on the perspective of digital transformation. Advances in Economics. *Management and Political Sciences, 52*(1), 91–99. DOI: 10.54254/2754-1169/52/20230701

Duan, D., & Liu, K. (2025). Development of Fintech, Green Credit, and Risk Taking in Commercial Banks. *Finance Research Letters, 86*, 108687. DOI: 10.1016/j.frl.2025.108687

Dwivedi, P., Alabdooli, J. I., & Dwivedi, R. (2021). Role of FinTech adoption for competitiveness and performance of the bank: A study of banking industry in UAE. *International Journal of Global Business and Competitiveness, 16*(2), 130–138. DOI: 10.1007/s42943-021-00033-9

Economic Times. (2025, April 23). *Digital payments comprise 99.8 percent of total transactions volume in H1 2025: RBI. The Economic Times.* https://m.economictimes.com/news/economy/finance/digital-payments-comprise-99-8-of-total-transactions-volume-in-h1-2025-upi-transactions-rbi/articleshow/124760861.cmsThe Economic Times

Elekdag, S., Emrullahu, D., & Naceur, S. B. (2025). Does FinTech Increase Bank Risk-taking? *Journal of Financial Stability, 76*, 101360. DOI: 10.1016/j.jfs.2024.101360

Elrefae, G., & Nuseir, M. T. (2022). Blockchain in global finance make-over: Exploring the mediating role of supply chain flexibility. *Uncertain Supply Chain Management, 10*(3), 983–992. DOI: 10.5267/j.uscm.2022.2.015

Elsaid, H. M. (2023). A review of literature directions regarding the impact of fintech firms on the banking industry. *Qualitative Research in Financial Markets, 15*(5), 693–711. DOI: 10.1108/QRFM-10-2020-0197

Elsinger, H., Fessler, P., Feyrer, J., Richter, K., Silgoner, M. A., & Timel, A. (2018). Digitalization in financial services and household finance: Fintech, financial literacy and financial stability. *Financial Stability Report*, (35), 50–58.

Engineering, N. U. (2023). Formation of the fintech sector: Opportunities and risks in the conditions of the digital economy. *Aktual'ni Problemi Ekonomìki, 1*(259), 24–34. DOI: 10.32752/1993-6788-2022-1-259-24-34

Erfan, N., Gangwani, S., & Belgacem, S. B. (2021). Impact of disposition effect on financial decisions among women investors. *Journal of management Information and Decision Sciences, 24*, 1-10.

Esoimeme, E. E. (2021). Identifying and reducing the money laundering risks posed by individuals who have been unknowingly recruited as money mules. *Journal of Money Laundering Control, 24*(1), 201–212. DOI: 10.1108/JMLC-05-2020-0053

European Union Agency for Cybersecurity. (2023). *ENISA threat landscape 2023: July 2022 to June 2023.* Publications Office. https://data.europa.eu/doi/10.2824/782573

FCA. (2025, September 30). FCA. https://www.fca.org.uk/

Feng, J., Jiao, W., & Wang, Y. (2025). Bank fintech and lending distance: The role of information asymmetry and risk management channels. *Economic Modelling, 151*, 107154. DOI: 10.1016/j.econmod.2025.107154

Fersi, M., Boujelbéne, M., & Arous, F. (2023). Microfinance's digital transformation for sustainable inclusion. *European journal of management and business economics, 32*(5), 525-559.

Fiordelisi, F., Girardone, C., Minnucci, F., & Ricci, O. (2020). On the nexus between sovereign risk and banking crises. *Journal of Corporate Finance, 65*, 101717. DOI: 10.1016/j.jcorpfin.2020.101717

Friedline, T., Despard, M. R., & Birkenmaier, J. (2018). Policy recommendations for expanding access to banking and financial services.

Frost, J. (2020). The economic forces driving fintech adoption across countries. *The technological revolution in financial services: how banks, fintechs, and customers win together, 838*(II), 70-89.

Frost, J., Gambacorta, L., Huang, Y., Shin, H. S., & Zbinden, P. (2019). BigTech and the changing structure of financial intermediation. *Economic Policy*, *34*(100), 761–799. DOI: 10.1093/epolic/eiaa003

Fundira, M., & Mbohwa, C. (2025). AI ethics in banking services: A systematic and bibliometric review of regulatory and consumer perspectives. *Discover Artificial Intelligence*, *5*(1), 1–25. DOI: 10.1007/s44163-025-00432-4

Fung, D. W., Lee, W. Y., Yeh, J. J., & Yuen, F. L. (2020). Friend or foe: The divergent effects of FinTech on financial stability. *Emerging Markets Review*, *45*, 100727. DOI: 10.1016/j.ememar.2020.100727

Fuster, A., Plosser, M., Schnabl, P., & Vickery, J. (2019). The role of technology in mortgage lending. *Review of Financial Studies*, *32*(5), 1854–1899. DOI: 10.1093/rfs/hhz018

Gai, K., Qiu, M., & Sun, X. (2018). A survey on FinTech. *Journal of Network and Computer Applications*, *103*, 262–273. DOI: 10.1016/j.jnca.2017.10.011

Gao, P. (2023). Analysis of the impact of digital currency on traditional banking and financial stability. *Advances in Economics and Management Research*, *8*(1), 326. DOI: 10.56028/aemr.8.1.326.2023

Garrouch, K. (2021). Does the reputation of the provider matter? A model explaining the continuance intention of mobile wallet applications. *Journal of Decision Systems*, *30*(2-3), 150–171. DOI: 10.1080/12460125.2020.1870261

Gekhaeva, P., Bolotkhanov, E., & Ismoilova, S. (2023). Global Digital Transformation Trends: Financial-Economic Sector. SHS Web of Conferences, 172, 02025. DOI: 10.1051/shsconf/202317202025

George, A. S. (2024). Finance 4.0: The transformation of financial services in the digital age. *Partners Universal Innovative Research Publication,* *2*(3), 104-125. https://doi.org/https://doi.org/10.5281/zenodo.11666694

George, A. S., Baskar, T., & Srikaanth, P. B. (2024). Cyber Threats to Critical Infrastructure: Assessing Vulnerabilities Across Key Sectors. *Partners Universal International Innovation Journal*, *2*(1), 51–75. DOI: 10.5281/zenodo.10639463

Gomber, P., Kauffman, R. J., Parker, C., & Weber, B. W. (2018). On the fintech revolution: Interpreting the forces of innovation, disruption, and transformation in financial services. *Journal of Management Information Systems*, *35*(1), 220–265. DOI: 10.1080/07421222.2018.1440766

Gomber, P., Koch, J.-A., & Siering, M. (2017). Digital Finance and FinTech: Current research and future research directions. *Journal of Business Economics*, *87*(5), 537–580. DOI: 10.1007/s11573-017-0852-x

Gong, X., Cheung, C. M., Zhang, K. Z., Chen, C., & Lee, M. K. (2020). Cross-side network effects, brand equity, and consumer loyalty: Evidence from mobile payment market. *International Journal of Electronic Commerce*, *24*(3), 279–304. DOI: 10.1080/10864415.2020.1767427

Gong, X., Zhang, K. Z., Chen, C., Cheung, C. M., & Lee, M. K. (2020). What drives trust transfer from web to mobile payment services? The dual effects of perceived entitativity. *Information & Management*, *57*(7), 103250. DOI: 10.1016/j.im.2019.103250

Goodfellow, I. J., Shlens, J., & Szegedy, C. (2014). Explaining and harnessing adversarial examples. arXiv Preprint arXiv:1412.6572.

Goodfellow, I., Pouget-Abadie, J., Mirza, M., Xu, B., Warde-Farley, D., Ozair, S., Courville, A., & Bengio, Y. (2014). Generative Adversarial Nets. Advances in Neural Information Processing Systems, 27. https://proceedings.neurips.cc/paper_files/paper/2014/hash/5ca3e9b122f61f8f06494c97b 1afccf3-Abstract.html

Gorai, S. K., & A. (2025). Artificial Intelligence In Personal Finance Management: Opportunities And Challenges. *IOSR Journal of Computer Engineering, 27*(1), 07–17. DOI: 10.9790/0661-2701010717

Grove, H., Patelli, L., Victoravich, L. M., & Xu, P. (2011). Corporate governance and performance in the wake of the financial crisis: Evidence from US commercial banks. *Corporate Governance*, *19*(5), 418–436. DOI: 10.1111/j.1467-8683.2011.00882.x

Gupta, M., & Gupta, A. (2025). Cyber security legal framework in India – overlaps, problems and challenges. *Journal of Business Management and Information Systems*, *12*(1), 11–20. DOI: 10.48001/jbmis.1201002

Haddad, C., & Hornuf, L. (2019). The emergence of the global fintech market: Economic and technological determinants. *Small Business Economics*, *53*(1), 81–105. DOI: 10.1007/s11187-018-9991-x

Hambrick, D. C., & Mason, P. A. (1984). Upper echelons: The organization as a reflection of its top managers. *Academy of Management Review*, *9*(2), 193–206. DOI: 10.2307/258434

Handarkho, Y. D., Harjoseputro, Y., Samodra, J. E., & Irianto, A. B. P. (2021). Understanding proximity mobile payment continuance usage in Indonesia from a habit perspective. *Journal of Asia Business Studies*, *15*(3), 420–440. DOI: 10.1108/JABS-02-2020-0046

Harmadi, U. W., Trinugroho, I., & Atmaji. (2022). The effect of fintech on conventional bank performance and bank risk. In Advances in Economics, Business and Management Research (pp. 140–152). Atlantis Press International BV. DOI: 10.2991/978-94-6463-066-4_13

Heimer, R. Z. (2016). Peer pressure: Social interaction and the disposition effect. *Review of Financial Studies*, *29*(11), 3177–3209. DOI: 10.1093/rfs/hhw063

Hendawi, R., Ineizeh, N. I., Hussein, O. J., & Alkahtani, M. (2024). The role of financial technology in improving performance in Jordanian Islamic banks. *Journal of Ecohumanism*, *3*(4), 279–290. DOI: 10.62754/joe.v3i4.3493

Hidayat-ur-Rehman, I., & Hossain, M. N. (2025). The impacts of Fintech adoption, green finance and competitiveness on banks' sustainable performance: Digital transformation as moderator. *Asia-Pacific Journal of Business Administration*, *17*(4), 987–1020. DOI: 10.1108/APJBA-10-2023-0497

Hikida, R., & Perry, J. (2020). Fintech trends in the united states: Implications for household finance. *Public Policy Research*, *16*(4), 1–32.

Hillairet, C., Lopez, O., d'Oultremont, L., & Spoorenberg, B. (2022). Cyber contagion: Impact of the network structure on the losses of an insurance portfolio. *Insurance, Mathematics & Economics*. Advance online publication. DOI: 10.1016/j.insmatheco.2022.08.002

Hmoud, A., Magableh, F. A., Badwan, N., & Almashaqbeh, M. (2025). *Impact of FinTech on capital allocation: Empirical evidence from Jordan and Palestine*. Borsa Istanbul Review.

Hoe, S. L. (2008). Issues and procedures in adopting structural equation modelling technique. *Journal of Quantitative Methods*, *3*(1), 76.

Hornuf, L., Klus, M. F., Lohwasser, T. S., & Schwienbacher, A. (2021). How do banks interact with fintech startups? *Small Business Economics*, *57*(3), 1505–1526. DOI: 10.1007/s11187-020-00359-3

Horváth, D., Kerényi, Á., & Szabó, R. Z. (2022). Intended benefits and challenges of cooperation between FinTechs and commercial banks. *Acta Oeconomica*, *72*(3), 289–308. DOI: 10.1556/032.2022.00023

Hou, X., Gao, Z., & Wang, Q. (2016). Internet finance development and banking market discipline: Evidence from China. *Journal of Financial Stability*, *22*, 88–100. DOI: 10.1016/j.jfs.2016.01.001

Hueske, A. K., & Guenther, E. (2015). What hampers innovation? External stakeholders, the organization, groups and individuals: A systematic review of empirical barrier research. *Management Review Quarterly*, *65*(2), 113–148. DOI: 10.1007/s11301-014-0109-5

Hussain, B. M. I., & Rafi, M. (2023). Online Financial Transactions in India: A Study of Its-Significance, Frauds and Security Models to Counter Frauds. *International Journal of Intelligent Engineering and Systems*, *16*(3), 455–469. DOI: 10.22266/ijies2023.0630.36

I.B, C., & M B, S. (2025). The Intersection of Fintech and Green Banking: Opportunities, Challenges, and Future Prospects. *IOSR Journal of Business and Management*, *14th*(15th), 35–41. DOI: 10.9790/487X-conf3541

Ibidunni, A. S., Ufua, D. E., & Opute, A. P. (2022). Linking disruptive innovation to sustainable entrepreneurship within the context of small and medium firms: A focus on Nigeria. *African Journal of Science, Technology, Innovation and Development*, *14*(6), 1591–1607. DOI: 10.1080/20421338.2021.1975355

Iglesias-Rodríguez, P. (2025). The future of instant payments in the EU: bank ownership, market contracting costs, and the accomplishment of financial regulation objectives: P. Iglesias-Rodríguez. *Journal of Banking Regulation*, 1-21. https://doi.org/DOI: 10.1057/s41261-025-00296-9

Indian Press Information Bureau. (2025, March 11). *Digital payment transactions surge with over 18,000 crore transactions in 2024–25*. https://www.pib.gov.in/PressReleaseIframePage.aspx?PRID=2110405 Press Information Bureau

Indian Press Information Bureau. (2025, October 8). *Curbing cyber frauds in digital India*. https://www.pib.gov.in/PressNoteDetails.aspx?ModuleId=3&NoteId=155384 Press Information Bureau

Investor Relations | Bank of America Corporation (BAC). (n.d.). Retrieved September 27, 2025, from https://investor.bankofamerica.com/

Investor Relations | JPMorganChase. (n.d.). Retrieved September 27, 2025, from https://www.jpmorganchase.com/ir

Iqbal, M. S., Sukamto, F. A. M. S. B., Norizan, S. N. B., Mahmood, S., Fatima, A., & Hashmi, F. (2025). AI in Islamic finance: Global trends, ethical implications, and bibliometric insights. *Review of Islamic Social Finance and Entrepreneurship*, 70-85.

Irfan, M., Kadry, S., Sharif, M., & Khan, H. U. (Eds.). (2023). *Fintech applications in Islamic finance: AI, machine learning, and blockchain techniques: AI, machine learning, and blockchain techniques*. IGI Global. DOI: 10.4018/979-8-3693-1038-0

Ishtiaq, M., Sher, F., & Shahid, M. N. (2024). Financial Inclusion, Fintech, Green Innovation, and Social Welfare: A Perspective of Environment Quality and Economic Development in China. *Global Management Sciences Review*, *9*(4), 156–168. DOI: 10.31703/gmsr.2024(IX-IV).13

Issa, A., Yousef, H., Bakry, A., Hanaysha, J. R., & Sahyouni, A. (2021). Does the board diversity impact bank performance in the MENA countries? A multilevel study. *Corporate Governance (Bradford)*, *21*(5), 865–891. DOI: 10.1108/CG-06-2020-0222

Jagtiani, J., & Lemieux, C. (2019). The roles of alternative data and machine learning in fintech lending: Evidence from the LendingClub consumer platform. *Financial Management*, *48*(4), 1009–1029. DOI: 10.1111/fima.12295

Jain, R., & Sonowal, B. (2025). Analyzing the Procedure for Investigation in Cybercrime and Admissibility of Electronic Evidence. In *Cybercrime Unveiled: Technologies for Analysing Legal Complexity* (pp. 265-289). Cham: Springer Nature Switzerland. https://doi.org/DOI: 10.1007/978-3-031-80557-8_12

Juengerkes, B. E. (2016). FinTechs and banks–Collaboration is key. *The FinTech book: The financial technology handbook for investors, entrepreneurs and visionaries*, 179-182.

K, S. (2025). Evolution of Neo Banking in India – A Paradigm shift in the banking industry. *International Journal on Science and Technology*. DOI: 10.71097/IJSAT.v16.i1.1774

Kaddumi, T. A., Baker, H., Nassar, M. D., & A-Kilani, Q. (2023). Does financial technology adoption influence bank's financial performance: The case of Jordan. *Journal of Risk and Financial Management*, *16*(9), 413. DOI: 10.3390/jrfm16090413

Kalai, L., & Toukabri, M. (2024). Risks, regulations, and impacts of FinTech adoption on commercial banks in the United States and Canada: A comparative analysis. *Thunderbird International Business Review*, *66*(6), 609–641. Advance online publication. DOI: 10.1002/tie.22404

Kalinić, Z., Liébana-Cabanillas, F. J., Muñoz-Leiva, F., & Marinković, V. (2019). The moderating impact of gender on the acceptance of peer-to-peer mobile payment systems. *International Journal of Bank Marketing*, *38*(1), 138–158. DOI: 10.1108/IJBM-01-2019-0012

Kalinic, Z., Marinkovic, V., Molinillo, S., & Liébana-Cabanillas, F. (2019). A multi-analytical approach to peer-to-peer mobile payment acceptance prediction. *Journal of Retailing and Consumer Services*, *49*, 143–153. DOI: 10.1016/j.jretconser.2019.03.016

Kamal, M., Rahmani, S., & Alam, M. R. (2025). Beyond traditional banking: How FinTech is reshaping financial access in India. *Available at SSRN* 5122110. https://dx.doi.org/DOI: 10.2139/ssrn.5122110

Kapliar, K. (2023). NEOBANKS IN THE AGE OF DIGITAL TRANSFORMATION. *International Scientific Conference Modern Science: Global Trends, Technologies and Innovations*. DOI: 10.30525/978-9934-26-354-5-2

Kapoor, N., Kapoor, T., Sisodiya, D., & Sushma, J. (2024). Impact of Fintech: Revolution in Banking and Financial Industry. *2024 IEEE 4th International Conference on ICT in Business Industry & Government (ICTBIG)*, 1–6. DOI: 10.1109/ICTBIG64922.2024.10911635

Karjaluoto, H., Shaikh, A. A., Saarijärvi, H., & Saraniemi, S. (2019). How perceived value drives the use of mobile financial services apps. *International Journal of Information Management*, *47*, 252–261. DOI: 10.1016/j.ijinfomgt.2018.08.014

Kartawinata, B. R., Fakhri, M., Pradana, M., Hanifan, N. F., & Akbar, A. (2021). The role of financial self-efficacy: Mediating effects of financial literacy & financial inclusion of students in West Java, Indonesia. *Journal of Management Information and Decision Sciences*, *24*(7), 1–9.

Karthika, M., Neethu, K., & Lakshmi, P. (2022). Impact of fintech on the banking sector. *Integrated Journal for Research in Arts and Humanities*, *2*(4), 109–112. DOI: 10.55544/ijrah.2.4.66

Kaur, S., Mishra, H., & Goyal, A. (2023). Cyber-security in UPI payments. *International Journal for Research in Applied Science and Engineering Technology*, *11*(5), 4955–4960. DOI: 10.22214/ijraset.2023.52175

Kavitha, S., & Krishnan, S. (2025). AI-based Personal Financial Management: Opportunities and Challenges. *ComFin Research, 13*(S1-i2), 68–73. DOI: 10.34293/commerce.v13iS1-i2.8737

Kayed, S., Alta'any, M., Meqbel, R., Khatatbeh, I. N., & Mahafzah, A. (2025). Bank FinTech and bank performance: Evidence from an emerging market. *Journal of Financial Reporting and Accounting*, *23*(2), 518–535. DOI: 10.1108/JFRA-09-2023-0526

Kazan, E., Tan, C. W., Lim, E. T., Sørensen, C., & Damsgaard, J. (2018). Disentangling digital platform competition: The case of UK mobile payment platforms. *Journal of Management Information Systems*, *35*(1), 180–219. DOI: 10.1080/07421222.2018.1440772

Kedziora, D., & Penttinen, E. (2021). Governance models for robotic process automation: The case of Nordea Bank. *Journal of Information Technology Teaching Cases*, *11*(1), 20–29. DOI: 10.1177/2043886920937022

Khadka, A., Sthapit, S., Epiphaniou, G., & Maple, C. (2024). Resilient Machine Learning: Advancement, Barriers, and Opportunities in the Nuclear Industry. *ACM Computing Surveys*, *56*(9), 1–29. DOI: 10.1145/3648608

Khanchel, I., Lassoued, N., & Khiari, C. (2025). Untangling the skein: The impact of FinTech on social and financial performance in microfinance institutions. *Regional Science Policy & Practice*, *17*(8), 100208. DOI: 10.1016/j.rspp.2025.100208

Khan, H. H., Khan, S., & Ghafoor, A. (2023). Fintech adoption, the regulatory environment and bank stability: An empirical investigation from GCC economies. *Borsa Istanbul Review*, *23*(6), 1263–1281. DOI: 10.1016/j.bir.2023.10.010

Khan, N. F., Ikram, N., & Saleem, S. (2023). Effects of socioeconomic and digital inequalities on cybersecurity in a developing country. *Security Journal*, *1*. Advance online publication. DOI: 10.1057/s41284-023-00375-4

Kharbanda, V., & Arora, C. (2022). Guidelines to build robust security standards for the financial technology sector in India. *Indian Journal of Law and Technology*, *18*(1), 4. Advance online publication. DOI: 10.55496/VMVA2405

Kharrat, H., Trichilli, Y., & Abbes, B. (2024). Relationship between FinTech index and bank's performance: A comparative study between Islamic and conventional banks in the MENA region. *Journal of Islamic Accounting and Business Research*, *15*(1), 172–195. DOI: 10.1108/JIABR-03-2022-0081

Khuan, H. (2024). Fintech and the future of banking: Collaboration and innovation for better financial services. [DEMAND]. *Economics Studies and Banking Journal*, *1*(2), 75–93. DOI: 10.62207/c0y42z81

Kjellman, A., Björkroth, T., Kangas, T., Tainio, R., & Westerholm, T. (2019). Disruptive innovations and the challenges for banking. *International Journal of Financial Innovation in Banking*, *2*(3), 232–249. DOI: 10.1504/IJFIB.2019.102308

Klapper, L., Singer, D., & Starita, L. (2025). *The Global Findex Database 2025: Connectivity and Financial Inclusion in the Digital Economy.*

K, M. S. R., & B K, D. S. (2025, February). Neo-Banks in India -Challenges and Expansion in Future. *IOSR Journal of Business and Management*, *14th*(15th), 18–22. Advance online publication. DOI: 10.9790/487X-conf1822

Koball, C., Wang, Y., Rimal, B. P., & Vaidyan, V. (2024). *Machine Learning Security: Threat Model*. Attacks, and Challenges., DOI: 10.1109/MC.2024.3396357

Kodali, P. (2025). The evolving threat landscape: Examining predominant cyber fraud methodologies in e-commerce ecosystems. *World Journal of Advanced Research and Reviews*, *26*(1), 2552–2560. DOI: 10.30574/wjarr.2025.26.1.1308

Königstorfer, F., & Thalmann, S. (2020). Applications of Artificial Intelligence in commercial banks – A research agenda for behavioral finance. *Journal of Behavioral and Experimental Finance*, *27*, 100352. DOI: 10.1016/j.jbef.2020.100352

Kumar, S., Lim, W. M., Sivarajah, U., & Kaur, J. (2023). Artificial intelligence and blockchain integration in business: Trends from a bibliometric-content analysis. Information Systems Frontiers: A Journal of Research and Innovation, 25(2), 871–896. DOI: 10.1007/s10796-022-10279-0

Kumar, A. (2024). Redefining finance: The influence of Artificial Intelligence (AI) and Machine Learning (ML). *Transactions on Engineering and Computing Sciences*, *12*(4), 59–69.

Kumar, A., Choudhary, R. K., Mishra, S. K., Kar, S. K., & Bansal, R. (2022). The growth trajectory of UPI-based mobile payments in India: Enablers and inhibitors. *Indian Journal of Finance and Banking*, *11*(1), 45–59.

Kumari, S. (2025). Rise of UPI and its impact on traditional payment systems in India: A digital transformation analysis. *International Journal of Research Publication and Reviews*, *6*(6), 6403–6408. DOI: 10.55248/gengpi.6.0625.2216

Kumar, S., & Rao, A. (2024). Assessing And Mitigating The Impact Of Geopolitical Risk Uncertainty On The Indian Financial Sector: A Policy Perspective. *Bulletin of Monetary Economics and Banking*, *27*(3), 483–526. DOI: 10.59091/2460-9196.2278

Kushwaha, D., & Malpani, D. (2025). The Impact of Fintech on Financial Inclusion in India: An Empirical Analysis of Digital Payment Adoption and Banking Access. *International Journal of Environmental Sciences, 11*(12s), 218–227. DOI: 10.64252/g845vb32

Ky, S. S., Rugemintwari, C., & Sauviat, A. (2025). Is fintech good for bank performance? The case of mobile money in the East African Community. *International Journal of Finance & Economics, 30*(4), 3918–3949. DOI: 10.1002/ijfe.3100

Lai, P. C., & Liew, E. J. (2021). Towards a Cashless Society: The Effects of Perceived Convenience and Security on Gamified Mobile Payment Platform Adoption. *AJIS. Australasian Journal of Information Systems, 25*, 25. DOI: 10.3127/ajis.v25i0.2809

Lamey, Y. M., Tawfik, O. I., Durrah, O., & Elmaasrawy, H. E. (2024). Fintech adoption and banks' Non-Financial performance: Do circular economy practices matter? *Journal of Risk and Financial Management, 17*(8), 319. DOI: 10.3390/jrfm17080319

Lekshmi, A., Atul, J., Pillai, A. J., Dhanya, M., & Kaladharan, S. (2024, August). Risks in Instant Loan Apps: Analyzing User Perceptions Using Machine Learning Approach. In *International Conference on ICT for Sustainable Development* (pp. 461-471). Singapore: Springer Nature Singapore. https://doi.org/DOI: 10.1007/978-981-97-8602-2_41

LendingClub Reports Fourth Quarter and Full Year 2023 Results. (n.d.). Retrieved September 26, 2025, from https://ir.lendingclub.com/news/news-details/2024/LendingClub-Reports-Fourth-Quarter-and-Full-Year-2023-Results/default.aspx

Lenz, R. (2016). Peer-to-Peer Lending: Opportunities and Risks. *European Journal of Risk Regulation, 7*(4), 688–700. DOI: 10.1017/S1867299X00010126

Leo, M., Sharma, S., & Maddulety, K. (2019). Machine learning in banking risk management: A literature review. *Risks, 7*(1), 29. DOI: 10.3390/risks7010029

Leong, L. Y., Hew, T. S., Ooi, K. B., & Wei, J. (2020). Predicting mobile wallet resistance: A two-staged structural equation modeling-artificial neural network approach. *International Journal of Information Management, 51*, 102047. DOI: 10.1016/j.ijinfomgt.2019.102047

Le, T., Ngo, T., Nguyen, D. T., & Do, T. T. M. (2024). Fintech and banking: Friends or foes? Evidence from bank–fintech cooperation. *International Journal of Bank Marketing, 42*(7), 1513–1535. DOI: 10.1108/IJBM-09-2023-0525

Levi, M., Doig, A., Gundur, R., Wall, D., & Williams, M. (2017). Cyberfraud and the implications for effective risk-based responses: Themes from UK research. *Crime, Law, and Social Change*, *67*(1), 77–96. DOI: 10.1007/s10611-016-9648-0

Lew, S., Tan, G. W. H., Loh, X. M., Hew, J. J., & Ooi, K. B. (2020). The disruptive mobile wallet in the hospitality industry: An extended mobile technology acceptance model. *Technology in Society*, *63*, 101430. DOI: 10.1016/j.techsoc.2020.101430

Li, Y., Shahid, M. N., Islam, M. U., & Deme, F. (2024b). *Fintech, and Mineral Resources Deteriorate Climate Sustainability: A Significant Role of Institutional Quality and Social Capital* (No. hal-05101044).

Li, Y., Yang, X., Wu, B., & Lyu, S. (2019). Hiding faces in plain sight: Disrupting ai face synthesis with adversarial perturbations. arXiv Preprint arXiv:1906.09288.

Li, C., He, S., Tian, Y., Sun, S., & Ning, L. (2022). Does the bank's FinTech innovation reduce its risk-taking? Evidence from China's banking industry. *Journal of Innovation & Knowledge*, *7*(3), 100219. DOI: 10.1016/j.jik.2022.100219

Liébana-Cabanillas, F., Marinkovic, V., de Luna, I. R., & Kalinic, Z. (2018). Predicting the determinants of mobile payment acceptance: A hybrid SEM-neural network approach. *Technological Forecasting and Social Change*, *129*, 117–130. DOI: 10.1016/j.techfore.2017.12.015

Liébana-Cabanillas, F., Molinillo, S., & Ruiz-Montañez, M. (2019). To use or not to use, that is the question: Analysis of the determining factors for using NFC mobile payment systems in public transportation. *Technological Forecasting and Social Change*, *139*, 266–276. DOI: 10.1016/j.techfore.2018.11.012

Liem, N. T., Son, T. H., Tin, H. H., & Canh, N. T. (2022). Fintech credit, credit information sharing and bank stability: Some international evidence. *Cogent Business & Management*, *9*(1), 2112527. DOI: 10.1080/23311975.2022.2112527

Li, J., Li, J., Zhu, X., Yao, Y., & Casu, B. (2020). Risk spillovers between FinTech and traditional financial institutions: Evidence from the US. *International Review of Financial Analysis*, *71*, 101544. DOI: 10.1016/j.irfa.2020.101544

Li, L. (2023). The digital transformation of the banking industry in the era of big data. Advances in Economics. *Management and Political Sciences*, *39*(1), 24–30. DOI: 10.54254/2754-1169/39/20231929

Lim, S. H., Kim, D. J., Hur, Y., & Park, K. (2019). An empirical study of the impacts of perceived security and knowledge on continuous intention to use mobile fintech payment services. *International Journal of Human-Computer Interaction*, *35*(10), 886–898. DOI: 10.1080/10447318.2018.1507132

Lim, W. M. (2021). Toward an agency and reactance theory of crowding: Insights from COVID-19 and the tourism industry. *Journal of Consumer Behaviour, 20*(6), 1690–1694. DOI: 10.1002/cb.1948

Lin, S. L. (2007). Risk management of banking industry in Taiwan. *International Journal of Services Technology and Management, 8*(4-5), 421–451. DOI: 10.1504/IJSTM.2007.013928

Lin, X., Zhang, S. S., & Zachariadis, M. (2025). Open data and API adoption of U.S. banks. *Journal of Financial Intermediation, 63*, 101162. DOI: 10.1016/j.jfi.2025.101162

Liu, H., & Hu, J. (2025). Bank Fintech and firm leverage adjustment speed: Evidence from China. *Research in International Business and Finance, 73*, 102613. DOI: 10.1016/j.ribaf.2024.102613

Liu, J., Li, X., & Wang, S. (2020). What have we learnt from 10 years of fintech research? ascientometric analysis. *Technological Forecasting and Social Change, 155*, 120022. DOI: 10.1016/j.techfore.2020.120022

Liu, R., Wu, J., & Yu-Buck, G. F. (2021). The influence of mobile QR code payment on payment pleasure: Evidence from China. *International Journal of Bank Marketing, 39*(2), 337–356. DOI: 10.1108/IJBM-11-2020-0574

Liu, Z., Li, X., & Li, Z. (2024). Inclusive FinTech, open banking, and bank performance: Evidence from China. *Financial Innovation, 10*(1), 149. DOI: 10.1186/s40854-024-00679-3

Li, W., Li, T., Shi, W., Long, Y., & Liu, W. (2025). A protective shield for banks: How fintech curbs earnings manipulation through information transparency and financing constraints. *International Review of Financial Analysis, 107*, 104622. DOI: 10.1016/j.irfa.2025.104622

Li, Y., Shahid, M. N., Islam, M. U., & Deme, F. (2024a). Fintech, Financial Development, and Digitalization Derive the Sustainable Economic Recovery: COVID 19 Pandemic and Post Pandemic Perspectives. *Asian Journal Of Economics. Business And Accounting, 24*(6), 317–327. DOI: 10.9734/ajeba/2024/v24i61364

Li, Y., Shahid, M. N., Islam, M. U., & Deme, F. (2024c). The Role of Green Technological Innovation, Fintech, and Financial Development in Environmental Sustainability: A Study on Selected Asian Countries. *Journal of Economics, Finance, and Accounting Studies, 6*(3), 32–39. DOI: 10.32996/jefas.2024.6.3.4

Lu, M. P., & Kosim, Z. (2022). An empirical study to explore the influence of the COVID-19 crisis on consumers' behaviour towards cashless payment in Malaysia. *Journal of Financial Services Marketing*, •••, 1.

Lu, X., & Lu, H. (2020). Understanding Chinese Millennials' Adoption Intention Towards Third-Party Mobile Payment. [IRMJ]. *Information Resources Management Journal, 33*(2), 40–63. DOI: 10.4018/IRMJ.2020040103

Lv, S., Du, Y., & Liu, Y. (2022). How do fintechs impact banks' profitability?—An empirical study based on banks in China. *FinTech, 1*(2), 155–163. DOI: 10.3390/fintech1020012

M, D. K. (2025). An analysis of unified payments interface (UPI): Payer and payee PSP performance, UPI apps, and P2P and P2M transaction trends in India. *ICTACT Journal on Management Studies*. DOI: 10.21917/ijms.2025.0318

M., , & Anwarul Islam, , K., & Saifuddin Khan, M. (2024). The role of financial literacy, digital literacy, and financial self-efficacy in FinTech adoption. *Investment Management and Financial Innovations, 21*(2), 370–380. DOI: 10.21511/imfi.21(2).2024.30

Mabe, Q. M., & Simo-Kengne, B. D. (2025). The impact of FinTech risk on bank performance in Africa: The PVAR approach. *Journal of Risk and Financial Management, 18*(8), 456. DOI: 10.3390/jrfm18080456

Madan, V., & Kour, M. (2023). Mobile payment usage: Systematic literature review. In *Emerging Trends and Innovations in Industries of the Developing World: A Multidisciplinary Approach* (pp. 89–93). CRC press, Taylor & Francis. DOI: 10.1201/9781003457602-16

Madan, V., & Kour, M. (2024), "Fintech and Mobile Payments in Transition: A Study of Adoption Challenges", *2024 IEEE International Conference on Interdisciplinary Approaches in Technology and Management for Social Innovation (IATMSI)*, (Vol. 2, pp. 1-6).

Manjunath, M., & Selvi, S. (2024). A study on cyber frauds post digitalization in India. *International Journal for Research in Applied Science and Engineering Technology, 12*(IV), 60191. Advance online publication. DOI: 10.22214/ijraset.2024.60191

Martínez Resano, J. R. (2022). Digital resilience and financial stability. The quest for policy tools in the financial sector. *The Quest For Policy Tools In The Financial Sector*. https://dx.doi.org/DOI: 10.2139/ssrn.4336381

Martín-Oliver, A., Ruano, S., & Salas-Fumás, V. (2017). The fall of Spanish cajas: Lessons of ownership and governance for banks. *Journal of Financial Stability*, *33*, 244–260. DOI: 10.1016/j.jfs.2017.02.004

MAS Announces Successful Applicants of Licences to Operate New Digital Banks in Singapore. (2020). https://www.mas.gov.sg/news/media-releases/2020/mas-announces-successful-applicants-of-licences-to-operate-new-digital-banks-in-singapore

Matemba, E. D., & Li, G. (2018). Consumers' willingness to adopt and use WeChat wallet: An empirical study in South Africa. *Technology in Society*, *53*, 55–68. DOI: 10.1016/j.techsoc.2017.12.001

Mayo, K., Grabill, N., & Wellman, M. P. (2024, January). Fraud risk mitigation in real-time payments: A strategic agent-based analysis. In *33rd International Joint Conference on Artificial Intelligence* (pp. 157-165). https://doi.org/DOI: 10.24963/ijcai.2024/18

Mbama, C. I., & Ezepue, P. O. (2018). Digital banking, customer experience and bank financial performance: UK customers' perceptions. *International Journal of Bank Marketing*, *36*(2), 230–255. DOI: 10.1108/IJBM-11-2016-0181

Mdluli, G., & Staschen, S. (2022). Pitfalls in MFI digitization: Overlooking the regulatory environment. CGAP Blog. https://www.cgap.org/blog/pitfalls-in-mfi-digitization-o verlooking-regulatory-environment

Meero, A. (2025). Islamic vs. conventional banking in the age of FinTech and AI: Evolving business models, efficiency, and stability (2020–2024). *International Journal of Financial Studies*, *13*(3), 148. DOI: 10.3390/ijfs13030148

Mehta, A. (2024). Impact of technological advancements on banking frauds: A case study of Indian banks. *emergence*, 11. https://doi.org/DOI: 10.33545/26175754.2024.v7.i1c.308

Mellyana, D., & Hasan Basri, M. (2024). Business solution for profit optimization at PBS clinic. *International Journal of Current Science Research and Review*, *07*(08). Advance online publication. DOI: 10.47191/ijcsrr/V7-i8-03

Merton, R. C., & Thakor, R. T. (2019). Customers and investors: A framework for understanding the evolution of financial institutions. *Journal of Financial Intermediation*, *39*, 4–18. DOI: 10.1016/j.jfi.2018.06.002

Mhlanga, D. (2020). Industry 4.0 in Finance: The Impact of Artificial Intelligence (AI) on Digital Financial Inclusion. *International Journal of Financial Studies*. DOI: 10.3390/ijfs8030045

Mhlanga, D. (2024). The role of big data in financial technology toward financial inclusion. *Frontiers in Big Data, 7*, 1184444. DOI: 10.3389/fdata.2024.1184444

Migozzi, J., Urban, M., & Wojcik, D. (2024). "You should do what India does": FinTech ecosystems in India reshaping the geography of finance. *Geoforum, 151*, 103720. DOI: 10.1016/j.geoforum.2023.103720

Mishra, D., Kandpal, V., Agarwal, N., & Srivastava, B. (2024). Financial Inclusion and Its Ripple Effects on Socio-Economic Development: A Comprehensive Review. *Journal of Risk and Financial Management, 17*(3), 105. https://www.mdpi.com/1911-8074/17/3/105. DOI: 10.3390/jrfm17030105

Molnár, J. (2018). What does financial intermediation theory tell us about fintechs? *Vezetéstudomány-Budapest Management Review, 49*(5), 38–46. DOI: 10.14267/VEZTUD.2018.05.04

Morgan, P. J., & Long, T. Q. (2020). Financial literacy, financial inclusion, and savings behavior in Laos. *Journal of Asian Economics, 68*, 101197. DOI: 10.1016/j.asieco.2020.101197

Mosayebi, P., Nejad, S. M., Minoei, M., & Mehrani, A. (2024). Evaluation of Financial Technology (FinTech) Indicators Using a Mixed-Methods Approach in the Banking Industry. *Management Strategies and Engineering Sciences, 6*(5), 52–58. DOI: 10.61838/msesj.6.5.7

Mothobi, O., & Kebotsamang, K. (2024). The impact of network coverage on adoption of Fintech and financial inclusion in sub-Saharan Africa. *Journal of Economic Structures, 13*(1), 5. DOI: 10.1186/s40008-023-00326-7

Murinde, V., Rizopoulos, E., & Zachariadis, M. (2022). The impact of the FinTech revolution on the future of banking: Opportunities and risks. *International Review of Financial Analysis, 81*, 102103. DOI: 10.1016/j.irfa.2022.102103

Nadkarni, S., & Prügl, R. (2021). Digital transformation: A review, synthesis and opportunities for future research. *Management Review Quarterly, 71*(2), 233–341. DOI: 10.1007/s11301-020-00185-7

Nalluri, V., & Chen, L. S. (2024). Modelling the FinTech adoption barriers in the context of emerging economies—An integrated Fuzzy hybrid approach. *Technological Forecasting and Social Change, 199*, 123049. DOI: 10.1016/j.techfore.2023.123049

Narayan, P. K., Narayan, S., Rahman, R. E., & Setiawan, I. (2019). Bitcoin price growth and Indonesia's monetary system. *Emerging Markets Review, 38*, 364–376. DOI: 10.1016/j.ememar.2018.11.005

Naser, H., Sultanova, G., & Nahar, S. (2024). The impact of Fintech innovation on bank's performance: Evidence from the Kingdom of Bahrain. *International journal of economics and financial issues, 14*(1), 136-143.

National Payments Corporation of India. (2025). *Unified Payments Interface (UPI) product statistics*. https://www.npci.org.in/product/upi/product-statistics NPCI

Navaretti, G. B., Calzolari, G., Mansilla-Fernandez, J. M., & Pozzolo, A. F. (2018). *Fintech and banking. Friends or foes?* Friends or Foes. DOI: 10.2139/ssrn.3099337

Naz, S., Asif, M., & Hameed, S. (2023). Fintech's role in sustainable banking performance: Are green banking policies driving sustainability in Pakistan's banking system? *Gomal University Journal of Research, 39*(03), 294–312. DOI: 10.51380/gujr-39-03-04

Ng, A. W., & Kwok, B. K. B. (2017). Emergence of Fintech and cybersecurity in a global financial centre: Strategic approach by a regulator. *Journal of Financial Regulation and Compliance, 25*(4), 422–434. DOI: 10.1108/JFRC-01-2017-0013

Ngo, X. T., Le, K. A., Nguyen, T. T., & Nguyen, K. D. (2025). Does FinTech curb bank risk-taking? Insights from an emerging economy. *Finance Research Letters, 86*, 108722. DOI: 10.1016/j.frl.2025.108722

Nguyen, T. T. T. (2025). The Impact of Fintech on Bank Profitability and Bank Stability in Emerging Country. *Journal of Organizational Behavior Research, 10*(2-2025), 12-19.

Nguyen, H. V. (2018). *Cash or cashless? Promoting consumers' adoption of mobile payments in an emerging economy*. Strategic Direction.

Nguyen, L., Tran, S., & Ho, T. (2022). Fintech credit, bank regulations and bank performance: A cross-country analysis. *Asia-Pacific Journal of Business Administration, 14*(4), 445–466. DOI: 10.1108/APJBA-05-2021-0196

Nguyen, Q. K. (2022). The effect of FinTech development on financial stability in an emerging market: The role of market discipline. *Research in Globalization, 5*, 100105. DOI: 10.1016/j.resglo.2022.100105

Nguyen, T. T., & Reddi, V. J. (2023). Deep Reinforcement Learning for Cyber Security. IEEE Transactions on Neural Networks and Learning Systems, 34(8), 3779–3795. *IEEE Transactions on Neural Networks and Learning Systems*. Advance online publication. DOI: 10.1109/TNNLS.2021.3121870 PMID: 34723814

Nikkel, B. J. (2020). Fintech forensics: Criminal investigation and digital evidence in financial technologies. *Forensic Science International Digital Investigation, 33*, 200908. Advance online publication. DOI: 10.1016/j.fsidi.2020.200908

Niroula, A., & Adhikari, S. (2024). Machine learning, banking, industry, digitalization, innovation. *American Journal of Finance and Business Management, 3*(1), 62–72. DOI: 10.58425/ajfbm.v3i1.286

Nugraha, D. P., Setiawan, B., Nathan, R. J., & Fekete-Farkas, M. (2022). FinTech adoption drivers for innovation for SMEs in Indonesia. *Journal of Open Innovation, 8*(4), 208. DOI: 10.3390/joitmc8040208

Nurlaela, N., Luthfiyana, M., Sulastri, A., & Wahyunita, E. S. (2020). REVIEWING THE FATWAS RELATED TO FINTECH APPLICATIONS IN ISLAMIC FINANCIAL INSTITUTIONS IN INDONESIA. *Share: Journal of Islamic Economics & Finance/Jurnal Ekonomi dan Keuangan Islam, 9*(2).

Obeidat, M., & Saxena, J. P. (2015). Customer's acceptance of internet banking in Dubai. *IOSR Journal of Business and Management, 17*(12), 61–80.

Oduro, D. A., Okolo, J. N., Bello, A. D., Ajibade, A. T., & Muritala, A. (2025). AI-powered fraud detection in digital banking: Enhancing security through machine learning. https://doi.org/DOI: 10.30574/ijsra.2025.14.3.0854

Oentoro, W. (2021). Mobile payment adoption process: A serial of multiple mediation and moderation analysis. *The Bottom Line (New York, N.Y.), 34*(3/4), 225–244. DOI: 10.1108/BL-09-2020-0059

Oladipo, J. O., Okoye, C. C., Elufioye, O. A., Falaiye, T., & Nwankwo, E. E. (2024). Human factors in cybersecurity: Navigating the fintech landscape. *International Journal of Science and Research Archive, 11*(1), 1959–1967. DOI: 10.30574/ijsra.2024.11.1.0258

Omarini, A. E. (2018). Banks and FinTechs: How to develop a digital open banking approach for the bank's future. *International Business Research, 11*(9), 23–36. DOI: 10.5539/ibr.v11n9p23

Othman, M. (2025). Fintech and sustainability: Charting a new course for Jordanian banking. *Journal of Risk and Financial Management, 18*(6), 328. DOI: 10.3390/jrfm18060328

Owusu, A., & Gupta, A. (2024). Identifying the risk culture of banks using machine learning. *International Journal of Managerial Finance, 20*(2), 377–405. DOI: 10.1108/IJMF-09-2022-0422

Pal, A., De', R., & Herath, T. (2020). The Role of Mobile Payment Technology in Sustainable and Human-Centric Development: Evidence from the Post-Demonetization Period in India. *Information Systems Frontiers*, *22*(3), 607–631. DOI: 10.1007/s10796-020-09982-7

Pal, A., Herath, T., & Rao, H. R. (2021). Why do people use mobile payment technologies and why would they continue? An examination and implications from India. *Research Policy*, *50*(6), 104228. DOI: 10.1016/j.respol.2021.104228

Pamarthi, K. (2024). Analysis on opportunities and challenges of AI in the banking industry. *Journal ID*, *1232*, 1214.

Panda, K., Sahoo, A., & Kumar, A. (2023). From the Margins to Mainstream: Fintech's Quest for Financial Inclusion in Emerging Markets. *European Economic Letters*, *13*(5), 341–361. DOI: 10.52783/eel.v13i5.762

Panjwani, K., & Shili, N. (2020). The impact of fintech on development of islamic banking sector in the contemporary world. *Saudi Journal of Economics and Finance*, *4*(7), 346–350. DOI: 10.36348/sjef.2020.v04i07.006

Pan, X., Zhang, J., & Huang, X. (2025). How Bank Fintech Facilitates Firm-Level New Quality Productive Forces. *Available at SSRN* 5269661. DOI: 10.1016/j.frl.2025.108308

Paramesha, M., Rane, N. L., & Rane, J. (2024). Artificial Intelligence, Machine Learning, Deep Learning, and Blockchain in financial and banking services: A comprehensive review. *SSRN*, *1*(2), 68–83. DOI: 10.2139/ssrn.4855893

Parboteeah, P. (2016). *LICENCE CC BY-NC-ND 4.0 REPOSITORY RECORD.*

Parera, M. P., & Molina, E. B. (2020). *BBVA Case Study: The effect of financial performance on shareholders wealth before and after Fintech acquisition.*

Parmar, M. (2024). The Impact of Cybercrime on Consumer Trust in E-Commerce. *Available at SSRN* 4843094. https://dx.doi.org/DOI: 10.2139/ssrn.4843094

Parsheera, S. (2022). Understanding state-level variations in India's digital transformation. *The African Journal of Information and Communication*, *2022*(30), 1–9. DOI: 10.23962/ajic.i30.15082

Patil, P., Tamilmani, K., Rana, N. P., & Raghavan, V. (2020). Understanding consumer adoption of mobile payment in India: Extending Meta-UTAUT model with personal innovativeness, anxiety, trust, and grievance redressal. *International Journal of Information Management*, *54*, 102144. DOI: 10.1016/j.ijinfomgt.2020.102144

Peer-to-Peer Lending Market Size, Share & Growth | 2032. (n.d.). Retrieved September 26, 2025, from https://www.alliedmarketresearch.com/peer-to-peer-lending-market

Peihani, M. (2022). Regulation of Cyber Risk in the Banking System: A Canadian Case Study. *Journal of Financial Regulation*, *8*(2), 139–161. DOI: 10.1093/jfr/fjac006

Petralia, K., Philippon, T., Rice, T. N., & Veron, N. (2019). *Banking disrupted?: Financial intermediation in an era of transformational technology*. ICMB International Center for Monetary and Banking Studies.

Philippon, T. (2016). *The fintech opportunity* (No. w22476). National Bureau of Economic Research.

Philippon, T. (2019). *On fintech and financial inclusion* (No. w26330). National Bureau of Economic Research.

Pinto, A., Herrera, L.-C., Donoso, Y., & Gutiérrez, J. A. (2023). Survey on Intrusion Detection Systems Based on Machine Learning Techniques for the Protection of Critical Infrastructure. *Sensors (Basel)*, *23*(5), 5. Advance online publication. DOI: 10.3390/s23052415 PMID: 36904618

Qiang, X. (2024). Digital transformation in the financial sector through FinTech. Advances in Economics. *Management and Political Sciences*, *76*(1), 226–234. DOI: 10.54254/2754-1169/76/20241656

Qian, S., Yang, Z., & Fang, X. (2025). Bank Fintech and Corporate Green Transformation Quality Improvement: Based on Greenwashing Governance Perspective. *Economic Analysis and Policy*, *87*, 401–423. DOI: 10.1016/j.eap.2025.06.017

Qi, J., Chatterjee, S., Worthy, S., Herndon, K., & Wojdynski, B. (2024a). Using an extended post-acceptance framework to examine consumer adoption of fintech. *International Journal of Bank Marketing*, *42*(3), 642–668. DOI: 10.1108/IJBM-10-2022-0448

Qu, Y., Rong, W., Chen, H., Ouyang, Y., & Xiong, Z. (2018). Influencing factors analysis for a social network web based payment service in China. *Journal of Theoretical and Applied Electronic Commerce Research*, *13*(3), 99–113. DOI: 10.4067/S0718-18762018000300106

Radenković, S. D., Hanić, H., & Bugarčić, M. (2023). Applying Artificial Intelligence in the Digital Transformation of the Banking Sector. *Proceedings*, *85*(1), 1. Advance online publication. DOI: 10.3390/proceedings2023085019

Rafiq, M., & Sohail, M. K. (2025). Adopting regulatory technology for anti-money laundering in banking: Key enablers and barriers in a RegTech model. *Sustainable Futures : An Applied Journal of Technology, Environment and Society*, *10*, 101377. DOI: 10.1016/j.sftr.2025.101377

Rahim, N. F., Bakri, M. H., Fianto, B. A., Zainal, N., & Hussein Al Shami, S. A. (2023). Measurement and structural modelling on factors of Islamic Fintech adoption among millennials in Malaysia. *Journal of Islamic Marketing*, *14*(6), 1463–1487. DOI: 10.1108/JIMA-09-2020-0279

Rajput, S. (2024). Building Robust Securities in PSO'S: Adopting RBI's Baseline Controls for Business continuity. *Planning (Chicago, Ill.)*, *ii*. Advance online publication. DOI: 10.2139/ssrn.4947696

Rane, N., Choudhary, S., & Rane, J. (2023). Blockchain and Artificial Intelligence (AI) integration for revolutionizing security and transparency in finance. SSRN *Electronic Journal*. DOI: 10.2139/ssrn.4644253

Ranković, M., Gurgu, E., Martins, O. M. D., & Vukasović, M. (2023). Artificial intelligence and the evolution of finance: Opportunities, challenges and ethical considerations. *EdTech Journal*, *3*(1), 20–23. DOI: 10.18485/edtech.2023.3.1.2

Rao, H. S. (2019). Cyber crime in banking sector. *International Journal of Research-Granthaalayah*, *7*(1), 148–161. DOI: 10.29121/granthaalayah.v7.i1.2019.1043

Rathi, C., Varshney, A. K., Chaudhary, S., Prakash, V., & Garg, A. (2024). A paradigm shifts in fintech and rural inclusion challenges in India. *International Journal of Science and Research Archive*, *12*(1), 299–311. DOI: 10.30574/ijsra.2024.12.1.0763

Ravikumar, A. S., & Mamadiyarov, Z. (2025). Mitigating risks through AI-powered fraud detection systems in digital banking. In Innovating Cost-Efficient and Scalable Business Models in the Digital Era (pp. 343–376). IGI Global Scientific Publishing. DOI: 10.4018/979-8-3373-2120-2.ch011

Ravirajan, K., & Shanmugam, K. R. (2023). *Determinants of Efficiency of Commercial Banks in India After Global Crises*. Madras School of Economics., DOI: 10.33423/jaf.v23i4.6456

Raza, M. S., Zhan, Q., & Rubab, S. (2020). Role of money mules in money laundering and financial crimes a discussion through case studies. *Journal of Financial Crime*, *27*(3), 911–931. DOI: 10.1108/JFC-02-2020-0028

Redrawing the lines: FinTechs growing influence on Financial Services—PwC Channel Island. (n.d.). Retrieved September 27, 2025, from https://www.pwc.com/jg/en/publications/fintech-growing-influence-financial-services.html

RGHL_Annual Report 31 Dec 2024-2025-04-22-17-42. (n.d.). Retrieved September 26, 2025, from https://assets.revolut.com/pdf/annualreport2024.pdf

Ridzuan, N. N., Masri, M., Anshari, M., Fitriyani, N. L., & Syafrudin, M. (2024). AI in the financial sector: The line between innovation, regulation and ethical responsibility. *Information (Basel), 15*(8), 432. DOI: 10.3390/info15080432

Rita, E. (2018). Fintech Transaction Volume Continues to Increase. Berita Satu., Retrieved October 2018, from.

Rizkyandy, R., Setyohadi, D. B., & Suyoto, S. (2018). What should be considered for acceptance mobile payment: An investigation of the factors affecting of the intention to use system services T-Cash. *Advances in Science, Technology and Engineering Systems Journal, 3*(2), 257–262. DOI: 10.25046/aj030230

Ross, R., Pillitteri, V., Graubart, R., Bodeau, D., & McQuaid, R. (2019). *Developing cyber resilient systems: a systems security engineering approach* (No. NIST Special Publication (SP) 800-160 Vol. 2 (Draft)). National Institute of Standards and Technology.

Ross, S. What percentage of the global economy is comprised of the financial services sector? Invest 5 (2015), 2015. Available online: https://www.investopedia.com/ask/answers/030515/what-percentage-global-economy-comprised-financial-services-sector.asp

Sabilika, K. (2024). *Green Fintech Market Review*.

Safiullah, M., & Paramati, S. R. (2024). The impact of FinTech firms on bank financial stability. *Electronic Commerce Research, 24*(1), 453–475. DOI: 10.1007/s10660-022-09595-z

Salah Mahdi, I. B., Bouaziz, M., & Boujelbène Abbes, M. (2025). The moderating effect of fintech on the relationship between CSR and banks' financial stability: Baron and Kenny's approach analysis. *EuroMed Journal of Business, 20*(2), 300–324. DOI: 10.1108/EMJB-03-2023-0082

Salampasis, D., & Mention, A.-L. (2018). FinTech: Harnessing Innovation for Financial Inclusion. In Lee Kuo Chuen, D., & Deng, R. (Eds.), *Handbook of Blockchain, Digital Finance, and Inclusion* (Vol. 2, pp. 451–461). Academic Press., DOI: 10.1016/B978-0-12-812282-2.00018-8

Salloum, S. A., & Al-Emran, M. (2018). Factors affecting the Adoption of E-payment systems by university students: Extending the TAM with Trust. *International Journal of Electronic Business, 14*(4), 371–390. DOI: 10.1504/IJEB.2018.098130

Sannino, G., Di Carlo, F., & Lucchese, M. (2020). CEO characteristics and sustainability business model in financial technologies firms: Primary evidence from the utilization of innovative platforms. *Management Decision*, *58*(8), 1779–1799. DOI: 10.1108/MD-10-2019-1360

Sardar, S., & Anjaria, K. (2023). *The future of banking: How neo banks are changing the industry.* *2*(2).

Sarfraz, M., Ye, Z., Banciu, D., Dragan, F., & Ivascu, L. (2022). Intertwining digitalization and sustainable performance via the mediating role of digital transformation and the moderating role of FinTech behavior adoption. *Studies in Informatics and Control*, *31*(4), 35–44. DOI: 10.24846/v31i4y202204

Saroy, R., Jain, P., Awasthy, S., & Dhal, S. (2023). Impact of digital payment adoption on Indian banking sector efficiency. *Journal of Banking and Financial Technology*, 1–13. DOI: 10.1007/s42786-023-00047-2

Saxena, R., Budki, A., & Gupta, A. (2024). A Study on the Consumer Risk Perceptions for FinTech Platforms in India. *Advances in Economics and Business*, *12*(3), 33–41. DOI: 10.13189/aeb.2024.120302

Schmidthuber, L., Maresch, D., & Ginner, M. (2020). Disruptive technologies and abundance in the service sector-toward a refined technology acceptance model. *Technological Forecasting and Social Change*, *155*, 119328. DOI: 10.1016/j.techfore.2018.06.017

Sebastian, D. (2025). Modernizing Credit Risk with Data Mesh: A Large Bank's Transformation to Real-Time Credit Intelligence. *Journal of Computer Science and Technology Studies*, *7*(10), 650–664. DOI: 10.32996/jcsts.2025.7.10.65

Setiawan, B., Nugraha, D. P., Irawan, A., Nathan, R. J., & Zoltan, Z. (2021). User innovativeness and fintech adoption in Indonesia. *Journal of Open Innovation*, *7*(3), 188. DOI: 10.3390/joitmc7030188

Shadrooh, S., & Nørvåg, K. (2024). SMoTeF: Smurf money laundering detection using temporal order and flow analysis. *Applied Intelligence*, *54*(15), 7461–7478. DOI: 10.1007/s10489-024-05545-4

Shah, M. A., Harish, K., Shradha, Hansda, K., Chowdhury, D., & Yadav, S. (2024). Beyond Mobile Payments: Exploring the Evolution and Future of Fintech (BY IJISRT). *International Journal of Innovative Science and Research Technology (IJISRT)*. DOI: 10.38124/ijisrt/IJISRT24APR259

Shahid, M. N., Sher, F., & Ishtiaq, M. (2025). Impact of FinTech and Control of Corruption on Environmental Sustainability. *Journal of Economic Criminology*, 100162.

Shah, P., & Agarwal, A. (2020). Cybersecurity behaviour of smartphone users in India: An empirical analysis. *Information and Computer Security*, *28*(2), 293–318. DOI: 10.1108/ICS-04-2019-0041

Shanti, R., Siregar, H., Zulbainarni, N., & Tony, . (2023). Role of digital transformation on digital business model banks. *Sustainability (Basel)*, *15*(23), 16293. DOI: 10.3390/su152316293

Shao, Z., Zhang, L., Li, X., & Guo, Y. (2019). Antecedents of trust and continuance intention in mobile payment platforms: The moderating effect of gender. *Electronic Commerce Research and Applications*, *33*, 100823. DOI: 10.1016/j.elerap.2018.100823

Sharma, P., Gallani, V., & Maheria, S. (2024). Digital payments and fraud connection: Insights from the Indian economy. *International Journal of Management. Economics and Commerce*, *1*(2), 102–111. DOI: 10.62737/spqxve67

Shaukat, K., Luo, S., Varadharajan, V., Hameed, I. A., & Xu, M. (2020). A Survey on Machine Learning Techniques for Cyber Security in the Last Decade. IEEE Access, 8, 222310 222354. IEEE Access. DOI: 10.1109/ACCESS.2020.3041951

Shekhar, V., & R, S. (2025). Navigating the dark side of fintech: A developer perspective. *Management Practice Insights*, *3*(Sp1, SI1), 58–64. DOI: 10.59571/mpi.v3si1.10

Shmuratko, Y. A., & Sheludko, S. A.Ya. A. ShmuratkoS. A. Sheludko. (2021). Financial technologies' impact on the development of banking. *Financial and Credit Activity Problems of Theory and Practice*, *4*(31), 61–69. DOI: 10.18371/fcaptp.v4i31.190792

Siddik, A. B., Rahman, M. N., & Yong, L. (2023). Do fintech adoption and financial literacy improve corporate sustainability performance? The mediating role of access to finance. *Journal of Cleaner Production*, *421*, 137658. DOI: 10.1016/j.jclepro.2023.137658

Siek, M., & Sutanto, A. (2019, August). *Impact analysis of fintech on banking industry. In 2019 international conference on information management and technology (ICIMTech)* (Vol. 1). IEEE.

Singh, A. (2025). Generational Perspectives on Fintech Adoption: Challenges, Demographics, and Digital Inclusion. *Mercados y negocios, 26*(56). https://doi.org/ DOI: 10.32870/myn.vi56.7827

Singh, N., Sinha, N., & Liébana-Cabanillas, F. J. (2020). Determining factors in the adoption and recommendation of mobile wallet services in India: Analysis of the effect of innovativeness, stress to use and social influence. *International Journal of Information Management*, *50*, 191–205. DOI: 10.1016/j.ijinfomgt.2019.05.022

Singh, R., Malik, G., & Jain, V. (2021). FinTech effect: Measuring impact of FinTech adoption on banks' profitability. *International Journal of Management Practice*, *14*(4), 411–427. DOI: 10.1504/IJMP.2021.116587

Singh, U. G. (2021). Investigating Mobile Payment Adoption in Mauritius. *African Journal of Business and Economic Research*, *16*(3), 257. DOI: 10.31920/1750-4562/2021/v16n3a13

Skała, D., & Weill, L. (2018). Does CEO gender matter for bank risk? *Economic Systems*, *42*(1), 64–74. DOI: 10.1016/j.ecosys.2017.08.005

Sobers, R. (2022). Data Breach Response Times: https://www.varonis.com/blog/data-breach-response-times

Solanki, R., & Sujee, L. S. (2022). Fintech: A disruptive innovation of the 21st century, or is it? *Global Business and Management Research*, *14*(2s), 76–87.

Sottet, J. S., Grandry, E., & Bjeković, M. (2018). Managing regulatory system with megamodelling. Proceeding - 2018 20th IEEE International Conference on Business Informatics, CBI 2018

Srivastav, A., & Hagendorff, J. (2016). Corporate governance and bank risk-taking. *Corporate Governance*, *24*(3), 334–345. DOI: 10.1111/corg.12133

Stankevičienė, J., & Kabulova, J. (2022). Financial technology impact on stability of financial institutions. *Technological and Economic Development of Economy*, *28*(4), 1089–1114. DOI: 10.3846/tede.2022.17093

Stulz, R. M. (2019). Fintech, bigtech, and the future of banks. *The Bank of America Journal of Applied Corporate Finance*, *31*(4), 86–97. DOI: 10.1111/jacf.12378

Subanidja, S., Sorongan, F., & Legowo, M. (2022). Leveraging Financial Technology Entity into Sustainable Bank Performance through a Competitive Advantage. *Emerging Science Journal*, *6*(1), 53–63. Advance online publication. DOI: 10.28991/ESJ-2022-06-01-04

Sujatha, D., Sudheer, A. K., & Balasundaram, E. (2025). Black swan dynamics: A network-based framework for systemic risk detection and mitigation [Article]. *Risk Management*, *27*(4), 24. Advance online publication. DOI: 10.1057/s41283-025-00177-5

Su, P., Wang, L., & Yan, J. (2018). How users' Internet experience affects the adoption of mobile payment: A mediation model. *Technology Analysis and Strategic Management, 30*(2), 186–197. DOI: 10.1080/09537325.2017.1297788

Suseendran, G., Chandrasekaran, E., Akila, D., & Sasi Kumar, A. (2019). Banking and FinTech (financial technology) embraced with IoT device. In *Data Management, Analytics and Innovation* [Singapore: Springer Singapore.]. *Proceedings of ICDMAI, 1*, 197–211.

Swan, M. (2017). Is technological unemployment real? An assessment and a plea for abundance economics. In *Surviving the machine age: intelligent technology and the transformation of human work* (pp. 19–33). Springer International Publishing. DOI: 10.1007/978-3-319-51165-8_2

Syed, A. A., Grima, S., & Sood, K. (2024). Assessing the Role of the Fintech Era on the Banking Stability of an Emerging Economy: Interaction Analysis of the Indian Banking Industry. *Folia Oeconomica Stetinensia, 24*(1), 182–202. DOI: 10.2478/foli-2024-0011

Tamraparani, V. (2022). Ethical Implications of Implementing AI in Wealth Management for Personalized Investment Strategies. [IJSR]. *International Journal of Science and Research (Raipur, India), 11*(3), 1625–1633. DOI: 10.21275/SR220309091129

Tanchangya, T., Islam, N., Naher, K., Mia, M. R., Chowdhury, S., Sarker, S. R., & Rashid, F. (2025). Financial technology-enabled sustainable finance for small-and medium-sized enterprises. *Environment. Innovation and Management, 1*, 2550006.

Tang, H. (2019). Peer-to-peer lenders versus banks: Substitutes or complements? *Review of Financial Studies, 32*(5), 1900–1938. DOI: 10.1093/rfs/hhy137

Tarawneh, A., Abdul-Rahman, A., Mohd Amin, S. I., & Ghazali, M. F. (2024). A systematic review of fintech and banking profitability. *International Journal of Financial Studies, 12*(1), 3. DOI: 10.3390/ijfs12010003

Tariq, H., & Hassani, M. (2023, September). Topology-agnostic detection of temporal money laundering flows in billion-scale transactions. In *Joint European Conference on Machine Learning and Knowledge Discovery in Databases* (pp. 402-419). Cham: Springer Nature Switzerland.

Temelkov, Z. (2020). OVERVIEW OF NEOBANKS MODEL AND ITS IMPLICATIONS FOR TRADITIONAL BANKING. *CHALLENGES OF TOURISM AND BUSINESS LOGISTICS IN THE 21ST CENTURY. ISCTBL, 2020*, 156–165. Advance online publication. DOI: 10.46763/YFNTS2031156t

Teng, S., & Khong, K. W. (2021). Examining actual consumer usage of E-wallet: A case study of big data analytics. *Computers in Human Behavior, 121*, 106778. DOI: 10.1016/j.chb.2021.106778

Thakor, A. V. (2020). Fintech and banking: What do we know? *Journal of Financial Intermediation, 41*, 100833. DOI: 10.1016/j.jfi.2019.100833

Tong, X., & Yang, W. (2025). Empirical analysis of the impact of financial technology on the profitability of listed banks. *International Review of Economics & Finance, 98*, 103788. DOI: 10.1016/j.iref.2024.103788

Tounekti, O., Ruiz-Martínez, A., & Skarmeta Gomez, A. F. (2022). Research in electronic and mobile payment systems: A bibliometric analysis. *Sustainability (Basel), 14*(13), 7661. DOI: 10.3390/su14137661

Tripathy, S. S. (2025). A comprehensive survey of cybercrimes in India over the last decade. *arXiv preprint arXiv:2505.23770.* http://dx.doi.org/DOI: 10.2139/ssrn.5048282

Ujunwa, A. (2012). Board characteristics and the financial performance of Nigerian quoted firms. *Corporate Governance (Bradford), 12*(5), 656–674. DOI: 10.1108/14720701211275587

Untoro, W., & Trinugroho, I. (2022, December). The effect of FinTech on conventional bank performance and bank risk. In *International Colloquium on Business and Economics (ICBE 2022)* (pp. 140–152). Atlantis Press.

Varma, P., Nijjer, S., Sood, K., Grima, S., & Rupeika-Apoga, R. (2022). Thematic analysis of financial technology (Fintech) influence on the banking industry. *Risks, 10*(10), 186. DOI: 10.3390/risks10100186

Venkatachalam, P. (2020, December). Influence of FinTech companies on banking landscape an exploratory study in Indian context. In *International Working Conference on Transfer and Diffusion of IT* (pp. 523-528). Cham: Springer International Publishing. https://doi.org/DOI: 10.1007/978-3-030-64849-7_46

Venkatesh, V., Morris, M., Davis, G., & Davis, F. (2003). User acceptance of information technology: Toward a unified view. *Management Information Systems Quarterly, 27*(3), 425–478. DOI: 10.2307/30036540

Vettriselvan, R., Velmurugan, P. R., Regins, J. C., Maheswari, S. U., & Joyce, R. (2025). Best Practices, Ethical Challenges, and Regulatory Frameworks for AI Integration in Banking: Navigating the Future. In *Artificial Intelligence for Cloud-Native Software Engineering* (pp. 377-410). IGI Global Scientific Publishing.

Vives, X. (2017). The impact of FinTech on banking. *European Economy*, (2), 97–105.

von Horn, R., & Kudic, M. (2025). Systemic risk in the fintech-banking system: Assessing instabilities and vulnerabilities in Central Europe [Article]. *The Quarterly Review of Economics and Finance*, *104*, 102071. Advance online publication. DOI: 10.1016/j.qref.2025.102071

Von Solms, J. (2021). Integrating Regulatory Technology (RegTech) into the digital transformation of a bank Treasury. *Journal of Banking Regulation*, *22*(2), 152–168. DOI: 10.1057/s41261-020-00134-0

Voshchak, O. (2024). THEORETICAL FOUNDATIONS OF NEOBANKS DEVELOPMENT. *Scientific Opinion: Economics and Management*. DOI: 10.32782/2521-666X/2024-88-13

Wahga, A. I., Majid, S., Ahmad, N., Aftab, I., & Awais, M. (2023). FinTech and Pakistan's banking industry: An exploratory study. *Journal of Policy Research*, *12*(4), 19–28. DOI: 10.61506/02.00122

Wang, H., Mao, K., Wu, W., & Luo, H. (2023). Fintech inputs, non-performing loans risk reduction and bank performance improvement. *International Review of Financial Analysis*, *90*, 102849. DOI: 10.1016/j.irfa.2023.102849

Wang, L. (2024). Impact of FinTech on Commercial Banks. Advances in Economics. *Management and Political Sciences*, *72*(1), 211–216. DOI: 10.54254/2754-1169/72/20240699

Wang, L., Luo, X. R., Yang, X., & Qiao, Z. (2019). Easy come or easy go? Empirical evidence on switching behaviors in mobile payment applications. *Information & Management*, *56*(7), 103150. DOI: 10.1016/j.im.2019.02.005

Wang, Q., & He, Y. (2025). Platform-Based Fintech and Bank Loan Maturity Structure: Evidence from Chinese Commercial Banks. *Finance Research Letters*, *86*, 108667. DOI: 10.1016/j.frl.2025.108667

Wang, R., Liu, J., & Luo, H. (2021). Fintech development and bank risk taking in China. *European Journal of Finance*, *27*(4-5), 397–418. DOI: 10.1080/1351847X.2020.1805782

Wang, X., Hou, S., Kyaw, K., Xue, X., & Liu, X. (2023). Exploring the determinants of Fintech Credit: A comprehensive analysis. *Economic Modelling*, *126*, 106422. DOI: 10.1016/j.econmod.2023.106422

Wang, Y., Xiuping, S., & Zhang, Q. (2021). Can fintech improve the efficiency of commercial banks?—An analysis based on big data. *Research in International Business and Finance*, *55*, 101338. DOI: 10.1016/j.ribaf.2020.101338

Wang, Z., Zhu, H., & Sun, L. (2021). Social Engineering in Cybersecurity: Effect Mechanisms, Human Vulnerabilities and Attack Methods. *IEEE Access : Practical Innovations, Open Solutions*, *9*, 11895–11910. DOI: 10.1109/ACCESS.2021.3051633

WEF_Future_of_Global_Fintech_Second_Edition_2025.pdf. (n.d.). Retrieved October 22, 2025, from https://reports.weforum.org/docs/WEF_Future_of_Global_Fintech_Second_Edition_2025

Wenner, G., Bram, J. T., Marino, M., Obeysekare, E., & Mehta, K. (2018). Organizational models of mobile payment systems in low-resource environments. *Information Technology for Development*, *24*(4), 681–705. DOI: 10.1080/02681102.2017.1311830

Wernerfelt, B. (1984). A resource-based view of the firm. *Strategic Management Journal*, *5*(2), 171–180. DOI: 10.1002/smj.4250050207

Widarwati, E., Fajar, I. Y., Nurmalasari, N., & Wityasminingsih, E. (2023). Digital Finance and Microfinance Risk Level. In *10th International Conference on Management and Muamalah*.

Wolters, P. T. J., & Jacobs, B. P. F. (2019). The security of access to accounts under the PSD2. *Computer Law & Security Review*, *35*(1), 29–41. DOI: 10.1016/j.clsr.2018.10.005

Wonglimpiyarat, J. (2017). FinTech banking industry: a systemic approach. *foresight, 19*(6), 590-603.

WSC. S. (2024, September 23). Seaya Ventures leads a €6 million round in Dotfile to automate regulatory compliance with AI. *Seaya*. https://seaya.vc/seaya-ventures-leads-a-e6-million-round-in-dotfile-to-automate-regulatory-compliance-with-ai/

Xu, F., Kasperskaya, Y., & Sagarra, M. (2025). The impact of FinTech on bank performance: A systematic literature review. *Digital Business*, 100131.

Xu, F., Kasperskaya, Y., & Sagarra, M. (2025). The impact of FinTech on bank performance: A systematic literature review. *Digital Business*, *5*(2), 100131. DOI: 10.1016/j.digbus.2025.100131

Yan, C., Siddik, A. B., Yong, L., Dong, Q., Zheng, G. W., & Rahman, M. N. (2022). A two-staged SEM-artificial neural network approach to analyze the impact of FinTech adoption on the sustainability performance of banking firms: The mediating effect of green finance and innovation. *Systems*, *10*(5), 148. DOI: 10.3390/systems10050148

Yao, M., Di, H., Zheng, X., & Xu, X. (2018). Impact of payment technology innovations on the traditional financial industry: A focus on China. *Technological Forecasting and Social Change*, *135*, 199–207. DOI: 10.1016/j.techfore.2017.12.023

Yao, T., & Song, L. (2023). Fintech and the economic capital of Chinese commercial bank's risk: Based on theory and evidence. *International Journal of Finance & Economics*, *28*(2), 2109–2123. DOI: 10.1002/ijfe.2528

Yaramolu, L. S. K. G. (2025). AI-Powered Portfolio Management: Transforming Wealth Management Through Intelligent Automation. *Journal of Computer Science and Technology Studies*, *7*(3), 14–23. DOI: 10.32996/jcsts.2025.7.3.3

Yin, F., Jiao, X., Zhou, J., Yin, X., Ibeke, E., Iwendi, M. G., & Biamba, C. (2022). Fintech application on banking stability using Big Data of an emerging economy. *Journal of Cloud Computing (Heidelberg, Germany)*, *11*(1), 43. DOI: 10.1186/s13677-022-00320-7 PMID: 36093281

Yuan, X., Puah, C. H., & Marikan, D. A. B. A. (2025). An Empirical Study on the Impact of Financial Technology on the Profitability of China's Listed Commercial Banks. *Journal of Risk and Financial Management*, *18*(8), 440. DOI: 10.3390/jrfm18080440

Yudaruddin, R. (2023). Financial technology and performance in Islamic and conventional banks. *Journal of Islamic Accounting and Business Research*, *14*(1), 100–116. DOI: 10.1108/JIABR-03-2022-0070

Zainal, N., Md Nassir, A., Kamarudin, F., & Law, S. H. (2021). Does bank regulation and supervision impedes the efficiency of microfinance institutions to eradicate poverty? Evidence from ASEAN-5 countries. *Studies in Economics and Finance*, *38*(2), 272–302. DOI: 10.1108/SEF-10-2019-0414

Zavolokina, L., Dolata, M., & Schwabe, G. (2016). The FinTech phenomenon: Antecedents of financial innovation perceived by the popular press. *Financial Innovation*, *2*(1), 16. DOI: 10.1186/s40854-016-0036-7

Zebari, G. M., & Al Musalhi, N. (2025). A comprehensive review of integrating AI and blockchain security: Innovations, challenges, and future directions. *Security and Privacy*, *8*(5), e70094. Advance online publication. DOI: 10.1002/spy2.70094

Zhang, X., & Li, Z. (2025). FinTech: The disruptive force reducing bank competition pressure. *Emerging Markets Review*, *65*, 101237. DOI: 10.1016/j.ememar.2024.101237

Zhang, Y., Ye, S., Liu, J., & Du, L. (2023). Impact of the development of FinTech by commercial banks on bank credit risk. *Finance Research Letters*, *55*, 103857. DOI: 10.1016/j.frl.2023.103857

Zhao, X., Sun, X., Zhao, L., & Xing, Y. (2022). Can the digital transformation of manufacturing enterprises promote enterprise innovation? *Business Process Management Journal*, *28*(4), 960–982. DOI: 10.1108/BPMJ-01-2022-0018

Zheng, C., Rahman, M. A., Hossain, S., & Alam Siddik, M. N. (2024). Construction of a composite fintech index to measure financial inclusion for developing countries. *Applied Economics*, *56*(52), 6498–6515. DOI: 10.1080/00036846.2024.2313600

Zheng, C., Rahman, M. A., Hossain, S., & Moudud-Ul-Huq, S. (2023). Does Fintech-driven inclusive finance induce bank profitability? Empirical evidence from developing countries. *Journal of Risk and Financial Management*, *16*(10), 457. DOI: 10.3390/jrfm16100457

Zuhroh, I. (2021). The impact of Fintech on Islamic banking and the collaboration model: A systematic review studies in Indonesia. *Jurnal Perspektif Pembiayaan Dan Pembangunan Daerah*, *9*(4), 302–312. DOI: 10.22437/ppd.v9i4.12054

About the Contributors

Muhammad Naeem Shahid earned his PhD (Finance) from Bahria University, Islamabad, Pakistan. He is currently serving as a Senior Lecturer at School of Accounting and Finance, Taylor's University Malaysia. He has also served as an assistant professor of finance and In-charge of the Department of Business Administration at Government College University, Faisalabad, Chiniot Campus, Pakistan. During his career, he taught a wide range of finance courses and served as the head of the Department of Business Administration at different Universities. Moreover, he has been serving his potential in various capacities, such as In-charge of academics and budget planning. So far, he has served as In-charge of the entrepreneurial society and a research associate in ORIC. He also initiated new academic programs at the bachelor's, Master's, and PhD levels. He received an APU Research Development Internal Grant (RDIG) from Malaysia and Travel Grants from the Higher Education Commission of Pakistan (HEC) to present his research overseas. He is also serving as the editor-in-chief of the Asia Pacific Journal of Emerging Markets and a member of the editorial board of the Academy of Accounting and Financial Studies Journal and New Horizon. Furthermore, he serves as a reviewer for many Impact Factor Journals. His research interests are Sustainable Finance, FinTech, behavioral finance and corporate finance. He has published his research papers in various renowned journals, including Energy Economics, International Journal of Islamic and Middle Eastern Finance and Management, Journal of Financial Economic Policy, and International Journal of Emerging Markets, among others.

Muhammad Umar Islam is a Senior Lecturer at the Asia Pacific University of Technology and Innovation in Malaysia. He Earned his PhD from INCEIF, Malaysia. His research interests include Fintech, Bank Performance, Sustainable Finance, and Islamic Finance. He has published in Energy Economics, the International Journal of Islamic and Middle Eastern Finance and Management, Cogent Business and Management, the International Journal of Business and Management, and the Bulletin of Monetary Economics and Banking.

***

Umadevi.B Associate Professor in Department of Management Studies at R.M.K Engineering College, Chennai. She is MBA with Finance & HR specialisation with UGC Net qualification. She is pursuing Ph.D in the stream of Finance at Anna University. Has a 18 years of experience in handling Finance, HR and Operations Management classes. She too possess few years of corporate experience as Process executive with International exposure.She is a qualified trainer on “Entrepreneurship Development Programme” (Learn-Wise course) by EDII. She has completed IIC’s training program and been certified as Innovation Ambassador.She is a Life Member of “Indian Society for Technical Education (ISTE)”. Has wide contributions to profession through many research journals and hold patents on Supply Chain area and Information system field. She is currently exploring research on Artificial Intelligence in Management field. She has received fund for a research project on farming community from Tamilnadu State Council for Science and Technology under Student Project Scheme during 2024. To her Credit, she has published Indian patents titled, “Programming The Supply Chain Network For Customers With Uncertain Demand”, “Block Chain-Based Shopping Cart” and received Grant for Australian patent titled, “Block Chain Based Rice ATM”. She is been recognized as NPTEL discipline star during the year 2024 for her continuous learning of courses in the field of management.

Aaleyah Behera is a graduate student of Business Administration (Finance and International Business) at Christ University, Bengaluru, India. Her academic interests include financial markets, ESG investing, fintech adoption, and financial risk analysis. She has engaged in research examining market behaviour during periods of economic and systemic shocks. Aaleyah actively participates in academic conferences and research initiatives, aiming to contribute to evidence-based discussions at the intersection of finance, sustainability, and technology.

Santhapalli Gautami is a seasoned academician and researcher with over 25 years of experience in teaching (20 years) and research (5 years) in Management Studies. She currently serves as a Professor at the Department of Management Studies, S.V. College of Engineering, Tirupati. Her areas of expertise include Finance, Human Resource Management, and Educational Empowerment. She has successfully served as Principal Investigator for the AICTE AQIS PRERANA Scheme (2019–2022) and completed Andhra Pradesh State Tourism Department

Funded project for Home Stay Survey and State Policy framework at Tirupati District submitted report to Tirupati District Collector on 1st May 2025, she has been shortlisted for DST SHRI-SATYAM and File Number: ANRF/SSH/2025/000097/DH Project titled "Tech-Integrated Heritage Research Centre (TIHRC) Revitalizing Andhra Pradesh Crafts through Innovation " research funding schemes. She has also applied for SERB POWER GRANT and DST-NIDHI iTBI SC, ST special Call demonstrating her active involvement as Principal Investigator in funded research projects amounting to over 5 crore. Dr. Gautami is a recognized Ph.D. Supervisor at JNTUA Anantapuramu and currently guides four research scholars. She has authored seven books with reputed international publishers and has published 45 research papers, including 9 UGC and 3 Scopus-indexed publications. Her contribution to academia includes organizing and participating in national and international seminars, conferences, and faculty development programs. Her academic leadership and commitment to excellence have been recognized through prestigious honours such as the "Leading Educationist of India Award 2019" (Saint Martin Council of Research Accreditation Commission, Melbourne, Australia) and the "Academic Excellence Award" (I2OR International Institute of Organized Research). She earned her Ph.D. in Management Studies (2015) from Sri Venkateswara University, Tirupati, and was the University Topper in Finance Specialization (2001 batch). She is APSLET qualified, a certified trainer by APSHE–British Council, and has completed various online certifications including SPSS, NPTEL, and MOOCs courses. Dr. Gautami has mentored over 218 MBA students in project work and continues to contribute as a resource person in academic seminars, workshops, FDPs, and management meets. Her professional affiliations span six academic societies, and she is known for her dedication, interpersonal competence, and result-oriented approach toward research and teaching excellence.

K. Mirudhula is a Research Scholar currently pursuing her Ph.D. in the field of financial literacy and sustainable finance. She holds a Master's degree in Commerce from SASTRA Deemed University and possesses prolific knowledge in the domains of finance and commerce studies. Her academic and research interests focus on exploring the intersections of financial literacy, sustainable financial practices, and their implications for individuals and institutions.

Ashifa Kariveliparambil is a faculty member in the Faculty of Health Sciences at Istanbul Gelisim University, Türkiye. She is an interdisciplinary scholar working across social work, public health, community development, and gender studies, with growing expertise in AI and data analytics for social research. Her work focuses on women's health, disaster resilience, social capital, and rights-based practice. She has published widely in Scopus and WoS indexed journals, led national and EU-funded projects, and holds a patented intervention model integrating social, health, and data-driven approaches.

Manjit Kour is working as Professor at University Business School at Chandigarh University. She holds a PhD in Business Management from IK Gujral Punjab Technical University, India. She has a good research record with several research papers published in reputed journals. She is an editorial board member and reviewer of many reputed journals including Scopus and ABDC-indexed journals. Her areas of interest include sustainability, green practices, Fintech, online marketing trends and business ethics.

V Lava Kumar is an accomplished academician with a diverse educational background and over 13 years of enriching experience in the field of education. Holding an impressive array of qualifications including an MBA, M. Com, PhD in Management, PGDTTM, along with certifications from APSET in Management and APSET in Commerce. His area of specialization is Finance and Accounting. Currently serving as an Assistant Professor at GITAM School of Business, GITAM Deemed to be University, Bengaluru, Dr. Lava Kumar is dedicated to nurturing the minds of future business leaders. His teaching methodology is grounded in both theoretical knowledge and practical insights, ensuring that students receive a holistic understanding of their subjects. Dr. Lava Kumar's contributions extend beyond the classroom, evident through his prolific research endeavours. He has authored numerous research papers, with 3 publications in prestigious Scopus-indexed and ABDC journals, and an impressive tally of 10 research articles in international and peer-reviewed journals. He co-authored a Book which is published in Surana publications. His research interests primarily revolve around contemporary issues in management and finance, where he strives to contribute to the academic discourse with valuable insights and innovative perspectives.

Rashi Modi is a graduate student specializing in Finance at Christ University, Bengaluru, India. Her research interests include financial markets, ESG and sustainable finance, fintech adoption, and systemic risk analysis. She has worked on empirical research examining market dynamics across asset classes during periods of economic and financial shocks. Alongside her academic work, she has gained practical exposure through internships and leadership roles, strengthening her analytical and research-oriented skill set.

Priyakrushna Mohanty (PK) is an Assistant Professor at the Department of Business and Management, Christ University, Bengaluru. Holding a Ph.D. in Tourism Studies from Pondicherry University, where he was a UGC Senior Research Fellow, Dr. Mohanty is a recipient of the prestigious Travel Corporation (India) Gold

Medal for his Master's in Tourism Studies. His academic qualifications extend to an M.Com. in Finance and PG Diplomas in Rural Development, Research Methodology, and Teaching Skills. With prior industry experience at Indian Railway Catering and Tourism Corporation Ltd., he brings a practical perspective to his role. A prolific researcher, Dr. Mohanty has authored over forty publications and co-edited five books with renowned publishers such as Routledge, Emerald, Springer Nature, and CABI. His research interests encompass Research Methodology, Tourism Sustainability, Livelihood, Events Tourism, e-Tourism, and Gender issues in Tourism Development.

Vettriselvan R. an Associate Professor, AMET University, specialized in HRM and Marketing. He is acting as Mentor, Saraswathi Institute of Medical Sciences, Hapur. He served as Review Board member, National Council for Higher Education, Malawi, Head of the Department, School of Commerce and Management Studies, St. Eugene University, Zambia, and Director, Research and Publication, St. John the Baptist University, Malawi. He has published 28 books and 105 articles in peer reviewed journals and edited book chapters. Under his guidance three have completed and Seven are pursuing their PhD.

Ravikumar R. N. is currently a Postdoctoral researcher at Universiti Malaysia Perlis, Malaysia. Also, working as an Associate Professor in the department of Computer Engineering at Marwadi University, Rajkot, Gujarat. He has 12+ years of national and international teaching experience. He completed his PhD at Amity University, Rajasthan, M.E at VMRF Deemed University, B.E at Anna University, Chennai. He is the co-founder of the Research Activities Club at Marwadi University and trains students on research activities, which leads to the publication of 7 Scopus/SCI journals, 20 Book chapters, 25 Conference papers, and 10 patents. His specialization is ML, DL, Federated Learning, Recommendation Systems, and Optimization Techniques.

Palanivel Rathinasabapathi Velmurugan is associated with BSBI, Berlin, as a professor in the Human Resource Management and Finance Stream. Prior to joining BSBI, he held the designation "Head" Faculty of Management at Sharda University, Uzbekistan, Central Asia, and "Dean of Arts" assignments at DMI St. John the Baptist University, Malawi, Central Africa. Also, he has been associated earlier with DMI St. Eugene University in Zambia, MAM Business School and various Engineering Colleges in India. He has a Ph.D. in Management from Mannonmanium Sundaranar University in India. Besides this, he holds an MBA Degree from SRM University in India and a BE Chemical Engineering degree from Annamalai University in India. Also, he completed six NPTEL Certificate

Programs conducted by various IITs in India. He brings with him 15 years of rich working experience in teaching and research. Furthermore, he has a keen interest in the Case Method of teaching and research. He is an academic out of passion. Not only that, but he also takes a keen interest in guiding Ph.D. students. He has supervised three Ph.D. research scholars under his supervision at DMI St. Eugene University in Zambia.

Aarthi S is a dedicated Assistant Professor in Computer Science with over six years of teaching experience. She is currently pursuing her Ph.D. at Marwadi University, Gujarat, and holds an M.Phil. and MCA from Bharathiar University, Tamil Nadu. Throughout her academic career, Aarthi has specialized in programming languages such as C++, Java, and C, and contributed to research in recommender systems and AI-related data privacy. She has published journal articles, contributed to book chapters, and actively participated in technical workshops. Known for her student mentorship and engagement in academic events, Aarthi remains committed to fostering innovation and excellence in computer science education.

N Sathyanarayana has over 17 years of teaching experience at both undergraduate and postgraduate levels. He holds a Master of Business Administration degree from Visvesvaraya Technological University (VTU) and a Master of Commerce degree from Periyar University. He has completed his Ph.D. in Banking and Finance from Dayananda Sagar University. Currently, he serves as an Assistant Professor in the School of Commerce at Jain (Deemed-to-be University), Bangalore. He has published 24 research papers in international journals, including three indexed in Scopus, and seven papers in national journals. Additionally, he has presented 14 research papers at international conferences and 11 at national conferences. He has co-authored two books at the national level and contributed 21 Scopus-indexed book chapters.

S. Karthikeyan is an accomplished academic and professional with a strong background in Management. He holds a Ph.D. in Management and an MBA in Marketing & Finance. With nearly two decades of combined experience, including nearly 10 years in academia and 4.5 years in industry, he has a diverse skill set. Dr. Karthikeyan is currently working as an Assistant Professor at SASTRA Deemed University and held roles as a Head of the Department. His expertise spans financial services, business economics, and securities market operations. He has also contributed to various academic initiatives, by publishing research articles in peer reviewed journals indexed in Scopus, Web of Science, ABDC etc..

D. Srikanth Reddy is an accomplished academician and finance educator with over 16 years of experience in teaching MBA and BBA programs. Currently serving as Assistant Professor of Finance at the School of Management Studies, REVA University, Bengaluru. He holds a Ph.D. and M.Phil. in Management from Krishna University, with specialization in finance. His teaching expertise spans subjects such as Investment and Portfolio Management, Corporate Finance, Financial Derivatives and International Financial Management. A certified NCFM and AMFI professional, Dr. Srikanth Reddy has been actively involved in conducting certification programs on capital markets and equity derivatives. He has published and presented several research papers in UGC-approved journals and national and international conferences. His scholarly interests include retail investor behaviour, financial markets and derivative trading. Committed to academic excellence and student development, Dr. Srikanth Reddy also contributes to curriculum design, examination boards and institutional outreach initiatives.

Athish Venkatachalam is a Graduate Student at Clemson University, pursuing a Master of Science in Computer Science. He completed his Bachelor of Technology in Computer Science and Business Systems at SRM Institute of Science and Technology (SRMIST), where he held leadership positions as Chairperson of SRM IET on Campus and Convener of the Technical Team at the Directorate of Student Affairs. Athish is recognized for his expertise in Cloud Computing, Distributed Computing, and DevOps, and earned accolades in various hackathons, including being a finalist in the All-India Level Smart India Hackathon 2022. At Clemson, Athish serves as a Graduate Research Assistant at the Human-AI Empowerment Lab, where he is dedicated to exploring AI for Social Good. In addition to his research work, Athish is the President of the Clemson Graduate Student Government, having previously served as the Director of Clemson Graduate Travel Grants. In this capacity, he plays an essential role in advocating for and supporting the graduate student community. Athish was also honored with the Best Outgoing Student award in 2023 by SRMIST for his exceptional academic achievements, leadership, and contributions to the university.

Muhammad Zahid (PhD) is currently working as Dean of the Faculty of Transport and Logistics at Muscat University, Oman. Before joining Muscat University, he served as a Professor and Dean of Management Sciences at the Bahria Business School, Bahria University, Pakistan. He also has experience serving the Department of Management Sciences at the City University of Science and IT, Peshawar, Pakistan, as a Professor and Dean of the Faculty of Management Sciences. He obtained his Postdoctoral Fellowship from Universiti Malaysia Kelantan and a PhD in Management from Universiti Teknologi PETRONAS Malaysia. He received his MS in Management and Master of Commerce degrees from Pakistan earlier. After completing his master's degree, he served in the banking industry for eight years as a branch and customer services manager. His area of concentration is corporate sustainability and financial performance. He has published two books in the area of sustainability and numerous research papers in indexed journals. For his outstanding research work, he has been awarded "The Award for Excellence- 2016 Outstanding Journal Papers from Emerald Group Publishing" and the Best Paper Award (2014) in the International Symposium on Research in Innovation and Sustainability 2014 (ISoRIS' 14), 15-16 October 2014, Malacca, Malaysia. Moreover, he has experience in editorship and is an invited reviewer for well-reputed journals in the fields of management, corporate sustainability, corporate governance, finance, gender in management, financial performance, sustainable development goals, and education for sustainable development. He has also supervised more than 30 research students and worked on several research grants in the aforementioned areas with academic institutions in Malaysia, Saudi Arabia, and Pakistan. He also has expertise in working with regulatory bodies such as the Pakistan Stock Exchange (PSX) in designing sustainability guidelines and reports in the business and academic domains (Impact Ranking). He can be contacted at mianmz11@gmail.com.

Index

A

B

C

D

www.ingramcontent.com/pod-product-compliance
Lightning Source LLC
LaVergne TN
LVHW080901300926
849162LV00003B/502